D1602456

Kate Chase and William Sprague

Kate Chase and William Sprague

Politics and Gender in a
Civil War Marriage

~

Peg A. Lamphier

UNIVERSITY OF NEBRASKA PRESS

LINCOLN AND LONDON

Library of Congress
Cataloging-in-Publication Data

Lamphier, Peg A.
Kate Chase and William Sprague:
politics and gender in a Civil War marriage /
Peg A. Lamphier.
p.   cm.
Includes bibliographical references and index.
ISBN 0-8032-2947-X (cl.: alk. paper)
1. Sprague, Kate Chase, 1840–1899.
2. Sprague, William, 1830–1915.
3. Chase, Salmon P. (Salmon Portland), 1808–1873—Family.
4. United States—History—Civil War, 1861–1865—Biography.
5. United States—History—1865–1898—Biography.
6. Legislators' spouses—United States—Biography.
7. Legislators—United States—Biography.
8. Married people—United States—Biography.
9. Marriage—United States—Case studies.
10. Divorce—United States—Case studies.
I. Title.
E415.9.S76 L36   2003
306.89'0973'09034—dc21
2003002466

For
Leo J. Burke,
Jackie Lamphier, and
L. Paul Lamphier

Contents

~

Illustrations

~

Acknowledgments

$\sim$

I owe Kate Chase and William Sprague the greatest debt of gratitude for consciously creating a public record of their lives. The acknowledgment of my academic debts must begin with the members of the History Department at Montana State University, who helped me find my way out of the wilderness of the hard sciences to my more natural habitat. Of special note are Paula Petrik, Pierce Mullen, Jeffrey Safford, and Mary Murphy. The dashing Bill Jones directed me to Claremont Graduate University's Vicki Ruiz, who has been extremely important to my academic and personal development. Vicki took me to Arizona State University, where my academic career crystallized in ways I had not foreseen. I cannot say enough about the generosity of spirit that infuses all of her efforts, or of her outstanding dedication to lost historical voices. Brooks Simpson held me to particularly high standards of scholarship in matters of nineteenth-century politics. His encyclopedic knowledge of these areas has provided me with a model to emulate. All of these scholars are deeply talented academicians, and they all have my sincerest gratitude.

My mentors at the Salmon P. Chase Papers—John Niven, James P. McClure, and Leigh Johnson—deserve special mention. Jim receives my particular thanks, not only for the yeoman duties of teaching documentary editing to the uninitiated but also for his true friendship. Mark Brown, curator of the Manuscript Division at Brown University Library, provided invaluable assistance in this project's early stages. Thanks also go to the Rhode Island Historical Society, the South County Museum, the Cranston Historical Society, and the tireless archivists at the Pennsylvania Historical Society, the Library of Congress, and the National Archives for their contributions. Because I live far away from my degree-granting institution, the Los Angeles Public Library system became my primary research facility. Particular thanks go to Charles Kaufman and the outstanding staff at Claremont's public library for their unceasing efforts to keep me supplied with interlibrary loan materials, both inside and outside the system. All of the working documents from the now-finished Salmon P. Chase Papers ended up at the A. K. Smiley Public Library in Redlands, California. The staff there proved as gracious as the building in which they housed the collection.

My personal debts are just as large. First and foremost, my parents, Jackie and Paul Lamphier, have all my love and gratitude, not only for being excellent parents but for understanding about my delay in turning into a regular grown-up. Their help has come at several crucial junctures, and they never let me down. Marlene and Tom Burke also have my gratitude. They have gone above and beyond the call of duty in ways too many to enumerate here. Rachel and Derek Brown both provided invaluable child-care services after I discovered that one cannot write a book "while the baby naps." My good friend Claudine Barnes was always there when I needed encouragement, advice, or a place to stay in Arizona. My sister, Aimee Musgrove, remains a steady source of comic relief, moral support and reality checks. Leo Jr. and Cameron Burke not only watched the baby so I could write but actually helped with document transcription (and thought it was fun!). Emma Burke assisted by scribbling on papers, spilling juice on my desk, waking up in the middle of crucial paragraphs, emptying the contents of my desk drawers, and covering the dog with post-its. In short, she made this project both harder and more meaningful than I expected, while filling my life with inexpressible joy.

Leo Burke has carried the burden of this biography more than any other person. He has listened to me tell stories about people long dead, gone to libraries when he could have been watching football, and functioned as the main contributor to the unofficial Peg Lamphier scholarship fund. As my gratitude cannot be expressed with words alone, I'll have to show him every day for the rest of my life.

Kate Chase and William Sprague

Introduction

~

Through all the drama, whether damned or not
Love gilds the scene, and women guide the plot

Richard Brensley Sheridan

In 1904, only five years after Katherine Chase Sprague's death and nine years before William Sprague's demise, the journalist Henry Villard included the following story about wartime Washington in his autobiography:

> One of the points of attraction was the headquarters of Governor Sprague of Rhode Island, who had recruited three regiments in his State and led them to Washington. He had a very limited mental capacity, but had reached political distinction at an early age—he was then but thirty-one—through the influence of a real or reputed great wealth. It was at his headquarters that he became acquainted with Kate, the beautiful and gifted daughter of Secretary [of the Treasury Salmon P.] Chase. The acquaintance quickly ripened into an engagement that was the social sensation of the day. She was far superior to him in every way, and married him for the enjoyment and power of his money. It turned out one of the unhappiest marriages ever known in American society, ending in moral and material wretchedness for both parties.[1]

Villard was neither the first nor the last writer to summarize Kate and William's union as venal, unholy, or mismatched. Biographers and contemporary social commentators alike found in the pair a kind of black-and-white morality tale. This take on the Chase-Sprague story creates a compelling story, laden as it is with illicit sex, thwarted ambition, betrayal, and barbarous practices. No modern historian has attempted to illuminate the gray areas of these two life narratives, to explore the cultural, social, and political components of one Victorian marriage.

Although four published biographies of Kate exist, as well as two biographical theses of William, more yet may be said about this couple. [2] Letters between Kate and her father suggest that Kate desired love and approbation not often forthcoming from her father or her husband. The Chase-Sprague Papers paint a far different picture of Kate and William's relationship than the one most popularly accepted—in fact, even a brief perusal of this collection forces the reader to rethink the notion that Kate married William simply for his money, or that he married her to gain access to Treasury-controlled cotton permits. Finally, no biography of their marriage would be complete without an examination of the man who assisted in its demise—the New York senator Roscoe Conkling. A small collection of letters from Kate in the Chester Arthur Papers, which have gone virtually unnoticed by all other biographers, makes it clear that she and Roscoe did not discontinue their relationship after the disastrous events of 1879. Biographies of the "Adonis of the Senate" pay little attention to the relationship between the senator and Kate, and I contend that one must attempt to understand their joint marital unfaithfulness to begin to understand the actors in this domestic drama.

This biography explores a marriage and how it functioned in a social milieu charged with politics, both personal and public. To understand Kate and William's courtship begs the simple question, "What happened?" The incongruence of Kate's and William's individual stories, reflecting as they do an unhappy marriage, one filled with misunderstanding, disappointment, infidelity, and both emotional and physical violence, provides the historian with an excellent opportunity to explore the ideologies that underpinned Kate's and William's respective "imaginative patterns." [3] One historian has suggested that an unhappy marriage occurs when the couple's subjective fictions of that marriage conflict, while in happy marriages husband and wife agree about the "facts" of their relationship. But disharmonious marital stories may stem from unhappy marriages, rather than vice versa, and certainly some couples experience more understanding and less emotional and physical insult than others. Kate and William's marriage suffered both from differing ideas about how their marriage should have worked and from alcohol-fueled domestic abuse. Thus the Chase-Sprague marriage tests leading theses with regard to companionate marriage. Joined by romantic love rather than obligation, nineteenth-century couples placed new demands upon their relationships, including high expectations of intimacy and companionship. This companionate ideal, some theories suggest, empowered women by displacing domestic patriarchy. Kate's story suggests quite the opposite.

The greatest difference between Kate and William may be located in their expectations and applications of power. Defined most simply, power represents that ability of individuals or groups to control the behavior of others. Kate and William's marriage provided ample opportunities for each to attempt the control of the other. This marriage was, in multiple senses, a venue where each partner exercised power through political authority. First, and most obviously, both Kate, as the daughter of Salmon P. Chase (a leading antislavery Republican, a cabinet member for Lincoln, and chief justice of the U.S. Supreme Court), and William, Rhode Island's governor and senator, represent political people in the most traditional sense. They both concerned themselves, though in different ways, with local, state, and national governmental systems, with political parties and public policy. William professed to admire Kate's political proficiency and her familiarity with the leading political men of the Civil War, but he found her expertise quite daunting. His efforts to prove his manhood time and again, in the face of economic and personal challenges, caused him untold anxiety. The paradox of William's life may be found in the fact that because of his cultural position he believed himself entitled to power, yet he felt powerless.[4] Thus William wielded authority in its most negative manifestations—he physically and emotionally abused his wife. He did this, not because he was an evil man, but because he confused power with control and domination. As his control over his economic and political life slipped away, he increased his efforts to exert himself in the domestic sphere.

Kate, on the other hand, may be described as a political woman. Women entered nineteenth-century politics as feminists, reformers, or party women. Most party women acted in auxiliary roles and at the local level. As Jo Freeman cogently put it, "Whereas feminists had assaulted the citadel, and reformers banged on the door, party women infiltrated the basement of politics." Kate—and, I would argue, other women as well—infiltrated not the basement but rather the front parlor of politics: the convention hall, the Senate, and even the White House. In her role as daughter, wife, and mistress to powerful political men, Kate represents a particular version of political womanhood little studied by serious histori-ans.[5] Like Dolley Madison and Louisa Catherine Adams, Kate utilized her social position and access to the unofficial arenas of political power, parlors and dining rooms, to act politically—in both the private and the public sense.

Politics, as I have suggested, may be personal as well as public, and power relations may be more poignant in personal relationships. Marriage, John Stuart Mill suggested, must be viewed as the penultimate political exercise undertaken by most adults. This sense of "political" has been almost the exclusive intellectual property of historians of women.[6] A biography of Kate and William's marriage—a political and legal institution that functioned in a larger political framework—offers an interesting opportunity to meld women's history and political history. Kate has long been regarded as a woman intimate with Civil War and Reconstruction politics. She has rarely been defined as a nineteenth-century political woman, in part because both political history and women's history have often defined political women as those who agitated for suffrage or moral reform: women who took on "male" roles of political activism. Twentieth-century popular biographies have represented Kate as an example of a political woman gone bad—overwrought with ambition and meddling in affairs in which she should not have been involved. Many have suggested that Kate transgressed womanly behavior by operating within a traditionally male political realm, first for her father, then for her husband, and lastly, and most covertly, for her lover, Roscoe Conkling. Such interpretations of Kate's life implicitly accept the dichotomy wherein politics may only be practiced in public and by men (or by women acting the man's role), not in a more private realm. But such a reading of Kate's life belies a paucity of gendered analysis. Paula Baker suggests a starting point for a more sophisticated approach to politics and women. "Attention to the interaction between women's political activities and the political system itself," she says, "can tell us much about the position of women in the nineteenth century." The exploration of gendered political subcultures, Baker believes, can further refine any discussion of women and politics.[7] Kate's life offers us an opportunity to explore a different mode of political behavior, one in which many other women may have participated through their positions as wives and daughters of politicians.[8]

Kate's life powerfully suggests not only that women were integral to party politics but that gender played a central role in America's partisan ideologies.

Her involvement in not only several presidential elections but in day-to-day policy decisions suggests that Republican womanhood may be described as public activity including, but not limited, to agitation for universal suffrage. The prominence of Kate and of women like Jesse Benton Frémont (or even Amanda "Puss" Belknap) points to the gendering of political parties—to the fact that Republicans utilized concepts of female duty and loyalty in mass party politics. Antebellum Democrats, in contrast, decried the use of prominent women to garner votes. Kate's wedding, for example, may be viewed as more than the legal expression of a private relationship. Her father invited not just family members but cabinet heads, senators, diplomats, and even the president, turning the wedding into a kind of Republican rally. In this way Kate's political career is suggestive of a particular way in which the Republican Party not only appealed to women but made their support crucial to the party.[9]

Gender, though, must not be considered a euphemism for "woman," for if gender is indeed "a social category imposed on a sexed body," then necessarily men must be considered part of any gender study. Because "gender is a primary way of signifying relationships of power," it would seem a particularly useful analytical tool in this combination of political history and biography. But studies of manhood and womanhood have often been marked as "separatist scholarship."[10] A study of a marriage provides a convenient venue to combine the two fields. Happily, political historians have begun to think about gendered analysis, and women's historians came to consider the importance of political analysis. They have utilized "politics" in a sense that includes "any action, formal or informal, taken to affect the course or behavior of government or the community." Nineteenth-century political culture had significant gender divisions or political subcultures. Although women were most often involved via the private sphere, some combined domesticity and political action via motherhood and voluntary organizations.[11] Historians have also emphasized the role of women in developing the modern welfare state, creating sophisticated answers to questions of how government works.[12] But historians' work has largely focused on traditional female networks or on female reform organizations and how they affected local and national politics. This biography twists that approach, instead suggesting how one woman, and thus perhaps many others, placed her imprint directly upon the manly forum of traditional politics. This approach, and others like it, may broaden our understanding of mid-nineteenth-century politics to include both formal and informal kinds of influence and authority as the basis for political power. In fact, it is Kate's "backdoor" approach that suggests yet another way in which gender and power coincided in the politics of policy and candidacy.

William's personal notions of gender—that is, how he created his manly identity—provide another focus for this study. Historians have posited several prescriptive manhoods, each generally dependent upon geography. William appears to have embraced both southern, honor-bound tenets of masculinity and the ethoses of the self-made man and Christian gentleman more commonly associated with northern men. Yet another branch of gender studies posits a partisan basis for manhood, with Whig/Republican men defining manhood differently from Democrats. Republicans, for example, celebrated women's moral influence more than did Democrats, who resisted the policy implications of such a national view in favor of an ideology that embraced white male authority, both in public and at home. [13] Given Democrats' protective stance toward racial slavery, and thus the need to maintain authority in household economies based on slave labor, this elevation of male authority had deep-seated political implications. It had, as well, geographical implications, given the regional nature of slavery. Thus partisan and regional manhoods may not always fall into neat categories when taken out of theory and put into practice.

William's biography suggests that men made use of multiple notions of manhood, shifting from one to another as life stage and individual situations altered. Although William was for most of his life an avowed Republican, and the son-in-law of a leading Radical Republican, both times he ran for office he did so, if not as a Democrat, then as an alternative to the Republican candidate. As a wealthy industrialist with thousands of workers at his command, William may have felt some kinship with southern Democrats, for certainly he felt a paternalistic responsibility toward his employees. His political speeches—which, except for a flurry in 1869, were few and far between—also suggest that William felt less-than-perfect sympathy for the Republican ideology. His behavior during at least one fight with a Senate colleague, as well as his actions when faced with direct evidence of Kate's infidelity, also suggest that William adhered to an honor based notion of manhood. Down to the dueling pistols, William's behavior, his sense of himself as a man, suggests that he fashioned for himself a gendered ideology best described as northern Democrat, if one allows "Democrat" to encompass elements of southern manhood. Class must come into play when describing manhoods as well, for not only did working-class men figure gender differently from other men, but many of them were both Democrats and northerners. William's considerable wealth set him apart from so many northern men, encouraging him to think of himself as a kind of planter gentleman, but this wealth did not make him a member of the elite class. He had a firm middle- and even working-class background; northeastern elites never viewed the Spragues as anything but rich upstarts.

Nineteenth-century womanhood was no less bound by geography, class, or political alliance. The period's prescriptive standards for northeastern white women like Kate included purity, piety, submissiveness, and domesticity. Historians have posited the empowering abilities of this ethos, for in womanhood women found sisterhood, and in sisterhood they found a basis for moral authority, both within and outside the home. Domesticity however, reflects "bourgeois self-consciousness" in that these tenets had class and racial boundaries. Kate's life story suggests that some bourgeois women engaged in the subversion of prescriptive domesticity as well. Her father's influence on her life, amply documented in more than three hundred letters, suggests that Kate subscribed to the tenets of the new Republican Party's ideology—a belief system based on the claim that all Americans, black or white, "could achieve social advancement if given equal protection under the law."[14] Republican rhetoric demanded the right of individuals to own themselves, to freely determine the course of their future, and to freely contract their labor. As the daughter of a leading Radical Republican and the wife of a governor and senator, Kate not only learned the ideology of party but became a female party regular who acted with and upon other members of her partisan community.

Prior to the Civil War, women's recourse to republican rhetoric (of the nonpartisan kind of republicanism) centered upon "republican motherhood." This ideology engaged women in the political process as the educators of the new nation's citizenry. Although liberating in its emphasis on the reasonable abilities of all citizens and the moral leadership qualities of white women, republican womanhood nonetheless figured women as subject to paternalist interests—to the men in their households whose duty it was to protect the liberty of their dependents.[15] By the mid–nineteenth century, Republicanism (as figured by the political party of that name) offered women yet another opportunity to exploit a political ideology for liberatory ends. Just as abolitionists used the framework of the Republican Party to agitate for the end of slavery, so too did women use the party and its ideology to urge the enfranchisement of women.[16] As a leading Republican, Salmon P. Chase tried to mold his daughter into an "accomplished" and political woman, and Kate's reactions to his efforts stand as a historical record against which may be tested such historical constructions as "true womanhood," the doctrines of "separate spheres" and "women's culture," and the rise of the much-touted companionate marriage. Significantly, the ideology of Republican womanhood may have allowed Kate to reconcile the gap between her political activity and her subversions of prescriptive middle-class womanhood. It is her upbringing that allows historians to apply middle-class standards to Kate, for though she may have lived in the rarified world of the politically and economically elite, she was raised to be a respectable, middle-class woman. Just as William was never a member of the elite class, Kate also, by virtue of her background and marriage, never became an accepted member of the elite class, however much she may have wished to do so.

The connection between Republican rhetoric of self-ownership for men, regardless of race, and feminist demands for the greater independence of women makes the Chase family's politics particularly significant. Divorce, a marital remedy Kate would seek, provided a space where she and other women embraced the ideals of the Republican Party. As some women came to view marital enslavement as antithetical to self-ownership, and as freedom became tied to the ability to freely contract labor, pro-divorce activists recast marriage as a "contract dissoluble at will."[17] This contractual view of marriage became a powerful ideal of women's right to personal freedom. Women's rights supporters like Elizabeth Cady Stanton objected not only to midcentury divorce laws but to the cultural view of marriage as a legal, not emotional, bond. "I am opposed to the PRESENT legalized marriage," Stanton declared in 1869, "and the marriage and divorce laws. . . . I would have [marriage] more pure and holy than it is today by making women the dictator in the whole social realm."[18] Kate, no less than any other political citizen, subscribed to the tenets of her partisan community, and her community centered upon her antislavery father. Never one to think of herself as restricted to the private sphere, Kate engaged in a political act when she sued William for divorce. On 20 December 1880, when she filed her divorce petition, Katherine Chase Sprague declared her emancipation, an act she emphasized by requesting a legal name change. [19] The Rhode Island senator's wife took back herself when she took back her name.

The first chapter of this biography addresses the details of Kate's and William's lives before they met. Chapter 2 explores their courtship, utilizing a wealth of letters from William wherein he negotiated the tenets of romantic love. Kate and William's wedding closes this chapter, offering an excellent opportunity to analyze the cultural and personal meanings behind the series of rituals that combined to make the courting couple legally one. Against the backdrop of the Civil War and Reconstruction, the early years of the marriage provide the focus for chapter 3, emphasizing the cultural and personal meanings of marital rituals. Politics focus this section, particularly in 1868 when Kate acted as her father's campaign manager at the New York Democratic convention, placing herself in the middle of a traditional political venue. The next year she and William suffered their greatest marital crisis yet, bitterly fighting about his marital infidelities and his attempts to distance himself politically from the Chases. The time period from after the Democratic convention through 1873, when Salmon died and the Sprague business failed, occupies chapter 4. Chapter 5 concentrates on the mid-1870s, when Kate's friendship with Roscoe Conkling blossomed into an illicit relationship. The following chapter will shine the light on one month in 1879—the public disgrace of the Canonchet imbroglio, wherein private matters of alcohol and domestic abuse, sexual improprieties, and all matters of excess came to the public view—and indicate how the resolution of those matters became an intensely political matter. Chapter 7 examines Kate and William's divorce, particularly how it may be viewed as both exceptional and representative of divorce in Victorian America. This section also examines issues of child custody and politics, at both the state and national level, to determine not only why Kate chose to divorce William but why she timed that decision as she did. The final chapter follows William and Kate through to their deaths, and in so doing it explores post-divorce life as a highly gendered experience, one that penalized divorced women more than divorced men.

I close with a quick word about editorial procedure and naming. This biography includes a number of excerpted letters. I have tried to make my transcription as faithful to the original as possible, retaining original punctuation and spelling. I have used brackets to indicate words I found indecipherable, sometimes including within those brackets my guess as to the correct word. Although all of Kate's biographers have called her Kate, biographers have always called her father by his full or last name. Much the same might be said of William Sprague. Given the power dynamic inherent in naming, particularly in a gendered reading, I have chosen to call all of my principal players primarily by their first name. Lastly, it is important to realize that no amount of study can truly make any biographical subject entirely knowable. I began this book believing that I would come to fully understand Kate, and I have ended realizing that there are many, many things about her that I will never know or understand. And although I have come to better understand William, he was an abusive and unrepentant drunkard who spectacularly failed his family. No amount of objectivity can overcome my distaste for the man, and accordingly I will always be Kate's champion.

ONE

Before They Met
Family Life in the Mid–Nineteenth Century, 1830–1861

⁓

On 13 August 1840, after four hours of hard labor, nineteen-year-old Eliza Smith Chase gave birth to her first child, a girl. Her husband, Salmon P. Chase, got down on his knees and "prayed God to support and comfort my dear wife, to preserve the life of the child and save both from sin." "Lizzie" came through her travail unscathed, despite the fact that a doctor attended the birth. Although Lizzie probably thought the baby was the most beautiful child ever born, the new father thought otherwise. He confessed to his diary that "The babe is pronounced pretty. I think it quite otherwise. It is however well formed and I am thankful. May God give the child a good understanding that she may keep his commandments."[1] They named the new baby after Salmon's first wife and first daughter, both deceased Catherines, but this latest Catherine would always be known as Kate.[2]

From the moment of his daughter's birth, Salmon viewed her with mixed feelings. He loved her, but with reservations. His ambiguous reaction to her birth might be viewed in the light of his need to separate his political persona from his tragedy-plagued private life. Thus began Kate's relationship with her father, a perplexing mix of loving concern and emotional distance that would create a girl and a woman who yearned for demonstrative, unconditional love and who used politics as a means to achieve that end.

Born in New Hampshire in 1808, Salmon P. Chase dedicated his entire adult life to politics. His family counted among its members a state senator, an Episcopal bishop, several Dartmouth-educated lawyers, and one U.S. senator. His father, Ithamar Chase, went bankrupt and died before Salmon was ten, shattering the family's security. Uncle Philander Chase, the bishop, took his nephew in hand and provided the boy with both rigid discipline and high educational expectations. As a young man Salmon graduated from Dartmouth, tried his hand at teaching, and studied law under William Wirt, the attorney general for President John Quincy Adams.[3] Early in his career Salmon defended runaway slaves from the Fugitive Slave Act, and he was a leading member of the Liberty and Free-Soil Parties in the late 1830s and in the 1840s.

During the early 1830s he courted Catherine Jane Garniss, the daughter of a well-off Cincinnati family. In 1834 Rev. Lyman Beecher performed the marriage of twenty-three-year-old "Kitty" and twenty-six-year-old Salmon. Unfortunately, the new bride died before the end of her second year of marriage, probably of a relatively common childbirth complication, puerperal fever. Finding himself the single father of an infant daughter— named Catherine Jane after her mother, but called Kate—Salmon lived with his Garniss relatives until at least 1837. In the fall of 1839 he married Eliza Ann Smith (in a double wedding: his sister Helen married Rev. Henry Walbridge), no doubt both because he was fond of "Lizzie" and because his daughter needed a mother. Lizzie was six weeks short of her eighteenth birthday and had been one of Katherine Garniss's friends. Less than four months into their marriage, Lizzie and Salmon had to face little Kate's death. A victim of scarlet fever, the little girl died just before her fifth birthday. Not long afterward Lizzie gave birth to her first child, whom the Chases also called Kate. Unfortunately, the second Mrs. Chase fared no better the first—she died of consumption when Kate was five after having given birth to two more daughters, neither of whom survived infancy. "We are desolate," the grieving Salmon wrote a close friend. Nor were there many Smith relatives on the scene to help the Chases—tuberculosis ravaged the Smith family during the middle years of the nineteenth century.[4]

Salmon married for a third and last time in 1846, to Sara Bella Dunlop Ludlow. Salmon had done business for the Ludlow family since 1839 and had done some legal work after Belle's grandfather Israel Ludlow died leaving a rather confused will. Israel had been one of the original proprietors of Cincinnati and left a tangled heritage of lands and money to his heirs. Salmon probably first met Belle when working on these problems. Her family was as a large and vital one, complicated by the repetition of Chambers, Ludlow, and Dunlop names. Belle's parents, for example, were first cousins, and her grandmothers, Sarah Bella Chambers Dunlop and Charlotte Chambers Ludlow, were sisters. This family, like the Smiths, was also touched by tuberculosis, and both Belle and her youngest sister, Josephine, contracted the disease. Belle gave birth to two girls during her married years, but only Janet, called "Nettie," survived to adulthood. Belle died in 1852, and Salmon never married again.[5]

Salmon raised his daughters in a sea of emotional ambiguity, probably because he felt overwhelmed by death. After the death of his first wife, for example, he filled many pages of his diary with anguished prose. Nineteenth-century American culture romanticized death and ritualized mourning, a case most eloquently seen in Salmon's reaction to Catherine Garniss's death.[6] He reviewed her demise in painful detail, described the deathbed scene and how he felt about his loss, and admitted that his grief was "irreparable."[7] When his first daughter died he again turned to his journal for consolation, writing, "I cannot but mourn her loss, but I endeavor to imagine her celestial bliss and check ungrateful pining."[8] In the next few years he would grieve for three more baby girls, as well as for Lizzie and Belle, three of his brothers, and both of his parents. Salmon called the death of Kate's mother "the saddest affliction," but nevertheless these later deaths did not appear to have caused him the same level of anguish as his earlier encounters with the Grim Reaper. In fact, he did not mention the deaths of Belle or two of his daughters in his journals.[9] These lacunae though, may well represent Salmon's decreased ability to be as expressive with his grief as he had been in his first encounters with death.

In Salmon's repeated fears of Kate's demise one finds the seeds of his love for her. Finding comfort in the scriptural line "The Lord loveth he whom he chasteneth," Salmon interpreted his losses as evidence of divine love. His seemingly harsh letters to ten-year-old Kate on the occasion of the death of her baby sister "Zoe" may be viewed in this context. "I am very anxious for you," he wrote. "Your mother was extremely solicitous that you should become a sincere, devoted Christian. I do not like excuses," he added. "They are often not strictly true, and they are almost invariably in bad taste. . . . You have some peculiar difficulties to deal with. You are somewhat nervous and timid. You fear censure and displeasure. When, therefore, you feel you have done something for which you may be blamed, you are peculiarly tempted to swerve from the truth in order to conceal or excuse it." If God loved Kate, her father assured her, he would "assist" her by keeping her alive.[10] Salmon believed that his stern letters to Kate would make her more virtuous and thus more protected by God.

Nonetheless, young Kate must have found her father's emotional coldness disheartening. Once he wrote, "Remember too, that you may die soon, and cannot, in any event, live very many years, and make your peace with God." As if this were not enough, he added, "Already eleven years of your life are passed. You may not live another eleven years; perhaps only a very small part of that time; certainly or almost certainly not many times eleven years. How short life is!"[11] When he heard his that daughter was sick he became terribly worried: "I feel very much troubled when I hear of your being in the slightest indisposed: for you can hardly realize my anxiety about your health." Fathering her from afar, he admonished, "You must be careful with your health. Your constitution is not strong naturally; but by eating only wholesome food, and taking sufficient exercise, and avoiding everything which weakens, you may become a vigorous & healthy woman, and you may grow up."[12] Kate may have interpreted these worries as expressions of love, however guarded, but her father's parenting style left Kate hungry for more obvious signs of affection.

Had she lived, Lizzie might have provided her daughter with the emotional comfort so prized by Victorian culture. Advice literature celebrated the intense bond between mothers and daughter.[13] When Kate was eight months old, Lizzie told her husband that "if she should die she should have great pain in parting with little Kate, but did not doubt that the Lord would take care of her."[14] Lizzie may have found her faith comforting when her physician diagnosed tuberculosis in both lungs when Kate was only two, for she surely understood the seriousness of the diagnosis. Two of her sisters had already died of tuberculosis, and a third would die only months later; her brother Edmund would also die of the disease. Religion may also have helped her when her next two daughters died as infants.[15] These blows, combined with her own ultimately losing battle with tuberculosis, must have left Lizzie with a shortage of emotional and physical energy, particularly for raising a healthy and rambunctious child. No amount of nutritious diet, exercise, open air, or applications of the "water cure" could forestall Lizzie's fate.[16]

After Lizzie's death, Aunt Alice came to live with the little family. Salmon had five sisters, but Abigail had died in 1838, while Hannah, Helen, and Jane all had families of their own. As a single female relative, Alice acted as mother to her niece until the following year, when Salmon married Belle. Unfortunately for Kate, her new stepmother spent much of her married life traveling to sanitariums and warm environments seeking a cure for tuberculosis. In 1847 Belle gave birth to Janet, known throughout her life as Nettie. In 1849 another daughter arrived upon the scene, but little Josephine, or Zoe, died before her first birthday. In spite of her ill health, Belle tried to make herself a mother to Kate, but she succumbed to her disease in 1852, when Nettie was five years old. Alice again acted as Kate and Nettie's de facto mother, caring for her brother's household when the girls were away at school. Unfortunately, in 1859 she died literally on Salmon's doorstep, the victim of a heart attack on her walk home from church. Kate heard Alice groaning on the threshold and sent for a doctor. Despite everyone's best efforts Alice's life quietly slipped away that very night, leaving the household motherless once again.

Salmon confided in his journal, "I lost a dear & good sister," but Kate's and Nettie's feelings went unrecorded. A Columbus newspaper lauded Alice because her "amiable virtues," as well as her many charitable activities, "had endeared her to many friends."[17] Alice had represented, in short, a paragon of nineteenth-century womanhood that might have served Kate as a role model in her adult life. Nineteen-year-old Kate would have to take over mothering tasks for her twelve-year-old sister, particularly during the war years, when Salmon had little time to act as one parent, let alone two.

This veritable parade of maternal and infant death, among which her father stood physically, if not emotionally, unscathed, must have made quite an impression upon young Kate's psyche. Biographers and contemporary observers alike have excoriated Kate for her seemingly excessive attachment to her father, but to whom else should she have looked to for love? Only her father stood the test of time. Kate lived part-time with her father, mothers, and Aunt Alice at Clifton farm, outside Columbus, until she turned seven. After that she was often away at a New York school for girls. To this must be added the reality of being a young girl raised in a culture filled with romantic literature about the importance of the mother/daughter relationship, as well as a society where most girls had intense day-to-day interaction with other females.[18] Victorian culture held that mothers taught daughters what it meant to be a woman. Mothers also had more emotionally intimate relationships with their daughters than they did with their sons or than did fathers with daughters. Salmon loved

Kate, but he proved better at monitoring her study habits than teaching her how to be a girl. Nor did Kate's female relatives entirely fill the gap, for death and dislocations continually fractured her relationships with aunts and teachers. As a result, Kate transferred to her father the emotional dependency that a nineteenth-century middle-class girl was supposed to have on her mother—a dependency made painful by his recurring physical and emotional distance.[19]

Indeed, Salmon's busy political career would have precluded full-time parenting even if he were not a single parent. In the same letter in which he announced Kate's birth as "a certain interesting little stranger who has lately made her first appearance on this stage," he hoped that "before the next Presidential elections antislavery feelings will Overthrow the *Great Evil*."[20] His political prominence would only grow during the years of Kate's childhood and young adulthood. Salmon's journals record a man constantly on the move in the service of antislavery politics. He tried fugitive slave cases before the U.S. Circuit Court, arguing that when African Americans left slave territory they became free by natural right and the founding fathers' intentions. His deep involvement in the Liberty Party in the early 1840s took him to conventions in both Ohio and New York.

Salmon's political course and strong religious beliefs combined to make him a particular kind of nineteenth-century man. Although several models for Victorian manhood coexisted at this time, Salmon defined himself as a self-controlled, temperate, and peaceful man whose partisan affiliations were tolerant of female political activity. The Liberty, Free-Soil, and Republican Parties were all more tolerant of women's political activities than were the Democrats.[21] Salmon's diaries, which in and of themselves illustrate his attempts to discipline himself to daily reflection, contain a veritable litany of domestic, moral, and political concerns. In 1840, for example, Salmon read and began to emulate the journal and lifestyle system espoused by *The Student's Manual*. Popularly known as "Todd's manual," it set out strict schedules for daily writing, reading, and reflecting meant to inculcate self-control through regular habits.[22]

In 1847, soon after Nettie's birth, Salmon sent Kate to Henrietta Haines's school for girls on Madison Avenue in New York. Although she was often accused of "evil stepmother" syndrome, Belle had good reasons for sending Kate to boarding school. Struggling with tuberculosis at this point, she probably found that the rigors of caring for both herself and a new baby left little energy for coping with an older child. Nonetheless, Belle did try to act as a mother to Kate, even from a considerable distance. Her letters illustrate genuine warmth and provide vivid descriptions of Kate's little sister: "Nettie grows very fast and we often have long talks about you and think how pleasant it will be when I am well and you home from school. Nettie gets quite beyond herself when I talk to her of you, & she jumps about clapping her little hands and saying oh Katy, oh Katy come home!" In another letter, Belle's description of her and three-year-old Nettie's seasickness on a voyage to Texas makes the reader almost nauseous in its detail, while a letter describing undressing Nettie and finding a snake inside the little girl's petticoats resounds with humor.

However well intentioned, though, Belle's letters may have served to make Kate more homesick by providing such clear pictures of what she was missing. As if she understood the effect her letters might have on her adoptive daughter, Belle was careful to remind Kate that the family missed her. "Nettie talks a great deal about you," she assured ten-year-old Kate, "& if strangers are going to New York she immediately tells them her sister Katy is in New York, and they will see her, & sometimes she wants to go with them to see you." Belle always signed her letters to Kate "your affectionate Mother," trying to fill the void left in Kate's life by her own mother's death. [23]

Like Kate's mother, Belle traveled to take the water cure, going to hydropathic institutions in Massachusetts, New Jersey, and New York. A popular therapeutic treatment in the nineteenth century, hydropathy utilized a regimen of cold water drinking and bathing. Its emphasis on fresh air, exercise, and light clothing made a great impression on Kate's father, who would urge his daughters, throughout their lives, to live by these tenets. [24] Salmon found himself at home no more often than Belle during the years of their marriage. He helped frame the Free-Soil Party platform in 1848, campaigned for Free-Soil candidates, and emerged in Ohio as an antislavery leader. In 1849 the Ohio legislature elected Salmon to the U.S. Senate. This put Kate's father in Washington on and off for the next six years. After Belle died in 1852, Salmon wrote Kate an uncharacteristically affectionate letter in which he consoled her for her loss of "a kind and affectionate guide" and thanked her for her "sincere devotion" to her stepmother. [25]

After Belle's death, Kate continued to spend the bulk of her time at Miss Haines's school for girls (Nettie went away to school at about the same age as Kate). Salmon did not send his girls away simply to warehouse them or to acquire for them a finishing school education. Miss Henrietta Haines expected far more from her students than skill in embroidery and piano playing. She planned rigorous courses of study in history, languages, math, composition, and religion. [26] Kate's classical education, while exceptional in its degree, did not greatly deviate from the kind of education many nineteenth-century girls received, particularly white, native-born girls. Literacy rates for men and women increased tremendously during the first half of the century, with women's literacy rivaling men's for the first time in American history. The notion of a republican country, one that depended upon the informed will of the people, translated into a need for an educated citizenry. Although only some white men could vote, Americans supported both public and private education for white women so that they might better mother male citizens. [27] Salmon expected his daughters to become educated women in order to act as appropriate political foils for both himself and prospective husbands and children.

Salmon never seemed to regret that his two children were not boys or to expect less of them because of their sex. He regularly pressed nine-year-old Kate to keep a journal and to draw upon it in writing more descriptive letters to her father. "You are a little girl and can easily command time to write a journal every day, and can copy that journal once a week and send it to me with a short letter. This is all I have ASKED of you and this you might certainly have done." [28] It seems that Kate resisted this level of control, causing untold friction between father and daughter. Several times, while criticizing Kate's letter writing, Salmon nagged that "What is worth doing at all is worth doing well," in part because Kate seemed to purposely underperform in the academic arena. [29] This letter is also interesting because Salmon wrote it on Kate's birthday but failed to mention her special day. He believed that her success would depend on hard work and ability and was deeply worried that Kate would not live up to his exacting standards. Like many other nineteenth-century parents, Salmon parented Kate with a combination of love and guilt; unfortunately for his daughter, however, he emphasized the guilt and mishandled the love. [30]

The course Salmon prescribed for his daughters did sometimes step outside the boundaries of women's traditional roles at midcentury. Salmon knew and admired many women who fell outside the strict parameters of "true womanhood." These women included his mother, Jannette Ralston

Chase, who became a single parent when her son was quite young and ran her family with an iron will. His scholarly older sister Abigail advised rigorous courses of study for her younger siblings, and sister Hannah was "something of a bluestocking." Elizabeth Washington Gamble Wirt, the wife of Chase's mentor William Wirt, authored *Flora's Dictionary*, which described the symbolic language of flowers through poetry. In fact, the Wirts also held their children, girls and boys, to exacting scholastic standards and despaired when their son Robert resisted.[31] Salmon wanted his daughters to be like all of these women—accomplished but still womanly. He wanted to raise girls who could act intelligently in the public arena and act as the center of morally virtuous families. He wanted to turn Kate into an accomplished political woman, not a surrogate son.

The liberal arts, not mathematics and science, played the most important part in Chase's program for his daughters. Chase's own education, guided by the stern influence of his uncle Philander Chase, the Episcopalian bishop of Ohio in the 1820s, emphasized the classics, the Bible, historical narratives, and authors like Shakespeare and Milton.[32] The young scholar had early aspirations as a writer and poet (writing perfectly mediocre poetry), and he kept a journal for most of his life. Salmon's mentor William Wirt was a man known for his scholarly avocation as well as for his personal charm and oratorical gifts.[33] As a result of the influences of Uncle Philander and Wirt, Salmon's career in law and politics owed much to written exposition, though he never really developed any brilliance in speechmaking, much to his career's detriment.

In arguing several fugitive slave cases, for example, Salmon gained fame for both himself and the antislavery cause by developing "an interpretation of American history which convinced thousands of Northerners that anti-slavery was . . . fully compatible with the constitution."[34] He exhorted his daughters to hone their writing skills (through careful attention to penmanship) and develop their powers of observation. "You must keep your eyes open child," he wrote fourteen-year-old Kate. "They were given you expressly to see with: and you mind was given you expressly to observe with."[35] He incessantly reproached both girls for their grammar, style, spelling, and, ironically (given his famously illegible script), handwriting, advice Kate took more seriously than did the more free-spirited Nettie. Reiterating warnings he had given Kate a few years before, Chase wrote thirteen-year-old Nettie, "You must take a great deal of pains with your spelling my darling. Your handwriting will be very good if you do not become careless. Remember the old saying that whatever is worth doing at all is worth doing well."[36] Seven years older than Nettie, Kate offered her younger sister advice and criticism as well: "Your last letter was a great improvement upon the others, still the spelling is not perfect. When you are not perfectly sure about a word, you should look at it in the dictionary."[37] Nettie's letters to Kate and to her father indicate a young woman with more than a passing acquaintance with the liberal arts. In the middle of her fourteenth year she offered this opinion: "I have been reading Dickens a great deal lately I think his writings are the strangest mixture of the grotesque & delicacy of feeling joined up and scattered around in the queerest manner. I think sometimes I like him and them again I don't, he is so strange."[38]

Although Nettie would have some difficulty fulfilling her father's expectations, Kate had even more trouble. These failings also seem to have weighed more heavily on Kate than on Nettie. The problem lay partly in Salmon's high standards and partly in Kate's inability, or perhaps even stubborn refusal, to meet those standards. Whereas Kate was torn between intransigence and a desire to please, Nettie was blithely secure in herself and her father's love in spite of his cold manner. Indeed, Nettie's nature made people, including her father, kinder to her than to her sister. It is difficult to determine whether these differences were innate or the result of birth order—Nettie may have benefited from a kind of "second son" syndrome, whereas Kate bore the burden of heir apparent, despite her sex. For example, in July 1854 Miss Haines sent Salmon his daughter's report card. He wrote to Kate that "it is not so creditable to you as I hoped & expected." She had finished eighth in her class and had received an unfavorable report from her French teacher—with whom she also shared a room. "The time has come to put on your thinking cap & use your brains," Salmon commanded. He then made her study French over the summer break.

Salmon's concerns encompassed more than Kate's intellectual growth. She was to spend the summer with his cousin Eliza in Concord. "You are now just at that age when girls are apt to feel that they ought to be allowed to think & act for themselves a good deal more than they are capable of," Salmon wrote. He was worried that Kate might do something that would cause her friends to lose their regard for her—suggesting not only that Kate malingered over her studies but that she had been showing a streak of independence that he regarded as vaguely dangerous.[39] In a long-distance attempt to control her behavior, he demanded that she write him three times a week, then suggested that a composition she had recently sent him could not have been her own work.

Perhaps as an expression of his dissatisfaction with the turn that Kate had taken at Miss Haines's school, Salmon enrolled her in Mrs. Maria Eastman's school after the 1854 summer break. Just outside Philadelphia, Eastman's Female Seminary offered a rigorous program of rhetoric, logic, literature, history, mathematics, geography, Latin, French, German, and Italian. Science courses included astronomy, physiology, chemistry, botany, and geology.[40] At first Kate enjoyed the school, though her father expressed consternation when he learned that the young women had played cards one Sunday evening. "The most that can be said of such games is that they relax & divert the mind; but there is a danger that they may absorb and excite it," he warned, "and, as there are many modes of diversion and relaxation which are not dangerous, it is best to avoid those which are."[41]

By the end of the school year Kate had become disenchanted with Mrs. Eastman's school, perhaps beguiled by the pleasant thought of quitting school altogether and going into society. She had had a brief taste of society over her Christmas break, when she charmed prominent Massachusetts senator Charles Sumner and others with her agreeable and "discriminating" manner.[42] That summer she and her father apparently agreed that she had had enough formal education. Kate spent the summer in Ohio with relatives while Salmon campaigned for the Ohio governor's seat, and that fall she was in New York outfitting herself with a wardrobe suitable for a young lady stepping into adulthood.

Salmon won the governorship of Ohio in the 1855 election, and for the first time in ten years Kate made arrangements to make her full-time home with him. Because her father would not be inaugurated until January 1856, she went to Columbus before him to set up house. Salmon wrote his daughter page after page of instructions with regard to the minutiae of settling down in Columbus, instructing her on which carpets and beds went in which rooms, how much she might spend on chairs, and where to go shopping. No detail was too small for the new governor's eye. Since Ohio did not have an official governor's residence, Salmon bought a house, complete with an attached greenhouse that functioned as Nettie's principal play area when she was not at school in Philadelphia. Aunt Alice rounded out the Chases' "domestic felicity" that year.[43] Having set up house to her father's exacting taste, Kate enrolled in a finishing school, where she attempted to perfect her skills at painting and music. She went to church with her father every Sunday, sometimes both morning and evening, went to parties with relatives and on sleigh rides with friends, and took additional French lessons, along with her father. Together the father-daughter pair paid social calls, went riding, and attended lectures. Salmon appears to have immensely enjoyed their time together. He described Kate as "sprightly & intelligent & right minded" after she discussed local and party politics one evening with her father and Edward Pierce, a Free-Soil and Republican politician.[44]

What seems clear, at least in retrospect, about Kate and her father's relationship during the Columbus years is that Kate decided to make herself invaluable to her father. She determined to place herself so centrally in his life that he would never again send her away. And so from 1857 to 1860 Kate made herself over from a well-educated girl busy with a social whirl of calls and parties into an astute woman who could converse intelligently with any politician in America. Not coincidentally, she did so during the very years that the Republican Party gave birth to itself, grew quickly to maturity, and won a presidential election.

The political woman, particularly the Republican political woman, was no anomaly in prewar America. In the 1856 presidential campaign, Republicans nominated adventurer John Frémont against James Buchanan. The new Republican Party centrally featured his wife, Jessie Benton Frémont, in the campaign, capitalizing on her renowned intelligence, beauty, and antislavery stance. Kate probably saw Jessie as a role model. Campaign songs, posters, stories, and slogans like "Jessie's choice" not only touted a sparkling political wife but used Jessie as a symbol of Republicans' commitment to partisan women.

Democrats reacted to the campaign strategy with derision and suggested that it proved Republican effeminacy.[45] Although both parties used womanhood as a construct to understand partisanship, the Republican Party particularly encouraged women as individuals, rather than as symbols, to become engaged in the political process. Many women took to the stump for Republicans in the late 1850s. They marched in parades, gave and attended speeches, signed petitions, and otherwise influenced and strengthened the party's position. In 1856, for example, Clarina Nichols gave over fifty speeches to Kansas Republicans.[46] Sympathetic to the Kansas Free-

State movement, Kate had hanging on her bedroom wall a framed issue of the *Herald of Freedom*, a Kansas newspaper whose press had been destroyed in the first sack of Lawrence. Flanking the *Herald*, Kate had pictures of her father and Charles Sumner, who had recently suffered a caning at the hands of Preston Brooks as a result of his "Crime against Kansas" speech.[47]

Kate traded the feminine details of finishing school for the hard knocks of Civil War politics with considerable success. A woman who met Kate in 1858 described her as "cultivated to her fingertips, [she] had the manners that come from exquisite breeding and a charming heart, and had been, all through her father's public career, a daughter of whom any man could be extravagantly proud."[48] The memoirist and society lady Isabella Trotter also met Kate at the governor's house and described her "as full of intelligence and knowledge. Her figure is tall and slight, but at the same time beautifully rounded; her neck long and graceful, with a sweet pretty brunette face. I have seldom seen such lovely eyes and dark eyelashes; she has rich dark hair in great profusion, but her style and dress were of the utmost simplicity and grace."[49] Salmon's politicking during the winter and spring of 1860 offered plenty of opportunities for Kate to hone her social and political skills. The German American politician and journalist Carl Schurz provides one of the best descriptions of the young woman Kate had become, recorded after he attended one of the Chases' well-known political breakfasts.

> She saluted me kindly, and then let herself down upon her chair with the graceful lightness of a bird that, folding its wings, perches upon the branch of a tree. She was then about eighteen years old, tall and slender, and exceedingly well formed. Her features were not at all regularly beautiful according to the classic rule. Her little nose, somewhat audaciously tipped up, would perhaps not have passed muster with a severe critic, but it fitted pleasingly into her face with its large, languid but at the same time vivacious hazel eyes, shaded by long dark lashes and arched over by proud eyebrows. The fine forehead was framed in waving, gold-brown hair.[50]

Unfortunately, these qualities would not help Kate's father gain the 1860 presidential nomination, for the new Republican Party viewed him as entirely too radical in his antislavery stance. He also was not particularly notable at that all-important political talent, speechmaking. In early 1860 the Ohio legislature again elected Salmon to serve in the U.S. Senate, for a term to begin in March 1861. Months later, Abraham Lincoln won the

Republican nomination, and Salmon pledged his support to his rival.[51] Kate had accompanied her father on several campaign trips while he sought his own nomination, but she abandoned the political hunt when his efforts came to naught. While her father stumped for Lincoln, she spent the rest of the summer visiting relatives.[52]

The Chase family left Ohio in February 1861, several weeks before Salmon's tenure as senator began. He and the girls stayed for a few days with Elizabeth and Louis M. Goldsborough, William Wirt's daughter and son-in-law, before moving to a suite of rooms at the Rugby, a residential hotel. Soon afterward, Salmon rented the house on the corner of Sixth and E Streets that would become their Washington home for the next several years.[53] Nettie later reported her first impressions of the nation's capital as "very disappointing; the combination of grandioseness and squalor of Washington" at that time impressed even a fourteen-year-old girl's mind with a sense of incongruity. The enormously wide avenues "literally flow[ed] with yellow mud; the contemplative cows and pigs meander[ed] through the streets."[54]

Salmon took the girls to Lincoln's inauguration and introduced them to the "very tall man" who called 1600 Pennsylvania Avenue his home, an occasion that made quite an impression upon Kate's little sister. At the inaugural ball Kate was resplendent in a white satin, puffed-sleeved, décolleté gown, complete with an overskirt of cherry silk festooned with artificial white roses. A crown of matching roses completed her ensemble, setting her personal precedent (and much-emulated style) of adorning herself with flowers rather than jewels—at least until she became a millionaire's wife.

Soon after the inauguration the Senate confirmed Kate's father as secretary of the treasury, making Kate one of the leading ladies in Washington. Since the wife of William H. Seward, Lincoln's secretary of state, did not go into society, only Mary Todd Lincoln came before Kate in social precedence. Besides being the second-ranking lady in Washington, Kate had youth, beauty, and intelligence at her disposal. "Quite a belle in Washington" and "worthy of all the admiration she received," summed up Mary Lincoln's maid Elizabeth Keckley. Abraham Lincoln pronounced her "young and handsome." His wife thought just the opposite, finding in Kate a bitter rival for social eminence. The First Lady disliked Kate for a multitude of reasons. Kate was younger and prettier than she and certainly more at home in Washington's political culture. Mary also believed, perhaps correctly, that

Kate coveted her role as First Lady and failed to cede appropriate deference to her social superior. Mary went so far as to forbid her husband to dance, or even talk, with Kate.[55]

Indeed, as *La belle des belles*, Mary had every right to worry that capital elites might find Kate a superior candidate for the head of Washington society. Carl Schurz touched upon the double threat that lay at the heart of Kate's position as a Washington belle when he found that in political discussions "graceful" Kate could take "a lively and remarkably intelligent part."[56] Although belles are most often depicted as a frivolous social type, they actually had considerable power—more so than most young women would ever again experience in their lives. Kate's position as a belle placed her at the center of social power and near a significant arena of political action. Serving as a "model of empowerment" and able to "bend [men] to her will," a belle like Kate specialized in evoking intense emotions while controlling her own. This, combined with Kate's political acuity, made her a kind of belle not often described by historians.[57] Kate could add to her arsenal her unmarried state, which gave her access to avenues of social expression closed to married women. With such weapons Kate could defeat Mary Lincoln on both fronts of the social battlefield, for Salmon's daughter had as an astute a grasp of politics as she had a youthful and pretty face.[58]

There would be much to learn and many prominent political and military men with whom to have discussions in the months after Lincoln's election. Major Robert Anderson accompanied Kate and Nettie home to Washington from New York in April 1861. News that the Sixth Massachusetts had been fired upon in Baltimore made the trip an adventure (the rail lines having been destroyed in Baltimore), complete with cannon fire from a privateer. Anderson and the girls escaped harm and landed in Annapolis, where they were greeted by General Benjamin Butler and his troops. Men from the Eighth Massachusetts escorted the girls home to their father.[59] In the succeeding weeks Salmon introduced his daughters to Winfield Scott, Simon Cameron, William Seward, Charles Sumner, and other Union luminaries. John Garrett, the president of the Baltimore and Ohio Railroad, gave both the Chases and the Lincolns "a consignment of live terrapin" for their mutual gastronomic enjoyment. The Chases set theirs loose in the basement, from which the turtles made their way to freedom through benign neglect. Much concerned, Nettie asked Lincoln what he did with his shelled delicacies. "I felt so sorry for the poor little fellows," the president replied, "that I took them all out into the garden and let them run away." [60] Nettie and Kate were much relieved.

While Kate's future husband would experience Bull Run from an officer's perspective, Kate and her sister did so from a more domestic point of view. The rumbling of the ambulance wagons outside their house woke them the morning after the battle. Rather than seeing cowardly failure in the troops' panicked retreat, they saw "such lengths by which men of fair courage may be driven by a panic." Salmon ordered coffee to be served from the street-level kitchen door to haggard and woeful-looking men. As Union hospitals overflowed, the girls watched in amazement as "eight or ten . . . poor sufferers were brought into the house." A soldier about Kate's age used profane language in front of the girls until he was chastised by the Chases' friend Bishop Charles P. McIlvaine. "God can help you," the bishop warned, "much more than the devil can." Family friend General Irvin McDowell had come to the house not long before the battle. William Seward also stopped by, and he optimistically told the Chases that "in ninety days the rebellion will be over and the country at peace." [61] But that July chaos reigned in the capital, and eventually both sides settled in for a protracted conflict. The soldiers soon left the Sixth and E Streets house, and the Chase sisters did what so many Washington women did that summer and fall—visit hospitals, talk about the war, and wait to see what would happen next.

Nettie remembered that the earliest "political words or shibboleths that I can remember are the 'Solid South' 'Compromise,' and 'Cotton is King.'" She added that the girls heard all "the vital and absorbing topics of the day constantly talked about and debated by the elder members of the family and the prominent men of Ohio and such discussions being as it were, each part of our daily life while we were busy with our play." [62] Her description of the physical layout of the Chases' Ohio house reveals a fairly open floor plan wherein "the four presidential candidates became mingled with our play in the oddest ways." Nettie's stories vividly tell of the blurring between private and public spheres in the Chase household. The girls, for example, once enlisted future president James A. Garfield in "a physiological research, which consisted of the disinterment of several defunct canaries in order that their skeletons might be presented to a museum, in the nursery." [63] Another instance of this blurring focused on the first political event Nettie remembered: "the self immolating attempt of John Brown . . . to free the slaves in Virginia." Then twelve years old,

Nettie and her cohorts "constructed a little fort and raised a flag on which was painted redly and defiantly, 'Freedom forever and Slavery never.' " A friend of Chase's passed through the conservatory and pointed out the "little rebels" to their father, whereupon Chase took the children into his study for a talk about politics and the sacredness of national law. Nettie remembered that her father emphasized "that the right-thinking men and women of the country must work together by peaceful means for the liberation of the slaves." [64] It was clear to Nettie that her father took his antislavery stance into his private realm, and this must have made a great impression upon his daughters.

As edifying as they are amusing, these stories say a lot about the kind of household in which the Chase girls grew up, the ideology which circulated in that private sphere, and what it meant to them in later years. In other articles Nettie discussed her father's love for literature, his belief in the importance of languages, his interest in the military side of the war, and the trips they took together. Domestic matters, romantic issues, and feminine accomplishment do not figure in these family stories; rather, political and intellectual realms provide the focus. Although these realities may be attributable to epistolary conventions or to the wishes of a newspaper editor, the very consistency in content of Nettie's reminiscences suggests that Republican rhetoric played as large a part in the lives of Kate and Nettie Chase as did prescriptions of womanhood. This is not to suggest that young Kate and Nettie stepped entirely outside the bounds of womanhood or failed to adhere to a proper codes of dress or decorum—neither of them ever publicly espoused, for example, free love or woman suffrage—but rather that Kate's childhood prepared her for her life as a political woman.

THE MAKING OF A "BOY GOVERNOR"

William Sprague turned thirteen just two months before his father's murder. It happened, as they say, "on a dark and stormy night," in 1843, when someone set upon Amasa Sprague as he walked home, shooting him in the arm and then cracking his head open with the stock of the gun. The assailant then threw the offending firearm in a nearby ditch, where it would later be found and identified. A small, stocky man who always had a joke ready at his lips, Amasa had recently prevailed upon the Cranston, Rhode Island, city council to deny the Gordon brothers a liquor license renewal, effectively shutting down the little gin mill wherein so many of Sprague's workers undoubtedly spent their time and money. Nicholas Gordon publicly threatened Amasa after the revocation, while other people reported seeing William Gordon lurking around one of the Sprague cotton mills. Since Amasa was the area's largest employer, as well as the brother of Rhode Island's former governor and current senator William Sprague III, the murder had to be avenged. Senator Sprague resigned his seat, hunted down the Gordons, identified the murder weapon as Nicholas Gordon's possession, and prevailed upon the state judicial system to convict and execute Nicholas Gordon for the murder of Amasa Sprague.[65]

Many Rhode Islanders thought the Spragues had railroaded Gordon, and over two thousand people accompanied the Gordon coffin through the streets of Providence in protest. Doubts lingered about the Spragues' use of power to avenge the murder of one of their own while coincidentally and conveniently reinforcing worker sobriety. So many doubters existed that nine years later the Rhode Island legislature abolished hanging in that state in response to what came to be viewed as a politically and industrially motivated legal lynching.[66] Amasa's son William, however, did not see the events of that winter as an episode of industrial conflict or as an example of the rapacious power of the rich. For William the murder and trial were a great personal tragedy that haunted him for the rest of his life.[67]

At the time of his father's murder, William, along with his brother, Amasa, and his sisters, Almira and Mary Ann, attended private school. The boys had additional schooling at the Irving Institute in Tarrytown, New York, but their uncle William, who had taken over the mills after the murder, quickly determined that the boys should be educated in the family business. Uncle William might also have based his decision to pull the boys out of school on the fact that neither of them showed as much interest in academia as they did in the more adventurous side of adolescent boy culture.

So began William's uncomfortable relationship with education. He spent his formative years in the counting rooms of A. & W. Sprague, learning the cotton-milling and calico-printing business from the ground up. Rhode Island was a state uniquely suited to the kind of business that made the Sprague millions. Its numerous waterways, with particularly winding courses and uneven beds, created a myriad of potential waterpower sites. As early as 1795 the state boasted three spinning mills, a number that exploded

1. Senator William Sprague. Photo by Brady, courtesy of the National Archives.

after the 1817 importation of the power loom. Production value for cotton reached over $7 million by 1840 and leapt to in excess of $20 million by the eve of the war.[68]

In this burgeoning industrial world, Fanny Morgan Sprague, the daughter of a shoemaker, gave birth to William in Cranston on 12 September 1830. Two years earlier, her first child, a son named after his father, had been born. Daughters Almira and Mary Ann quickly followed.[69] As a child William had a fervent interest in things military. A friend of his remembered that young William organized a troop of twelve-year-old boys to drill and march in preparation for the social upheaval that became the Dorr Rebellion. In a struggle for political power, Thomas Wilson Dorr led the propertyless and thus disenfranchised workingmen in a revolt against Rhode Island's existing system—one that concentrated political power in the hands of old rural farming towns and wealthy industrialists. These class-based and geographic hostilities eventually caused a subtle transfer of power to the state's northern urban and industrial sections.[70] In the fall of 1841 Dorr's supporters passed a "People's Constitution" for which more than thirteen thousand white, male citizens voted. Dorrites claimed that this vote constituted a majority of voting Rhode Islanders and that the old state charter should be replaced. Rhode Island's legislature naturally refused to recognize the popular, if extralegal, constitution. The situation became increasingly tense until, in May 1842, Dorr's supporters mounted an unsuccessful attack on Providence.

At the outbreak of hostilities, William and forty other boys gathered together and began to march to the center of action. The miscreant group probably intended to defend the conservative faction, given the fact that William's uncle, the senator, had been sent to President John Tyler to request assistance against the Dorrites.[71] Earlier in the conflict, though, before switching his support to the conservatives, Uncle William had voted for the People's Constitution. Dorrites were outraged and considered him a traitor. Early-nineteenth-century boys' lengthy transition from dependence to independence often encouraged them to rebel against adult male authority. Thus the boys' march may have just as well been a rejection of, rather than support for, family politics.[72] State troops discovered the boys not far from their homes and escorted them back to their parents before anyone came to harm.

In his teens and twenties, William joined and drilled with the Providence Marine Artillery Company. The aspiring soldier found the group a sadly disorganized mélange of men dedicated mostly to public parades. This disorganization of the Rhode Island militia reflected a national trend. Although the Second Amendment to the Constitution guarantees the right of states to maintain militias, by 1850 compulsory militias had fallen into disrepute and had even become illegal in some states.[73] Within three years of his joining, the company promoted William from lieutenant to colonel, though undoubtedly the company was as impressed with the Sprague fortune as with William's organizational prowess. He paid all the company's bills, purchased a full battery of light artillery, and had a grand time playing at military games.[74]

William's enjoyment of this side of his adult life can be linked to his boyhood, when he ran around with a neighborhood gang of boys relatively unfettered by the domestic or business sphere. This play, far from being harmless fun, focused on self-assertion, conflict with other boys, sham battles, and a kind of guerrilla warfare against adults. Antebellum American boys attached themselves not only to local militias but to volunteer fire departments and political party activities—all opportunities for them to emulate adult men in a boy-centered subculture. William's martial life also allowed him to escape the serious business of textile manufacturing and a fatherless home life.[75]

While William's youthful activities, both in the artillery and in the mill counting rooms, provided early training in the art of manhood, they also did him a disservice. Because William was bereft of a father figure, his early assumption of manhood—or what a young, fatherless boy conceived as manly—created a young man ill at ease with himself. William's inability to create a convincing gender code for himself was only exacerbated by the fact that the early nineteenth century featured a number of models for manliness, many of them contradictory and in transition. His personal code of masculinity was often clumsily exaggerated in some aspects and atrophied in others. William's fondness for martial glory suggests that he based part of his definition of manhood on a code of honor more often used to describe southern men. Southern honor depended in great part on slavery, a social system that created a tremendous contrast between the abject dependence of slaves (and to a lesser extent white women) and the autonomous freedom, prestige, and power that came from white men's control of others. The Sprague manufacturing empire placed William in the middle of a world where Sprague men employed a vast number of workers—people whose labors made William's family extremely wealthy and politically powerful. In a manner similar to the mutual dependency of slavery and honor in the South, the wage labor system in the Northeast created a truncated version of honor-based manhood in the North. William's version of honorable manhood feared shame above all other public humiliations and protected itself with deeds of collective and individual aggression. That he learned this elaborate personal code without the benefit of a father not only skewed his sense of manhood but made that code all the more important to him.[76]

In 1856, after Uncle William died of typhoid fever, William's boyhood came to an end. With the death of the family patriarch, control of the business passed to the next generation of Spragues. Only twenty-six years old that year, William, along with his brother, sisters, mother, and cousin, formed a new company called A. & W. Sprague Company. William later reported, "I was thrust into the counting-room, performing its lowest drudgeries, raising myself to all of its highest positions," so that "I was left with the interest in my sole charge."[77] Brother Amasa and cousin Byron ostensibly also ran the company, but William did most of the work. Theoretically, Amasa's responsibilities encompassed the calico printworks, while William supervised cotton milling and dyeing as well as the maintenance of buildings and machinery. In reality, Amasa preferred to focus his energies on raising and racing trotting horses, while Byron practiced the family predilection for insobriety full-time.[78] Byron's misbehavior was so extreme that William, himself no stranger to alcohol-induced revelry, commented at Byron's death that "he died of drink and barbarous practices."[79] It is unclear just what "barbarous practices" might encompass, but a sexually transmitted disease may have played a part in Byron's demise. What does seem clear is that Byron's and Amasa's life choices left little room for the mundane details of textile mill operation.

Both William's contemporaries and his biographers have underemphasized his business acumen, particularly as a young man. Without a father's guidance, the young man turned a thriving but modest cotton-milling business into one of the largest and most profitable firms of the nineteenth century. One local history of mill towns reads like a laundry list of local businessmen who sold out to the Sprague company. A. & W. Sprague purchased land, water rights, and existing mills from anyone who would sell. William bought the newest equipment and refurbished mills in Cranston, Arctic, Quidnick, and Natick; built a state-of-the-art establishment at Baltic; and ran all the mills, at an enormous profit, through the Civil War years and after. At the Quidnick mill, for example, William had the buildings moved closer to the river, built new tenement houses, and enlarged the mill to hold 250 looms. The company paid workers promptly and in cash, maintained strict discipline, and never experienced a strike for wages. [80] William also designed mills, including a four-story granite mill at Arctic, complete with surrounding dam, waterfall, and machine shop. [81]

At the company's pinnacle, a New York newspaper reported that A. & W. Sprague ran nearly 280,000 spindles and employed 10,000 workers, including 1,200 in Cranston, 800 at Natick, 500 at Arctic, 500 at Quidnick, 600 at Central Falls, 1,000 at Baltic, and 700 at a lumber mill in Augusta, Maine. Combined, A. & W. Sprague had a payroll of $25,000 per day, out of which workers paid rent on Sprague-owned tenements and boardinghouses built near each mill. The company was, quite simply, the largest calico-printing mill system in the world. [82] Sources also reported that by 1873 the output of the Sprague operations exceeded that of any other textile company in the United States. The nine mammoth Sprague mills wove a combined 800,000 yards of cloth plus 1.4 million yards of calico per week, and legend had it that "whenever you saw smoke in Rhody it belonged to the Spragues." [83]

Not content to depend solely on the vagaries of the cotton-milling business, the Spragues also held timberlands in Maine, cattle land in Kansas and Texas, and a waterpower company in South Carolina. In Providence they controlled the Union Railroad (a streetcar rail line), the Perkins Sheet Iron Company, the Rhode Island Horse Shoe Company, the Sprague Mowing Machine Company, the Comstock Stove Foundry, and the American Horse Nail Company, in total employing an additional eight hundred workers. William was an economically independent man whose dedication to capitalism enhanced his claims to nineteenth-century manhood. As a "Self-Made Man," a nineteenth-century category for manhood, he had to be aggressive in business, but he, like other men, lived at the mercy of the market. The very instability of the market made men like William chronically anxious and insecure. Always a "work in progress" that might falter at the first economic failure, this configuration of manhood was both precarious and powerful. Men who linked their manhood to economic success risked their gender identity with every dip in the market. Time and again William emphasized his worldly achievements as proof of his manly self. [84]

Although William was an accomplished businessman, his background provided him less political and intellectual indoctrination than Kate had gained from her own upbringing. William's position as an extremely successful and wealthy businessman partially mitigated his need for higher-education credentials, but many prominent men were wealthy and well educated. His love of the military side of life provided him with a way in which to view himself as equal to his colleagues. In 1859 William took a trip to England, France, and Italy, perhaps partly in an attempt to acquire the kind of polish and credentials that would allow him entrée into high society. Just one year shy of thirty, he found himself touring the military establishments of Europe, where he found efforts for Italian liberty sufficiently interesting to generously contribute to Giuseppe Garibaldi's quest for Italian nationalism.[85] The Sprague family said that the titular head of the family had traveled to Europe as a "matter of health," seeking respite from the rigors of running a multimillion-dollar empire, but there was a more seamy reason for William's trip abroad: his paramour was pregnant.

William had chosen to dally with a respectable middle-class girl named Mary Eliza Viall. The Vialls were among Providence's finest families, but in spite of (or because of) their staunch conservatism, Mary believed in free love and William Sprague. She met William in his late twenties and found him a handsome young man. He had dark gray eyes, set so they turned down at the corners, and his hair was light brown and parted at the side. William possessed a fair, boyish complexion that his mustache did little to mature, complemented by clothes always a little rumpled, as if he lacked either the time or the grown-up inclination to take better care of his attire.[86] Many ladies thought he cut an eccentric and romantic figure. Men usually found him less impressive.

"Can you understand," Mary reasoned, "that a man may love a woman too well to marry her,—that in loving himself better,—and by himself we might mean destiny."[87] Her adoration of William bordered upon obsession; she compared him to Napoleon, Hamlet, and Lancelot, and described herself as her hero's "crowned queen." [88] She worshiped everything about William. Unfortunately, Mary became pregnant, and William made it clear that he had no intention of marrying her. With that he left for Europe, while the Vialls arranged a hasty marriage between their daughter and a military man named Anderson, who soon afterward abandoned his new wife.[89]

Mary's free-love ideology rested on the belief that women had a sexual nature and that they had a right to seek sexual gratification with a loved one or to refuse the unwanted advances of any man, husband or not. Advocates of free love did not believe that women should have sex anywhere with anyone but rather that the "instincts of love," rather than the law, ought to legitimize the sexual act. Mary's later writing makes it clear she agreed with Victoria Woodhull's claim that "people may be married by law . . . and they may also be married by love and lack all sanction of law. . . . Law cannot compel two to love." [90] In a thinly disguised biographical novel, *The Merchant's Wife, or He Blundered: A Political Romance of Our Own Day*, Mary excused William's behavior. She asked, "Who flees the sweet enervation of love, to pursue in the cold orbit of glory? What if, in so doing, he must needs sacrifice a human heart upon the altar of his ambition—call it what we may? Will not true love sacrifice itself for the beloved? Did he not honor her by believing she asked for his glory, though he must win it without her? *She* forgave him." [91] Mary, it seemed, was fully prepared herself to live without her Lancelot, but she had not expected to lose him to another woman. It would be Kate, not William, whom Mary would never forgive.

Woodhull and Mary Viall Anderson were not alone in their critique of mid-nineteenth-century marriage. As early as 1847, John Humphrey Noyes's community at Oneida practiced a system of "complex marriage" wherein every woman was considered married to every man. Noyes discouraged monogamy, believing it hindered the realization of a Bible-based communitarianism. Oneidans believed that sex should be joyous and that no one marriage was indissoluble. [92] Forces as disparate as the Shakers, the Mormons, and the nascent women's rights movement all challenged the sexual and marital status quo during the first half of the nineteenth century. Early feminists largely confined their efforts to divorce reform and property acts for married women, which guaranteed that a woman would not lose her personal property to her husband after they married, but even these reforms caused thousands of antebellum Americans to rethink their attitudes toward traditional marriage. [93] However scandalous Mary Viall must have seemed to her middle-class Providence neighbors, she had plenty of company in her rebellion against marital standards.

In 1859 a faction of the Rhode Island Republican Party, uneasy with their party's nomination of an abolitionist named Seth Padelford for governor, joined with state Democrats. This coalition nominated young William for governor. Although Rhode Islanders were among the citizens against the 1850 Fugitive Slave Act, and for Frémont in 1856 and Lincoln in 1860, many considered Padelford entirely too radical for the governorship. Padelford also had the backing of the locally powerful "Journal Ring," headed by former governor and current U.S. senator Henry B. Anthony, who had also once edited the *Providence Journal*. Democrats believed that only heavy infusions of cash into the electoral process would combat the power of the state's reigning political machine, and William Sprague had that kind of money. He had, as well, a sense of his manhood that eschewed moral reforms like abolition and embraced military heroics and economic power over workers.[94]

Four days after his nomination, on 23 January 1860, William debarked the steamship *Africa* from England and arrived in Providence to a hundred-gun salute and cheering throngs of well-wishers. He later said that he had received the grandest ovation Rhode Islanders had ever seen fit to bestow on a private citizen, and indeed it must have seemed so, particularly when he was surrounded by one hundred men in full military dress.[95] His old artillery group feted him that evening at the armory, and afterward a brass band accompanied him on his walk to a nearby hotel where many of Rhode Island's political power brokers were hosting a banquet in his honor. In his speech, William, never much of a rhetorician, promised "a government of enlarged liberty regulated by law."[96] The race for the governor's seat was in full steam.

William had initially refused the nomination, later claiming that he had "previously pledged myself that I would not enter politics. I was young; I had no political knowledge, and no knowledge of the real work at hand." In his protestations he emulated Kate's father, who always, and disingenuously, claimed that he did not seek public office. The tradition of political disinterest recalls the political style of the early Republic. The framers of the Constitution believed that ideal political candidates would accept the will of fellow citizens in accepting political office but that they would not actively seek that office. By the 1840s partisanship began to overrule the intentions of the founding fathers.[97] Like Salmon, who made faux protestations of disinterest his life's work, William had no real commitment to disinterested public service, and he accepted the nomination after only a week's hesitation. "I was told," he said, "that it was of national importance that the radical element should be suppressed."[98] The *Providence Daily*

Post weighed in that "Colonel Sprague will consent to take the post for governor with the view of concentrating the conservative, union loving sentiments of the State." The *Providence Daily Journal*, on the other hand, suggested that William had accepted the nomination in order to consolidate his company's power in the state. The *Providence Evening Press* forcefully decried the *Journal*'s accusation. The nominee controlled a too large and well-established business, it said, to politick as an advertising ploy. Each paper then began to accuse the other of bias and fraudulent reporting.

And so, in the tradition of mid-nineteenth-century politics, the mudslinging began in earnest. Padelford's backers invited Abraham Lincoln to speak on their candidate's behalf, as well as Frederick Brown, John Brown's brother. Democrats flung the epithet "abolitionist" about, suggesting that the Republicans would be happy with nothing less than disunion.[99] Radical Rhode Island Republicans claimed that Sprague wished to repeal the ten-hour law—a potentially disastrous claim against an industrialist candidate in a state full of textile workers. William denied the charge.[100] Just before the election, the *Post* ran a story claiming that Padelford had bribed a local tax collector to disenfranchise potential Sprague voters. Just as probable is the story that Democrats and the Sprague camp bought votes for upwards of fifty dollars each. William spent an astronomical $100,000 on the campaign, and witnesses later claimed that party regulars escorted voters to the ballot box, then paid them after they cast their vote. William's investment proved sound; he won the election by a scant 1,532 votes and paved the way for his transition from local tycoon to nationally known "boy governor."[101] Although one scholar claimed that "his victory was celebrated throughout the nation as a rebuke to the abolitionists," most of the nation barely noticed the Rhode Island gubernatorial race.[102]

The 1860 presidential election overshadowed all other electoral races. Although Lincoln was by no means an abolitionist, southerners found his politics, and the simple fact that he was a Republican, sufficiently inflammatory that in ten slave states he received no electoral votes. Conversely, in the free states he won over 50 percent of the popular vote in a field of four candidates, and he won all of the electoral votes in all of the free states except New Jersey (where Stephen A. Douglas won three to Lincoln's four).[103] Thus the election had strong antislavery implications for the nation, and this greatly alarmed many southerners.

Antislavery ideology like that espoused by Kate's father in his 1854

"Appeal to Independent Democrats" aimed more at limiting the spread of slavery and attacking "slave power" than at abolishing slavery. Abolitionists took a moral stance toward slavery, and some abolitionists advocated equal civil rights for black Americans. While abolition proved too radical for most northerners, who were by and large fairly racist, antislavery rhetoric, with its emphasis on free soil and free labor, provided a basis for the establishment of the Republican Party. Antislavery circumvented the problems of both the Whig Party, which split over slavery, and the American Party, which embraced both anti-immigrant and anti-Catholic stances, partly as a way to divert national attention from the slavery issue. Men like Salmon P. Chase and, to a lesser extent, William Sprague recognized that this new political party "escaped the odium of intolerance while creating a bridge to Protestant Americans" that could provide significant political power to those who could embrace antislavery but not abolition.[104] Lincoln's election represented a triumph of the new Republican Party, which not only opposed the expansion of slavery but supported the homestead program as well as internal developments like the transcontinental railroad and protective tariffs. The country could view Lincoln's victory as "the end of an era"; bisectional parties had once held the Union together, but they could do so no longer.[105]

The Rhode Island elections that year, like so many other elections in 1860, were part of a struggle to determine the course of the nation. Most northerners had no desire to vote for an abolitionist. Rhode Islanders did not wish to anger the region that produced the cotton so valuable to the state's economy. Hoping to illustrate their sympathy for the cotton states' plight, they encouraged Governor Sprague to authorize official state delegates to the Virginia Peace Convention in November 1860. William expected the delegates to lend an ear to any concessions the South might desire in order to quash the secession movement. Additionally, the Rhode Island legislature repealed the law it had earlier designed to thwart slave catching after the passage of the Fugitive Slave Act, hoping to thereby convince southerners that at least some northerners had no desire to interfere with their "peculiar institution." But Rhode Island's concessions came to naught as South Carolina seceded on 20 December 1860, with six more southern states following by 1 February 1861. On 12 April 1861 the Confederacy stuck the first blow of what would be a calamitous and defining war for the nation—firing upon Major Robert Anderson's garrison at Fort Sumter. Rhode Island's—and the Spragues'—hopes for a trouble-free industrial future disappeared in the smoke of Pierre G. T. Beauregard's bombardment of the outgunned fort.

When the Confederate artillery pinned down Fort Sumter, Rhode Island and its governor rose to arms. The time for concessions had passed, and the only clear path to restoring the cotton supply lay in swiftly bringing defeat to the Confederates. Furthermore, war is often good for industry, and this war would prove no exception for Rhode Island's manufacturing interests. The wealth and population of Providence, for example, doubled during the 1860s.[106] The day before the Confederacy fired upon Fort Sumter, William wrote Lincoln to apprise him of the state's readiness:

> We have a Battery of Light Artillery with Horses and Men complete and a force of 1000 men completely disciplined and equipped, unparalleled or at any rate not surpassed by a similar number in any country, who would respond at short notice to the call of the government in defense of the capitol. . . . I would be ready to accompany them. Would God grant his protecting care and guidance to you Sir in your trying and difficult position and a safe deliverance from our unhappy difficulties is the constant prayer of
> Your obedient servant, William Sprague[107]

Only days later, the eager warrior, astride a magnificent white horse (undoubtedly picked for him by his brother, who raised horses), led the First Rhode Island Detached Militia and Battery, under the command of Colonel Ambrose E. Burnside, to the nation's capital. The "Flying Artillery" was the second command to reach Washington, the Thirteenth Massachusetts beating them by one day. As they marched, the troops sang:

> *No state is more true or willing to do*
> *than dear little Rhode Island.*
> *Loyal and True. Little Rhody.*
> *Bully for you. Little Rhody.*
> *Governor Sprague was not very vague*
> *When he said, "Shoulder arms, Little Rhody!"*[108]

Ninety-six horses, purchased by Amasa, accompanied the artillery battery. Washingtonians thrilled to see the dashing "boy governor," his black felt hat festooned with a jaunty yellow feather, leading his men. Not the least among them was Kate Chase.[109]

That spring William appeared to be a romantic and daring figure, but not all believed what they saw. John Hay, Lincoln's private secretary, recorded in his diary that "I called on Sprague, the Gov. of R. I. . . . a small insignificant youth who bought his place. But who is all right now. He is very proud of his company, of its wealth and social standing."[110] The Rhode Island troops quartered at a camp outside Washington and inside the U.S. Patent Office. However unimpressed Hay might have been with William, he gushed at the splendor of his regiment: "Scattered through the rubbish and camp-litter . . . there was enough of breeding and honor to retone the society of the Gulf and wealth enough to purchase the entire state of Florida. . . . When men like these leave their horses, their women and their wine, harden their hands, eat crackers for dinner, wear a shirt for a week and never black their shoes—all for a principle—it is hard to set any bounds to the possibilities of such an army."[111] One observer called the unit "the million dollar regiment."[112]

In these heady opening days of the war, William shone as he never had before and never would again. He organized Rhode Island's Battery A and the Second Rhode Island Infantry and engaged in numerous military sorties. Having escorted Burnside's troops to Washington, William returned to Rhode Island and his business. Perhaps overestimating his own importance, the governor wrote to Secretary of War Simon Cameron that "the interest of the service should admit your making me a major-general." When offered a mere brigadier-generalship, William declined, saying that the people of Rhode Island could not accept a position of less rank.[113] William's refusal may have been wise, for it was said that one could not throw a stick in the nation's capital without hitting six brigadier generals.[114] William had no commission when, in mid-July, General Irvin McDowell began to move his troops against the Confederate army at Manassas Junction. On 18 July, William returned to the field of battle and accompanied Major John Barnard of the U.S. Corps of Engineers on a reconnaissance mission to Blackburn's Ford, near Manassas. Confederates fired upon the party, but all escaped unharmed. The sortie satisfied William's desire to "feel the enemy."[115]

Less than one month after their arrival in Washington, the Rhode Islanders faced the perils of the First Battle of Bull Run. On 21 July, as onlookers gathered on hills with picnic baskets, Confederate troops utterly routed the Union army. Federal troops fled the field with such alacrity that the ground that took them two and one half days to cover going in took one day to retreat from.[116] William had command of the Rhode Island regiment's artillery. Men and horses died where they fell, the bullets so thick in the air that William had holes in his "loose blouse," and survivors thought better of a charge. Then came William's shining moment: "The men will remember when I rode in front of them, struck down their muskets to a level with the enemy, and how they received me—the only officer they had whom they could see; and I shall never for get the sensation which I felt in the blast of the enthusiasm with which these twelve hundred men received me. We were ripe for a charge. I led. Sir, my horse was then shot. I took off his saddle in front of the line; and the men, without order, fell back."[117] The "million dollar" men fled the scene, led by their officers—an act William found reprehensible but which highlighted his own considerable fortitude. "The regiment was led away; but the artillery remained and I with it." To the end of his days the unofficial commander would insist that if Burnside's men had held they "would have carried the day," but instead they and others failed to guard the rear of the Union army. At the end of the day, exhausted from his labors, William finally fell asleep at the front, only to awaken in the middle of the night to a dark and empty field. He borrowed a horse, "jumped the fences," and made for Washington, hours after most everyone else. At Willard's Hotel he fell into bed, "prostrate with fatigue" and shaken with the "disgrace he had seen." [118] He also found himself exhilarated to have become, for a brief shining moment, his fantasy of himself.

Thus the first decades of Kate's and William's lives created young adults eminently suited to each other. Both had lost a same-sex parent when young and understood the vagaries of growing up without that model. Because of their partially orphaned state, both had been thrust into adult roles early in their lives, and both were intimately acquainted with midcentury politics. Many of their contemporaries viewed the two of them as paragons of achievement, though both had also felt the slings and arrows of disapproval. William, at thirty, was on the cusp of fame, moderate in his politics, politically ambitious and economically successful. He had created a life into which Kate would fit nicely—she was socially and politically connected where he was not, smart enough to help him with his career, and sufficiently beautiful to adorn a millionaire's home. Kate, too, was at the beginning of a tremendously promising life in 1860. As the head of her father's household in the nation's capital, she found herself a social hostess and political confidant for Lincoln's secretary of the treasury. Equipped with the tools of brilliance and in the bloom of youth, she looked around Washington for a suitable partner, and her eye would chance upon the young governor of Rhode Island.

Kate and William met briefly in September 1860 at a ball celebrating the dedication of an Oliver Hazard Perry monument in Cleveland, Ohio. William attended, with a staff of over one hundred military men, as the official representative of Perry's home state. Salmon and Kate also attended as guests of Chase's friend Richard Parsons, a Cleveland attorney and Republican politician. [119] Their attendance came with some resistance on Kate's part. Loyal Kate did not wish to so quickly to forgive the prominent Ohioans who had failed to support Salmon during the recent Republican presidential convention. A more sanguine and politically realistic Salmon persuaded his headstrong daughter of the political folly of this stance.

So fate found the Chases in Cleveland that September weekend. At midday William rode at the head of the military parade that opened the ceremonies, no doubt looking dashing and handsome. That evening Parsons made the appropriate introductions. The matchmaker later reported that Kate and William seemed much taken with each other and spent most of the evening together. Kate's beauty and William's political and economic prominence made the two seem, in Parsons's mind, "a perfect pairing off."[120] William later told Kate that "you became my gaze and the gaze of all obviously, and you left the house taking with you all my admiration and appreciation but more than that all my *pulsations*. I remember well how I was possessed that night and the following day."[121] After the party they went their separate ways, he back to Rhode Island, she to the heat of prewar Washington. They would meet again in the near future.

TWO

"My Former Self Has Lost Its Identity"
The Courtship and Wedding,
1861–1863

∿

At the outbreak of the Civil War, William led Rhode Island troops to the nation's capital, and into Kate's orbit. By the war's beginning she had solidly entrenched herself in Washington society and collected a number of admirers. It did not take long for the pair to rediscover their mutual interest. By the summer and early fall of 1861, Kate could be found visiting the many military camps around Washington, particularly "Camp Sprague." The First Rhode Island maintained a parade grounds outside the city, and there William held court as a dashing military figure and boyish governor.[1] The courting couple occasionally went riding together in the hills around the camp, as well as engaging in other, more intimate activities. William remembered: "I well remember the call [Godard] & I made upon you. I remember the troubled time that led to the battle of Bull Run and I remember with greater pleasure than ever the sail down the Potomac fraught with consequences of great importance to my personal relations and to my material interests. Do you remember the hesitating kiss I stole and the glowing, blushing face that responded to the touch. I will remember it all. The step forward from the Cleveland meeting, and the entranced poetical sensation. For it was poetry, if there ever is such in life."[2] Washington society began to link Kate and William together after Kate acted as hostess on several occasions at the Rhode Island headquarters. Such behavior carried particular significance in an age when generally only wives, daughters, or other close female relatives guided a man's social engagements. On another occasion William broke ranks at a public military review to present himself and his white horse, military plumage and all, at the Chase carriage.[3] This public declaration of interest struck General Winfield Scott as utterly inappropriate, but William's attentions probably flattered Kate. He seemed to most observers an economic, political, and military boy genius, as well as an exceptionally handsome young fellow in his tailored military dress and snappy yellow-plumed hat. William appeared entranced by Kate, who possessed beauty, intelligence, and tremendous social and political skill. That summer both were at the pinnacle of their powers, shining brightly in a social milieu that held many luminaries.

After Bull Run, William returned to his Rhode Island business. He also spent considerable time raising two more regiments of infantry and one of cavalry. It was during this period that the young couple began their correspondence. Although none of their letters from this early period of courtship have survived, we know of their existence from later letters. In one such letter William queried his intended, "My dear, did you know then you were taking a good deal more interest in me than just friendship?" [4] These letters must have been necessary given the peripatetic nature of William's existence. They acted as more than representatives of Kate and William's burgeoning relationship; their letters *were* the relationship. For nineteenth-century couples like Kate and William, writing represented a "significant arena of cultural expression," one where each could come to know the other. Through romantic letters, Kate and William sought to create a world with themselves at the center, a universe so defined by love that they could transcend the prescriptions of "separate spheres" that kept men and women apart. More than creating a romantic world, letter writing allowed William to create a romantic identity that would attract and flatter Kate, and presumably her letters did much the same for him. [5]

Kate and William needed to do their courting through the mails. In addition to his usual activities with the Sprague business, William attended two governors' conferences, one in Providence and another, larger one at Altoona, Pennsylvania. The Altoona conference garnered for William a further measure of fame. One reporter labeled Rhode Island's governor "original, intrepid, an eccentric genius." This same man believed William was a "mastermind" whose part in the conference "saved the Union." [6] The governors ratified Lincoln's preliminary Emancipation Proclamation, declared their support for Lincoln, and demanded McClellen's dismissal. Sprague and others then traveled incognito to Washington to personally deliver the results of the congress to Lincoln. Although ultimately the conference turned out to be far less influential than the governors had hoped, its short-term results may have further impressed William upon Kate's mind. The conference, like his military service, made the young governor appear a daring man of action, not just ideas. Comparing William to her staid statesman father, Kate may have found this version of manliness exciting and attractive.

COURTSHIP INTERREGNUM AND THE GREAT COTTON CAPER

The budding romance suffered a serious setback in the fall of 1862. William later described it as "the dark" that came after day. "In some countries the day is almost constant," he explained, "but the night commeth. So with us it came. We will cover that with a vail [*sic*]."[7] One of Kate's biographers has suggested that William broke off the relationship after he learned of some dubious moral conduct by Kate during her Columbus days. [8] But in an interview years later, William told a reporter that before he married Kate a Columbus man had informed him that Kate had been "indiscreet." William told the man that he believed she had never passed the bounds of respectability. William said he then demonstrated his confidence in Kate's high moral stature by calling on her the evening after the gossipy Columbus man's exchange.[9]

In fact, the business of running A. & W. Sprague may have been what brought the veil of darkness over Kate and William's budding romance. The Sprague business required cotton, which by late 1862 had become a rare commodity—rare enough that William ventured into treasonous waters to get it, and worse yet, attempted to enlist Kate's father in accomplishing the deed. Recognizing that a good portion of the Northeast's industry depended upon cotton, Lincoln and his cabinet developed a system whereby manufacturers could purchase cotton from southerners loyal to the Union—but only if they had appropriate permits. Chase and his cohorts intended this system to prevent cotton trading, which would give "aid or comfort to the enemy."[10] Coincidentally, the authority to issue cotton permits rested with Secretary of the Treasury Salmon P. Chase. That in and of itself might have been enough to damn William in Kate's eyes, for certainly she (and Salmon) understood the vital connection between cotton and the Treasury Department.

Unable to easily coerce permits from his suitor's father, William embarked upon an effort to get cotton out of Texas via one Harris Hoyt.

A Texan of dubious Union sympathies, Hoyt had a bogus letter of introduction from John Hay to President Lincoln, which the Texan passed off as a letter of introduction *from* Lincoln. [11] There is no evidence to suggest that Lincoln's private secretary ever wrote such a letter; in his voluminous writing, Hay never referred to Hoyt or the letter. With this faux seal of approval Hoyt breached the Treasury office twice in mid-September, only to be refused a permit both times. In an attempt to force the secretary's hand, Hoyt threatened Salmon, telling him that he would "send him to Governor Sprague." Salmon adamantly responded, "I wish you to understand that these gentlemen don't control me." Hoyt also tried the same dodge on Secretary of the Navy Gideon Welles and Secretary of War Edwin M. Stanton, with no more success. [12] Having been in Washington long enough to have heard about the romance between William and the treasury secretary's daughter, Hoyt arranged a meeting with the governor in late September 1862. They met at Willards, a hotel popular with politicians; it contained "more scheming, plotting, planning . . . than any building of the same size ever held in the world." Willards was situated on the northwest corner of Pennsylvania Avenue and Fourteenth Street. [13] During the early months of 1861, hotel proprietors kept the peace by arranging for southerners to stay on one floor and use the Fourteenth Street entrance, while northerners entered on the Pennsylvania Avenue side of the building. Soon after their first meeting at the infamous hotel, Hoyt and Sprague met again in Providence to further their plans. [14]

William and Byron Sprague, along with William H. Reynolds, lent Hoyt enough money to purchase three ships and cargo with which to trade for cotton. Besides being one of Salmon's oldest friends, Reynolds had been the treasury agent at Port Royal, South Carolina, in charge of cotton production until he lost his post under accusations of accounting discrepancies and lack of "sympathy with all the interests of the colored man." [15] William wrote to Kate's father, claiming that Hoyt had letters from the president proclaiming him a loyal Union man. William added that Hoyt desired to get his family and friends out of the South, while gathering "important information for the benefit of our Government," and thus needed cotton permits and a blockade pass. Reynolds wrote Salmon a similar letter, adding that he thought Hoyt should be paid "a nominal fee" for acting as a secret government agent. [16] A statement later made by the ship's captains claimed that "guns, and rifles, cartridges, caps, &c."

were on board the ship. The ship's log also lists nails, opium, quinine, whiskey, fabric, hoopskirts, corsets, foodstuffs, and many other items. In effect, the conspirators tried to force Kate's father to assist them in selling "stores" that included guns and other military equipment to southerners in return for cotton, to purchase more cotton with both real and counterfeit Confederate money, and to do so on the government payroll. Salmon did not procure the documents William and Hoyt wanted, but the scheme had a backup plan to do the same, without any permits. William wrote letters to both Benjamin Butler, then commander of the Department of New Orleans, and to "Officer Commanding Gulf Squadron, Gulf of Mexico, &c.," which Hoyt carried with him on his illegal mission. One ship, the *Ella Warley* (for which Sprague had paid $29,600), collided with the Union steamer *Star of the West*, and both sank about ten miles from New York. Hoyt sailed to Havana on the *Snow Drift*, changed her to British registry, renamed her the *Cora*, bought more gunpowder, and sailed to Matamoros, Texas, with his hold full of Sprague-funded trade goods.[17] The intrepid trader shipped his goods to Houston, traded them for cotton, and sold that for a $45,000 profit. He then made a contract with the Confederate government to furnish $400,000 worth of similar goods, to be paid in cotton which he planned to run through the Union blockade.

Precisely how much of this traitorous scheme William knew about remains unclear. He later claimed that his duties as governor, particularly his attendance at the 24 September Altoona conference (with three days' travel on either side of that date), had so absorbed him that he had not been aware of the details. Those, he insisted, he left to Reynolds and his cousin Byron (who was conveniently dead by the time of the inquiry). Nonetheless, William had written those two vaguely impressive but essentially meaningless letters of passage for Hoyt after he returned from the Altoona conference.[18] This, coupled with the fact that William told Kate repeatedly that matters of business came first with him, before his duties as governor or senator, suggests that William knew far more about the venture than he later claimed. In the meantime, Kate knew that William had attempted to use his acquaintance with her to influence Salmon in a highly suspect undertaking—something she could not possibly have looked upon favorably. And so in mid-October, around the time William and Reynolds wrote her father those preposterous letters, Kate and William ceased courting.

While William risked treason charges, Kate continued to hold sway over

Washington society. The same week that William wrote Salmon a letter pressuring him to help Harris Hoyt, James Garfield, an Ohio Republican recently elected to the U.S. Congress, wrote in his diary about life at the Chase house. Garfield had been staying with the Chases and had taken three of Salmon's female relatives sightseeing when Kate proved "too busy" for the task. He thought Kate "a woman of good sense and pretty good culture," but, like others, he believed that her pug nose marred an otherwise pretty face. "She has probably more social influence and makes a better impression generally than any other cabinet lady," he added. Although Garfield was a married man and thus not in the running for Kate's hand, he escorted her to General Carl Schurz's military camp, went horseback riding with her and her father, and kept the family company around the parlor fire. [19] Rather than retire to her bedroom in heartbreak, Kate continued on with her considerable social duties, probably determined not to let William's shortcomings get the best of her.

Undoubtedly, Kate felt genuinely offended by her suitor's heavy-handed attempt to manipulate her father into an illegal cotton caper, but this event proved to be an important passage in their courtship. Mid-nineteenth-century courting women often tested their relationship with a dramatic emotional crisis, either real or manufactured, to ensure the sincerity of a potential husband's love. Treason and conspiracy certainly offered the opportunity for such a crisis, which acted to test in a dramatic fashion William's attachment to Kate. Additionally, this test increased Kate's sense of self-worth by creating an opportunity for her to control the shape and tenor of the courtship. [20] She emphasized her personal and political power by stopping and starting the relationship as she desired. Later she created a smaller test when she required William to give up tobacco before the wedding—essentially identifying the evil weed as an obstacle he had to overcome to win her hand. But before William could set himself on a tobacco-free path he had to overcome the larger test, an obstacle in the game of love with exceedingly real and serious ramifications.

ROMANTIC LOVE AND THE FINE ART OF COURTSHIP LETTERS

The next year, on 5 March 1863, William resigned his post as governor to represent his state in the U.S. Senate. [21] A frenzy of military action, political intrigue, and social events surrounded Washington that spring.

News of African American soldiers and the aftermath of the Emancipation Proclamation, mixed with virulent racism, caused a multitude of violent episodes in the Union's capital. Congress continued to fight over the future fate of the South's inhabitants, both black and white, and the parade of generals in command of the Army of the Potomac continued. With the victory at Gettysburg still to come, copperhead Clement L. Vallandigham's campaign for governor in Ohio raised important issues in the nation's capital about the place of political dissent in a time of crisis. [22] In the midst of all this ideological upheaval, Washington transformed itself from a muddy backwater of 75,000 to an increasingly dignified national capital with over 200,000 inhabitants. The exodus of southerners in 1861 created a social void filled by new elites like Mary Todd Lincoln, who may not have been popular but whose position as the First Lady indisputably made her the head of capital society. After Willie Lincoln's death from typhoid fever in early 1862, the mourning Mrs. Lincoln may have remained the titular head of Washington society, but Kate reigned as its sovereign queen. In response to the rigors of war, social activities in the capital became increasingly frenetic, featuring more teas, receptions, and balls each successive year. One reporter described Washington as "mad with gaiety, reeling in the whirl of dissipation, before it sits down to the ashes of lent. There are three of four grand parties a night; theaters, operas, fairs, everything to make its denizens forget that war and sorrow are in the land."[23] Mixed with the capital's elites were thousands of soldiers, former slaves, ladies of the evening, confidence men, actors, office seekers, and others of low repute. Shanties sprang up along the malaria-infested canals, areas so dangerous that one was known as "Murder Bay," and a journalist claimed that "discomfort and disgust prevailed."[24]

It was in this harried milieu that William began his senatorial career, bringing with him his hopes for prominence in the Senate and his suit for the treasury secretary's daughter. As a result of his new post, William divided his time between his businesses in Rhode Island and his political duties. Like many other bachelor politicians, he stayed at Willards. The popular boarding hotel, while undeniably popular with politicians, was also noted (as were most hotels in the capital) for its lack of cleanliness, discomfort, and exorbitant rates. In the evenings William encountered air filled with tobacco smoke and floors slimy with tobacco juice, as well as ladies "whose exact status was uncertain."[25]

William also continued to spend a great deal of time in Providence and the surrounding mill towns as he supervised the spinning, weaving, and printing of A. & W. Sprague's calico. Soon after he began his appointment, the new senator's self-described veil of darkness parted and Kate and William again began keeping company and correspondence. [26] Since there had not yet been any unpleasant ramifications from the cotton caper, or because William could use the Altoona conference as a gallant excuse for only partial involvement in the unsavory matter, the Chase family put aside their reservations and welcomed him into their home. When William was in Washington, he and Kate probably followed a fairly predictable courting pattern. Balmy spring evenings on the Potomac provided a perfect atmosphere for walks together, particularly if they avoided Washington's smelly canal areas.

The many social functions incumbent upon the daughter of a cabinet member provided Kate with many opportunities to dazzle the young senator with her dress and wit. William probably called on Kate at home— taking tea or a meal, or sitting with the family after dinner when the Senate did not have an evening session. In the Chase parlor William would have had an opportunity to meet many of Washington's notable men and women, who came calling on a regular basis. At dinner one January evening, for example, the Chases entertained a cabinet member, a bank president, a prominent historian, nine congressmen, one judge, and a senator. [27] There must have been quiet evenings as well, when the press of business and war left the Chases' front parlor empty of everyone but Kate and William.

Fortunately, for historians and readers alike, if not for the courting couple, William rarely stayed in Washington very long. Thus, in the spring of 1863 surviving correspondence between Kate and William recommenced— beginning with short, factual letters that transformed into fervent love letters by the autumn months. William address his letters progressively to "My dear Katie," "My dearest Kate," and finally to "My darling Katie." [28] His closings also became progressively more intimate, from "Devotedly" or "Affectionately yours," to "affectionately, devotedly & longingly all yours." [29] William's courtship letters reflect a new ethos of love. Romantic love in the Victorian age had many components, existing as a highly structured ideology. By the mid–nineteenth century, romantic love, something that Americans of the previous century had considered of dubious value, had become the basis of a lifelong commitment. In other words, Kate and William *had* to "fall in love" in order to marry.

This transition stems from a number of cultural factors, chief among them the heightened value of emotions in America's First and Second Great Awakenings. Evangelicalism, allied with changing notions of personal liberty, challenged America's old, more hierarchical, and role-bound sense of social order.[30] Law, religion, family, and property issues became secondary compared to the experience of romantic love as it resonated with nineteenth-century individualistic concepts of self. As Ellen Rothman has noted, "Romance was defined as something to celebrate rather than mistrust."[31] In this way, finding "true love" became a normative middle- and upper-middle-class value, one so strongly held that it became compulsory rather than merely desirable. Kate exemplifies the generational nature of the new theology, for her father found his primary personal identification with a stern God, while Kate saved her emotional energy for her husband and children, putting religion at the periphery of her life.

The emotional openness or candor associated with romantic love posed a greater obstacle for men because nineteenth-century manhood required emotional self-control. Conveniently, William's openness with Kate offered him a safe arena to explore his inner life.[32] He became so involved in romantic expression that he seems to have blocked the outside world from his letters. Although as a cabinet member's daughter Kate had an interest in political and military events, William rarely discussed with her such public matters. From May through July, for example, Salmon wrote his daughters about the events at Chancellorsville, Gettysburg, and Vicksburg and about his resignation offer to Lincoln, believing that they cared deeply about the prosecution of the war. William, in contrast, rarely mentioned the war in his letters to Kate, and when he did it was more to curry favor with her than to actually discuss policy. In mid-July he wrote: "Speaking of what your father says of his great administrative qualifications that he reduced caos [*sic*] to method and regularity; in the Gubernatorial office, the best for Ohio ever had & the strongest man in the country and his daughter surpasses all his qualifications." William went on to compare himself to Napoleon and Kate to Josephine, telling Kate that his potential for greatness "all rests with you."[33] This passage strongly suggests that William's letters were apolitical, not because he underestimated Kate, but rather because he found himself caught up in romance and allowed the outside world to slip away.

Thus, though Kate might have had the advantage in engaging in emotional exchanges, William became quite accomplished at the fine art of romance.

Kate's courtship practices remain more difficult to ascertain. William wrote all the surviving letters from this period, so we can only guess about her letters. Kate did write to him, for William usually began his letters by mentioning the letters he had received—or failed to receive—from her. Seventy letters from William survive, mentioning within them thirty-three letters from Kate. Even accepting the possibility that Kate wrote some letters that William failed to mention, it appears that he was the better correspondent in the relationship. In nineteenth-century courtship, most courting men wrote longer, more careful, and more frequent letters than their female counterparts. "I have not let two days pass without writing to you," William proudly noted. "I fear my love you are so pressed with notes, that you forget when mine do come. I fear they are so numerous at times as to make them less appreciated."[34] He worked hard at love, just as he did at business.

The exact date when Kate and William became engaged remains uncertain, mainly because nineteenth-century Americans looked upon marriage engagements as a private matter.[35] In the eighteenth century, such announcements were most often made from the pulpit. By the nineteenth-century, couples personally spread the word or wrote letters to family and friends, with each partner taking responsibility for his or her respective social circle.[36] Late in May, in what Rothman describes as an "intensely private drama," William proposed and Kate accepted.[37] Not long after they became engaged, William explained to Kate how wholly their relationship had changed his life: "The business which takes my time, my attention, my heart, my all is of a certain young lady who has become so entwined in my imagination; that my former self has lost its identity. You will become jealous of her; perhaps will you not! or can you consent to share so close and intimate a relationship. I will surprise you by stating her name Katie Chase."[38] Kate, like many other nineteenth-century women, was in no hurry to end the courtship phase of her life, and she set a November wedding date. Young women of the time found the courtship phase of their lives exceedingly pleasant and empowering. They were content for a time to enjoy the ability to control their destinies, conform lovers to personal wishes, and engage in romantic interludes without the almost crushing responsibility of keeping house and raising children in Victorian America.

Although her father and William preferred that the wedding take place in September, Kate insisted that the date not be advanced.[39] Years later, she described her engagement in her diary: "Then in the full flush of social influence & triumph whose career had been curiously independent & successful, surrounded by some [word illegible] friends & many men ready to flatter & pay her homage, accustomed to command & to be obeyed & to be anticipated successfully beyond my right or dessert of her own to claim, & to get stood ready, without a sigh of regret, to lay all these and more, upon her alter of love in exchange for a more earnest and truer life!—one long dream of happiness & love."[40] Kate clearly viewed her impending marriage as a sacrifice of personal and social power. Although her many detractors have long maintained that she married William in a heartless attempt to gain power through his tremendous fortune, it appears that Kate viewed William's money as secondary to the high position and accolades due her as the treasury secretary's daughter and hostess.

In a 31 May letter, Salmon wrote family friend James Garfield, "I am going to lose a daughter and gain a son. Katie is to be married to Gov. Sprague: but the event will not probably take place before fall. What changes may take place between now and then makes me almost shudder to think of it. But let us hope the best."[41] On the same day, William, probably sensing Salmon's ambivalence about the match, assured his prospective father-in-law, "God bear me witness that it will be the object of my life to see that she receives no detriment in my hands. If a life of devotion to her, and to yourself can make me worthy of it all I shall deem it well spent."[42] It would appear that both Salmon and the prospective bridegroom felt concern for the couple's prospects.

PULSATIONS AND POWER: PHYSICAL
INTIMACY AND COMMUNICATING GENDER

A subtle but undeniable vein of physical passion and intimacy runs through William's post-engagement letters. Most Victorian courting couples did engage in physical intimacy. This is not to say that mid-nineteenth-century couples engaged in intercourse before the marriage, for physical intimacy allows for a wide range of private activities.[43] Kate's level of physical and emotional passion can only be inferred from William's letters and her later writing. William had gone back to Rhode Island after proposing to Kate, believing "a respite necessary." They intended to meet again at Niagara in late June, and again in July and August at Newport. Unfortunately, Salmon canceled his trip to Ohio, which was to culminate in the Niagara assignation, and would not approve Kate's plans to spend so much time in Rhode Island.[44] This meant that Kate and William did not see each other for most of June and July. William repeatedly hinted at sexual frustration in his summer letters. "I want you in all possible ways," he wrote in June, adding, "I dont know how I shall get myself up most acceptable to you."[45] In July he reminded Kate that she desired to "avoid the appearance of too close *intimacy* before marriage."[46] Both William's stress on the word "intimacy" and his use of "appearance" strongly hint at the physical aspect of their romantic life.

Late July brought William, and presumably Kate, some relief from the stress of separation. On 28 July they met in Philadelphia and from there went on to South Pier, Rhode Island. The two families spent the weekend there before William returned to Providence to catch up on business. Salmon, Kate, and Nettie took rooms at a boardinghouse and toured the countryside in a carriage William had left at their disposal. After less than a week's vacation, Salmon left Rhode Island for New York, where he conducted some Treasury Department business before returning home. Kate and Nettie stayed on at the Sprague summer residence at Narragansett Pier, with Fanny and William's sister, Almira, acting as chaperons. From Washington, Salmon cautioned Kate to "Be careful to do nothing which will in the slightest diminish his respect for you; for love cannot be forceful where respect is impaired."[47] After several weeks with the Spragues, the girls left to visit friends and tour the Portsmouth Navy Yard, the White Mountains, and the shops of New York City. Mid-September found them back in Providence with the Spragues. Fanny Sprague presided over Young Orchard, a three-story Georgian mansion near the center of town where various members of the Sprague family, including William, made their home. The Chase girls stayed for a few days before taking Nettie back to New York to start the fall school term.[48]

Kate and William's time together was not all felicity and kisses; they had several fights of sufficient fervor that William urged Kate that they must "be careful of each others temper—we must not be such cowards as to allow it to control us." Continued separation, though, made William's heart grow fonder. "I shall be so very glad," he wrote in October, "when I have you all to myself." The next day he reminded Kate how much he "suffered" as a bachelor and how his discomfort could have been avoided if she had only agreed to marry him sooner. "I shall soon become desperate & will then I hope have an antidote for that which is consuming me," he wrote. "This is the usual, evil man you have tied yourself to." [49] The diary Kate kept years later suggests she kept her virginity intact until her engagement, then allowed William favors she had granted no other suitor. Clearly, he had a strong expectation of sexual intimacy when they were together.

Kate was far less sexually experienced than her fiancé. Although she may have felt passionately about William, she was reluctant to indulge in forbidden premarital intercourse. Victorians placed a high value on female virginity. Eighteenth-century couples often experienced a pregnancy before marriage, but both community cohesion and economics encouraged couples to marry. Even women who did not marry faced minimal censure from their communities, and they often made good marriages to men who were not the father of their child.[50] By the early nineteenth century, however, this tolerant attitude toward premarital pregnancy had disappeared, in part because communities could no longer force young men to marry against their will. Advances in industrialization, urbanization, and transportation made it too easy for men to seduce a woman and disappear. In an effort to prevent such behavior, the "social punishment" for sexual adventurers rose precipitously—particularly for women, who became the living embodiments of illicit sexual behavior.[51] For Kate and William the temptations and dangers of physical intimacy disappeared after mid-September. Except for two weekend meetings in New York, they did not see each other until their November wedding.

As the wedding approached, it became increasingly clear that William's world left little room for same-sex friends. When Kate asked about his attendants for the wedding, he seemed at a loss to come up with three friends and suggested that Kate's father might provide the groomsmen. William finally chose, not friends or family, but three Rhode Island military officers with whom he had only the most formal relationships.[52] Kate also seems to have had no true female friends. Her socially prominent and busy life as Salmon P. Chase's hostess may have precluded such relationships, but it seems that if she had desired or needed a friend or two she certainly had the opportunity to meet and cultivate the friendship of many of Washington's young women.[53] Rather, Kate almost exclusively identified with men.

William's intensely romantic letters helped to cement the relationship between himself and Kate, and her letters no doubt did the same for him. Thus despite cultural assumptions that men and women belonged in separate spheres, grouped by gender because of overwhelming sexual differences, romantic love allowed people like Kate and William to develop heterosocial relationships that could be celebrated as sites where matched souls met.[54]

Mid-October found Kate back in Washington acting as her father's hostess, coming into daily contact with prominent political figures.[55] William felt compelled to remind her that he too had greatness within his grasp: "It is power that I contemplate daily. It is reputation and to excel that prompts me to action. When you view it all with judicious eye you will see the affluence and give your hand of encouragement to all my efforts. I am like a man full of latent ability to influence & control multitudes & to wield great power by stretching out my hand. . . . This is the feature which attracted you & this hereafter [will] be the one which will continue to satisfy your ambitions and tastes. Without it you will have nothing in me."[56] This passage is remarkable because it intimates that while William felt entitled to power, he did not really feel powerful. For example, he exposed his belief that Kate must find his great wealth his most attractive and manly attribute.[57] In a later letter William confessed that he suspected he had no right to Kate's devotion, though he was "safe so far as worldly means are concerned."[58] However much insecurity these communications might seem to reveal, William believed they served to remind Kate of his manly qualifications as good husband material. At the same time, William essentially waged a campaign to become more manly, for white Americans believed that men needed to be married. Marriage helped men control their sexual behavior and allowed women's superior moral natures to regulate men's avaricious and aggressive impulses—impulses that could threaten the nation's moral, social, economic, and political order. William's efforts to control his alcohol and tobacco intake, for example, gave him an opportunity to demonstrate self-control, while at the same time providing him a way to demonstrate his potential as a responsible family and national leader. In these ways, marriage—rather than women—transformed boys into men.[59]

William also told Kate about the qualities of manhood he did not possess, apparently believing that she would be all the more womanly in helping him to address his weaknesses. For her sake he determined to abandon the evils of tobacco before the wedding—an attempt that left him feeling grumpy. "Forgive yesterdays letter," he pled two weeks before the wedding. "When I commence to leave off the disgusting habit of chewing cigars I am cross and ugly. The soothing effect of tobacco quiets and destroys me. I am free today, never again I trust to be subject to such abject servitude."[60] He added that he did not think a woman like Kate should be subjected to anything as disgusting as tobacco. He also confessed to both Kate and Salmon that "nearly all our defects are occasioned by drinking, and I know that in my own life whatever improprieties I may be charged with, is from this cause."[61] He believed that Kate could help him overcome this weakness as well. In this way, William defined his own manhood not only by its cardinal characteristics but in relation to Kate's womanhood. In the months before the wedding, William made every effort to appear courageous, economically secure, generous, gentle, and in full control of his baser instincts. In return, Kate accepted the responsibility to act as a foil for William's masculinity and in so doing to emphasize her own womanliness.

In the end, it is difficult to know how well we understand Kate and William's emotional or intimate relationship. Cataloging how they fit into the ethos of romantic love or how they negotiated gender roles actually tells us little about what they felt for each other. They did go to fairly great lengths to be together, despite the rigors of their social and economic lives, and William's letters seem exceedingly fervent and sincere. Not long before the wedding, he wrote, "The devotion & love which is inspired as we contemplate the source of all love, of all good & full power, will reflect itself upon our whole life our relationship towards each other and towards those around us." [62] The following week he wrote, "This is indeed our month; and to think of always, always being lovers." [63] As the wedding approached, William's letters became longer, more frequent, and more explicitly romantic. The couple has often been condemned for their seemingly opportunistic pairing—William attracted to Kate for political advantage, she to him for mercenary reasons—but we can never really know how deep and how real his love for her was, or hers for him. Human beings have a tremendous talent for self-deception—for turning the real into the ideal by simple force of will. It is interesting to note that Kate chose a man who was the antithesis of her father: William drank, whereas Salmon abstained; William was small and mercurial, whereas Salmon was large and dignified; William wrote fanciful and romantic letters, whereas

Salmon filled his letters with blandishments and war news. Kate's longing for unconditional love and acceptance, along with William's desire for the kind of social position that familial association with a man of Salmon Chase's stature, as well as the confluence of time and place, convinced the two that their destinies were intertwined by the power of love—and perhaps, just perhaps, they really were.

THE WEDDING: RITUAL AND REVELRY

By 7:30 on the evening of 12 November, carriages lined both Sixth and E Streets to deliver their passengers at Salmon P. Chase's rented Greek Revival mansion. Traffic came to a veritable standstill for blocks while elite Washington society waited to gain entrance to the social event of the season. The "brilliant concourse of guests" included no less than the president of the United States, unaccompanied by his wife, who was still mourning the death of their son. President Lincoln had resumed his social calendar—three days before the wedding he had seen John Wilkes Booth in *Marble Heart*. Former secretary of war Simon Cameron attended, accompanied by his daughter. Cabinet members Edwin Stanton, Gideon Welles, Edward Bates, Caleb Smith, and William H. Seward donned their finest waistcoats in preparation for the dancing and politicking that would take place after the short marriage ceremony. News of the Army of the Potomac's continued success, this time at Rappahannock Station, must have contributed to the festive feeling, though tension continued over the Army of the Cumberland's straitened conditions in Chattanooga. [64]

Montgomery Blair made himself conspicuous by his absence—he and his brother had both recently made anti-Chase speeches, though Francis Blair, patriarch of the Blair family, did attend. [65] The always elegant Lord Lyons, British minister to the United States and considered by some the onetime front-runner for Kate's hand, also made an appearance. [66] Also in attendance was Kate's friend John Hay, Lincoln's private secretary, who called the assemblage "a very brilliant looking party." From Massachusetts came Senator Henry Wilson and Kate's great favorite, Charles Sumner. Rhode Island's Senator Henry Anthony, the mayor of New York, a host of the diplomatic corps, and officers of the army and navy, many accompanied by ladies, rounded out the wedding's five hundred invited guests. Crinoline, lace, satin, silk, ribbons, flowers, and costly jewels evidenced themselves

2. William and Katherine Chase Sprague shortly after their
wedding. Photo by Brady, courtesy of the National Archives.

everywhere as the wives and daughters of Washington's most powerful men "shed beauty and grace on the gay assemblage."[67]

Large mirrors cut to fit the first-floor windows blocked out the dreary reality of a November Thursday in a war-torn country where Union guns again bombarded Fort Sumter and Grant waited in Chattanooga for Sherman.[68] Instead, the mirrors reflected the national colors, "tastefully draped" for a "brilliant effect," the marine band in a rear alcove, and a full banquet upstairs for the guests' enjoyment.[69] Guests crowded into the lower rooms of the house until 8:30, when unseen hands threw open the doors to the back half of the double parlor. Kate stood resplendent in white velvet and lace, crowned by a magnificent diamond-and-pearl tiara. Nettie and two other attendants flanked the bride. Next to Kate stood her "boy governor," dressed in sober black, with three attendants of his own. The ceremony, conducted by the Episcopalian bishop Thomas Clark of Rhode Island, lasted less than thirty minutes; the subsequent "congratulatory manifestations by friends" as they passed through the receiving line took considerably longer.[70] Kate, partnered by her father's old friend Richard Parsons, led off the dancing. The "Kate Chase Wedding March," composed especially for the occasion by Frederick Kroell, was such a hit among the assemblage that they demanded the marine band play it twice more before the evening's close. Belles like Secretary Cameron's daughter and General Irvin McDowell's daughter wore out their dancing slippers in the whirl of waltzes that lasted past midnight.[71] Kate and William shone more brightly than they ever had or ever would again. Kate would look back on this November evening and write, "All this love and beauty, nobleness and gentleness. . . . I believed NO future brighter than that our united loves spread before us."[72]

Kate and William's wedding represented the crowning moment of their courtship. By the mid–nineteenth century, weddings had begun to take on a form easily recognizable to any modern purveyor of the society pages— white dresses, numerous guests, elaborate gifts, and, most important, a series of rituals in which the bride figured as the central figure while the groom became almost an afterthought. Some elements of wedding ritual meant different things than they do today, while other elements better represented holdovers from the previous century. The increasingly structured nature of nineteenth-century wedding rituals mirrored other changes in American life. As weddings grew ever more standardized, so too did they become increasingly personal. In the contest between public and private, between the highly personal romantic needs of a couple and the community's claims on their union, couples gained increasing control through the century. Even this wedding, by all accounts a spectacularly public event serving particular political ends, rested almost entirely in the hands of one twenty-three-year-old woman.

Weddings of the eighteenth and early nineteenth centuries were generally small affairs, attended only by close family members or friends, with little social display. Kate's father, for example, wed on three occasions but never particularly emphasized the event in his voluminous diaries and letters. Even Salmon's marriage to his first wife, Kitty, for whom he demonstrated the most public feeling, went unmentioned in his journals—this despite the fact that Lyman Beecher conducted the ceremony and that Kitty's early death of puerperal fever caused Salmon to write a lengthy memoir of their time together. Neither Salmon's wedding to Kate's mother, Eliza Smith, in 1839, nor to Sarah Bella Ludlow, Nettie's mother, in 1846, seemed any more remarkable to the groom.[73]

Clearly the Sprague-Chase wedding was on a different order of magnitude than any of Salmon's nuptials, given the political and economic prominence of the men involved and the midcentury shift in wedding ritual. Wedding arrangements absorbed Kate for most of the summer and fall. And the work was hers to do, for society increasingly regarded wedding planning as "women's work." William called their upcoming nuptials "YOUR wedding" on several occasions and deferred to his fiancée's wishes in all wedding matters.[74] She purchased much of her trousseau and goods for the new household on several trips to New York, beginning as early as three weeks after their engagement, and filled in what she could not get there with orders to European designers. Dresses from Paris arrived in September, while Kate and Nettie were in Rhode Island, so Salmon sent them on, via the New York Custom House, for the bride's perusal. They must have pleased Kate, for her father wrote, "I am glad your dresses suit you so well. To meet the demands of your taste they must be JUST right."[75] Kate also arranged for cases of claret, champagne, and brandy, and "segars" from at least two different purveyors, as well as over two hundred pounds of lamb, beef, and veal. Four dressmakers received fifteen hundred dollars' worth of business. Between fittings, Kate had to select music for the marine band, carriages, flowers, wedding cards from Tiffany, decorations, extra chairs, additional wine and sherry, and the reception catering. This orgy of spending left her father's bank account overdrawn by $156.98 on the day of the wedding.[76] The bride also had to attend all social events given in her honor, entertain out-of-town guests, and pay social calls right before the wedding to indicate whom she would receive when she became Mrs. William Sprague.[77] All of this must have consumed a tremendous amount of Kate's time, especially considering her already full schedule running her father's household. No wonder William, with only his mills and senatorial career to look after, had time to write more courtship letters than Kate.

As for William's wedding responsibilities, he had only to name his attendants (a job he tried to pawn off on his soon-to-be father-in-law), send out invitations to his side of the family, purchase the bride's wedding jewels, and get himself to Washington in time for the ceremony. The groom determined that he needed only about twenty invitations, for, as he wrote to Kate, "the company must be yours." Kate sent out over five hundred invitations and seems to have regarded William's guests as so secondary to the proceedings that he had not received any "cards" by late October, when he notified Kate that "People are becoming impatient." He plaintively added, "I have not received my invitation to the wedding. Must I do without." Then Tiffany "bungled" the card order, causing William to suggest that he move his jewelry order to some other house. His invitations arrived almost immediately.[78]

In keeping with his tremendous fortune, and in order to demonstrate his generosity, William ordered an ornate diamond-and-pearl tiara from Tiffany that would crown Kate on their special day. She wished it to be made so that the pearls in the lower part of the tiara could later serve as a necklace. The large rose diamond centerpiece would detach as a brooch, and the branches on either side of the main ornament could be formed into a cache-peigne, a type of ornament usually worn in a lady's hair. Tiffany also designed a bracelet to match the tiara, as well as a pair of diamond-and-pearl earrings. Those who commented on the jewels used words like "splendid," "unique," and "especially rich and artistic." Indeed, the set was so magnificent that people would later inflate the price of the set to upwards of $50,000. Actually, it cost considerably less. William told Kate that her friend General McDowell, who had supervision of the project because he lived near New York, had made improvements that increased the set's price from $5,500 to $6,500.[79]

Kate had no engagement ring, for such tokens did not become standard fare until the 1870s, but William did order Kate's wedding ring from

Tiffany.[80] He also ordered diamond studs for himself, all the while protesting to Kate, "I can hardly afford to wear such luxuries, but in honor of her to whom I confer my present welfare & external peace I will indulge." [81] More likely than economic penury as a cause was William's dislike of finery—at least for himself. One variant of manhood held that physical appearance was an indicator of manliness. A man who was too well dressed, for example, visibly separated himself from manual labor. [82] Democrats in particular held that manly attire should be plain, though ideas about masculine fashion crossed partisan lines. The groom wore a "black coat and pantaloons and best of white silk," as well as new boots and his diamond studs. His attendants, all of them military men, wore their dress uniforms— by request of the bride and groom. Captain Thomas Ives wore his naval uniform, while Major H. Baldwin and Captain Havens wore those of the army.[83] William's unease with adorning himself also illustrates his growing impatience with the culmination of the courtship process. Of the myriad wedding preparations, many of which must have impinged on both his time with Kate and the frequency of her correspondence, he could only admonish, "Had you married me at once, off hand, all this would have been passed, not thought of, much less said." [84] William, it would seem, longed for the old-style, less elaborate wedding.

Fifty honored guests gathered that Thursday in the Chase parlor to witness the religious ceremony joining William Sprague and Kate Chase. Neither the day of the week nor the location should be considered unusual. Nineteenth-century Americans often married and had their receptions at home, in the symbolic heart of the family. They also usually married on a weekday, sometimes on Sunday, and rarely on Saturday, which popular sentiment held to be unlucky. According to a popular ditty,

> *Monday for wealth,*
> *Tuesday for health,*
> *Wednesday the best day of all;*
> *Thursday for losses,*
> *Friday for crosses,*
> *And Saturday no luck at all.* [85]

Evidently unaware that the bride had picked an inauspicious day for her wedding, cabinet members, the president, and select congressmen outnumbered the bride and groom's families. The hundreds who attended the wedding in actuality attended only the reception, which commenced at 8:30 when the doors to the double parlor opened to permit sight of the newly married couple. This distinction reflects the older-style weddings, for by the 1880s the size difference between the private ceremony and the more public reception had all but disappeared. [86]

Kate's large reception served her father's need for public display. Salmon expected his guests' elegance to reflect his own prominence, and indeed newspaper accounts of the festivities at Sixth and E Streets emphasized both the august nature of the company and the magnificence of their costumes. One guest reported that the wedding "was a great display of elegance and riches." [87] Salmon could view the festivities as reflecting his high political status as well as to his increased political and economic aspirations. As his biographer put it, "Of all the Cabinet officers and including the President, Chase was the most active in making political points out of his socializing." [88] If the president could come to his daughter's wedding, then surely Salmon could claim sufficient social standing to one day occupy 1600 Pennsylvania Avenue. In this way the presidential aspirant displayed his own place in Washington hierarchy while simultaneously locating his family in the elite political strata of Washington society.

Kate did not share William's discomfort with fashion. Her wedding dress had a train considered large even by the standards of the day. While everyone who saw her reported Kate a vision of refined loveliness, the picture she created came at a heavy price. Mid-nineteenth-century women wore as many as seven layers of cloth between the outside air and their skin. Kate would have worn a chemise (without a "bust improver" given her statuesque build) and pantalets next to her skin, over which went a whalebone- or steel-reinforced corset laced to create the twenty-inch waist for which she was famed. Next she would have donned a shirtlike corset cover and a whalebone-, cane-, or steel-girded hoopskirt of such tremendously large, bell-like proportions as to require an eight- to ten-foot hem on both the under- and overskirts of her velvet dress. Indeed, skirts of the early 1860s grew to such prodigious size that two ladies could not walk or sit side by side with ease. William, with his small stature and relatively tight clothing, must have felt utterly eclipsed by his bride's physical and social prominence. [89] Kate's bridesmaids—Nettie, Alice, and Ida—were also all decked out and fulfilled their cultural function of representing the young, unmarried world to which Kate would no longer belong. [90]

In her attire Kate must be considered a new-style bride, for white weddings and veils did not become standard wedding attire until later in the century. Before that women wore variously colored dresses at their weddings, the choice dictated more by class, region, and individual taste than by strict bridal protocol. Bridal white did not signify sexual purity in the nineteenth century, as it would later. For Kate, the ornate white dress advertised her "hope so confident . . . that I might be the messenger of his joy & holding him above all the dearest & best I might become his companion, friend & advocate."[91]

Kate's chances for a successful marriage also depended, at least according to social theory, upon the kind and quality of gifts she received on her special day. The nineteenth century's increasing emphasis on the material culture of domesticity demanded that couples possess more things to set up housekeeping. In her *Treatise on Domestic Economy*, Catherine Beecher listed over twenty items and provided eleven pages of instruction for ironing alone, including three irons, three clothes frames, five different kinds of cloths, and a host of smaller items.[92] But Kate was no middle-class bride and had probably done little ironing during her life. Of the gifts the couple received, the *Washington Evening Star* wrote, "The bridal presents are said to exceed those of any modern date," estimating their worth at $100,000, while the *New York Times* opted for the $60,000 range.[93] Many of Kate's later detractors would point to her wedding gifts and spending habits as evidence of both economic and moral profligacy. Quite to the contrary, her role as arch-consumer fulfilled an essential wifely function by establishing her husband as a man who could afford a wife with "duties of vicarious leisure and consumption."[94] Nor did she become a professional consumer of her own making; William encouraged her time and time again to think of money as something with which to obtain pleasurable items.

After the wedding ceremony and once the guests had passed through the receiving line, servants cleared the Chase's rear parlor for dancing. The marine band entertained guests until midnight.[95] The president enjoyed himself enough to stay until almost 11:00. Tired dancers could avail themselves of a wide variety of beverages, and there was a lavish buffet set up on the second floor. Washington caterer F. P. Crutchet provided galantines of truffles, pâtés, terrines, aspics, a veal "salade," eighteen gallons of oysters, fourteen dozen roast partridges, and three hundred dinner rolls, for all of which he charged less than two hundred dollars.[96] At the end of the evening, the Chases certainly regarded the wedding as a rousing social and political success. Even Francis Preston Blair Sr., patriarch of the family currently feuding with Salmon, "enjoyed the wedding," though his daughter reported that he had "reproached Sprague" for having recently been seen in the company of another woman. After the wedding, John Hay wrote in his diary, "Kate looked tired out and languid especially at the close of the evening when I went in to the bridal chamber to say good night. She had lost all her old severity and formal stiffness of manner, & seemed to think she had *arrived*."[97]

THREE

No Future Brighter
Braving the Perils of Marriage and
Reconstruction Politics,
1863–1868

~

Happiness in marriage is entirely a matter of chance.
Jane Austen

"WE ARE HAPPY"

At 5 P.M. the day after the wedding, Kate and William took the train from Washington to Philadelphia, accompanied by a large bridal company. The happy group included Kate's sister, Nettie; her cousin Alice; the groomsmen Haven, Baldwin, and Ives; and a large Sprague contingent making their way home to Providence. This group consisted of William's mother, Fanny; his sisters, Almira Sprague and Mary Ann Nichols; Mary Ann's daughter Ida; William's brother, Amasa; and Amasa's wife, Mary.[1] The bridal party avoided publicity by traveling in a private train car. The master of transportation for the Baltimore and Ohio Railroad, William Prescott Smith, had offered private cars and special trains to the Chase family on several occasions, though more often for reasons related to the war.[2] The group stopped overnight in Philadelphia, then went on to the Fifth Avenue Hotel in New York the next morning—a logical stop on the bridal trip in spite of the waves of violence that had convulsed the city in the recent draft riots.[3]

Unfortunately, relative political and racial harmony did not make New York safe for the wedding party. The trip took a calamitous turn when the hotel erupted in fire, not once, but twice in the same night. On Monday, 16 November, a fire began in the boiler room and rapidly spread to the laundry, drying, and engine rooms of the hotel basement. A scarcity of fire hose hindered the firemen's work, but after two hours they had the blaze sufficiently controlled that hotel guests could return to their rooms.

At 2 A.M. the Spragues and all their fellow hotel guests were yet again roused from their rooms, "and again a scene of consternation and confusion ensued." The *Times* suggested that the two fires were neither unrelated nor accidental but rather the work of some nefarious characters bent on stealing property from the hotel. As the woodwork on the Twenty-fourth Street stairway blazed, the Spragues decided they had enjoyed New York quite enough.[4]

However distressing New York must have been for the wedding party, good news from Tennessee surely lifted everyone's spirits. In September, Confederates had trapped Rosecrans's Army of the Cumberland in Chattanooga, but on 15 November Sherman arrived with another seventeen thousand men.[5] George Thomas then replaced Rosecrans as commander of the Army of the Cumberland, while Grant assumed command of the newly created Western Military Division. This, combined with the addition of not only Sherman's troops but two corps from the Army of the Potomac, made the siege at Chattanooga appear less desperate. In a move that only helped Union troops, Confederate president Jefferson Davis ordered General Braxton Bragg to detach Longstreet and fifteen thousand men to Knoxville.[6] Things were looking up in the West that fall.

While soldiers set the stage for the next major battle, the bridal party happily ferried across the Long Island Sound and up Narragansett Bay to Providence. When William, Kate, Nettie, and Alice arrived at Young Orchard they found the house ornately decorated for their welcome. Red, white, and blue bunting festooned the house and archway, which bore a large gilt WELCOME HOME sign. Streamers hung from the house's central tower, with flags and more bunting decorating the windows and doors. In a letter to her uncle Salmon, Alice described the effect: "The large appearance of the decorations as seen from the street gave one the idea that it was intended to make the happy pair feel a kind of rapturous emotion of welcome. Oh! It was very funny." Alice thought the house looked ready for a "horse fair," while Kate, utterly aghast, professed fatigue and retired before the welcome party was over. Although William wrote his father-in-law that "the reception passed off quite brilliantly," the gardeners immediately took down Young Orchard's festive adornments.[7] Perhaps Kate had also noticed that none of Rhode Island's social elite attended her reception, neither the former governor nor old school friends who had so graciously received her father and her on earlier trips. Now a Sprague, Kate may have begun to realize that elite Rhode Islanders did not socially receive members of her new family. As one arbiter of taste put it, "Governor Sprague never had the manners of a gentleman, only the veneer of refinement, and in a mental lapse might put his feet upon a rose satin chair. That was a Sprague trick—they all did it." [8] Providence society also remembered the matter of Mary Viall Anderson and how carelessly William had treated her and her family. Thus Kate's entrance into Providence society as Mrs. William Sprague proved somewhat less triumphant and elegant than she might have wished.

Not to be confused with a honeymoon, Kate and William's wedding trip represented an older-style ritual in which a newly married couple, accompanied by family and friends, journeyed to relatives' homes. [9] By the early nineteenth century, as the growth of railways made wedding trips more accessible for the middle class, short trips became more common and popular. Popular resort areas like Niagara Falls developed as a result. Although the vast majority of eighteenth- and nineteenth-century newlyweds could not afford vacations, either long or short, those who did embark upon a bridal trip fulfilled an important social task. If the marriage ceremony severed some of their previous individual ties to their respective families, visits to those same families served to reestablish those links while including the new family member in an expanded circle of joint family relations. [10] William suggested to Kate that after the wedding they visit Niagara as well as Montreal and Quebec. Salmon also attempted to arrange the wedding trip, offering the bridal party the use of a revenue cutter for cruising the coast. Kate, who wanted to use her bridal trip to visit Chase relatives in Ohio, overruled both men. [11]

While the new couple visited in Providence, Salmon wrote William about Lincoln's impending trip to Gettysburg. Salmon could have gone with the president, but he opted to stay home to work on his annual treasury report. [12] Kate's father also hoped Kate would get Nettie back to school in a timely manner, but his hopes went unfulfilled. Nettie had such a good time in Rhode Island that she returned to Mrs. Macaulay's school several days late. By Monday, 23 November, after ten days of bridal touring, William and Kate dropped Nettie off in New York and set off for Ohio. [13]

When Kate and William finally found themselves alone, the trip became a honeymoon. Honeymoons differed from wedding trips by emphasizing a couple's separation from their family—an emphasis entirely in keeping with the ethos of romantic love. The honeymoon highlighted the personal, emotional, and erotic voyage of discovery Kate and William undertook when they wed. The fact that the Spragues embarked on both types of trips exemplifies both their class status and the fact that the transformation of the bridal trip into the honeymoon would not be complete until later in the nineteenth century. [14] The couple visited Cincinnati, Columbus, and Cleveland, the last home of Richard Parsons, the man who had introduced them in the fall of 1860. Parsons arranged a large party in their honor.[15] The first week of December found them in Loveland, Ohio, visiting Kate's cousin Jane Auld, who reported to Salmon that Kate looked "well and happy." [16] William wrote his father-in-law, "I am delighted that you see a brighter future for us. As I have known that you trembled a little. . . . We are Happy. We feel we have it upon a foundation that will not give way. With God on our side and the ever watchful eye & council of one so dearly loved we share with you in feeling that misfortune can never come tho trials may." [17] William also reported that they both had colds, but even stuffy noses could not mar the new couple's happiness with one another.

Days later the honeymoon ended. Kate and William returned to Washington together, but William soon left for Rhode Island by himself to catch up on business matters.[18] His letters during this period offer a stark contrast to his long, emotive courtship letters. Having successfully won Kate, he confined his missives to dry rehearsals of facts and instructions, sometimes only a few lines long. Kate, on the other hand, expressed herself as if still in the throes of honeymoon ardor: "Shall I tell you how much I miss you & how the sunshine has all gone from our beautiful home. Paradise is no paradise without a God & my life is indeed deserted. I absolutely felt afraid of the dark last night in my longing for my own darling. I prayed God very earnestly before going to rest for your protection and safe return. The fire in your Sanctum burns cheerful and bright. . . . Oh darling I hope these separations will not come very often. They are hard to bear." [19] Not long after he received this letter, William decided to spend the holidays with his mother and siblings in Rhode Island while Kate stayed in Washington with her father and Nettie. He blunted the news by sending Kate a shawl as a Christmas gift. "Forgotten so soon?" she half teased, "Oh darling how could you serve me so?"[20] In an effort to lure her new husband home, Kate invited the Spragues to Washington for the holiday season, but William's sister Mary Ann offered a polite refusal on behalf of the family, citing exhaustion from their Washington trip four weeks previous.[21] Although Kate had written her new husband every day of their separation, and twice on Christmas, William wrote sent a letter after Christmas reproaching her for forgetting him. Kate fired back a letter saying she "thought it hard" that she had gone four days before hearing from him. She added that he sent her an envelope with official papers and no personal note, and that when he did write it was "one poor note," accompanied by a letter to her father which announced that he would not return to Washington for New Year's Day either. "That it was a bitter disappointment to me you will know. New Years day promises to be a great failure."[22] Still, she closed the letter with a cheery story of her recent shopping trip in New York and her boat trip through icy waters. However cold her trip, though, it could not have been as frosty as William's next letter: "That your January fortune will promise a failure sorry much regret. I would that you would make it a success in consequence of my inability to be with you and you would lighten my burden this much by exhibiting a willingness to deny yourself for that purpose. I am in every moment engaged in large & numerous duties & engagements to trying to do my duty in every way and I have a right to ask your aid and sympathy. You my love are not I hope to prove an additional burden to me, as you will certainly do if my acts are the cause of any unhappiness." He went on to tell his lonely bride that this day twenty years ago his father had been murdered and that her letter brought him further "vexation" and "disappointment."[23] While William professed to give "every spare moment that comes to me" to business, his mother wrote Kate of her son's leisurely breakfasts with the family and the New Year's Day party he had attended with his sisters, his niece Ida, and his brother.[24]

Kate and William's early married years suggest that they experienced difficulty in sustaining the romance of courtship. If courtship centered upon the ideals of romantic love, companionate marriage represented those ideals applied to marriage. The romantic and companionate ideal for marriage created heightened expectations with regard to personal intimacy—levels never before expected between American spouses. Observers have suggested that the increasing emphasis on affection and loyalty between spouses (and between parents and children) improved the position of women in marriage.[25] Other historians have noted that the high goals of companionate marriage could prove elusive for many couples when combined with the tensions inherent in the ideology of separate spheres.[26]

Companionate marriage created another difficulty. Many couples could not sustain the fervor of first attraction through several years of day-to-day contact, nor could they feel content with a marriage that functioned as a comfortable, economic relationship. This kind of marriage, so acceptable in the seventeenth and eighteenth centuries, did not meet mid-nineteenth-century society's demand for emotional intimacy. The new-style marriage may have created as much unhappiness as it did connubial bliss. Certainly the Spragues experienced just such a disappointment.

Expectations of increased sexual intimacy, brought about both by the romantic ethos and by improved reproductive control, could also create conflict between couples—a conflict exacerbated by the imbalance of power between men and women.[27] Women, for example, could not legally refuse their husbands, even though the tenets of companionate marriage suggested that men should be considerate of their wives' wishes. This legal and social reality may have been the basis for some of the Spragues' marital tension. On two notable occasions William would attack his wife in her bedroom, suggesting that that intimate venue was fraught with dangerous levels of tension.

Kate would have four carefully spaced children, so birth control may also have been an issue. American couples had a wealth of contraception and abortion options available to them during this period. The marital birthrate among white, native-born couples dropped almost 50 percent during the course of the nineteenth century. Both the potential market for contraception and the wide dissemination of birth-control information suggest that deliberate attempts to curtail fertility played an important part in many marriages.[28] Unfortunately, no sources provide any clues about the method of family limitation that Kate and William used. Nonetheless, it appears that the heightened demands of physical as well as emotional intimacy would prove stressful to the Sprague marriage.

It did not take long for the cracks to begin to show in their relationship. While William busied himself with A. & W. Sprague business in Providence, Cranston, and Baltic, Kate arranged household matters to her satisfaction and once again acted as political hostess for her father. These were not such separate undertakings as one might think, for Kate and William had agreed to share the Sixth and E Street house with Salmon. A three-story neoclassical brick building with side bay windows, the mansion had a prestigious address, six blocks to the west of the White House in a town where many functionaries did not maintain permanent establishments. Charles Sumner, for example, lived at the Arlington Hotel until his 1866 marriage. [29] The matter had taken some negotiation over the summer, for William at first resisted the idea of living with Salmon. In June he wrote, "I could never consent to occupy any house with dimmed authority. Where I live the house which is to come to us must have no power within it but yours. We may visit. We may journey. We may do anything which we think it excellent to do but our permanent home must be that which we command without the first hint of conflicting authority. No house is large enough for two families is a familiar saying." [30] By mid-July, though, William had come around to the idea of sharing a house with the treasury secretary. He professed himself "delighted" by his correspondence with Kate's father, for the two had agreed that they would split the rent, payment of servants, and use of the stable. Once this was decided, workmen commenced remodeling and repainting the house so as to provide private quarters for the two branches of the family—an undertaking that considerably distressed Salmon given the extent and the cost of the improvements. By the fall, William, with Kate as his agent, had commenced negotiations with Joseph B. Varnum to purchase the house for $30,000. Salmon, William, and Kate agreed to arrange private rooms for each family member, with the Spragues paying table expenses and Salmon paying the servants. Since Salmon already had two carriages and appropriate horses, he told William to forgo the purchase of yet another conveyance and "give the money it would cost to the hospitals." William wrote Kate that he thought he might just as well "throw that money in the ocean," and he bought a fine new carriage of Kate's choosing for their Washington use. [31]

March 1864 found Kate so sick as to require constant care—care neither her husband nor her father had the time or inclination to provide. Instead, General Irvin McDowell and his wife, Helen, took her into their home in Buttermilk Falls, New York. Kate missed the funeral of her sister-in-law, Mary Sprague, in late March because of her repeated bouts with colds and respiratory infections. [32] These episodes caused Salmon great anxiety, particularly given that tuberculosis had destroyed his personal life on several occasions. Not until June did Kate feel well enough to join her husband in Washington. Congress was in session, and William found her assistance an important part of his day-to-day life. In one cross-town note he hastily scrawled, "There is a bundle of papers under my table which I wish you to send by the bearer. They are papers that Mr. Hazard needs published. Please look them up & oblige your absurd one."[33]

THE FALL AND RISE OF MIGHTY MEN

Salmon also needed Kate's political services. The Missouri congressman Francis Blair had made a January speech from the House floor charging the secretary with "profligate administration of the Treasury Department . . . rank and fetid with fraud and corruption's." This, coupled with the fallout from the Pomeroy circular (a pamphlet that Chase's unofficial presidential election committee had used as an attack on Lincoln), caused Salmon to tender his resignation to the president in February 1864. Lincoln, however, refused to accept the offer.[34] Kate must have breathed a sigh of relief.

By April, Lincoln had made it clear he would not discipline Blair for his attack on Chase. In the same letter in which he had refused Salmon's resignation, the president wrote that he believed his cabinet members had the right to run for president. Nonetheless, that Salmon had availed himself of this right exacerbated Lincoln's growing disillusionment with him. The gulf between Lincoln and his treasury secretary widened to unacceptable proportions. Kate attempted to mediate her father's political crisis. She brokered meetings between her father and leading Republicans such as Albert Riddle, who reported that Chase was "in a frightful rage" over the president's refusal to discipline Blair. A series of political maneuvers eventually created a temporary truce, but Salmon would soon discover the extent of his fall from favor.

In defending his father-in-law, William also found himself at odds with Senate Republicans, particularly the Radicals whom he believed had deserted Salmon in his hour of need. Unfortunately, the kind of help Kate's husband could provide did little to bolster Salmon's flagging reputation. Elizabeth Blair Lee wrote her husband, the naval officer Samuel Phillips Lee, that Sprague and other senators "all dined & drank too much" and as a consequence got into "quite an undignified" brawl over the matter.[35] Kate apparently gave up trying to assist her father and husband in their dubious political actions. Soon after William's drunken fight, she and Nettie left Washington for Newport, where they stayed for much of the summer.

Although one resignation bullet was successfully dodged, neither Kate nor William could prevent the scene from repeating itself in June, this time over a patronage dispute. Having negotiated a bitterly contested New York Custom House appointment, Salmon warned Lincoln, "I cannot help feeling that my position is not altogether agreeable to you; it is certainly too full of embarrassment and difficulty and painful responsibility to allow me the least desire to retain it." He enclosed his resignation, hoping to force the president to publicly admit that Salmon might appoint whomever he wanted to Treasury Department posts. Instead, Lincoln agreed with Salmon that they had "reached a point of mutual embarrassment in our official relation which it seems can not be overcome" and accepted the resignation.[36] Three months after Blair's accusations, Kate's father became a private citizen. Five days later, William stood up in the Senate and defended his father-in-law, rebutting Blair's attack. Coming on the last day of the session and months late, the speech made little impression on anyone in the Senate chambers or in Washington. Salmon mentioned the speech to Nettie in a letter and confessed: "I am heartily glad to be distanced from the administration; though a little sorry to miss the opportunity of doing the real work I feel confident I could with Gods blessing accomplish." To Kate he suggested that William's fervent defense was a bit misplaced, however enthusiastic. He also refused her offer to come to his side. Finally, he warned her, "If you think me wronged or not appear to let nobody THINK you THINK so. People never sympathize with such [sentiment]." Salmon and William soon joined Kate and Nettie in Newport, though Salmon stayed less than a week.[37]

Not willing to withdraw entirely from public life, Salmon campaigned for Lincoln and other Republicans the rest of that summer and fall. William eventually went back to Providence, and Kate went home to Washington with her father. Once again the Spragues commenced writing angry letters to each other. Where once William had relished everything about Kate, he now felt free to chastise and lecture his "bridy." "I should not my darling," he wrote Kate, "have you unwomanly. . . . I would have you act womanly, religiously, lovingly—such is your nature controlled by pride." He added that should she be able to forget their "disagreements," he thought "we shall have a happy and useful future."[38] That Christmas William gave Kate, then three months pregnant with their first child, a gift of money. He urged her to remember that cash signified "power for happiness and usefulness, the power to procure precious stones, fine raiment and benefits to others through its proper distribution."[39] If she did not already, Kate would come to despise such gifts. In her diary she wrote of another Christmas when she had looked forward "with glad anticipation" to the gift of a particular jewel she had admired at Tiffany. She had been afraid to confess to William her desire for the object, as she confided to her diary: "It seemed to me so like begging that I could not bring myself to say what was the truth, 'oh yes, I do want it very much!' it was the only thing we saw that I did long to possess, as I do like things that are rare and beautiful, & I fancied that he saw how much I did want it & that he meant to surprise me with it as a treat . . . [believing] that at length my husband had anticipated & prepared a pleasure for me & more than that, than at the rich jewel I expected to possess, did this thought make me feel joyous & happy. And the money was a bitter disappointment." [40] Bringing a millionaire into the family caused both Kate and Salmon to make many adjustments, but Salmon's discomforts did not match the romantic disappointments faced by the new Mrs. Sprague. William had not gotten what he had bargained for either, for he had married the daughter of a cabinet member and presidential hopeful and now found himself the son-in-law of a man isolated by the political fallout of his presidential aspirations. It seems, as well, that Kate resisted William's attempts to force her to adhere to nineteenth-century standards of submissive womanhood. Neither she nor Salmon was what William wanted (or needed) them to be.

One thing did go right for the Chase-Spragues in 1864. Not long after his election, Lincoln nominated Salmon to fill the deceased Roger B. Taney's position as chief justice of the U.S. Supreme Court. The Senate promptly confirmed the nomination, and the house on Sixth and E once again became a center for official state business. Many have since suggested that Lincoln put Chase in the Supreme Court in order to keep him out of presidential politics, and that Kate, suspecting this motive, was enraged. She is said to have shaken her finger at Charles Sumner and taken him to task for "this business of shelving papa," crying, "Never mind, I will defeat you all." The sources for this oft-repeated story cannot be considered reliable, though it has been repeated so many times it has taken on a certain authority. Lincoln had already handled Salmon's presidential aspirations and appointed him to keep the Radicals happy. Additionally, no other report has Kate speaking so rashly and clumsily, and it seems unlikely that she would have publicly chastised Sumner, whom she greatly admired. Lastly, no correspondence between Salmon, William, and Kate suggests that Kate believed the attainment of the highest judicial post in the land to be anything other than a plum assignment. Indeed, Salmon did not let the highest judicial post in the country prevent him from running for president in 1868.[41]

The winter social season of 1864–65 found Kate confined to the house, too pregnant with her first child to play the belle of Washington. She had plenty of time on her hands to worry about her husband's troubles—the cotton caper had been resurrected. In late November, on the same day Lincoln sent Salmon's nomination to the Senate, the army arrested Charles Prescott. Prescott had been the captain of Harris Hoyt's blockade-running ships—ships that carried guns to trade for southern cotton. On 6 December 1864, Prescott gave a full and detailed confession of his activities over the past few years. The arrests of William Reynolds and Byron Sprague, both of whom had been partners in the scheme, followed Prescott's confession. The arrests of his partners caused William to frantically cover his tracks. Kate and Salmon never would have forgiven him for the disgrace of being arrested for treason, nor would the charges have been good for the Sprague business.

William wrote to General John A. Dix, who had charge of the matter, and claimed he had no connection to Hoyt. William told Dix that the whole matter was nothing more than a politically motivated attack on himself through his friend and cousin. He also laid the blame for any possible A. & W. Sprague involvement in the affair at his cousin Byron's door, claiming that Byron "had the management of the business [then], I being engaged in the field and in executive duties." William also contended that he had severed his partnership with Byron when he learned that his cousin had "hostile intentions."[42] William offered this smoke screen to Dix, hoping the general did not have access to the letters William had written in support of the cotton scheme. This denial also relied on Dix's ignorance of the fact that William had always controlled A. & W. Sprague, regardless of his other activities. Two months later William sent Dix another letter, this time explaining that the A. & W. Sprague Company was "comprised of women, children, executors, administrators, and guardians" who had never seen a penny from the enterprise. The family, he claimed, had actually had met with "heavy losses" in their attempt to keep the mills open through the war. Here William overplayed his hand, for few Americans would believe that Sprague women and children faced penury, particularly in the light of William's recent, well-publicized, and expensive wedding.

Next, William did what many politicians before and since have done to avert attention from a seamy personal episode. He stood up in the Senate and made two patriotic speeches: one decrying the fact that American flags were being manufactured from British cotton (evidently Confederate cotton seemed a better solution), and a second wherein he bravely came out for "perpetuating all races of man," a declaration that could be read as a support for the expanded rights of either black or white Americans, depending upon the sentiments of the listener.[43] Despite William's bravado, the army arraigned Hoyt on six charges of treason. At the same time, Prescott continued to confess to the judge advocate, further implicating the Spragues, though by that time Salmon had already been sworn in as the chief justice of the Supreme Court.[44] Dix did write to Secretary of War Stanton, notifying him that he had paroled Reynolds and Byron Sprague and that Hoyt had made a full confession implicating William and Byron Sprague and Reynolds. "The high standing of those gentlemen makes the case one of great delicacy," Dix wrote, effectively putting the case against William into Stanton's hands.[45]

Kate made one of her few public appearances that winter at her father's swearing-in ceremony, but no letter, no diary entry, no observer can give us a clue to what she thought of the fallout from her husband's cotton acquisitions or what part she played in the cover-up. She did continue to cooperate with William in his political interests, sending packets of letters and instructions to Rhode Island for his attention. On New Year's Eve he wrote her a thank-you letter, though he jokingly qualified his gratitude by writing, "I might be entirely displeased with you as my wife is far more competent to discharge my duties than myself. How would you like that duty?"[46] He added that he believed her more accomplished at "attending to the love letters," given her greater experience. Although William had written nearly two letters to every one of Kate's during their courtship, in married life those roles had been reversed. The balance of power had shifted.

Events of the spring of 1865 pushed the Texas adventure onto political back burners for a time. Dix's letter to Stanton arrived just before Lincoln joined Grant outside Richmond in April. That month Grant's Union forces took control of the Confederate capital. Northerners went wild with jubilation, and the president made a speech on reconstructing the Union. John Wilkes Booth heard it and swore, "That is the last speech he will ever make."[47] Late on the night of 14 April, Salmon recorded in his diary that a gentleman had come to his door to tell him that "the President had been shot in his box by a man who leaped from the box upon the stage & escaped the rear—He could give no particulars & I hoped he might be mistaken. . . . My first impulse was to rise immediately & go to the President, whom I could not yet believe to have been fatally wounded." Salmon stayed home, believing he could be of no service, and later that night guards came, "for it was supposed that I was one of the destined victims—and their heavy tramp-tramp was heard under my window all night. . . . It was a night of horrors."[48] Kate and Nettie, in their rooms that night, heard the solemn boots as well, a sound that brought the war home as vividly as the bleeding and cursing men who had lain in the parlor four years previous. They would have done well to imagine the sound to be the changing of the guard. Their father administered the oath of office to Vice-President Andrew Johnson the next morning.

Kate came out of confinement again to attend Lincoln's funeral. The minute guns boomed that day, and the church bells tolled the nation's desolation. One of only seven women present, seven months pregnant and swathed in black, she stood in the sweltering crowd in the White House's East Room for over four hours. Down from Providence for the occasion, William stood by her side. Salmon recorded in his journal that "every body seems overwhelmed."[49] Forty thousand mourners followed the hearse up Pennsylvania Avenue to the Capitol, where the fallen president again lay in state. Two days later a special train carrying Lincoln's body, as well as that of his disinterred son Willie (who had died in 1862), began the seventeen-hundred-mile trip to Illinois. For the next ten days the funeral cortege slowly made its way across the country.[50]

The Texas adventure disappeared for the time being, a beneficiary of the assassination and the new president's Reconstruction policies. Domestic matters also distracted Kate and William from their political woes. After converting the house on Sixth and E, the Spragues set about remaking a 350-acre property William had bought on Narragansett Bay. In the summer of 1865 they began the conversion of the "Sprague Farm" into "Canonchet," a sixty-eight-room mansion named after a seventeenth-century Indian chief. A. & W. Sprague Company purchased the farm from the Robinsons, a family that had owned the property since the early 1700s. Kate and William lived in the Robinson farmhouse for several summers while they completed the big house. The finished building had four stories, two large towers, and two smaller ones. It took six years to build, and Kate furnished it "with disregard for cost." Described most often as Mansard architecture, Canonchet predated the mansions at Newport. It contained a four-story grand staircase, a music room, a ballroom, $40,000 worth of hand carving in the dining room alone, a well-stocked library, apartments for Kate's father, a room just for Horace Greeley, and a tiled dairy in the basement.[51] Kate essentially became the project supervisor. If William had no real political future and her father's presidential chances looked dimmer and dimmer, she had Canonchet to engage her lively mind. There also exists the possibility that some of the thousands of dollars Kate would spend on Canonchet over the years were retribution for William's marital transgressions—years later she would claim that William had been violating his wedding vows since the first year of the marriage.

Kate did much of the early work at Canonchet while pregnant—a circumstance that greatly worried her father. Nonetheless, her first pregnancy was relatively trouble-free. Born in June 1865, the baby made his father and grandfather deliriously happy. Aunt Eliza assisted the birth, and as with all her children, Kate delivered the baby boy easily and with no complications. Kate wanted to name him after her father, but William vetoed this idea. Salmon agreed, reminding Kate that "William is not only a better one: but is the name of one to whom your first duties belong, and it was the name of his father was it not? and should be borne by his first boy."[52] Salmon was mistaken, because William's father's name was Amasa, and the baby was always called Willie. Salmon and Nettie visited Narragansett in July, and the new grandfather reported, "baby all that had been told. . . . Katie quite well—in better health and handsomer than for years."[53] By the time Willie reached six months of age Kate found herself back in Washington, making the rounds of New Year's Day receptions. Salmon, Laura Cooke (the financier Jay Cooke's sixteen-year-old daughter), and Kate called on President Johnson at the White House, where they encountered several Supreme Court judges, cabinet members, and senators. William showed up later with Nettie, and then the whole group went home to receive guests of their own. William went back to Providence before the week was out, leaving Kate to attend the winter balls with her sister and father.[54]

DISTANCE DOES MAKE THE HEART GROW FONDER

In 1866 Kate and her sister took their first trip to Europe, leaving from New York with Willie and his nurse Maggie in tow. In the first month of their trip the party traveled from London to Paris and Brussels and finally back to London. Kate saved William's letters to her during her European sojourn. These letters, unlike those of the previous two years, bear a striking resemblance to his courtship letters. They are longer and more emotive, and concentrate on four major themes: politics, spending money, William's desire to be a better man, and his need for Kate. These letters are rarely critical, as the following, written from the Senate chamber in mid-May, illustrates:

My Dear Wife,

Your letter received;—the one you wrote on the eve of your journey to Paris. I am glad you have been away during my trouble, as I should have visited it upon you. My mind is sadly disconnected. Trouble at home, growing out of Ida & engagement, which I cannot write about.[55] Trouble of the business nature with my people at home. Trouble from more anonymous correspondence and trouble from comments in newspaper letter writers, who speak of me so correctly. I am more and more in the belief that I am unsuited to my post. I am afraid that my physical infirmity will prevent my being useful. I dont want to resign. I dont want to again go into business and I am quite sure unless I change my present habits I shall go down hill fast or faster than I have. If I count back, one two or three years and see how little I have accomplished, it is enough to discourage any one. My wickedness has placed me in a very base & uncomfortable positions [sic]. I will *not* let you see the newspaper slips. I have shown them to your father, but I write you just as I feel. I feel the public notice of my unfitness very sorely because I believe that criticism is just. I am sorry my letter seems so disconnected—so abstracted. When writing I lose my connection the same as I do when [talking] hence my great trouble— . . . You cannot tell how happy your happy journeyings gives to your husband. Do not trouble yourself about him. He will go on, strive to overcome the weakness and short comings of his character and let the future overcome the weakness and short comings of his character and let the future determine his success or want of success. I am glad you are on the way to Paris. Do not let a moment pass that is not passed in enjoyment. I think that your father will not be able to go to England, as there is now a probability of his holding court. . . . I have felt it as you have since your absence. I have felt alone, homesick and heartsick. I have acted strangely, but as I wrote you some time since[,] I am safe. All temptations all pass by me. If I die I will not die subject to any [word illegible] whiskey or otherwise—You need hereafter have no fears on that subject. I will not drink one drop until I again see you. I write it in order that I may face up to a proper standard—decaying mental strength— and I hurt myself far more than I do myself good. Do not consider this a random letter, as you will deal with me as the hostile correspondence that I have refused to.

Yesterday we had quite a spicy debate between Fessenden and Sherman about funding the public debt. I sent you through the Dept of State some large [photographs] of the Chief Justice 1/2 for yourself 1/2 for Nettie—I am going to send you this letter. I find it is rambling. I jot down my thoughts as I feel them. I suspect I cannot write you better. The next note I promise you shall be more coherent. That I miss you [you] may very well imagine, but it will endure the separation—for your good, for your happiness. How is baby. Does he grow. My love to Nettie. Regards to Maggie and devotion to

Your W Sprague[56]

References to personal vice (as well as general incoherence) are common in William's letters during the spring and summer of 1866, letters he hoped would woo Kate back to his side. One suspects that the self-denigration in this and other missives was meant to make Kate admire his candor and induce her to assure him of his worth. William's self-criticism also functioned to remind Kate that he really was trying to make himself into the kind of man she wanted him to be. "I should be better prepared to fill a senatorial position," he wrote in June. "I dont know as I am less useful than others, or some others, but I am far from being satisfied with what I am doing." In his next letter he denigrated his own manhood: "I find I am still a boy. Do you not feel so, boys are good in places. I am a man in some ways, boy in others. I dare everything. I can consider everything. I have accomplished some things. I am not 36. Can I do more. How can I do more without my wife. I want her help."[57] In this way the senator made his immaturity a positive attribute, pointing out how much unexplored potential Kate might help him uncover.

The letters also reveal William's emotional ups and downs. "I have done badly today," one letter begins. "I made a poor show in opposing a postponed cut in the Tariff. I could not get it the proper spirit and my mind worked very sluggish. I am tonight to present an urn to the orphans in the Soldiers fair. I hope I may do better, but I fear that it will turn out that being a poor speaker I shall make myself as such more conspicuous." William went on to describe his "want of legislative ability," his lack of learning, and the burden of bearing up against "such a state of things." [58] Other letters emphasized what he believed to be his progress in matters Kate thought important: "I am delighted in my attention to dress (your own dear work) I think my associates see in me a great improvement." He proudly told Kate, by then back in England among such august company as English radical reformer John Bright, "I wear silk stockings every day . . . I have the neatest pair of boots known to any individual." [59] He dressed well for church, which he attended with Salmon, as well as taking walks, carriage rides, and dinners with the old gentleman, all of which he took great pride in relating to his wife.

William did all of this to please Kate. In stark contrast to the letters he wrote her right after they married, he constantly wrote her of how much he missed her and needed her: "I never knew my dear how hard the separation would be." [60] Later in the summer he admitted that "Your presence has my dear not called for such expressions. It is your absence my dear when your worth is acknowledged." He needed Kate to control his baser instincts—a role expected of many nineteenth-century women. "Teach me to satisfy your every longing & keep me in such control that my poor ability will be able to meet your every wish." Nineteenth-century writers had reversed an earlier view of women as the embodiment of carnal desire, transforming men into the lustful gender. Prescriptive literature not only claimed women's lesser interest in passion but believed that "the purity of women is the everlasting barrier against the tides of man's sensual nature urge." [61] William consistently reminded his wife of the consequences his lack of control could have. "I am glad I am not pleased anymore with the rattle of other women's dresses," he wrote in June, though only weeks earlier he had reminded her of his terrible weakness. "However much I wander and stray away I am always brought back with further stronger sentiments of love and affection for my wife." In the same letter he wrote a thinly veiled tale about his old lover Mary Viall Anderson, telling Kate that she had asked him for a loan. Calling the episode "the old story," William suggested that Mary had appealed to him as the father of her child. "I wonder if it is true—I know that I know some more than I did 6 years ago."[62] William had apparently begun to doubt whether he was the father of Mary's son. As Kate would find out later, he knew enough about his lover's life to know that sexual discretion was not one of her virtues. Kate must have wondered if all this marital honesty was worth the cost.

That summer, Kate received a letter from her husband describing in great detail his attraction to another woman. While promenading around Lafayette Square he noticed two ladies: "I was at once interested, and put myself in their way, and stationed myself where I could have a full view. The lady that interested me was a little shorter than my wife. She was developed where a woman to be a real woman must be developed, nearly as much as my wife." He reminded Kate that "you told me to admire the beautiful women."[63] Kate appears to have encouraged her husband's philandering on more than one occasion. "In your last letter you gave me encouragement to admire beautiful women," William wrote, though he suggested that his association with Kate had sharpened his taste to include only "beautiful & intellectual women." Given that she yearned for his love, and his love alone, it seems unlikely that Kate really wanted William to ogle other women, but rather that she disguised how much his actions hurt her with a brave front. In encouraging her husband, she may have been looking for some assurance from him that he did not want to look at other beautiful women. She seems to have given her husband just enough rope with which to hang himself, and William unwittingly fell into the noose.

These letters reveal how much William missed his wife and wanted her back. Before she had left they had been on less than amicable terms, at least once sparring in public. At a state dinner early in the Johnson administration, dining companions noticed that the Rhode Island senator's wine consumption had begun to affect his comportment. Someone warned him not to drink any more, saying, "There are a pair of bright eyes looking at you." "Damn them," William retorted, "They can't see me." Kate, blushing to match her pink silk gown, leaned across the table and angrily replied, "Yes, they can see you, and they are heartily ashamed of you."[64] The story quickly make the rounds, attaining legendary status when, for the few weeks after the incident, Salmon, rather than Kate's "boy governor," acted as her escort to parties.

William's predilection for alcohol became a major bone of contention quite early in the marriage. "I have been into whiskey since you left," he

confessed in a letter to Kate, "and I am still sleepy."[65] In May he promised
to give up liquor until Kate's return. Many other letters refer to bouts
of "dyspepsia," a code word the Spragues and Salmon used for William's
ruinous hangovers.[66] The centrality that William's battle with vice had in the
relationship may certainly be found in the previously quoted letter, with its
references to "physical infirmity," "wickedness," "weakness," "shortcomings
of . . . character," and "temptations," as well as his direct promise to abstain
from whiskey until Kate's return.

Not coincidentally, in a letter where William told Kate he had been
drinking again, he went on to urge her to "go where you like to go, and to
live as you desire to live so far as the expenditure of money is concerned. . . .
Buy all you desire to buy any mementos that will be pleasing for you to have
in your hands. Dress as becomes a refined intelligent lady of great refinement
and accomplishment & see your sister is not in anyway less in that respect
to yourself." He reminded her that he wanted her to spend money that
and she should not refuse to obey him in that matter.[67] Thus early in their
relationship William established a pattern whereby he redressed his marital
inadequacies by throwing money at his wife. That she took him up on his
largesse, offerings he could well afford, sheds a different light on his later
claims about her financial profligacy. That he urged her time and again to
buy whatever she wanted suggests that she did not easily take to this new
spending habit. Nor is it likely that she found it adequate recompense for
her husband's marital shortcomings. Rather, the couple used liquor, sex,
and money to negotiate the political landscape of their relationship, with a
considerable amount of marital power seesawing back and forth as a result.

William also curried favor with Kate by writing her about the latest
political news. He often wrote to her from the Senate chamber, reporting
on the latest debates. Twice he outlined for her the civil rights bill, noting
where the amendment stood in the congressional process.[68] The repetition
of this bit of news suggests either that William was exceedingly impressed
with his part in the process or that he, like many other senators, was not
in a state of perfect sobriety when he wrote. Ironically, while he may have
wished to impress upon Kate the effort he was making to pay attention to
the political process, his letters from the Senate chamber suggest quite the
opposite. Nonetheless, his letters did demonstrate his understanding that
the road to Kate's heart was paved with politics.

While William tried to curry favor with his absent wife, Salmon did quite the opposite. He had again forgotten her birthday. Two months after the date, she wrote William of the matter, partially because he too had forgotten her special day. William then told Salmon of Kate's anger. Salmon wrote her, "It was a mean thing that your birthday was not commemorated. I am quite ashamed of that Yankee habitude which leads me to neglect such occasions."[69] Admitting that he undervalued outward signs of affection, he declared his intention to do better in the future.

It seems that Kate had a matched set in her life, for neither man ever fulfilled her need for voluble affection. It is this need that her trips abroad served, for each time she left William he resumed courting her—assuring her of her superiority to other women and his own deep inadequacies when he faced a life without her. Their relationship did better in the mails than it ever did when they were faced with the reality of each other's presence. Kate's need for love reflected the high value American culture placed on affection. In affection-based marriages, men granted the object of their affection power in the relationship because she provided him and his children with emotional, spiritual, and physical nurturing. This theoretically created a family relationship less hierarchical than in the previous century. The companionate model "denied patriarchy" by permitting increased marital choices based on the tenets of romantic love and encouraged mutual affection as a replacement for male authority.[70] But to say that Kate had power because her husband had affection for her seems to conflate power with influence. Affection-based marriages did little to ameliorate the inequalities between men and women.[71]

And what of Kate and William's relationship, where marital affection consistently failed? Marriage has always been a relationship of power. Thus the question becomes, can historians assign to husbands and wives differing grades of power, or must power be considered absolute? William's 1866 letters to Kate, written because she had withdrawn from him, do suggest that she had recourse to some marital authority. She had the ability to leave William, to make him want to do better, to effect some change in the relationship. Ultimately, though, she did not have the power to create any meaningful, long-term change. For example, for the duration of the marriage William came and went as he pleased, drank as much as he wanted, and behaved, time after time, erratically in public. Their marriage clearly illustrates the divide between wifely authority and marital happiness within the companionate model. Kate and William's relationship also suggests the limits of female power in less-than-felicitous marriages. Kate could influence William to behave or dress in a particular manner, but she could not make him do those things if he did not already wish to do so. Fundamentally, the basis of real power lies in just that ability—to make someone do something he or she does not want to do.

Charles Sumner's 1866 marriage to Alice Mason Hooper illustrates just how quickly the struggle for supremacy could destroy marital happiness. The beautiful and elegant Alice was the widow of the son of Sumner's friend Samuel Hooper, a congressman from Massachusetts. Married on 17 October 1866, the couple had dinner parties almost every night and began building a $30,000 house on Lafayette Square. The social and economic strain proved too great for Sumner, who vainly attempted to keep his young wife quietly at home. Alice violently revolted from his attempts to control her, and by February 1867 she began going out socially without her husband, often in the company of a dashing Prussian diplomat. She was heard to tell Sumner that she would go where she pleased and "God damn you, 'tis none of your business."[72] By the fall of 1867, Washington was abuzz with rumors that Mrs. Sumner was to divorce her husband on the grounds of impotence, rumors probably started by Alice. Sumner responded by speaking ill of his wife, writing to Mrs. John Lodge, a member of the prominent Massachusetts political family, "She is a bad woman—at home in the house a devil self-willed and infernal; in every respect forgetful of her marriage vows."[73] Unlike Kate, Alice had little trouble feeling angry about her marital disappointment, and no patience to heal the breach. The Sumners separated after eight months of marriage and never spoke again. Alice reverted to her maiden name, though she and Sumner did not divorce until May 1873, ten months before his death.[74]

Kate tried again and again to find a balance between her expectations for a romantic and egalitarian relationship and William's (and her father's) desire that she play the submissive wife. She found the submissive role William and Salmon expected difficult to maintain for a sustained period of time. Kate also repeatedly failed to turn William into a model Republican man—one who rejected aggressive masculinity, valued self-control, and showed deference to the moral guidance of his wife.[75] She responded to these failures with deep disappointment and a seeming incapacity to adjust her expectations accordingly. Only in letter writing could she revive the romance in her marriage.

Whatever marital difficulties the Spragues experienced in their first years of marriage were temporarily mended by separation. William met Kate, Nettie, Willie, and Maggie in Baden-Baden in mid-October and soon after accompanied his small family home. Nettie stayed on in Dresden through the winter, though Salmon confessed himself unhappy with her plan to remain abroad another year.[76] Once the Spragues were back home, their second courtship did not last the winter. Back in Washington by mid-December, William left again for Providence, leaving his wife and son in Salmon's care. Willie's croup and Kate's disappointment at being so soon abandoned made Salmon predict a "dull" Christmas.

In spite of his dire predictions, Grandpa had great fun with his daughters and grandson, and the confused state of politics during the winter of 1866–67 did little to dampen the capital's social season. Washington elites continued to express their relief at the end of the war with endless parties and balls. In her reminiscences, the Washington socialite Elizabeth Ellet described the 1866 social season as "almost a carnival. Washington seemed to have gone wild." She noted "the mixed character of the assemblages," where the nouveau riche mingled with the solidly respectable, much to the latter's dismay.[77] President Johnson's receptions, hosted by his daughter Martha Patterson, proved a high point of the social season. At the presidential New Year's reception, people noticed the chill that had already settled on Charles Sumner's two-and-a-half-month-old marriage to the lovely Alice Hooper, as well as the fact that the marine band played "Hail to the Chief" when the Grants entered the room. Kate was there, surrounded by a circle of the most imposing men in the room. She had a conversation with Ulysses and Julia Grant, no doubt cognizant of the fact that he represented a major stumbling block to her father's presidential aspirations.[78]

Kate spent most of the rest of the winter at home, only occasionally attending a ball or hosting a morning reception for her father. She did give one dance that season, a matinee that attracted an immense crowd. Curtains were closed and candles lit to imitate night so that the revelers might dance for hours and still get home before dawn. One attendee noted, "The engaging manners of Mrs. Sprague gave her an ascendancy in society." Kate and her father also attended Adele Cutts Williams's parties. Stephen Douglas's widow, the new Mrs. Williams had once been the object of Salmon's amorous attentions, but even the widow's obvious physical attractions had been unable to breach Kate's father's resistance to yet another marriage.[79]

Salmon's letters to Nettie that winter describe a felicitous family atmosphere, one made joyous by little Willie's baby steps into toddlerhood. Like
so many other babies, Willie enjoyed stair climbing, and he made his mother
accompany him up and down the main staircase until he could negotiate
them without any "little tumbles." His indulgent grandfather described
him as a "really sweet child. His occasional bursts of temper are like April
storms—soon come, soon gone." Salmon described Willie to Nettie as "that
baby of babies before whom all other babies hide their diminished heads."
Grandpa believed that though all families believed their babies the best,
Willie truly was a paragon of perfection. "He knows perfectly how to say
dinner—to me seems he says it rather a new way 'deenar' but he knows, the
little rogue, what it means. . . . If he considers himself as at all slighted he
gets mad as quick as anybody you ever saw. But he is politic too: as soon as
he is convinced that he can make nothing by crying he comes out of it at
once. See what a diplomatist he is going to be!"[80] Kate must have had her
hands full with the two of them, however much domestic help she had.

RECONSTRUCTION AND THE IMPEACHMENT TRIAL

The spring of 1867 found Kate and Willie still in Washington with Salmon,
while William toiled on in Rhode Island and Nettie lingered on the
Continent. William, when he did spend time in Washington, forgot his
protestations of sobriety and suffered from repeated attacks of "dyspepsia."
As his willfully blind father-in-law put it to Nettie, "Last night he felt so
badly he could not come down. No woman could have a kinder or more
indulgent husband than he has been to Katie. Sometimes I feel she doesn't
feel it quite enough; though I know she loves him and is proud of him."[81]
By summer Kate met Nettie in Paris. The sisters, Willie, and his nurse went
on to Italy together.[82] William and Salmon forgot Kate's twenty-seventh
birthday in August, as well as Nettie's twentieth birthday one month later,
though Salmon blamed William for confusing the dates for him.[83]

While the sisters traveled in Europe, Radical Republicans and President
Andrew Johnson continued to square off over Reconstruction. The two
essential missions of Reconstruction were to determine the place of former
Confederates in the Union and to fashion a workable civil rights program for
former slaves. Johnson concerned himself far more with reintegrating white
secessionists than with the political rights of black Americans. Although he

had once been a slave owner himself, the president disliked the southern white aristocracy almost as much as he did former slaves. Radical Republicans, Salmon P. Chase among them, saw Reconstruction as a "golden moment" to effect black suffrage and civil rights as well as to explore more fully the potential of congressional power. [84] By proclamations, Johnson offered amnesty to former Confederate military men, restitution of all property not human, and a plan by which southern white men determined the new state constitutions. As a result, not one constitutional convention in the former Confederate states would provide for black suffrage. Sumner called Johnson's proclamations "madness," while Thaddeus Stevens asked, "Is there no way to arrest the insane course of the President?" [85] Stevens's alarm was not unjustified, as white southerners attempted a return to the prewar status quo, demanding states' rights and instituting a series of harsh "black codes" that functioned to keep former slaves as de facto chattel.

By mid-1866 many northerners had acknowledged the failure of Presidential Reconstruction, a postwar period when Johnson was remarkably lenient with former Confederates and not particularly concerned with black civil rights. Johnson antagonized Congress by vetoing a Freedman's Bureau bill, and he accused Radical Republicans of treason. He had lost control of the Republican Party. Republicans gained a three-to-one majority in both congressional houses. [86] Virtually spoiling for a fight, they held sway over the political process. As Salmon put it, "Congress just now is our King." By early 1867 Congress enacted the Tenure of Office Act, which required that Johnson get Senate approval before removing from office any Senate-confirmed federal officeholders. Having essentially crippled Johnson's patronage power, the Senate moved on a series of Reconstruction acts that set up provisional governments in the former Confederate states, determined who would vote and hold office and how, and set the terms for state conventions and constitutions. Johnson vetoed, and Congress overrode his vetoes on three separate Reconstruction acts by July 1867. [87] These acts served as battleground between executive and congressional power, setting the stage for the larger struggle.

The year 1867 also saw the senatorial debut of the man who would eventually occupy the center of Kate's life. Thirty-eight-year-old Roscoe Conkling had already served a number of years in the House and, as the "Adonis of the Senate," was admired by multitudes of ladies and heartily disliked by many of his colleagues. Hearing of Conkling's election, Secretary of the Navy Gideon Welles recorded in his diary that "Conkling is vain, has ability with touches of spread-eagle eloquence, and a good deal of impetuous ardor. He may improve and he may not."[88] Having been on the Joint Committee on Reconstruction when in the House, Roscoe had immense interest in how best to manage the reunion of seceded states. Although he had missed the vote on the Reconstruction Act of 2 March, which divided the South into five military districts (he had been installed in office two days later), Conkling declared his intention to take an active part in the Senate by participating in debate on the Supplementary Reconstruction Bill and by engaging in oratorical jousting with Senators Drake and Morton.[89] Kate could not have failed to notice the new senator's enthusiastic debut, contrasting Conkling's performances with those of her husband, who was so often mute or missing entirely from the fray. She would also have known that the acerbic radical Thaddeus Stevens had championed the new senator's previous career as a congressman. Positioned as he was in the radical camp, Roscoe may have attended the soirees Kate gave on her father's behalf. But that summer, while Roscoe commenced his lifelong addiction to matters of patronage, Kate bade her adieus to her father and husband and sailed across the Atlantic once again.

That fall, coinciding with Kate and Nettie's return to Washington, Congress reconvened to determine how next to subvert the president's attempts at Reconstruction. Thaddeus Stevens led a faction that began preaching impeachment, even though both houses had essentially disempowered Johnson with Republican majorities large enough to override any veto. The Tenure of Office Act would precipitate the impeachment crisis when Johnson asked for the resignation of Secretary of War Edwin M. Stanton in August 1867, while Congress was not in session. Stanton, who reported the contents of Johnson's cabinet meetings to leading Radical Republicans, refused the order, prompting Johnson to suspend him from office. Congress failed to concur with the suspension—a move that prompted the president to oust Stanton from office in February 1868, in direct violation of the Tenure of Office Act.[90]

Four days after Stanton's removal from office, Stevens and John Bingham moved to have Johnson impeached. A committee of seven, including Roscoe Conkling, determined the rules for the proceedings. That committee consulted Kate's father, who as chief justice would preside over the trial.[91] Salmon found himself in a "peculiarly difficult position" with regard to the trial. To his friend Gerrit Smith he wrote, "Coming into the Senate to preside I feel and am felt as a sort of foreign element. The Senate, like all other bodies has a good deal of Esprit de Corps. I as Chief Justice look for my powers & duties in the Constitution and very naturally find myself disagreeing as to their nature & extent from many senators."[92] As usual a master of understatement, Salmon well understood that his belief in the unconstitutionality of the proceedings, and thus apparent sympathy with the unregenerate Johnson, would nullify his chances for a Republican presidential nomination. Nonetheless, to Salmon "the whole business seems wrong . . . [suggesting] that Congress is above the Constitution." Salmon believed that the impeachment had more to do with partisan power than with real evidence of high crimes.[93]

More than Salmon's impeachment stance compromised his presidential chances with the Republican Party. The 1867 elections in his home state of Ohio had turned the legislature over to Democrats. Ohio and other northern states had also failed to pass suffrage measures for black males, signaling northern voters' unwillingness to comply with the Radical Republican platform. Many white Republicans did not want blacks enfranchised, and Salmon's adherence to that cause did little to enhance his party standing. In an 1868 letter to the banker and diplomat August Belmont, Salmon carefully laid out his political philosophy. He believed he might be considered a Democrat in the principles of "finance, commerce and administration," but he continued to assert that suffrage should not be limited to white citizens.[94] While Democrats hailed the 1867 elections as a great victory for their principles, they exaggerated the level of their success. Nonetheless, Republican Party leaders came to understand that moderates, rather than radicals, would win the day in the next election.[95]

Throughout the bitter impeachment trial, William publicly said nothing. Not coincidentally, Stanton still held the file that contained Hoyt's testimony as to William's treasonous involvement in the cotton caper. No doubt aware of that fact, Kate took an intense interest in the impeachment trial. Each day found Nettie and Kate in their front-row Senate gallery seats, probably carefully evaluating the course of the trial and storing up nuggets to discuss with William and Salmon at the dinner table. The society columnist Emily Edson Briggs reported Kate as "autumnal sweetness and perfection . . . a picture of delicacy and grace, arrayed in silk tinted with the shade of dead forest leaf, with dead gold ornaments to match." She continued, "Paris has Eugenie; Washington has Mrs. Senator Sprague, the acknowledged queen of fashion and good taste." [96] On another occasion Kate sat in the gallery attired in a royal purple gown and matching bonnet that caused one writer "to feel that her eyes rested upon the most graceful, distinguished and queenly woman that she had ever seen in the capitol, or elsewhere on the face of the globe." Kate also appeared as "a lilac blossom," her violet bonnet "fastened to its place by lilac tulle so filmy that it must have been stolen from the purple mists of the morning. An exquisite walking dress of pale lilac silk has trimmings a shade darker, whilst lilac gloves conceal a hand that might belong to the queen of the fairies." [97]

More than merely fashion hyperbole, or an effort by Kate to outshine all other women, her elegant clothes marked Kate as a virtuous woman. Literally pounds of fabric, draped in multiple layers, created, in the mid-nineteenth-century mind, a picture of feminine modesty, a proper visual display of womanhood. Kate's adherence to strict fashion decorum helped fix her as a respectable woman—and, more important, as an acceptable political woman. Elaborate descriptions of Kate's costumes served to distract men's eyes and minds from Kate's political identity. Feminists and dress reformers' insistence that fashionable dress made women dependent upon luxuries and prisoners of their own clothes added to the disguise element of Kate's wardrobe. When reformers, on the outside of the political mainstream, insisted that corsets and hoopskirts debilitated a woman's "self-mastery," they implicitly suggested that a woman so attired could never be a legitimate political actor. To be a citizen, and thus a political person, one had to be independent and virtuous, and thus a categorical male. When Stanton, Bloomer, and other advocates of dress reform adopted the "new costume," the tremendous uproar they caused could be traced to a cultural perception that these women desired to usurp the active and independent public sphere inhabited by men. [98] While political cartoons lampooned dress reformers as promiscuous, ugly, unladylike female monsters, Kate donned her haute couture and slipped, relatively unresented, into the political fray. In effect, her velvet and silk dresses acted as a kind of drag, allowing her political mind and female body entrée into a male venue.

Gossip and newspaper reports had it that by her lovely presence Kate sought to influence her husband and other Republicans to vote for Johnson's acquittal. Rumors suggested that she threatened to leave her husband if he did not vote as she wished, or that her dinner parties at the Sixth and E

Street mansion functioned to control the trial from behind the scenes. A Philadelphia paper suggested that Salmon's dislike of Benjamin F. Wade, a longtime Ohio political opponent who would inherit the presidency if the Senate voted to convict Johnson, made the chief justice favor the president. The paper then quoted Kate as saying, "the idea of that horrid Ben Wade being put over my father!" [99] Whether or not Kate actually said this or threatened to leave William—and both seem unlikely given her political sagacity—her father had real concerns about what the trial meant to the country's judicial and governmental systems. William, on the other hand, had more personal worries. Even Gideon Welles assumed that William's vote would go the way Kate desired, but William remained silent on the matter. [100] So vociferous were Kate's demands that William bend to her will, or so the rumors went, that they quarreled violently. Washington insiders believed so strongly in Kate's unwavering support for her father and his political positions that no one could believe that she would not demand that William vote the Chase family line and find the president innocent. Stanton's hold over William had so far remained a closely guarded secret, so even Washington insiders were unaware that William's career, and even his freedom, may have depended upon a vote against Johnson. Thus when Kate suddenly left for Narragansett many Washingtonians believed that her inability to convince William to vote for acquittal had driven her away. The gossip was simply incorrect.

Kate did leave Washington with a cold, though whether reasons of health or stress over her family's political situation prompted her departure remains unclear. Salmon wrote her, "I was dreadfully frightened about your cold, and very uneasy about you going north when you did." He also worried that "the Governor says you have found the Narragansett air too bracing and his uneasiness increases mine." This suggests not only that Kate and her husband were corresponding, an unlikely happenstance if she were enraged with him, but that she was relatively unwell. Salmon added, "How I wish you would take a different view of your social duties, & cease [injuring] yourself, by attending those wretched night parties." Salmon did refer to an argument between the Spragues, but his letter suggests that the argument was not about impeachment:

> How well I love you my darling! My whole heart seems to go towards you while I write and tears come into my eyes. How wrong it is for

those who love to express their love. I remember how often you have felt hurt by my apparent indifference to what interested you: and I feel sorry that I ever occasioned any such feelings to you. I see now in your husband something of that which I blame on myself. But I know how strong my love really was, and I know how strong his is. And I am very glad that, while you have sometimes forgotten that the happiness of a wife is most certainly secured by loving submission & loving tact, you, generally, conquer by sweetness. I never saw him so much affected as by the difference that occurred between you just before you went away. He was almost unmanned—moved to tears. I have not thought it best to refer to it; but [I will] try to make my society pleasant for him & hope I succeed. You must love away all his reserve—and help yourself to do so by reflecting how generous, self sacrificing & indulgent a husband he is to you. . . . If he were only a true Christian he would be nearly perfect.[101]

Whatever had moved William to tears, it had not been Kate's insistence that he antagonize Stanton in voting to acquit Johnson. Whether or not Kate believed her husband innocent of treason, she must have known of the charges Hoyt and Prescott had leveled against the three Sprague men. Certainly William's letters to Dix suggest he had something to cover up, and Dix's letter to Stanton strongly suggests that Hoyt had fully implicated William. Kate must have been aware of most, if not all, of these realities.

Thus, given the fact that Stanton held evidence that could virtually ruin her husband, it seems unlikely that Kate would have blindly urged her husband to defy Stanton and vote in agreement with her father. She would hardly have demanded that her husband openly antagonize the secretary of war, nor could she publicly subvert her father's position. By leaving town, Kate removed herself from the sticky situation. Salmon seems equally aware of the moral ambiguity of his son-in-law's position. One must remember that until Salmon's resignation, Stanton and he had been co-cabinet members as well as good friends. It seems extremely unlikely that these two wily old politicos had not had a frank discussion about the Sprague family's cotton-acquisition practices. Although newspapers reported that the chief justice would influence his son-in-law to vote for acquittal, Salmon denied the very idea. "Sprague was not influenced by me," he wrote Horace Greeley, "nor did I seek to influence him."[102] Kate's father dismissed all the stories of his and Kate's influence over the trial as "mere bosh," and when William voted Johnson guilty of high crimes and misdemeanors, the senator and chief justice went on amicably living under the same roof for a better portion of the next year. And contrary to the rumors, Kate did not leave her husband. Salmon and Kate well understood the meaning of William's vote, and silence was their only recourse to the awkward rumors.

THE 1868 PRESIDENTIAL ELECTION

Before vacationing at her house on Narragansett Bay, twenty-eight-year-old Kate had important political business to accomplish. Her father, who had long nurtured presidential ambitions, scuttled any remaining hope he might have had of gaining the 1868 Republican nomination by his insistence that the impeachment trial be a judicial rather than political event. Radical Republicans denounced him as a traitor to their cause, and by March they began to accuse him of courting the Democratic Party. Their accusations were not unfounded. In April, popular journalist Theodore Tilton publicly renounced his support of Kate's father, writing, "We now have reason to believe that Mr. Chase would not accept the Republican nomination even if it were tendered. We have equal reason to believe, also, that he would accept the Democratic nomination, if it could be tendered on a platform not inconsistent with his well-known views of Negro suffrage." [103] Because the immense popularity of Ulysses S. Grant made the general's nomination an almost foregone conclusion, and because of his unpopularity with the Republicans, Kate's father sought the nomination elsewhere. Salmon's lust for the presidency, what Lincoln had called his "maggot in the brain," led him straight to the Democratic Party. [104]

As the Chase movement gained momentum, the chief justice's old friends expressed disbelief at his political defection. Others suggested that he run as a third-party candidate, supported by anti-Grant Republicans. In fact, newspaper reports of a third party were fairly common that spring, though Salmon's correspondence suggests that he never viewed the idea as a viable alternative. [105] The *New York Herald* blamed Kate for the early rumors of Salmon's move to the Democrats. "Mrs. Sprague is, and for some time has been, not only foolishly ambitious to be recognized officially as the first lady in the land . . . to gain this end she has been and is playing the game of a remorseless politician." The paper went on to claim that "being a lady of spirit and decision of character, who will not take no for an answer, she has led her father, the Chief Justice, into this unseemly pursuit of the Presidential Succession." [106] A few days later, the *London Times* reported that Kate was "lobbying for the President" and that her husband had given money to New Hampshire Democrats. [107] It did not seem odd to these sources that Kate might take a political part, only that she might be doing so against her father's better impulses.

Indeed, not only did both Republicans (and before them Whigs) and Democrats define their political goals in domestic terms, each side claiming that their policies would best protect the American home, but the deeply partisan issues of the war years had drawn a good number of women into the process. Elite, middle-class, and working-class white women arranged campaign suppers, receptions, dances, and community barbecues, observed conventions, and attended rallies and speeches. Black women also participated in these events, though they sometimes faced violent reprisals. The Republican Party particularly became "the party of the home," accepting the ideology of women's moral superiority and emphasizing the importance of women's influence in politics. Republicans, for example, offered a "gender-based critique of slavery" that emphasized the threat slave labor posed to white families in both the North and the South. The party's wartime conversion to abolitionism also attracted a great number of women— women who had found the Whig Party's inaction in the face of Democrats' expansion of slavery distasteful and immoral. Republicans not only declared an allegiance to women's needs and services but attracted large numbers of nonvoting supporters. Democrats attacked this ideology as destructive to white male authority and, ultimately, as threatening to womanhood.

Both parties agreed that women's virtue provided the foundation for political virtue, though they disagreed on the extent to which women should directly influence politics.[108] Some of the hostility Kate faced might have been based on the degree of her political participation—hostility her detractors expressed by attributing Salmon's ambition to his daughter. Kate's ingress into party politics, then, was less surprising than the fact that she did so under the Democratic umbrella. Doubtless her familiarity with Republican women's partisan activities made her feel perfectly at home at any political convention.

Salmon, as Lincoln and so many others had recognized, hardly needed Kate to drag him into the presidential fray. He had been a candidate for the Republican nomination in 1856, 1860, and 1864. As early as 1865 he surreptitiously began his 1868 campaign with a trip to the South. Pregnant with Willie, Kate stayed home, effectively elevating Nettie to the position of primary companion on a two-month trip along the southern coast. Poor Nettie suffered the effects of seasickness on the revenue cutter they used for travel. Salmon's diary leaves little doubt that he used the trip to reinforce his old ties to Treasury agents, federal officeholders, and military men in positions of power. His letters to Stanton and Sumner also support the notion that Salmon had not given up the dream of installing his political ambitions at 1600 Pennsylvania Avenue.[109] Additionally, the chief justice wrote seven long letters to President Johnson detailing his belief that the national government should assist recently freed slaves, particularly with regard to suffrage, and that white southerners would accept any Reconstruction plan the president might propose.[110] Although Johnson rejected Chase's advice, the letters illustrate how badly Salmon yearned to determine the course of the country.

Although Kate did not force her father to pursue the Democratic nomination, neither did she discourage him. Instead, the two worked together, as they had so often before, to attain his political goals. In May, only days after the impeachment verdict, the Republicans unanimously nominated Grant on the first ballot.[111] That month and the next, Salmon continued to correspond with a number of men about his possible candidacy, commenting on favorable newspaper editorials and laying out the platform upon which he would run. Salmon believed that "suffrage for all, amnesty for all; good money for all; [and] security for all citizens at home and abroad against governmental invasion" were essential to democracy, and he told a friend that should the Democrats embrace these issues, "I could not be at liberty to refuse the use of my name."[112] After Grant's nomination, the *New York Herald* suggested that only Chase could unite conservative Republicans and "sensible" Democrats to defeat the Civil War hero. Chase contended that he had always been, at heart, a Democrat, except with regard to slavery. "On that question," he assured August Belmont, "I thought the democratic party failed to make a just application of democratic principles, and regarded myself as more democratic than the democrats. My old friend General Cass would sometimes say to me, when we served together in the Senate, 'Why, Chase, you are as good a democrat as any of us.' "[113] Salmon earnestly (if incorrectly) believed that southern Democrats would accept universal suffrage if it were teamed with universal amnesty as the basis for

Reconstruction, thus making his candidacy as a Democrat tenable, at least to himself.[114]

The issues before the country that year were not only suffrage but also the complicated matters of Reconstruction and national finances. Reconstruction encompassed blacks' voting rights as well as the where, when, how, and who of admitting southern states and their representatives back into the national political process. The division of the South into military districts also figured into the Reconstruction issue. Salmon joined Johnson and others in believing that martial occupation of the old Confederate states served to alienate white southerners, though he thought the president "wrong in limiting by his Reconstruction Proclamations the right of suffrage to whites." The encroachment of the military into the judiciary of the South also worried Salmon. As the former secretary of the treasury, Kate's father obviously had strong opinions about national finances, particularly the question of the day—whether Civil War bonds, issued under Chase's tenure as treasury secretary, should be repaid in gold or in "greenbacks." Democratic front-runner and Ohioan George Pendleton, for example, favored repayment in paper, while New Yorker Horatio Seymour supported the Democratic Party's more traditional hard-money line. While the Republican Party's platform skirted these issues with ambiguous language, the Democratic Party came firmly down on the side of a "out-and-out greenback plank."[115] Although Chase was, in fact, the father of greenbacks, he favored a return to specie payment. This hard-money stance, combined with his insistence on universal (and thus black) suffrage, meant that Kate and his more official supporters had their work cut out for them at the convention. To many, Salmon P. Chase appeared no more than a shameless opportunist.

In July, while Salmon enjoyed a vacation at Canonchet, Kate installed herself at the Fifth Avenue Hotel in New York. From this headquarters she acted as her father's de facto campaign manager for the Democratic convention. The hotel could not have been a more convenient place from which to operate. Situated near the Tammany Wigwam (where the Democratic convention would be held), the new building had been adorned for the occasion with $20,000 worth of blue satin, gold fringe, and other decorations. The hotel also functioned as an informal convention center for many candidates and delegations, including the headquarters for Indiana, Illinois, Massachusetts, West Virginia, and Maine. The Ohio delegation, upon which Kate and her father counted to support the Chase movement, took up rooms in the floors above Kate's suite.[116] Kate also spent a good deal of time at the Clarendon Hotel, where the Chase movement had its headquarters. William Hudson, at the time a self-described "cub" for the *Brooklyn Eagle*, described Kate as "in supreme control, in the flush of beautiful womanhood, tall and elegant, with exquisite tact, with brains of almost masculine fiber, trained in the political arts by her father." Hudson admitted that he "fell under her sway" so completely that he believed it necessary that her father get the nomination.[117]

William's cousin Susan Sprague Hoyt and her husband, Edwin Hoyt, lived in New York, just one block down Fifth Avenue from the hotel, and Kate slept at their house—the hotel room must have been too much a political hotbed to allow for a lady's private needs.[118] William's brother, Amasa, headed up the Committee of 100 to elect Chase, working from Providence to raise money.[119] Kate met with Horatio Seymour, Roscoe Conkling's brother-in-law and convention president; John Bigler, one of California's first governors; and August Belmont, who gave the convention's opening speech.[120]

In her first letter from the convention, Kate professed to her father, "I am glad you are not going to be greatly disappointed if the nomination is not for you. I should like to see this bright jewel added to your list of earthly distinction & I BELIEVE it will be. But we can love & be very happy & just as proud of you without it. Will the COUNTRY do as well?" Kate thought she might go to Narragansett to see "dear little Willie" before the convention officially began, but her next letter suggests that she became too quickly and deeply embroiled in political details to leave town, even though she did "long very much to see the boy."[121] Both Kate and Hamilton Smith, who was also working for the Chase effort, believed that the New York delegation and the faction that supported George Pendleton were acting "fractious" and needed to be cultivated. On Kate's stationery, Smith wrote her father, "What a magnificent woman Kate has become—With her shrewdness & force, & with ninety days time, I could have you nominated by acclamation & elected by an overwhelming majority."[122] The day Kate postponed her trip to Rhode Island, the *New York Herald* reported that although the New York delegation preferred Chase, they would vote for Sanford Church on the first ballot. New York probably intended to force the candidacy of yet another man, in an effort to break up the coalition behind front-runner

George Pendleton. [123] The *Herald* claimed that the state's defection from Chase was intended to "harmonize the New York, Ohio and Pennsylvania delegations upon the Chief Justice before presenting his name." [124] Under the circumstances, Kate had good reason to stay in the muggy atmosphere of New York and forestall any precipitous political rout.

Because convention rules did not allow women on the floor, Kate acted primarily behind the scenes while John Dash Van Buren officially acted as the Chase campaign manager. Nonetheless, Kate had the pulse of the machinations, warning her father against those men whom she considered intemperate and untrustworthy and apprising him of the platform nego-tiations. She also kept track of the whereabouts of the men authorized to act for her father. When asked about her father's chances of success, Kate quipped, "It is all a question of whether the Democratic Party has the sense to seize its opportunities. I fear that when the South seceded the brains of the party went with it. Since then it has rarely missed an opportunity to blunder." [125]

Salmon's letters matched Kate's in political detail. He continued to play both sides of the fence with her, one paragraph discussing the breakdown of the ballots, or the debt and suffrage planks, and in a later paragraph denying any desire for the nomination or her assistance. "You know how little I desire a nomination and how averse I have been to making any efforts to secure it," he disingenuously pled. Like many other politicians of his era, Salmon liked to create the illusion that the public sought his service, rather than the other way around. He closed one political missive by saying, "I am afraid my darling, that you are acting too much the politician. Have a Care. Don't do or say anything which may not be proclaimed on the housetops. I am so anxious about you that I cannot help wishing you were in Narragansett or here where I take all things very quietly & play croquet nearly every evening." [126] Three days later he wrote her again, urging her to consult with Van Buren and others to get the Chase name before the convention. Denying his desire for the presidency while arduously pursuing it had become an established pattern with Salmon. Kate had spent enough time with her father during the last two campaigns to understand the meaning behind his protestations. Coincidentally, both Grant, who received the Republican nomination, and Horatio Seymour, who would get the nod from the Democrats, also professed an unwillingness to run for president. Salmon's reluctance was probably less genuine than either

Grant's or Seymour's. [127] Kate labored on through the heat, taking long interviews with the New York Republican Samuel Tilden and Seymour in an effort to gain their support.

On 9 July, Kate came to understand that all of her labors had been for naught. On 7, 8, and 9 July the convention considered twenty men for the nomination, but not one had enough support to gain the nomination. Then, late on the ninth, a virtual stampede for Horatio Seymour ended the struggle. On the twenty-second ballot, Seymour received all 317 votes, becoming the Democratic presidential nominee in the coming election against Grant. Kate felt the failure most keenly.

> My dearest father,
> You have been most cruelly deceived & shamefully used by the man who you trusted implicitly, & the COUNTRY must suffer for his duplicity. I would not write you yesterday in the excitement of the result of the action of the Convention, & until I had carefully gone over in my mind all the circumstances that had come under my *knowledge* of the action of Mr. Van Buren. When I get comfortably settled at Narragansett, I will write out a full & detailed history of my Knowledge of this matter that can not fail to convince you of his bad faith. Nothing more would be needed, than that since the result of the nomination was [word illegible] Mr. Van Buren [mingles] constantly at the Manhattan Club, next door has not been near me, & has passed both Mr. Kennedy and Mr. Schuckers this morning without recognition. Had Mr. Kennedy had the authority to act for you, you would have been as certainly nominated on the wave of the enthusiasm created in the Convention by the 1/2 vote cast by California day before yesterday, as anything could be. Mr. Van Buren's telegraph to you to answer no questions in regard to the Platform, was the block he put in the way of your nomination, & when at the critical juncture he was at last found, (for he has scarcely been seen in the Convention) he refused to take the responsibility of speaking for you, & said he would now do the responsibility with Mr. Long *but took no action* & the moment had gone by. Had I received my letter at the hour it was due, or any time before 3 1/2 P.M., I believe all would have been different. Mr. Kennedy & Mr. Long were both true as steel, but neither of them were equal (or so situated as to be equal) to the combinations against them. Mr. Tilden & Mr. Seymour have done this work & Mr. Van Buren has been *their tool*—This is my honest belief, but I will write it out carefully—So dear father in the future, be guided by the advice of some of those who are

devoted to you but who are more suspicious than your own noble heart will allow you to be.

With all this *you personally* can have nothing to regret. Your friends have worked nobly, & the universal disappointment today is amazing. Not a flag floats nor is the semblance of rejoicing visible anywhere.

Your name is the watchword with the people, & they have been outraged & deceived. I am perfectly well & go to the country to kiss Willie & see the Governor. I may return, & think I shall, to Washington with the Governor when I hope we can capture you & take to Narragansett. Mr. Cisco, is as true as tried steel. Mr. Long has gone home broken hearted. You can form no conception of our depression here.

Your devoted Katie[128]

This letter highlights the depth of Kate's involvement in her father's political life and her astute understanding of the details of the political process. In her affection for her father, though, she failed to comprehend the larger scheme of the convention until too late. The letters of leading Democrats, in addition to Van Buren, Seymour, and Tilden, suggest that party leadership never took the Chase camp seriously, instead using the chief justice to force the nomination of a more traditional Democrat. In a letter to Tilden, for example, Samuel Church wrote, "Chase is out of the question. . . . [W]e will use him well, but must not think of nominating him."[129] Days before the convention officially began, the *New York Times* reported: "The Chase movement has reached its limit and amounts to very little indeed. A large majority of men scorn the idea of his nomination."[130] Democrats may also have also been using the chief justice's name to broaden their appeal, and he probably never had much of a chance of succeeding with the Democratic Party.

Kate was right about John D. Van Buren—for not only had Van Buren proposed Tilden's name for nomination months before the convention, but Tilden's private papers reveal that he had used Van Buren as his personal, confidential agent.[131] Tilden and Seymour may have supported Chase that spring, but western Democrats favored Pendleton, and eastern Democrats jumped on and off the Chase train enough times to derail the whole effort. By June, Tilden (and thus probably Van Buren) no longer supported Chase. Significantly, during the convention Seymour stayed at Van Buren's home who confirmed Kate's suspicions of his disloyalty by avoiding her and those working at the Chase headquarters. Kate took better measure of Van Buren than her father ever did, for Salmon continued to support him and other men until the bitter end. "I was told that Seymour was for himself before the convention met, but would not believe it," Salmon wrote Van Buren, adding, "I thought *you would not be* deceived & know you would not deceive."[132] Kate's father preferred to believe that Van Buren had been tricked than to recognize his treachery. During the early days of the convention Kate had believed her father's nomination unlikely, or at least unnecessary, but once she was caught up in the excitement of power brokering she seems to have forgotten those realities. Once home she must have reassessed the facts of the convention—that her father's home state had not voted for him en masse; that his views on universal suffrage made him an unlikely postwar Democrat, as did his views on debt payment; and that southern delegates reviled his name. On 9 July the Chase movement had its brightest moment. A test vote revealed he had a 37–24 lead among New York delegates and that 11 Ohio delegates favored him as their second choice.[133] As shining moments go, it hardly dazzled the convention. Salmon never received more than 4 votes out of a possible 317. "Presidential fever is a deadly malady," Carl Schurz had once noted, but Salmon had lived with the illness for two decades.[134] His daughter turned out to be no less immune.

The 1868 elections proved beyond a doubt that politics do indeed make odd bedfellows. Eight years before, no one would have thought that Salmon P. Chase, who had so valiantly argued fugitive slave cases and urged the end of slavery, would allow his name before a convention of Democrats. Clement Vallandigham, a notorious wartime copperhead found guilty of sedition in 1863 and banished to the Confederacy, supported the Chase movement, believing he gave the Democrats their only chance to regain the White House.[135] Conservative eastern Democrats liked Chase's hard-money stance, but in the end he wobbled on that issue, as he had on suffrage. His proposed platform suggested that universal suffrage be administered by the states, rather than federally mandated, and that debt be repaid "honestly," saying nothing specific about gold.[136] These planks, both unspecific and easily manipulated, left many with the impression that the chief justice would adopt any stance in order to gain the presidency.

This impression, though, does not fit the man. If Salmon had been more willing to bend his political ideology to the whim of party and popular sentiment, he might have been more successful in his ambitions. He had a tremendous capability for self-deception, and his overweening ambition to gain the presidency for himself did not match his sincere political beliefs. He recognized the unseemliness of his passion and struggled against his desires. His voluminous correspondence reveals a man who trusted men unworthy of his faith in them. Certainly Vallandigham's unsavory war record should have marked him as outside the bounds of respectability, and just as certainly, Kate was correct that her father unwisely placed his trust in men like Van Buren who spent more time drinking than gathering support for Chase. Salmon repeatedly ignored her advice on matters of men and platform—apparently unable to appreciate the political woman he had helped to create. Just as his principles did not mesh with the political realities of the day, neither did his view of womanhood correspond with the Republican Party woman his daughter had become. When a Washington journalist told Salmon about the outcome of the convention, he immediately asked, "Does Mrs. Sprague know? And how does she bear it?"[137] Some see Salmon's response as proof that he desired the nomination far less than did his daughter, but his correspondence does not bear this out. Rather, given the spectacular failure of his movement, he may have immediately perceived his error in ignoring Kate's astute advice and understood that he had failed her as surely as Van Buren had failed them both.

FOUR

"Argument and Pertinacity"
The Difficult Years,
1868–1873

~

*The capacity of women to make unsuitable marriages must
be considered the cornerstone of society.*

Henry Adams

Salmon was neither the first nor the last man to undervalue Kate. Her husband did so time and time again—a fact that became increasingly evident as the 1860s came to a close. By the end of 1868, Washington society acknowledged that the marriage was an unhappy pairing; the Spragues continued to move in polite company, though often not together. The couple did experience a brief period of happiness that fall, when William broke his leg while at Canonchet and Kate took up full-time nursing duties. Apparently she found William's dependence a pleasurable experience, but it did not last long. Once William was up on crutches he went back to Providence, dismissed his wife, and returned to work. From Canonchet a disconsolate Kate wrote her father: "I feel as though my occupation were gone." She soon left for shopping in New York, then went back to Washington.[1]

During this period, the nation's capital, still only half built, was a study in contrasts. Ornate carriages often got bogged down in muddy streets, opulent mansions of the bejeweled elite stood near shacks filled with recently freed slaves, and cows competed with the new horse-drawn trolleys for space. An English tourist thought Washington looked "like the card-board cities which Potemkin erected. . . . [I]t is impossible to remove the impression that, when Congress is over, the place is taken down and packed up till again wanted." Many senators, representatives, diplomats, and lobbyists stayed in the capital for only two or three sessions, creating a largely transient society. Everyone noted the poor quality of the hotels, even the famed National and Willards, which were "eternally shabby." [2] Many of the senators were rich men and their money primed both the political and social pumps, though few had as much money as Senator Sprague. It cost the White House fifteen hundred to two thousand dollars to feed twenty people dinner, where upwards of thirty-five dishes took elegant diners only two hours to consume. Henry Adams noted that "politics and reform became the detail, waltzing the profession" in postwar Washington.[3]

As the president's wife, Julia Dent Grant reigned supreme in this society, though the elegant Julia Fish, the wife of Secretary of State Hamilton Fish, ran her a close second. One society columnist assessed the new First Lady by writing, "Born without the natural gifts or graces which could have made her a leader of other minds, she is, nevertheless, very fond of social entertainments, and enters into them with good nature and visible enjoyment, which at times goes far to take the place of higher and more positive attainments." Mrs. Grant gave a reception every Tuesday afternoon, and each could guarantee the attendance of the best-dressed and most prominent ladies of Washington. Although Mrs. Grant's parties were called "morning receptions," they actually took place in the afternoon. In elite society, any call or event that took place before dinner was designated a "morning" call. Journalist Emily Edson Briggs noted that the First Lady "possessed a wonderful power of conciliating all distracting elements which helps to unite social and political society."[4]

Fashion reflected the age's excesses. "Dresses were magnificent almost beyond precedent," one contemporary wrote. "The fashion prevalent of loading one skirt above another with trimmings, and the bright contrasts of colors, were abundantly exhibited." Kate, for example, wore pink hair adornments and a blue silk dress with a pink over-tunic and blue lace trimmings to President Johnson's last reception. Considered by many to be in the full bloom of her beauty, she figured prominently in the gilded social scene that was Reconstruction Washington. The American poet and author Elizabeth Ellet noted that "Mrs. Sprague's receptions continue to be a prominent feature of society. Gifted with beauty and brilliant mental qualities, her reign is undisputed." [5] While Kate waltzed in Paris gowns, William remained in the background. Mary Logan, herself a politician's wife, noted that Kate and Nettie were "fascinating and brilliant women" who "presided over the home of the chief justice and made it one of the most attractive in the city." Logan left William out of her picture of the "eminent statesmen and learned men and women of the time" who were entertained so lavishly at the Sixth and E Street house.[6]

"UNPLEASANT WORDS"

Kate and William had fought through the summer months after the Democratic convention, first over the treatment of Kate's horse, which had to be destroyed after a drunken groom rode him too hard, and then about William's drinking problem. Kate eventually discovered that her husband had not only continued his relationship with Mary Viall Anderson but had engaged in illicit relations with at least one of the servants at Canonchet. After Willie's birth Kate had hired a nursemaid named Maggie to help her with the baby, the same maid who accompanied her and Nettie to Europe. Later, in her divorce petition, Kate claimed that William "frequently attempted to have criminal intercourse with the female domestics and guests in the family, causing them to leave the house . . . that said Sprague by indecent advances to female servants, and other violations of decency, which had increased in frequency and enormity, had made said residence at South Kingston an unsuitable abode."[7] This, coupled with a specific accusation of adultery "with Maggie English, in South Kingston and elsewhere, in the years 1866 and 1867," strongly suggests that Maggie, Willie's maid, and Maggie English, partner in William's infidelity, were one and the same.

The couple's fights became more frequent and furious until Salmon, who had left Canonchet for circuit court duty in West Virginia, began offering his daughter marital advice. On one occasion William had done something that caused "unpleasant words" between the couple, and Salmon urged:

> You must reflect, my darling that there can be only one head to a family, and that while a husband will always find happiness of both increased by mutual counsels, yet that it is the wife's part when the husband chooses to act, in any matter upon his own judgment without asking hers, to acquiesce cheerfully and affectionately. . . . Few wives ever had a more indulgent husband, and a husband to be more justly proud than you. You love & honor him I know; but sometimes you complain when he thinks it unreasonable & contend with him when duty & prudence require submission. You can conquer only by love & submission—not by argument & pertinacity. An end gained by pertinacity is really lost.[8]

In these few lines Salmon illuminates both his expectations for his married daughter and her resistance. He also places himself on William's side, leaving Kate without an ally.

The unhappy couple may have created some kind of reconciliation, because they conceived their second child early in January 1869. [9] The possibility exists, though, that Kate became pregnant without any marital rapprochement, given William's escalating abuse. In the fall of 1868 Kate began a diary in an attempt to come to terms with the state of her marriage. Alone at Canonchet while William was in Providence with his mother, Kate wrote and asked him to come home. He answered that as a "man of business" with "ways of life of his own," he would not see her. Kate then heard that he was complaining about her to employees, friends, and family—a rumor that deeply wounded her. She also disliked the fact that her husband allowed his brother, Amasa, to "offer me sorry redresses short of personal insult, without a thought of chiding him, or protecting me." William also paid heed to "some malignant tongue, seeking to destroy his peace, or mine, or both, & claim to know of me, which if true, would make me unworthy to be a wife—, any man's wife!" [10] Apparently, someone had accused her of infidelity.

In spite of these insults, Kate went to Providence on the eve of their anniversary to "secure some little token of love & affection from my husband." Having not seen his wife for ten days, William forced Kate to wait in an outer office with his clerks, though he could see her from where he stood. Kate described their meeting as follows:

> William saunters indifferently in the room, looking shabby and unkempt & with a careless nod to me, makes this remark about the matter. I answer as cheerfully as I can, but with my heart in my throat. I ask of him is he coming home this week. Why no, he has not thought of such a thing. He then picking up the papers upon his desk as though impatient at the interruption, turns again & asks me if *I want anything* of him. He thought of money, again uppermost on his mind, not a question of home, not an inquiry for the boy, not even the extended courtesy of a chair. I went away disappointed, chagrined, & indignant, at this breech of the commonest good breeding. A careless good-bye from William in the same breath with a laugh, what a coarse, dirty boar (who is of course very interesting, a power) & I am allowed to find my way out in the rain, & to my carriage as best I can. This is a bald, hard picture, but true to life.

It is a matter of wonder that I feel so hard & bitter that I almost hate this man, who calls himself my husband, & yet has so little title to the name. For five years, every sensibility has been on the rack, impulses & feelings crushed back for the want of a response, tasks contemptuously ridiculed, motives impugned, acts misconstrued, charges both immodest & unjust proffered, & finally, with his own hand, William has added the drops which have caused my cup of sorrow to overflow, forcing upon me to the knowledge which a merciful enemy would have spared me.[11]

Kate's diary entries of 1868 make it clear that the marriage had not only failed to live up to its promise but had disintegrated into small and large acts of cruelty. Her indignant references to William's charges that she had been unfaithful suggest not only that had she not yet crossed that line but that William was engaged in a pernicious form of misplaced guilt, hurling at his wife the charges of a sexual impropriety which he himself practiced. Kate's diary entry from days earlier reinforces this view: "Great God, is this the woman-hood, alone, & single-handed I fought for so jealously those long years . . . my motive to safeguard strength all. It is fitting perhaps that the only man who found me weak, though he be now my husband, should reproach me with it & make it the excuse for with holding that love, confidence and trust my heart has so ached to possess? Was my weakness, my [word illegible] of this long punishment?"[12] This entry also suggests that Kate and William engaged in premarital sex and that William used that fact as proof to himself that his wife had transgressed her marital bonds as much as he.

Kate, like most nineteenth-century women, had little recourse to a bad marriage. Her father counseled submission and reconciliation, and she continued to yearn for the romantic dream. She prayed for hours that "my marital vision might be cleared" and that she would find the strength to stamp out her "stubborn pride" and "high moral ambition." She sought harmony, regardless of its cost, and for short periods of time her efforts would prove successful. "It has been a month & more since I have written here & such a bright, happy month, so full of gladness & delight, & so fraught and blessed with promise for the future. And yet to-day has been spent in another long fierce battle with myself, in the effort to subdue & force back the old bitterness of spirit I have not yet conquered, but I will strive!" She chastised herself for "passionate impulses," despising herself for being "weak & defenseless" in the face of her desire to burst her bonds of self-restraint. She raged at her inability to influence her husband to more considerate and family-oriented behavior. She "moved every personal consideration to do right & please others" and then found herself "ready to abandon all effort for the future."[13] This after William gave her money for Christmas and her father forgot her entirely.

William's abuse and Kate's attempts to behave "perfectly" mirror a common dyad in dysfunctional relationships; William's occasional violence controlled Kate's day-to-day behavior. She attempted to act in a womanly enough manner to influence her husband to good behavior, but the prescriptions of "true womanhood" could not help her in this real-life situation. The ideals of romantic love and companionate marriage did little more for Kate than create expectations that her union could not meet. She could do nothing more than manufacture sporadic periods of relative marital harmony.

In the spring of 1869, Salmon wrote Kate yet another set of fatherly advice letters. Reelected to the Senate in March, William took his political success as a sign to spend more time in Washington. His reelection, which gave him a feeling of increased political self-confidence, corresponded with his father-in-law's waning political power. The debacle of the 1868 Democratic convention had finished Salmon's political career, and for the first time in his life William felt like the master of his own house—no longer in the great man's shadow. Increased contact caused Salmon to lose patience with the new William, and in April Chase sympathized with Kate: "It is hard to be loving & affectionate when met by unkind words & acts. I know it is; but I know that she who thus acts will have her reward." Two days later he began his letter, "My heart is full of sympathy for you my precious child; but I Pray earnestly & hope humbly that out of this great trial might come true peace for you."[14]

The source of her father's sympathy lay not in an ordinary marital squabble but in William's public attack on Kate from the Senate floor. In a series of well-publicized speeches, the senator accused fellow legislators, the press, and American women of corruption and immorality. In his second speech he attacked lawyers, who made up most of his fellow congressmen. William claimed that his colleagues had failed to warn the American people about the coming of the Civil War, wrote laws no one but other lawyers could understand, and had become corrupt in their belief that they had more power than the president. In rebuttal, Senator Joseph W. Nye suggested that lawyers could be no worse than manufacturers "with no regard to their fitness for the place." He also apologized for the lawyers who had made legislation too complicated for William to understand. "Perhaps if he had been a little more of a lawyer," Nye suggested, "he would not have been puzzled so much." [15] The Senate floor and gallery erupted in laughter.

William, who had admitted to being more afraid of giving a speech than of "storming a line of presented bayonets," answered with another speech. He called Nye "the Charlatan of the Senate" and admonished the gallery for laughing. The senators "have been educated to laugh and to make light of the most serious things," William charged, but as representatives of the people the gallery should not have exhibited the same "thoughtless, senseless disposition." He also attacked fashionable dress, questioning "whether those adornments clothe any more virtue and integrity than do garments of a less gaudy and less luxuriant quality." [16] Kate, seated in the gallery and dressed in black cashmere and lace, suffered through her husband's newfound love affair with oratory. [17]

After reading a long passage on English history and extolling his own war record, William continued to impugn everyone in sight. He believed "that American society to-day has perhaps less virtue, less morality, in it, than that of any civilized government in the world." In striving to be rich, "the contest [of] virtue is lost." Of women he asked, "Where is the husband who closes his door with satisfaction?" William's sexualized language represented a larger nineteenth-century political trend that centered on feminizing political opponents or attacking their sexual purity. After the Civil War, Democrats attacked Republicans for "embodying the sins of corruption and extravagance." Democrats also conflated black men's political power with rapacious sexuality, using white women's purity to bolster hierarchical relationships. William, a Democrat at heart, especially with regard to his obsession with sexual corruption, fits into this larger pattern. [18]

William continued his speech with an attack on his father-in-law: "I favored the election of General Grant in opposition to the aspirations of one connected with me by family ties. I did that because I felt that Grant had not learned the practices of those who had charge of the Government," practices William believed to be tyrannous and poisoned by party politics. He worried about revolution, stridently claiming again and again that the people would not stand for "the present condition of the country." William was correct about the widespread governmental corruption of the postwar years, though he overestimated the public's degree of outrage. Henry Adams's *Democracy* and Mark Twain's *The Gilded Age* broadly lampooned the political, moral, and intellectual corruption of the nation's capital, but many Americans found the novels more amusing than provoking.

Six days later, William again took the Senate floor. By this time his oratory had become the wonder of Washington, and the gallery was packed full of those eager to see who would next suffer the little senator's attention. He wasted no time attacking "Americans who travel abroad, mix and mingle in that filth, and come home here to inoculate the immoralities they have seen into their own society." Kate had been abroad twice since their wedding. William then charged the Supreme Court justices, including his father-in-law, with consistently failing to consider new evidence when deciding an old subject. "It is for the purpose of maintaining their prestige, regardless of the merits of the case."[19] One week later he likened the powers that controlled public credit to "the virtue of a woman, easily stabbed in secret." The Senate, he claimed, engaged in an "arbitrary grasp of power," the president had fallen victim to the "canker that possessed the body politic," and the Supreme Court appeared uninterested in justice.

William next accused the Brown family, also prominent in Rhode Island manufacturing, of unfairly attacking himself and his business, cheating the state out of thousands of dollars, and generally imperiling the liberties of all Rhode Islanders. From this arena William slipped into yet another remembrance of his own courageous action in the war, particularly when compared with what he believed to be the cowardly and treasonous behavior of General Ambrose Burnside and the "million dollar men." Significantly, William recognized that his state now suffered from the "increasing growth of two great houses," each of whom struggled for economic and political supremacy. He placed Burnside and Senator Henry B. Anthony in the camp of those "at war" with the Spragues. He accused the Browns of mismanaging Brown University and of using the school as a front for illegal real-estate dealings. He also held the Browns personally responsible for the "cowardice" of the First Rhode Island Regiment, though in fact they had nothing to do with the veritable stampede of soldiers who had quit the field at the First Battle of Bull Run. Burnside, on the other hand, had been the regiment's commander. Anthony, the senior Rhode Island senator, would answer William's charges by reading a letter from John C. Brown and Robert Ives calling the charges "false and malicious." [20]

Among the short-term results of William's brief affair with the spoken word was yet another marital rift. By the time William made his last speech on 8 April 1869, Kate had fled Washington. She, Nettie, and Willie traveled to Aiken, South Carolina, a resort area noted for its beneficial effects upon well-to-do sufferers of respiratory diseases. [21] Kate and William continued to write hostile letters to each other, while Salmon took the attacks on himself and his daughter in fairly good humor. Although he admitted that Kate had been "sorely tried," the chief justice pretended ignorance of just how far his son-in-law had gone. As he politely phrased it, "the Governor's speeches have attracted a good deal of attention throughout the country. I have not considered what he proposes sufficiently to have any opinion as to the merits of it." Having feigned ignorance of the great insults his family had publicly sustained, Salmon told Kate that she had brought much of this upon herself and yet again counseled her to greater submission: "Humble your pride—yield even when you know you have the right on your side— remember the sacred obligation of your marriage vow—read it over & pray for strength and affection to keep it *fully*, in spirit as well as in act." [22] Kate must have heeded her father's advice, for his letter two weeks later reported that William "seemed much gratified by something you had said," though he expressed irritation at Kate's disapproval of the "Mastiff and puppy story," yet another piece of trouble cooked up by William. [23]

After William's last speech, Senator Joseph C. Abbot of North Carolina attempted to defend Anthony and Burnside. William, sensitive to any slight, responded by calling Abbot a "mongrel puppy dog," at the beck and call of the Senate's powerful "mastiffs." [24] Abbot and Sprague publicly hurled insults at each other, and the newspapers reported that Abbot both threatened to shoot William and hired "thugs" to menace him. Charles Sumner and John Sherman averted potential bloodshed by arranging a truce between the two factions, most probably at the behest of Salmon, whom they visited the morning before the story of the truce broke in the newspaper. [25] In a letter to Nettie, Salmon tried to minimize the situation: "I think he is doing much to attract public attention . . . showing unexpected honor and resource; and may be safely left to find his own way." He compared William to a child who, if left to his own devices, will pick himself up when he falls. Nettie's father also pointed out that advice only works when "the adviser loves the advised," suggesting the depth of the emotional estrangement between himself and William. [26]

The Abbot imbroglio was not the first time William personally insulted one of his fellow senators. Seemingly unaware of how people had come to think of him, William gave a newspaper interview in mid-April as part of an effort to portray himself as "a great reformer" and potential presidential candidate. During the course of the interview he called Senator Alexander Cattell a "mutton head" and Senator Willard Warner a "puke." The language William used with these senators, as well as with Abbot, also has partisan roots. Democrats, more often than Republicans, invoked the spirit of workingman's street culture in political speeches. Indeed, manly candor, like the candor required during courtship, demanded that a man reveal his thoughts, however insulting. In this variant of manhood, it was more important for a man to be candid, consistent, and unafraid of approbation than to consider rules of polite society. [27] Thus William probably thought that his vivid insults illustrated his fearless and frank masculinity. To have curbed his language would have been, at least in his own mind, effeminate and dishonest.

In spite of, or perhaps because of, William's rough verbal style, the *New York Herald* found him something of an admirable character. Indeed, if Horace Greeley's *New York Tribune* represented the reform element of the Republican Party, the *Herald* appealed to more conservative Americans— particularly Democrats who had supported the war effort but denounced abolitionists. Described by biographer Douglas Fermer as a "wilful and roguishly eccentric old man," the newspaper's editor, James Gordon Bennett, prized his lack of editorial consistency, his ability to play devil's advocate, and his appeal to popular sentiment. Although Bennett had retired by 1866, his son, also named James Gordon Bennett, continued the paper's conservative and sometimes whimsical policies. [28] In April the newspaper ran a laudatory piece on William. Calling him the "lion of the hour, if not the coming man of the Nineteenth Century," a *Herald* journalist described "LITTLE RHODY AT HOME":

> We found the Senator from Rhode Island in his study, reclining before
> the fire, wrapped in a loose and well-worn dressing gown, and apparently
> lost in thought beyond all hope of awakening. The study appeared itself
> a study, with all kinds of curious traps laying around loose. Books on
> top of Bohemian vases, wonderfully carved paper knives, odd-looking

ink bottles. . . . and the New York Herald spread out to throw a flood of light over all. . . . Near the Senator's chair stood a small tray holder, laden with the abstemious fare of a student, consisting of coffee minus milk and toast minus butter.

The journalist thought nothing of the fact that the interview, scheduled for late in the afternoon, took place with a man so obviously just out of bed. In fact, both he and William seem determined to create a picture of a man too busy to attend to the social niceties of life:

> We took a long look at the Senator's face to see if we could find therein any trace of the malady called craziness, which his enemies conveniently attribute to him. There was none in his eye at least. . . . Sprague looks old on first acquaintance. He has a small head, small features, large, lustrous eyes. . . . Sprague might have been a fast young man at some period of his life or he might have been a very hard working student of business; for on the outer edges of his face there are furrows that one of his age should not have. He wears his hair somewhat long and with extreme carelessness as though the comb that nature provides in the fingers had been the only one he ever made use of. It certainly presents a very disheveled appearance; but it shows at least he is above the small vanity of lavishing on the outside of his head the time that is better bestowed on the inside.[29]

The journalist made a virtue of the same slovenliness that so irritated Kate. But nineteenth-century gentlemen did not appear in public looking like a rumpled bed, nor did they receive guests in their home while in a state of undress. *Herald* readers may have interpreted William's personal style as a manly dislike of finery or even as a boyish disregard for grown-up rules of hygiene. His disheveled appearance might also be attributed more to his fondness for late-night carousing than to incipient genius. In reality, the person described in the *Herald* sounds like a man prematurely aged by the debilitating effects of alcoholism—a disease that must have ravaged William's brain as surely as it had his face.

The *Herald* representative, though, was not the only man to see in William a prophet for change. For several nights running, crowds of working people and "mechanics" gathered outside the Spragues' Washington house to serenade the David who dared fling stones at political Goliaths. One night they took up the cry "Sprague for President" until the hero of the hour appeared at the door and made a short speech.[30] But even if the people in the street did not know it, Kate certainly understood that her husband would never get close to the presidency.

It did not help William's public persona that Emily Edson Briggs, a journalist who had always written admiringly about both Kate and William, wrote a quietly scathing column lampooning William's program for the country. Briggs acknowledged that workingmen hailed William as their new leader and that his assessment of political corruption had some truth, but as to William's demand that more money be printed to ease the nation's financial burdens, she scoffed, "Why not? If Senator Sprague wants ten thousand yards of calico, he manufactures it. If workingmen want more money, he is advised to manufacture the same. It is a great deal easier to print a paper dollar than to earn the gold the paper is expected to represent." William's plan would do no more than make more money for himself, Briggs charged, while his plan to create a government department to prevent political fraud would only create "a new set of dishonest officials." Briggs added, "Only a lunatic attempts to extinguish a fire by throwing on more fuel."[31] Although she ended the column by suggesting that a number of good men had wrecked themselves in the dangerous waters of financial planning and that the senator had at least meant well, her words helped sound the death knell for William's political career.

After 1869 neither Kate nor her father could ignore William's infidelities any more than they could his political peccadilloes. Before she had left for South Carolina, Kate found in her husband's coat pockets some letters which, according to her father, infuriated her. She had, as well, searched her husband's trunks and removed some items, including some letters to her from "Col. Crosby." A sporting man and adventurer, John S. Crosby was the kind of exciting, well-educated, and well-traveled man who would have intrigued Kate. He served with Philip Sheridan in the Indian campaigns from early 1869 until late 1870 and may have corresponded with Kate about his western experiences.[32] Evidently William had taken Crosby's letters from Kate, Kate retrieved them, and then William searched her room and reclaimed the letters and other items. When Salmon questioned William about the matter, the younger man lost his temper and "made it impossible to get a hearing." William did tell Salmon that he "should not be controlled by [Kate] any longer."[33]

William's reelection had given him confidence and helped him to feel, for the very first time, powerful in his relations with Salmon and Kate. No doubt the end of his father-in-law's presidential ambitions contributed to William's sense of freedom. Exultant at what he perceived as his success, accomplished not only without the Chases but at odds with them, William crossed yet another moral boundary. In early May he moved one of his paramours into the Sixth and E Street house. Salmon, who lived in the same house with William but could not get him to speak to him, wrote William a mild letter of reproach: "Mackay dismissed Annie yesterday as he said by your order, and has put in her place a very fine looking English woman who appears very well. . . . But is it not a little risky to bring such a woman into the house while there are not other women here?"[34] In his letters to Kate, Salmon said nothing about the recent household rearrangements, but somehow she found out anyway. In her divorce petition she named "Harriet Brown, in the year 1869 at Washington in the District of Columbia." Having had sex with the serving women under his roof, even with his child's nurse, William apparently thought little of bringing "such a woman" into his wife's home while she was away. After this incident Salmon began to distance himself from the Spragues' relationship and quit offering Kate advice. He maintained his silence until his death, perhaps finally recognizing that his intelligent daughter's gifts had been wasted on a dissolute man.

This silence did not provide Kate with much support in what must have been an exceedingly difficult period of her life. Salmon seems to have been almost incapable of connecting with his daughters on any more than a superficial level. He could write them letters full of concern for their health and accomplishments, but he could not face the messy daily details of their lives. Indeed, his willful ignorance of his daughters' needs helped to create a woman who chose William Sprague out of a field of eligible men, an intemperate, rich, military adventurer who appeared the exact opposite of her father. Unfortunately, at the heart of the matter Salmon and William were much the same. Both men were emotionally and physically distant, careless with those who loved them, and more concerned with public power than private happiness.

Salmon did more than emotionally distance himself from the harsh realities of Kate's marriage. He also physically removed himself from the Sixth and E Street house. In a letter in which he first commented on the strained relationship between himself and William, Salmon told Kate that he was "sorry—very sorry—to part even so far as to have a separate house in the same city, but I really think it for the best." Salmon used twenty-two-year-old Nettie as his excuse, saying that she "naturally feels she wants a house of her own, or rather father should have a house & that she should be at the head of it."[35] Nettie and her father rented a house on I Street and moved there in mid-September. William Tecumseh Sherman's family lived on I Street as well, in the house the Grants had vacated with their move to 1600 Pennsylvania Avenue.[36] In September Salmon also purchased the thirty-acre Edgewood estate just outside Washington. Built in 1830, the Federal-style house had been used as a hospital during the Civil War.[37] It would require two years' work to make it habitable, and until then Salmon and Nettie lived alone together for the first and only time in their lives.

As she always did, Kate temporarily forgave William his sexual and oratorical transgressions. Eventually he went down to Aiken and accompanied Kate and Nettie home to Canonchet. Later Salmon joined them for a vacation on Narragansett Bay. He found it a "great delight . . . to see the restoration of the old affection" between Kate and William. Salmon, with his usual inattention to the important elements of his daughter's life, failed to notice that Kate was seven months' pregnant by the end of his visit. In a later letter Salmon chastised his daughter, "It was wrong of you to leave me to be informed by others that you expect to be a mother again in October."[38] Biographers have interpreted Kate's reticence, combined with William's repeated references in his spring speeches to female immorality, as evidence that the baby did not belong to her husband. But certainly Kate might have expected her father to notice her condition, since he had spent the better part of the spring and summer with her. It is not as if she ran off to Europe to hide the pregnancy or concealed the baby's birth date—remedies she most surely had at her disposal. That Salmon failed to notice her pregnancy must have hurt her feelings and caused her to remain mute upon the subject. This inability to speak with her father about such an important event suggests that Kate had begun to emotionally distance herself from Salmon as well as William. Her father had failed her so many times that she quit trusting him with her personal life. It should also be noted that William never disclaimed paternity for this child, or any of the other children, until much later, during and after the divorce.

In October, Kate gave birth to a healthy baby girl whom she named Ethel. Cousin Eliza Chase Whipple attended the birth and wrote Nettie and Salmon that the mother and baby "escaped without serious consequences." Jubilant about the birth of a new grandchild, Salmon wrote his daughter,

"I am glad the baby is a girl. For my part, I like girls rather better than boys though I would, I believe, have put up with one—perhaps two—for the sake of having a brother apiece for you and Nettie. But girls are nice."[39] Thus the tumultuous year of 1869 finally staggered to a close, the family larger by one and savaged by discontent.

DISTANCE, DISGRACE, AND DEATH

Family matters went on much the same the next few years. Kate bore two more daughters, Kitty and Portia, in 1872 and 1873.[40] Sometimes the Spragues got along, sometimes not. Time might have helped William recognize the dubious results of his speeches, or perhaps he had released all of his frustrations, for he remained silent during the remainder of his Senate tenure. In the summer of 1870, while touring Minnesota and Niagara Falls with Nettie, Salmon suffered a mild stroke. She took him to the Hoffman House in New York and sent word to her older sister. Kate and William came at once, and a week later they moved Salmon to Canonchet to convalesce. Kate, William, Willie, and baby Ethel enjoyed Grandpa's company until late December, when he moved from the chilly environs of Narragansett Bay to New York.[41] Kate and William appear to have made an effort to appear happy in front of the ailing man. To Nettie, who was in New York shopping for her approaching nuptials, Salmon observed that "the Governor, as long as Katie was absent, was very constant in his attendance."[42] Kate, who hated to be out of the center of political action as much as her father did, traveled between Rhode Island, Washington, and New York. She continued to practice politics. When offered the post as minister to Sweden, John Hay called on Kate for advice. He reported that Kate "slept on it and she said no."[43] Hay refused the job.

Although society columns commented upon William's increasingly public habit of finding comfort in the bottle, he managed to stay relatively sober around his father-in-law.[44] However much Salmon professed himself satisfied with William's behavior, the fall of 1870 proved an enormously shameful time for the Chase-Sprague family. On Halloween, William's part in the Harris Hoyt cotton caper finally became public knowledge. Thomas Jenckes, a Rhode Island congressman of long standing, announced at a reelection meeting that "in the darkest days of the war . . . [Sprague violated] the Articles of War of the United States in holding commerce with the enemy, and aiding them with money and munitions of war." Jenckes read to the assembly the judge advocate general's report to Stanton as proof of his allegations. This report not only described Hoyt's activities during the war and his involvement with the Spragues but also summarized General Dix's report—the same report that had turned the matter over to Secretary of War Stanton because of its "great delicacy."[45] William answered Jenckes's charges, claiming that Hoyt had a letter from Lincoln, that Hoyt had merely wanted to help loyal Union men get their cotton out of the South, and that he had no contact with Hoyt after their initial meetings. All of these claims were bald lies.

Next, in a move that should have been familiar to anyone who had read his 1869 Senate speeches, William cited his own stellar war record and attacked Jenckes as a man too cowardly to serve as a "soldier in the field." Dix released a cautious statement in the *Providence Press*, a Sprague mouthpiece, stating that a full investigation had found "no ground for instituting proceedings" against any of the men and that William's "conspicuous patriotism" should act as a guarantee of his integrity. Dix and Stanton had probably closed the matter of William's wartime treason after the senator voted guilty in President Johnson's recent impeachment trial. The *Press* also accused Jenckes of buying votes in the Republican primary.[46]

Jenckes continued to press his allegations, but Hoyt's full confession, which had allegedly implicated William, had disappeared after the impeachment trial. This made the congressman's case fatally weak. William, in an effort to silence Jenckes, gave large amounts of money to Jenckes's opponent, virtually ensuring the congressman's defeat. The *Providence Journal* cited this as yet another example of the disgraceful way the millionaire used money to subvert the political process. The paper also announced the arrest of a number of voters. Calling these men "five-dollar Republicans," the newspaper maintained that Sprague money had paid for their votes.[47]

Aware that he had made a tactical mistake, William next asked the Senate to investigate the matter. Conveniently, the new secretary of war, William Belknap, showed no more interest in prosecuting William than had Stanton, and he did not forward to the Senate committee the documents that demonstrated William's guilt. The committee then commanded Jenckes's appearance so summarily that he had no time to gather witnesses who might attest to the missing documents. In fact, powerful men in the Senate had no desire to help Congressman Jenckes because he had been pushing for civil service reform since the end of the war. Patronage provided the basis for many a senator's power, and any regulation of civil service appointments and tenure struck at the heart of that power. Although Jenckes told the investigating senators that "the confidential statement of Hoyt" did exist and that "its contents could be proved by three or four witnesses," the investigating committee concluded that there was "nothing in the paper implicating Senator Sprague."[48] It seems likely that Kate and her father understood the dirty dealings that spawned such a verdict. Even as they sighed in relief over the fact that the chapter on William's treasonous activities during the war had officially closed, they must have been privately mortified.

Jenckes's attack on William was motivated by more than moral outrage. Indeed, since Jenckes was not only a Republican but running for a seat in the House of Representatives, it would seem that he had little reason to expose a fellow Republican's dirty laundry. But political parties often divided into factions, and nowhere were two competing factions more corrupt or personally motivated than in Rhode Island. Brown & Ives, a prominent Rhode island manufacturing company that William had attacked in his Senate speeches the previous year, could count among its allies Henry B. Anthony, the other Rhode Island senator. This cooperative used the 1870 congressional election as another sortie in their ongoing battle with their economic and political rival. That each faction had the support of a Providence newspaper only magnified the fracas. The *Providence Journal* and the *Providence Press* squared off over William's dubious personal history as part and parcel of the Rhode Island Republican Party's internal factional struggles.[49]

A few months later William once more broke his father-in-law's heart and antagonized Kate, this time over that matter of the justices' pay. The chief justice made just $6,500 per year and his brethren $6,000. An appropriations bill attempted to raise those salaries by $4,000, but it failed to pass the Senate by one vote. Instead, the justices received a $2,000 raise.[50] As Salmon summarized the matter, "What particularly grieves the Judges is, that, that vote was given by Gov. Sprague. Why would he not help us in this emergency? Even had he left the Senate or not voted, we should have won the day." The bewildered Salmon, who had made every attempt to act kindly and fatherly to his son-in-law for the past seven years, felt "really distressed" about the whole matter.[51] Once again, William had used the political process to demonstrate his independence from Salmon—and, by proxy, from Kate.

Although William's increasing vindictiveness may have partially stemmed from the ruinous effects of his alcoholism, he probably believed his growing independence was a wise idea given the waning of his father-in-law's public power. Not only had Salmon lost all hope of ever becoming president, but by the early first years of the 1870s it was clear that his influence on the Supreme Court was also under attack. In February 1870 the Court decided *Hepburn v. Griswold*, which in a five-to-three vote had declared the Legal Tender Acts unconstitutional, with Justice Chase voting with the majority. As secretary of the treasury, Salmon had pushed the issuance of paper money as a wartime necessity, but he regarded greenbacks as dangerous for the nation's economy. U.S. notes, called greenbacks, had become the national currency and were not redeemable in gold coin, or "specie payment." Bond payment lay at the center of the greenback controversy. The federal government had sold millions of dollars' worth of bonds to underwrite the war, but it had not specified how those bonds would be repaid. Much of the country wanted the bonds paid in gold, and thus any plan to pay in greenbacks was labeled "repudiation." The 1868 Republican platform "denounced all forms of repudiation as a national crime," but Republican leaders understood that resumption of specie payment, while desirable, was not immediately practical. As one of his first official acts, the newly inaugurated Grant signed the Public Credit Act of 18 March 1869, which did nothing more than pledge to eventually redeem greenbacks and bonds in coin. Although in his first inaugural Grant demanded that "every dollar of Government indebtedness should be paid in gold," he and other Republicans carefully failed to specify when resumption would occur.[52]

The day of the *Hepburn* decision, the Senate confirmed President Grant's two choices for vacancies on the Supreme Court. Both men supported the Legal Tender Acts. By late March the chief justice had solid evidence that the Court's anti-greenback majority would be reversed, causing an acrimonious split among the justices that left Salmon on the minority side. For the time being, though, *Hepburn* held, and a veritable storm of opposition threatened to overwhelm the chief justice. Observers noted that he had begun to look old and tired. In 1872 the Court upheld the constitutionality of the Legal Tender Acts (reversing *Hepburn*), causing Salmon to predict dire consequences for the country if it continued to rely on irredeemable paper money.[53]

William, like many others, believed that a specie-based money system chiefly helped the rich stay rich. His championing of greenbacks was not only popular with the working class but beneficial to his business. Debts, of which A. & W. Sprague had many, could be repaid more easily with paper money. William proposed a United States Council of Finance—a poor man's bank that would underwrite cheap money for both small and large investors.[54] The laboring men who serenaded William and suggested him as a presidential candidate in 1869 had done so primarily in support of these ideas. Harried by high prices, cheap immigrant labor, and a growing population of freedpersons, northern white working men and women acclaimed "Little Rhody" as an alternative to those who would push high tariffs, the gold standard, racial equality, and the politics of the rich and middle-class down their throats. William could also portray himself as a Washington outsider, capitalizing on people's post-impeachment disgust with political regulars. That same sentiment had helped sweep Grant into office not long before, and it was Grant's judicial appointments that had overturned Salmon's money stance.[55]

However much this latest series of scandals and betrayals hurt her, in the early months of 1871 Kate turned her eye to her sister's marriage to William (Will) Hoyt. No relation to Harris Hoyt, Nettie's intended was the son of one of William's cousins. Nettie most probably met him when visiting Kate in Narragansett, where other family members also had summer homes. Kate also visited the Hoyts in New York when she was in town on shopping trips.

Kate spared no expense or effort in order to make her twenty-three-year-old sister's wedding "one of the most beautiful and elegant affairs ever given."[56] She hosted pre-wedding parties for the couple, arranged for the marine band to play at the reception, and made sure Nettie's dress and the decorations shone with the same brilliance they had at the last Chase wedding. Nettie married Will at St. John's Church on Lafayette Square rather than at the house, though the reception, attended by President Grant and members of the cabinet and Supreme Court, took place at home. Nettie, though less socially prominent than her elder sister, had always been popular in Washington. Senator John Logan's wife, Mary, recalled that "there could not possibly have been sisters more unlike each other than were the Chase sisters, not only in personal appearance but in disposition, talents, and characteristics. Nettie, though of a plainer face, was one of the most gentle, modest, retiring, and lovable characters that one could possibly imagine."[57]

John Hay, who had once been in the running for Kate's hand and who held a dim view of William, summed up the match: "He is a very nice fellow—and no end of cash. She is a very nice girl—and no end of talent."[58] The press praised the event as "one of the most beautiful and elegant affairs ever given," though "queenly Mrs. Sprague," in her turquoise velvet dress with a pink silk train, appears to have nearly eclipsed the bride.[59] The press generally ignored William, though one newspaper did mention the presence of "Mrs. Sprague's husband." He had no official position in his cousin and sister-in-law's wedding—a fact that also went unremarked by the press. Washington society had begun to pretend that Senator Sprague did not exist. His wife, on the other hand, still held her social position as if "one born to royalty."[60]

A week after the wedding, Nettie and Will set out for their honeymoon in Wales and Germany, beginning a remarkably long and happy marriage. Although Nettie was never as socially prominent or politically involved as her sister, everyone acknowledged that she had a sunny and obliging nature. One society columnist wrote that "Miss Nettie Chase is, perhaps, more universally liked than her more haughty sister."[61] Certainly Nettie made a far better choice of marriage partner than did Kate. Ten months after the wedding she gave birth to a daughter named Janet, and fifteen months later a son named Edwin, after Will's father. Two more babies would follow Edwin, including a son named Franklyn and a daughter named Beatrix.[62] Nettie turned out to be as good a mother as she had been a daughter—a loving, artistic woman who wrote and illustrated books of nursery rhymes for children's pleasure.

Kate also took great pleasure in her role as mother. In one of the few surviving letters from Kate to her father, she described Ethel and Willie at home at Canonchet.

> My curly-headed girl came to me today, with the paper weight containing your photograph (& which I always keep on the table before me, though Willie claims you gave it to him) & said "I want Grandpa Chase to prom, (read come) I hurrah for Brobner Sprague & I huzzah for Chase"—her sentence was a little less connected but that was what she intended. When I tell you that after mashing her "Poupets" nose the other day, she came to me to "wipe the tears from [word illegible] eyes," you will no wonder that her little tongue is so ready. She is only twenty two months old & she has many of Mother Gooses melodies, as well as such epics as "Goodby John"

& "Up in a Balloon" quite pat. Willie has been made proud & happy by having received from his Aunt Nettie a miniature mitrailleuse [machine gun] which I have the honor to be saluted by most every morning before I am up & find cocked & elevated for the purpose at night, at the foot of Willie's bed, beside my own.[63]

One wonders why Willie's bed was in his mother's bedroom. Its proximity may have been Kate's attempt to limit sexual contact with her husband. In her children Kate found and could express unquestioning love. In fact, in the same letter she noted that she had just received a "Birthday Greeting" from Nettie: "I was so pleased that she remembered to think of me on that day. I fear I am a good deal of a child about such things yet, though the yearning for love is hardly one of the childish things one would wish to put away."[64]

In the spring of 1872, after giving birth to her second daughter, Kate returned to Washington society. By this time bustles had replaced hoopskirts and bonnets had made way for tiny tilted hats on puffs of false hair. Kate's parties were noted for their elegance, dancing, and ice sculptures. No one, though, could compete with the Belknap house for unadulterated opulence. The second Mrs. Belknap, who had succeeded her sister as the wife of Grant's secretary of war, was known for her beauty, sense of fun, private fortune, and friendship with Julia Grant. Only Kate could equal Amanda Belknap for richness of dress—the French designer Worth dressed them both.[65]

That spring Kate marked her father's possible candidacy for the presidency with a magnificent reception. An immense wheel of violets, carnations, roses, and camellias took pride of place at the center of the garden, where Kate had a pavilion erected to serve dinner to Supreme Court justices, cabinet members, and various congressmen and their wives. Salmon, though, looked one stroke past his prime, particularly when standing next to Kate—radiant in pale blue satin and turquoise and diamond jewelry. Reporters likened her to a "goddess" at the zenith of her beauty and power, while her father seemed a sun that had already set. Even Carl Schurz found the chief justice's post-stroke frailty too "pathetic" to make him a viable contender for the next election. As usual, Salmon's correspondence contained both protestations that "I shall not seek the nomination" and promises that he would "not refuse the use of my name." He had played this game, unsuccessfully, over the course of the last five presidential elections, but at no time with less success than in 1872. As usual, Kate's detractors blamed her for Salmon's final attempt at a nomination, suggesting he did it just to make her happy. Salmon's maniacal drive for the presidency makes this scenario unlikely.[66]

Even Kate had less than perfect faith in her father's chances. She invited two other presidential hopefuls to the big soiree, but once the party concluded she offered her father little more in the way of practical help toward realizing his ambitions. Grant's nomination, as it had been four years before, was a foregone conclusion—the Republican convention nominated both the president and Vice-President Henry Wilson on the first ballot. Earlier in the year, Liberal Republicans had bolted the Republican fold in antagonism to Grant and nominated Horace Greeley, a devout antislavery man of long standing. This move signaled the virtual end of any third-party hopes for victory, since the Liberal Republicans needed considerable Democratic support to beat Grant. The Democratic Party had in fact adopted the Liberal Republican platform and ticket at their June convention in Philadelphia, but southern Democrats had a hard time accepting Greeley (a longtime antislavery advocate) into the fold. In all this ferment Salmon figured hardly at all, though he did receive thirty-two votes on the sixth and final ballot at the Liberal Republican convention.[67] Greeley died weeks after Grant's reelection, and Salmon, who had supported his old friend in his last contest, traveled to New York to serve as pallbearer.

Several weeks after the birth of Nettie's first child, Salmon went to New York to see his new granddaughter. Kate and her children, who by this time included Willie, Ethel, and fifteen-month-old Portia, stayed at the nearby Clarendon Hotel, leaving room for the proud grandfather at Nettie's house on West Thirty-third Street.[68] Salmon took the train to New York on Saturday, 3 May, and enjoyed two days with his daughters and five grandchildren around him. Sometime Monday night or early Tuesday morning he suffered a fatal stroke. Unable to wake him, his valet, William Joice, called out for help. There was nothing that doctors or his girls could do but watch the old warrior struggle for every breath. Wednesday morning, with Kate, Nettie, Will, the valet, and two doctors standing by, Salmon P. Chase breathed his last.[69]

Kate, then halfway through her final pregnancy, stood the blow like the political soldier her father had trained her to be. Salmon's body lay in state at the Capitol, his casket covered with a floral cross from Nettie and a crown of white rosebuds from Kate, before being moved to the Supreme Court chambers for the funeral. Kate went home to the house on Sixth and E Streets, and though many of Washington's elite made condolence calls, she did not receive them. She wrote her friend John Nicolay that she suffered from "the distress of returning to this house so full of memories of my dear father," and for most of the summer she remained in seclusion.[70] Friends predicted that she would not recover from her father's death, but she did. However much she would miss her father, his demise may have been a blessing in disguise. No longer did she have to suffer the slights of his affection, no longer did she have to live up to his expectations of accomplishment and submission, and no longer did she have to pretend that her marriage had turned out to be anything but a failure. She was free to remember her father as she chose—as a great man and perfect parent.

Before 1873 came to an end the Spragues faced another crisis. Already in economic trouble over expansion into southern cotton mills and an ill-fated attempt to map a new Panama Canal route, A. & W. Sprague leaned heavily on financing by Jay Cooke & Company.[71] Cooke had gained fame as an investment banker when he helped then–secretary of the treasury Salmon P. Chase sell war bonds to the public on a grand scale.[72] By 1872 railroad expansion had outpaced earnings, causing a wave of market speculation and eventually the collapse of the stock market. In September, while President Grant relaxed at Cooke's opulent estate, Ogontz, Jay Cooke received the news that his New York office had closed, a move precipitated by the failure of Northern Pacific Railroad financing.[73] Before lunch Cooke closed his Philadelphia and Washington branches as well. Stocks plummeted on Wall Street. Panic ensued. Runs on banks made money increasingly unavailable, and businesses large and small became embroiled in a veritable vortex of financial ruin. "Boom times became gloom times" as over five thousand businesses went bankrupt.[74] By late October, A. & W. Sprague Company announced its failure, as did Hoyt and Sprague Company, Nettie's husband's business, which had acted as buying agents for Sprague cotton.

A. & W. Sprague had been worth $3 million in 1856, $6 million in 1865, and $19 million on the eve of the 1873 panic, employing more than eight thousand people. Because the company's assets exceeded its debts, William might simply have closed shop, liquidated the company's assets, and retired on the surplus, but bankruptcy was not in the state's best interests. The company's demise would have cost thousands of jobs, and the collapse of Sprague-supported banks would have torn the "financial fabric of Rhode Island." Also, though A. & W. Sprague had assets of nearly $19.5 million, creditors demanded payment of $14 million worth of debt, an amount that far exceeded the company's liquid assets.[75] Thus, because of the firm's financial power and because A. & W. Sprague was not bankrupt in the usual sense of the word, Sprague's creditors (largely banks holding Sprague paper) agreed to place the company into a trusteeship. The provisions of the trust mortgage allowed William to offer promissory notes to his creditors at 7.3 percent interest, to be paid after three years.

In December 1873 control of A. & W. Sprague shifted, for the first time in William's adult life, out of his hands and into those of company trustee Zechariah Chaffee. Chaffee also assumed control of the Hoyt company, whose debts outweighed its assets by $10 million. Brother Amasa stayed on with the company, acting as the manager of the printworks. William admitted to Chaffee that he had "given no personal attention whatever to any of the business concerns" for the past five years, and he removed himself almost entirely from not only the business but from the state of Rhode Island.[76] The business would do no better under Chaffee. In 1874, Hoyt & Francklyn, a company led by Nettie's husband, brought civil suit against A. & W. Sprague to strip that company of its holdings. An 1876 flood so seriously damaged the Sprague mills in Connecticut that they had to be closed, putting more than a thousand employees out of work. Even the company's Rhode Island mills reduced their labor force after 1873 in an attempt to curb costs as creditors continued to press for payment. Chronic depression in the cotton-manufacturing business only exacerbated the company's problems, hastening the death of the Sprague empire. By the late 1870s matters had disintegrated to such an extent that William went back to work for the company and publicly charged Chaffee with gross mismanagement.[77]

With the death of Salmon and the Sprague empire in 1873, the tenor of Kate and William's marriage entirely changed. William's 1869 attempt to move one of his mistresses into the Sixth and E Street house had signaled the beginning of the end. The marriage limped along until 1873, in large part because Kate continued to appease William and her father by acting the submissive and forgiving wife. Salmon's death, however, freed both of the

Spragues from their charade of happiness. Significantly, William's business failure seriously undercut his sense of manhood because he defined himself as a man of industrial power and business acumen. After the business failure he quit acting the part of hardworking manufacturer and devoted himself to full-tilt marital infidelity and insobriety. Prostitutes from Washington to Providence and from New York to Alexandria all benefited from William's patronage, while maids and guests of the Sprague family, particularly at Canonchet, became increasingly at risk of suffering William's dubious attentions. After her father's death, Kate was doubly set free—free from her father's expectations and free to no longer act the part of wife of a successful industrialist. One of William's biographers claims that after Salmon's death, "life had nothing to offer [Kate]."[78] Her letters and actions after 1873 suggest quite the opposite.

The Beginning of the End
Domestic Infidelities and Family Life,
1874–1878

~

Morality is a private and costly luxury.

Henry Adams

THE ADONIS OF THE SENATE

Variously described as "commanding," "magnificent," and "splendid," Roscoe Conkling, who stood over six feet tall, had what one contemporary described as "the figure of Apollo . . . the face of an Adonis, an intellectuality second to none of his day, the steadfast convictions of a fanatic and a will of iron."[1] Others found him haughty, overbearing, and vindictive, but no one disputed his impressive oratorical powers. He wore highly decorated waistcoats and held his ground in the Senate with what his arch-enemy, the Republican politician James Blaine, called "his majestic, super-eminent, overpowering, turkey-gobbler strut."[2] Olivia Edson Briggs gushed, "His beauty is of the aqua-marine type. It resembles a very fine diamond considerably off color, unless one is fond of flame." Mary Logan called him "the handsomest man in the Senate and the most fastidious in his style of dress and manner." Of Roscoe's less tangible characteristics, Logan noted that "he was ever ready for a debate and made many enemies by the sneers with which he treated the remarks of brother senators with whom he disagreed. He was so intense in everything he did that he sometimes apparently forgot there was any other person in the Senate besides himself."[3] He supported the enfranchisement of women, eschewed tobacco and liquor, and liked horses and boxing. This last gave Roscoe "the finest torso in public life" upon which to balance his full head of flaming red-gold hair and blue eyes.[4]

Rumor had it that Conkling had only one vice—the ladies. Long before

3. Senator Roscoe Conkling. Courtesy of the National Archives.

he became intimate with Kate, tales of his exploits had circulated around Washington. One journalist, or so the story goes, wrote a long exposé of Roscoe's extramarital adventures. Supposedly, the senator confronted the newspaper editor and threatened to kill him if he published the article. The editor's assistant claimed "there was . . . something so unspeakably fierce and cruel in his savage gaze" that they killed the story.[5] Conveniently, Mrs. Conkling did not live in the capital, preferring the comforts of her Utica home to the company of her husband. The ladies in the Senate gallery took this absence as permission to send him long-stemmed pink roses and other tokens of affection.[6] Men seemed less susceptible to Roscoe's charms. Henry Adams believed him one of the most "aggressively egoistic" men he had ever met.[7]

A sixth-generation New Yorker, Roscoe's mother, Elise Cockburn Conkling, "the belle of the Mohawk," gave birth to him on 30 October 1829. His father, Alfred Conkling, served for twenty-seven years as the federal judge for the Northern District of New York. In 1853 Millard Fillmore appointed him minister to Mexico. Growing up in Albany in the 1830s and 1840s, young Roscoe came into daily contact with men like Thurlow Weed, editor of the *Albany Evening Journal;* William H. Seward, governor and senator for New York; and former presidents Martin Van Buren and John Quincy Adams. Like Kate, he was sent away to school in New York. At sixteen he deemed his formal education at an end, disappointing his father by refusing to go on to college. Instead young Roscoe decided to read law with a Utica firm—a practice whereby young men were trained to be lawyers while providing free clerking services.[8] Kate's father had done much the same thing with William Wirt. Thus, while his formal schooling may have been more abbreviated than that of some of his colleagues, Roscoe enjoyed a substantial apprenticeship in politics at his father's house.

Admitted to the bar when he was only twenty years old, Roscoe was remembered by one New Yorker as being "like a tall, blond young lady. . . . his cheek as fresh as a rose, with long red ringlets clustered about his neck."[9] Only months later, Whig governor Hamilton Fish, a friend of Roscoe's father, appointed the younger Conkling as district attorney for Oneida County. In 1855 Roscoe wooed and wed Julia Catherine Seymour, sister of the New York politician Horatio Seymour, who had recently been defeated as governor of New York. A friend described Julia as "amiable" and "without much force of character." Although Julia lived with him at a boardinghouse in Utica for a short time, the couple spent very little of their married life together.

Roscoe served two terms as mayor of Utica before being elected as the county's representative to the U.S. House of Representatives in 1860. At the congressional convention a Conkling delegate had argued that given the current political climate New York ought to send muscle, as well as brains, to the Senate. Roscoe proved the delegate correct when, just days after his arrival in the House, he stood over Thaddeus Stevens and effectively prevented southern hotheads from assaulting the elderly but peppery-tongued Pennsylvanian. Julia and their baby, Bessie, accompanied Roscoe to Washington, but Julia soon found either life in Washington or life with "Lord Roscoe" a little too much to bear and returned to Utica to stay. In 1864 the Conklings bought a house in Utica, but when in town Roscoe kept a room at Utica's Baggs' Hotel. The estrangement had become entrenched.[10]

When he was in the capital Roscoe stayed at Willards, establishing a long tenure as Washington's most eligible married man. In 1867 he switched from the House to the Senate, where he would gain his fame and create the power behind his political machine. Van Buren's Democratic "Albany Regency" controlled political power in early-nineteenth-century New York. Thurlow Weed's Whig organization balanced against the Albany Regency until the latter's collapse in 1848. Weed eventually took his machine into the Republican fold and consistently championed William H. Seward for the presidency. By the time Roscoe became a senator, a power vacuum existed in New York. Democrats' power was distributed through a variety of "rings," most notable among them Tammany Hall. Reuben E. Fenton led the state's Republicans. By 1869 Fenton's tenuous hold on the New York Republicans began to slip as anti-Fenton forces gathered around Roscoe Conkling. In July 1870 Conkling and Fenton squared off over New York Custom House appointments, the same sticky issue that had precipitated Salmon's resignation from Lincoln's cabinet. Roscoe supported President Grant's choice for the collectorship, while Fenton chose another. Grant's man won the post, placing Conkling in the enviable position of virtually owning "the most powerful patronage instrument in the country." In September 1870 Roscoe consolidated his power at the Republican state convention in Saratoga, demolishing Fenton's forces during the gubernatorial balloting.[11]

After that people called him "Boss Conkling," but only behind his back.

The New York Republican Elihu Root summed up Roscoe's power in a few succinct sentences: "I do not remember how many years, Mr. Conkling was the supreme ruler in this state; the Governor did not count, the legislatures did not count; comptrollers and Secretaries of state and what-not, did not count. It was what Mr. Conkling said."[12] Political bosses were ubiquitous during the Gilded Age, and machine politics ran more states than not. A boss organized, centralized, and utilized political power by awarding state or federal jobs to loyal party members, thereby ensuring continued loyalty. Bosses appeared outwardly friendly and respectable, but they had to be extremely flexible in matters of political virtue. Often having less interest in principles than in brokering power, bosses functioned more as political businessmen than as ideologues or reformers. Quickly grasping these realities, the new senator had created a political empire that eventually outmaneuvered the formidable Tammany Hall.[13]

In politics and many other matters, Roscoe and Kate had much in common. Both were children of prominent men and had grown up in houses permeated with local and national politics. They had similar educational and political backgrounds. Early in his career Roscoe considered himself a "Seward Whig," advocating antislavery and free soil; predictably, he became a Republican after 1856. Kate's father had helped to develop the antislavery ideology that would guide the new party. Salmon was a leading Radical Republican, and even dour old Gideon Welles called Roscoe "an intense radical. . . . with spread eagle eloquence."[14] Washington society considered Kate and Roscoe as physically attractive as they were intelligent and socially prominent. Kate concurred with her father about the evils of drink and tobacco, as her continued battles over these substances with her husband can attest, and Roscoe, as everyone knew, drank little and loathed tobacco. The two also shared a mutual fondness for horses and political intrigue, and each had an unhappy marriage. It seems little wonder that they would find each other exceedingly congenial company.

Ironically, when Salmon died, President Grant offered the chief justiceship to Roscoe. Grant had vowed not to nominate a new chief justice unless Congress was in session, but almost seven months elapsed between Salmon's death and the time Congress reconvened. This created much grist for the rumor mills. Writing to his friend Roscoe in November 1873, Grant admitted, "My own preference went to you at once. But I determined—and announced—that the appointment would not be made until the meeting of Congress—that I thought a Chief Justice should never be subjected to the mortification of rejection. The possibility of your rejection of course was not dreamed of."[15] Two weeks later Roscoe wrote back to the president: "I ask you to let your choice fall on another, who, however else qualified, believes as man and lawyer, as I believe, in the measures you have upheld in war and in peace."[16] Roscoe understood, as Salmon had not, that the chief justiceship paled in comparison to the presidency and that the White House became out of reach from the bench. Roscoe had more immediate political concerns as well. If he had taken the Court appointment, his Senate seat would have fallen empty and the Democrat-controlled New York State legislature would fill the post. As a Republican boss he could not allow this to happen.[17]

Biographers had suggested that Kate discouraged Roscoe from taking the appointment, but there is little evidence that she had that degree of influence over him in 1873. Although many have dated the beginning of their illicit relationship to as early as the beginning of the Grant administration, no solid evidence supports this claim.[18] Salmon's letters and journals never mention Roscoe, suggesting that before Salmon's death Kate and Roscoe were at best casual acquaintances. In February 1870, Senators Conkling and Sprague sat down together at a dinner given by Julia and Hamilton Fish and engaged in friendly conversation. Both Julia Fish and Julia Grant received Kate, which they most certainly would not have done if they had suspected sexual improprieties. On New Year's Day 1873, Julia Conkling, arrayed in black velvet and lace, and Kate, in a yellow Worth gown, both attended the Grants' reception.[19] It is possible that in the half year between Salmon's death and Roscoe's refusal of the chief justiceship Kate and Roscoe had become close. It is more likely, however, that Roscoe refused the seat because of his involvement in the powerful game of patronage and machine politics—because ruling the Supreme Court was simply not as powerful a position as ruling New York politics or living at 1600 Pennsylvania Avenue. Nor did he have the temperament to be a judge. When asked by a friend why he had declined the prestigious position, Roscoe declared that "he would have been continually gnawing at his chains."[20] He found himself far more suited to flowery and fiery oratory in the Senate, where his flashy waistcoats and flamboyantly colored ties might be admired as much as his political power.

Honest about his predilections, Roscoe once declared that "when Dr.

Johnson called patriotism the last refuge of a scoundrel he forgot the possibilities in the word 'reform.'" [21] The practical Roscoe believed that reformers hid a lot of hypocrisy behind their supposed moral high ground, using their "moral authority" to attain political power while attacking those, such as himself, with a more politically pragmatic approach. At the same time, Roscoe portrayed himself as a Republican gentleman. Republican men defined themselves by what they were not—Democrats. By the 1870s Republicans spent a good deal of energy depicting Democratic men as violent, lustful, and intemperate. At the base of all these charges lie Republicans' portrayal of Democrats, regardless of class, ethnic, or regional concerns, as lacking in habits of self-control.

In fact, Democrats agreed with this assessment, but with a more positive spin. They often portrayed Republican men as effeminate for rejecting patriarchal control over their households. Republicans, on the other hand, embraced a type of male behavior that included temperance, self-control, and deference to the moral guidance of mothers and wives. [22] Although Roscoe did not give his wife much control over his day-to-day behavior, ladies like Julia Fish and Julia Grant found him extremely congenial. Even talk of his prowess in the boxing ring fed into this version of manhood because of the controlled nature of this type of fighting. Roscoe's body, "the finest in public life," reflected taut self-control, unsullied by the debilitating effects of tobacco and drink. Kate must have found him tremendously appealing, particularly in comparison with her more self-indulgent husband.

However much Kate and Roscoe enjoyed each other's company, she spent most of the four years after her father's death traveling back and forth to Europe. If their relationship had slipped from the licit to the illicit in the months after Salmon's death, Kate was not sufficiently impressed to stay in Washington. She remained abroad from October 1874 until midsummer 1875, came home briefly to attend to some matters of her father's estate, and returned to Germany until the fall of 1876. In August 1874 Julia Grant invited Julia Conkling to visit the Grants' summer retreat in Long Branch. "Bring the Senator, too," she jestingly wrote, "just for company while traveling and to look after the baggage." The eminently proper Julia Grant knew of the Conklings' estrangement, but it seems unlikely that she would have tolerated the senator's presence if she had any suspicions of infidelity. More likely a passionate relationship did not spring up between Roscoe and Kate until after her semi-permanent return from abroad.

"IN A STRANGE LAND"

While Kate was in Europe, Rhode Island's legislature declined to return William to the Senate. In March 1875, Rhode Islanders elected in his place Ambrose Burnside, one of the men whom William had so defamed in his 1869 speeches. Burnside's election not only functioned as a stern rebuke to William from the political leaders of his home state but also undermined William's manhood. In an age when politics were highly charged with gendered rhetoric, election winners were portrayed as more manly than losers. After elections, for example, popular iconography portrayed victors as crowing "roosters" and losers literally limp with defeat. Another sexually fraught political metaphor was found in the popularity of pole raisings. Partisans would affix party banners to poles, raise them, and then brag about their size and uprightness, particularly compared to rival poles. [23] From France, Kate attempted to support her husband through this latest crisis of manhood. She wrote William's brother, Amasa, "My living alone as I am doing alone & in a strange land, with my children, is no small sacrifice, but I contribute cheerfully hoping to relieve my husband of care & expense, that he may have his mind & time for work." She went on to describe her husband as a man with "a rare fund of strength and wisdom" and urged Amasa to support and trust his brother in his effort to rebuild the business.[24] She also wrote William T. Sherman, thanking him for letters of introduction and discussing his future in politics. She mentioned a meeting between him and William and thought Sherman ought to take her husband's advice. "No man perhaps is more familiar than he through actual knowledge & experience," she wrote, "experience dearly bought with the crushing incubus under which the Industrial Masses of our American people are now staggering. Governor Sprague is a brave, independent, public spirited, deep thinking man & such a remedy as he would offer for the relief of this prolonged financial stress would at least be worthy of a hearing." [25] Kate may not have been willing to speak ill of her husband to either his brother or Sherman, but she could certainly have chosen to say nothing at all. She seems to have been attempting to bring about yet another reconciliation.

Kate and William exchanged several letters over the course of the summer and fall, and in November William must have unburdened himself about his worries for A. & W. Sprague. Kate's reply suggests that distance had once again made her heart grow fond. From Paris she advised:

My dear husband, . . . Now let me give you the drift of my thoughts. I gather there is a danger that Mr. Chaffee will not be able to pay his interest in January. If this is imminent why is it not the *Golden Moment* for you to seize the dilemma by the horns & strike your [word illegible]. . . . I think your attitude if you would only take advantage of it is splendid! & I would rather have it as a base which to reconstruct than the whole fabric as it stood intact before suspension.

How does a programme like this strike you? You call in advance of a crisis (forseeing it, & showing the world courage to proclaim, which few would have), a meeting of your Creditors. Flatter their choice & satisfy Mr. Chaffee by giving him as much credit as you can, for his administration, plainly & forcibly. The true reasons for his failure to fulfill what he undertook in the best faith, try & make your creditors see & understand the existing conditions as large in the country, as *You* see them. . . .

Offer to assume the Entire management of the interests of the A & W Sprague Manufacy. Co. with the full co-operation of the Hoyt faction if it can be obtained.

Kate went on to explain how William might get the cooperation of the Hoyt branch of the family and how to proceed if that cooperation were not forthcoming. She discussed the business's debt, the interest that had to be paid, and the amount of work it would take to turn the company around. She then assured William:

If you take up this burden I go home at once to help you bear it with heart & soul. I will provide the children with proper instruction & settle them in the country & you may make me General Inspector of the factories or the head of the Corps or gather up the waste & fragments that nothing is lost, everything to be of use.

I do not disguise it. When I think of the possibility of that grand enterprise which you have done so much to create, & which well wielded would be worth more to you than his Scepter is a King on his throne slipping from your grasp. The thought is intolerable.

She concluded by proposing that William leave business matters in a lawyer's hands for the time being if he could "see your way clear to come abroad." Kate thought markets could be found for Sprague goods in Italy and Spain if only he would help her "make special study of this question." She closed, "Faithfully, as always, your wife."[26]

Kate also wrote Will Hoyt, Nettie's husband, urging him to cooperate with her husband. She warned Will that however brilliant a businessman William might be, "He has been wounded & goaded to a dangerous extent & I have at times held my breath in fear of such a man as I felt he might make." She admitted that her husband was "peculiar & difficult to approach," but she believed that only William could keep the utter destruction of the company at bay.[27] It would appear that Kate attempted to negotiate a marital as well as business truce and that she blamed William's poor behavior on his business troubles. She hoped that by becoming involved in the company she might rekindle their earlier romance. Her eagerness to step into the day-to-day running of A. & W. Sprague speaks both to her desire to have a meaningful and powerful occupation and to her willingness to do whatever it took to be close to her husband. Her tactics failed. William did not seize control of the business, he did not go abroad to explore markets with Kate, and he did not seek her help. No letter exists to explain how he rebuffed is wife—in fact, there are few letters between Kate and William after December 1875, and none of them are friendly. He may have found Kate's attempts to enter his world tremendously threatening, fearing that she might use her considerable intellectual gifts to co-opt the one arena where he had once reigned supreme.[28]

During Kate's brief trip home in mid-1875, accompanied by Ethel and Portia, she and Nettie negotiated the division of their father's estate. The meetings did not go well, further complicating the sisters' relationship. After A. & W. Sprague's 1873 failure, Kate and Nettie found themselves married to men in competing and unfriendly branches of the family. Kate soon returned to Paris. She disliked leaving her children, often moving them with her from house to house and from country to country in a peripatetic existence. In early 1876 she left Willie at Mr. Lauteren's school in Heidelberg while she and the girls went on to a hotsprings at Carlsbad, Bohemia, where they stayed for part of the summer. Kate bought each of the girls a new doll, which she took great delight in describing to Willie. Kate's letters to her son over the next two years describe the rich family life she tried to create with Ethel, Kitty, and Portia as well as the amount of time she spent playing with them and caring for them. She reassured Willie, "Dont feel disappointed that your Papa does not write oftener, he is preoccupied & perplexed with his affairs." Once home at Edgewood, Kate sent Willie pictures of his sisters and constant assurances that they had not forgotten their "beau boy." [29] She described the "babies" in their white fur coats, "looking like little polar bear cubs," playing in the snow with Don, the family dog:

> It is a very funny sight to see Ethel start down the hill on her sled coasting (Don sitting up grandly looking on) with the puppies at her heels, seizing her coat, biting her legs, pulling her hood & then rolling all over in the snow together. Ethel is so bright, so full of fun. I have seldom seen her as well as this winter. She sleeps in the little room adjoining mine, alone she dresses & undresses herself, makes her own bed, [cleans] her room and keeps it tidy. . . . Portia & Kitty are improving very much. They now begin to speak a little English. They advance all the while instead of losing their German. They send you lots of love & kisses. [30]

Although she was a loving and indulgent mother, Kate had high expectations for her children, paralleling her father's expectations for her. She often wrote her children advice that sounded as if it had been copied verbatim from Salmon's old letters. By the time Willie was eleven, for example, Kate expected that he write her in both German and English and that his letters be neat and interesting and arrive regularly. "Write as you would talk." Kate urged. "Tell what interests you & be sure it will interest your parents, who follow your every little act with affection & solicitude." She softened her criticisms as her father never had, perhaps remembering the pain his stern letters had caused her: "Confide your troubles to your dear Mama & know that in her you have loving friend always ready to help & sympathize with you. A little boys grief are just as great as those of older people & it is a relief to tell them to someone. Besides there is no trait better worth cultivating than FRANKNESS. Speak right out & speak from your heart . . . & seize every opportunity to do little kindnesses that you may be beloved by all who know you." Worried that her son would grow up too much like his father, Kate urged him to cultivate an ordered sense of self-control:

> Habits of neatness & order I covet for you, but can only be acquired with great patience & while you are small. You will feel the benefit of them all your life & without them you will be a trial to yourself & to all who are connected with you. A careless disorderly person can have but a faint idea of the discomfort they create, the time they waste & the injustice they do themselves, in many ways. Even ones outward appearance must not be disregarded. You are quite old enough to under stand a quotation from

Shakespeare—"The apparel oft bespeaks the man" and others respect
a man in proportion to the respect which he shows for himself. If he
abuses & neglects himself others will abuse and neglect him & he can
not complain. There is danger too that he will not have the confidence
of his associates for they will be sure to believe that a very nice sense of
horror is hidden under slovenly neglect.[31]

Kate hoped to influence Willie as she never could his father. By the
beginning of 1877 she no longer believed she could change William, nor
did she harbor any false hopes for his potential, but she still had aspirations
for his son.

William seems to have taken a much smaller part in parenting the
children. When Kate returned to the States in the fall of 1876, she and the
girls moved into Edgewood, the house her father had left her, and not into
the Sixth and E Street house where William stayed when in Washington.
From abroad, Willie wrote his father, often at Kate's urging. One of these
letters goes far to explain the relationship between father and son. "My dear
boy," William wrote in November 1877, "I have received all your letters to
me. I am very thankful to you for continuing to write me, although not
having your letters replied to." William then complimented his son on his
letter-writing ability, saying he had never mastered the art:

> I could not write or express myself as well as you do now, by a good
> deal. I had difficulty from want of concentration, and habits instilled in
> me. My mother, your grandmother, was quite rigid with her sons. Your
> father and Uncle Amasa. A good deal like what your mama felt and acts
> towards you. Constantly reminding one of defects and worrying us into
> obedience. You are a long way off and a long time away. I must make
> a bargain with you before your mama bribes you away from me. Your
> sisters Mama takes with her and leaves me here alone. She complains a
> good deal because I have so little to do with the family, now you must
> make me a part of your family by joining me when you come home.

William added that if Willie would come live with him they could go
to the Paris Exposition in the spring. His fatherly letter also contained
a lengthy account of how he had been "making laws for the Country,"
designing machinery for the mills, and otherwise attending to business in
Providence and New York. What laws William might have been making
remains unclear, for he no longer held public office. He closed his letter by

complaining to his son that Kate had kept him in the dark about Willie's living situation and that she had failed to pay the boy's considerable school bills.[32] Clearly, the break between Kate and William had become irreparable.

William's fathering style represents an exaggeration of the national trend. Since the Revolution, mothering had begun to overshadow the centrality of fathering in the American family. As John Demos put it, "As mother's importance waxed, father's inexorably waned." In an industrializing world, middle-class men became the family breadwinners. Women stayed home with the children, while men left the home to labor in a world that increasingly defined work as waged work. Thus white America shifted family models from a male-dominant family to a mother-centered view of the domestic circle. This is not to say that fathers had no authority in the nineteenth-century family—their economic supremacy demanded children's (and wives') respect and obedience, which merged with senti-mental ideals of paternal affection to create a sometimes contradictory and difficult model of fathering.[33]

Kate, like most other nineteenth-century American women, had almost sole control of child rearing, while William provided economic support for her and his children. In so doing he fulfilled the greater part of the unwritten fathering contract. The geographical distance required by William's business translated into emotional distance between him and his children. William rarely wrote to his son, and when he did his efforts seem stilted and unsure. We have no record of correspondence between the girls and their father.[34] Ethel, Portia, and Kitty, like most other Victorian girls, probably identified a great deal with their mother, who traveled with them, took care of them, and generally doted on them. Their father must have been a shadowy and strange figure on their emotional landscape. In a world where many fathers played a minor role, the Sprague girls probably felt no exceptional pain at their father's physical and emotional absence. This is not to say that all Victorian fathers matched William's disassociation from his family, but certainly many men had little to do with the physical and emotional labor of child rearing. More difficult to measure is the degree of affection William felt for his children. No letter or reminiscence suggests that a loving father/child relationship existed in the Sprague household, though evidence of such emotions often eludes the historical record.

During the spring of 1876, while Kate lived in Germany, one of her social rivals became embroiled in one of the many scandals that marred Grant's second term. Amanda Belknap, the third wife of Secretary of War William Belknap, was noted for her gorgeous gowns and lavish parties. Indeed, some Washingtonians publicly wondered how the Belknaps funded such extravagant living standards. The Belknap scandal began in the fall of 1870 when the second Mrs. Belknap, Amanda's sister Carrie, offered to obtain a government appointment for an office seeker. John Evans, the current holder of the post, wanted to retain his lucrative position as trader at an Indian post, so he agreed to pay Carrie Belknap six thousand dollars per year, in quarterly installments of fifteen hundred dollars, to keep his job. Shortly thereafter Carrie died after giving birth to a baby girl, leaving her baby and husband to the tender mercies of her widowed sister, Amanda. Amanda made a deal with Evans to continue the payments, though the money was ostensibly for her sister's child. The Belknap baby died in June 1871 but the payments continued, both before and after Belknap married his dead wife's sister. In total Belknap and his wives collected about twenty thousand dollars' worth of bribes, or about two and a half times the secretary of war's official salary.

When the scandal broke in March 1876, Belknap maintained that he knew nothing of the sisters' arrangements. Amanda professed that she had not desired the payments but had not known how to stop Evans from making them. Julia Grant, who liked the current Mrs. Belknap a great deal, asked Amanda why she had not told her husband about the illegal transactions. "Tell Belknap," Amanda exclaimed. "Why he would have annihilated me." Unfortunately for the Belknaps, no one believed that all that money had flowed into the household without Belknap's knowledge or against the flamboyant Amanda's will. Belknap, in an effort to forestall his impending impeachment, offered his resignation to President Grant, who accepted it. The ruse was successful, because although the House impeached Belknap he was not convicted of any crime, primarily because the Senate did not believe it had jurisdiction over Belknap once he became a private citizen.[35]

This seamy episode illustrates yet another way in which women could wield political power. One of Belknap's wives illegally sold a tradership, and another brokered the continuation of the monetary relationship. Surely Carrie and Amanda Belknap were neither the first nor the last women to have had tremendous access to extralegal political machinations through a powerful husband. Kate would have been familiar with similar situations, but she never chose to use her position in such a heavy-handed, greedy manner. Although Kate had her detractors, men and women who resented her gifts and her influence, no one ever accused her of overstepping the bounds of legal propriety. By the time Kate returned to the States, Amanda Belknap's reign as a leading Washington hostess had ceased, though Kate would not fill the vacancy.

The roots of Kate and William's unofficial separation lay in the events of late 1876. One night, in a drunken rage, William made a bonfire on the front lawn at Canonchet. Unfortunately for all concerned, he used bedding and furniture from the house, which he broke up and flung upon the flames. Kate later said that William had threatened to kill her that night, though she and the children escaped physical harm. A few months later, in February 1877, he attacked again. Storming into Kate's bedroom in the middle of the night, apparently more drunk than usual, William dragged Kate from her bed, hauled her over to the bedroom's second-story window, "and attempted to throw her therefrom." Kate described the attack as "extreme cruelty" and even years later remembered the event as one of "great violence." [36] Neither she nor William ever explained the precipitating event of these two episodes, but the first assault probably came at about the time Kate and Roscoe initiated their affair. Kate's attempts to rekindle her relationship with William through the business had been rebuffed by the beginning of 1876. She remained in Europe until that fall, but no correspondence exists between the couple, suggesting a permanent marital rift. She returned to Washington, established her own residence, and reentered the social scene. Not long afterward, people began to notice Roscoe and Kate often in each other's company.

William's decision to express his anger by attacking expensive furniture suggests that money may have been the immediate precipitating factor. Kate, undoubtedly short on funds after her European sojourn, may have gone back to Canonchet in an effort to secure money from her husband. Money had always been an issue between them. William would urge her to spend when he felt beneficent or guilty, while Kate would engage in bouts of conspicuous consumption when she felt wounded. She disliked his gifts of money (which she believed thoughtless), but after 1873 she repeatedly charged that he failed to support his family. This last fact offers the strongest hint as to why Kate continued to come in contact with William after 1873. Her father's estate had yielded very little in the way of actual cash. Nettie had forced Kate to buy her half of Edgewood (leaving

Kate cash poor and property rich), but Kate, unlike Nettie, had no funds from her mother's side of the family on which to depend in financial hard times. This may also help explain why Kate was so eager to help William's business in 1875. Kate, like many other wives in her social location, needed William's economic support. Clearly, neither Kate's infidelity nor her financial dependence excuses William's violence, but they do make his actions more comprehensible.

William's infidelities also played a part in the violence of 1876 and 1877. Kate accused her husband of infidelity with one "Elisabeth R. McCue, formerly Elisabeth Rhing" at "South Kingston" between 1877 and 1880. Kate knew the woman well enough to know both her unmarried and married names, and "South Kingston" is Kate's code name for Canonchet. William was probably having yet another "affair" with one of the household servants, and when Kate came back to the States she discovered it. Given William's habit of projecting guilt, one or both of the attacks may have been caused or exacerbated by his own offenses. He would have viewed violence as an acceptable outlet for his frustrations. Indeed, class-specific notions of masculinity granted non-working-class men's violence a certain cultural legitimacy. A laborers' bar fight, for example, was deemed dishonorable and animalistic, while senators' verbal and physical attacks on each other were affairs of honor. Additionally, because nineteenth-century society primarily acknowledged working-class and immigrant men as domestic abusers, William (and the people around him) did not have to think of himself as a wife beater. He could instead view himself as an honorable man, protecting his patriarchal authority.[37]

The outcome of the sensational Sickles and McFarland cases a few years earlier may have reinforced William's view. In 1859, Daniel Sickles, a Democratic congressman from New York, discovered that his wife, Teresa B. Sickles, and Philip Barton Key (son of composer Francis Scott Key) were having an affair. Although Daniel Sickles's reputation was tarnished with several extramarital affairs of his own, his wife's infidelity was personally and socially unacceptable. Daniel forced Teresa to write out her confession, including the secret signal the lovers had arranged for their assignations. Sickles waited at his house for Key to walk by and give the signal, and when he did Sickles shot and killed him. A jury acquitted Sickles on the grounds that he had acted as a "true man" by violently defending his right to control his wife. After murdering Key he would become a prominent Civil War general, a military governor of one of the five southern Reconstruction districts, and minister to Spain. New Yorkers would even return him to Congress in the 1890s. Sickles was a friendly acquaintance of the Chases until 1865, when his politics would put him on the other side of the fence from Salmon in the impeachment proceedings.[38] Clearly, murder did not particularly affect his career or social standing.

Although very different in many respects, the McFarland case bore a striking similarity. Abby and Daniel McFarland had an unhappy marriage, exacerbated by Daniel's drinking and chronic unemployment. Abby supported herself and her two children by giving dramatic readings and acting. She lived for sixteen months in Indiana and obtained a divorce in 1869. She had promised Albert D. Richardson, a correspondent for the *New York Tribune*, that she would marry him after her divorce, but before she could make good on her promise her ex-husband attacked Richardson in his *Tribune* office and shot him in the stomach. Abby and Albert were married on his deathbed, and McFarland was arrested for murder. In a highly charged newspaper battle, journalists depicted Abby as a woman of dubious morals, calling into question the legitimacy of both her divorce and her relationship with the murdered Richardson. A jury acquitted McFarland of any crime, agreeing with his lawyer's argument that "the husband had as much right to shoot him down as though Richardson had been guilty of her forced abduction. . . . [W]oman is the weaker vessel, and is meant to be under the protection of the stronger vessel, man; and any attempt from any quarter to interfere with that supremacy, even though it be with the consent of the woman, is as much an infraction of the husband's rights as though it were the infliction of absolute violence upon her or upon her."[39] Thus the law sanctioned violence in the defense of a man's marital tie, even after divorce had severed that tie. Certainly the McFarland and Sickles cases allowed William to view himself not as a debased wife beater but as a man honorably and legally defending his marriage.

Like Daniel Sickles, William viewed his own marital indiscretions as less serious violations of morality than those of his wife. Marital infidelity rested on a gendered double standard. No case more aptly illustrates this than Beecher-Tilton affair. In 1870, Elizabeth Tilton, the wife of famous newspaper editor Theodore Tilton, confessed to her husband that she had been having some kind of passionate relationship with her pastor, Henry Ward Beecher. The Tiltons espoused a tepid free-love ideology that backfired when "Lib" refused to break off her relationship with Beecher. In late 1872 the notorious free-love advocate Victoria Woodhull learned of the illicit relationship. She disapproved, not of the love affair, but of Beecher's monumental hypocrisy. As self-appointed guardians of the nation's morality, Beecher and his sisters Harriet and Catherine had been vocal in their disgust at Woodhull's advocacy of free love. Woodhull broke the story in her weekly newspaper, which in turn caused a great outpouring of support for Beecher. The public denounced Woodhull as a liar and pornographer and labeled Lib an immoral woman of the worst type. In 1874, Theodore Tilton sued Beecher for alienation of affection. Tilton lost his suit, and the following year he and his wife divorced. While Beecher survived the affair with his reputation only slightly tarnished, Lib retired from society and spent the rest of her unhappy life as a recluse. [40] The real lesson to be learned from the affair concerned the inequalities of the sexes when breaching the bonds of marriage. Men could stray from the monogamous fold, but women could not. William and Kate must have both understood the lessons in the Sickles, McFarland, and Tilton-Beecher controversies.

After William's second attack, Kate and the girls moved out of Canonchet and back to Edgewood. Although William later accused her of "willfully and without cause desert[ing] the bed and board" he provided, he had encouraged her to move out that February, probably to give him greater freedom to conduct his extramarital affairs. [41] The move also gave Kate greater access to Roscoe, both geographically and emotionally, and their relationship would quickly escalate into a nearly public affair. Significantly, Kate did not discuss William's attacks at the time they took place, understanding that many would perceive his actions as a reasonable response to her own behavior. Not until her petition for divorce would these episodes come to light, and then under extremely charged conditions.

Indeed, William's fondness for illicit sexual relations became a matter of public record on more than one occasion, most notably with Mary Viall Anderson. In 1876, Anderson published a thinly veiled autobiographical novel in which she not only admitted to "loving" her hero outside the bounds of nineteenth-century propriety but also attacked Kate, calling her "coarse," "indelicate," full of "personal vanity," and lacking in "natural" manners. Mary claimed that William had married Kate for her political connections, that William's "blind infatuation" and Kate's beauty had lured

"Caesar" into a loveless marriage. Mary's ramblings make it clear that she still yearned for William and believed they would "be reunited one day."[42] Her accounts of William's 1869 speeches glow with vivid and detailed description, making it clear that she found his oratory quite stirring. Mary's unqualified admiration for William's political abilities suggests that she had a greater grasp of hero worship than of Reconstruction politics.

In Mary's defense, if she believed in free love—and her novel suggests that she did—then she did not view her affair with William as immoral. Rather, because the tenets of free love held that "marriage without love is a sin against God," Mary could believe that her claim to William was greater than Kate's. According to this way of thinking, it was Kate, not Mary, who acted the paramour for engaging in a sexual relationship with William outside the bonds of love. Mary, like most of Kate and William's other contemporaries, assumed that their marriage had always been loveless.[43] Mary's novel must have been utterly embarrassing and galling to Kate. To be publicly mocked and reviled by her husband's mistress, to have the cherished beginnings of her marriage claimed as false, and to have her husband's early love called into question—each of these charges must have landed a terrible blow. William had also continued his relationship with Mary after the publication of her book, effectively doubling the insult to his wife and encouraging his mistress in her beliefs.

If the romance of her courtship seemed distant and unreal, Kate had Roscoe Conkling to console her. In the fall of 1876 the New York senator attempted to win the Republican presidential nomination, but he gained only 99 of the required 379 votes at the nominating convention. Instead, compromise candidate Rutherford B. Hayes won the day, in part because New York threw its votes to him at the last minute.[44] Roscoe had no love for either Hayes or his vice-presidential running mate, William Wheeler. Wheeler had once turned down Conkling's offer of a New York Custom House post by saying that it would not "compensate me for the forfeit of my own self-respect."[45] Hayes made civil service reform *the* issue of his campaign, thus threatening the power base of party bosses like Conkling. Roscoe refused to campaign for Hayes, claiming that a debilitating eye disease forced him to stay in a darkened room that fall.[46]

Republicans, sullied by the scandals of Grant administration and the post-1873 depression, did not enjoy the same certainty of winning the election that they had in other recent elections. In the 1874 elections

Democrats seized control of the House, marking a resurgence of that party's power. On only two ballots the Democrats nominated Samuel J. Tilden, the same man who Kate correctly believed had betrayed her father at the 1868 convention. In November 1876, Tilden won the popular vote by a majority of over a quarter of a million votes, but the electoral vote count was not so clearly in his favor. The problem centered on the returns in Florida, South Carolina, and Louisiana. Republican leaders contended that Democrats had cheated the vote count in Tilden's favor and had forcibly prevented black men from voting. Republicans needed all three states to place Hayes in the White House by a margin of 185 to 184. Backroom maneuvers and sneaky dealings abounded as each party, and camps within parties, attempted to control the manner in which the electoral votes from the three southern states were counted.[47] In the sordid battle over the Tilden-Hayes election, Roscoe helped to craft an electoral commission bill that proposed five senators (three Republicans, two Democrats), five representatives (three Democrats, two Republicans), and five Supreme Court justices to decide the electoral vote. Two justices were Democrats, two Republicans, with a fifth to be chosen by the four judges. They ultimately chose Judge Bradley, who would weight the commission in favor of the Republicans.

Before the commission could do its work, though, the bill to create it had to pass both houses. During the height of the excitement, Billy Hudson, the same man who had fallen under Kate's spell at the 1868 convention, happened upon her at a local train station. She had just disembarked from a train, and he watched as she swept across the waiting room and dropped her scarf. He picked it up and "lowered his dignity" sufficiently to run after her. He faced his "political divinity of 1868!" She thanked him and noted that he looking tired and dissipated. "Ah, I know the habits of you boys," Kate teased. After a polite social exchange she told him, "Senator Conkling will support the Commission with a speech." Hudson contended that Kate was at the train station because she was returning from a secret meeting with Conkling in Baltimore—a meeting Kate set up at the behest of Republican leaders to sway Roscoe to give the commission a Republican majority.[48] He did, and the bill passed both houses.

Privately, Roscoe believed that Tilden had won the election, and evidence suggests he was correct. Nonetheless, the commission began its work by counting Florida's votes for Hayes on a straight partisan eight-to-seven vote. Rumors flew around Washington that Roscoe would make a speech against the corruption of Louisiana's votes, but he did not. Tilden supporters believed themselves "fearfully deceived." Others claimed it an "open secret" that Kate had swayed Roscoe to remain silent on the Louisiana question to avenge Tilden's part in Salmon's 1868 defeat. [49] In keeping with the myth about Kate's ruthless ambition to see her father elected president, biographers and historians have suggested that she harbored a deep animosity against Tilden for his part in Chase's defeat at the 1868 Democratic convention. Unfortunately, this story underestimates her ability to understand the complexity of the politics at that convention and fails to account for Roscoe's party loyalty (and Kate's understanding of that loyalty). Roscoe would not have supported a Democrat, even against a Republican whom he considered an enemy. Such a move would have accomplished for him what the impeachment trial did for Salmon, namely, to make him forever persona non grata in the Republican Party. Conkling was not the kind of man who would have damaged any chances he had for a cabinet post or the presidency with party disloyalty, particularly if the only thing at issue was virtuous adherence to political principle.

This is not to say that Kate had no opinion or influence with Roscoe in the matter, but rather that it seems unlikely that she did more than support his decision to abandon Tilden. In fact, when Kate originally spoke to Hudson she implicitly suggested not only that Roscoe supported the commission but that she did as well. The commission, as originally planned, would have consisted of eight Democratic votes rather than eight Republican votes. At the last minute, Illinois elected Judge David Davis (who was nominally a Republican but would have voted with the Democrats) to the U.S. Senate. Davis resigned his Supreme Court seat after the Senate passed the commission bill, and Judge Bradley (a Grant nominee) took his place. In its first configuration the commission would most probably have given the disputed votes to Tilden. Thus a good case can be made that Kate had little real political animus for Tilden. The rumor that Kate swayed the outcome of an election, though, speaks eloquently both to how much political power she did have and to how many powerful men came within her sphere of influence. The rumors also suggest that while some people found Kate's political prowess admirable, others disapproved of her involvement to such an extent that they could find only dastardly motives for her actions. However much the Republican Party encouraged women's partisan activities, Kate presented a case of a woman who acted, in some Americans' minds, too prominently in a process that had been defined as the province of men.

Kate's letters to Willie also suggest that she had a busy life outside politics. Still at Edgewood, the girls, particularly Portia, had colds that lingered all spring. The day before Easter found them all well enough to attend a play featuring Gulliver and the Lilliputians. The "giant" gave the children quite a fright, making them afraid that he might eat them. [50] In June, Kitty battled and defeated a life-threatening case of scarlet fever. "The disease has been thoroughly thrown out of her system," Kate wrote Willie, and "the other two sisters escaped infection and are very well."[51] Never a very strong child, Kitty suffered from a developmental disability that would keep her physically weak and intellectually childlike all her life.

Significantly, though Willie was still in Mr. Lauteren's school in Heidelberg, Kate's June letters make no mention to him of her imminent trip abroad. Her late-June trip back to Europe had a private purpose. Not long after Kate sailed, Roscoe left for the Continent as well—without his wife and daughter. Washington noticed the coincidence. Although Kate preserved no letters from this trip abroad, we do know that the New York senator arrived in Southampton on 27 June, toured Henry VII and Anne Boleyn's house and other attractions, and soon afterward left for London. Roscoe wrote his daughter, Bessie, that once in the city he had not presented any of his letters of introduction, nor had he registered his name at the hotel. In London he attended a dinner given by Minister Edwards Pierpont and his wife in the Prince of Wales's honor. Julia and Ulysses S. Grant attended as well, though they left England for Brussels soon after. Undoubtedly secretly together, Roscoe and Kate must have breathed a sigh of relief at the Grants' departure. The Grants were particular friends of Julia and Roscoe Conkling, and Mrs. Grant went so far as to point out to her dinner companions at Pierpont's dinner that no one "knew so well the right thing to do as Mrs. Fish or Mrs. Conkling." Roscoe agreed with Julia Grant, or so he told Bessie.[52] Kate's release from her father's censure, from the abuse she suffered in her marriage, and perhaps even from sexual standards she had learned as a girl all encouraged her to view "the right thing" with a jaundiced eye—and that quality, as much as anything else, brought her and Roscoe together in Europe during the summer of 1877.

The next year found Kate once again regularly attending Senate sessions. One day, while she sat in the gallery "in a black robe with threads of gold in delicate tracery, a bonnet of black lace crowned with a double tiara of roses," Roscoe and the Mississippi senator Lucius Q. C. Lamar engaged in fierce verbal fisticuffs over an army appropriations bill. Democrats had attached a rider to the bill that provided a fine of five thousand dollars or five years' imprisonment for any federal officer, the president included, who used the army to "interfere" with elections. Roscoe gave a grandiloquent speech on the bill, denouncing the rider as a usurpation of presidential authority and an invitation for "thugs and . . . all the fraternity of bucket-shops, the rat-pits, the hells and the slums" to interfere at will with elections.[53] Hayes had vetoed the bill after it passed both houses (each of which had Democratic majorities), and so June found the bill back in the Senate, with the Democrats determined to push it through before the end of the session. When Roscoe denounced the attempt as "an act of bad faith," Senator Lamar jumped to his feet and "in a voice almost choked with passion" accused the New Yorker of lying and general low moral character. The gallery took notice and strained forward to hear the great orator's retort. Conkling paced to the back of the chamber, stood within a few feet of Lamar, and told the chairman that if he were not in the Senate he would call Lamar "a blackguard, a coward and a liar." Lamar answered by reiterating that though his words had been "harsh" he had meant what he said. The southerner then virtually issued a call for a duel by saying that his language "was such that no good man would deserve and no brave man would wear." The Senate erupted in applause and hisses.[54] Kate was said to have turned ghastly pale and been near fainting, though one journalist reported that "she looked about her with the mien of an empress but her face was the face of a Sphinx."[55]

The chairman finally brought the floor to order, but for weeks afterward talk of duels and violence circulated in the capital. Southerners like Lamar believed that the duel, and the code of honor it enforced, provided a bulwark against chaos by reinforcing social hierarchy and male authority. As an affair of honor, the duel provided an "outer show of inner worth" for elite-class men.[56] One man, who expected to be Lamar's second if the duel did take place, believed Conkling would not fight. "I don't regard him as a man of courage."[57] Roscoe laughed off the idea of a duel, saying that in New York they had other ways of settling personal differences.

Indeed, as early as 1804, when Aaron Burr had mortally wounded Alexander Hamilton in a duel, northerners had repudiated the duel as a socially acceptable form of violence. New Jersey indicted Burr for murder, while Georgia and South Carolina provided him with refuge until the furor could die down. After Burr's disgrace, dueling became the cultural property of planter-class southern men—men who implicitly understood both the rules and the reasons for invoking an affair of honor.[58]

In the Lamar-Conkling affair, two competing visions of manhood ran up against each other. Roscoe's ethic of masculinity denied physical violence as a solution for verbal disagreements, while Lamar's sense of honor demanded that he redress the insults the northerner had hurled at him with a duel, or at least an offer to duel. Indeed, to "win" the battle, Lamar did not actually have to fight; he only had to be appear *willing* to fight. Northern papers attacked Lamar's "plantation" ethic, while southern or Democratic papers thought Conkling's refusal to meet Lamar at dawn exposed him as a coward. William would have better understood the southern Democrat's vision of manhood than Roscoe's, as later events would bear out. Word had it that Roscoe's troubled personal life, particularly his daughter's upcoming nuptials to a man of whom he disapproved, had made him quite cranky.[59] Washington believed that only Kate could console him.

By the time of the Lamar exchange, Kate and Roscoe's affair had progressed so far that the two were openly passing notes in the Senate. Kate sat in the gallery on many days, though her husband no longer had a seat on the floor. Colleagues noticed that Roscoe was more likely to give a speech on the days Kate attended. He would sometimes scribble a note in lavender ink and hand it over to a Senate page, who would minutes later transfer the missive to Kate. Kate generally let the note sit in her lap a few minutes before opening it, as if to suggest that its contents had little to do with her. The messages were probably little more than the usual stuff of lovers, but just as often Roscoe appealed to Kate for advice on some political problem, believing that her "bright mind will solve [political problems] quicker than mine." Once she had composed a reply, a servant would take it out of the gallery. Roscoe would casually got up from his seat, walk to the rear of the chamber, and stand with his back to the Senate doors. A door would crack open, and an unseen hand would slip Kate's answer into his waiting palm. Notes did not always suffice the two's needs, for on some occasions a private secretary would escort Kate to a Senate committee room and stand guard at the door after Roscoe joined her. What actually took place in the room was a matter of much conjecture.[60]

Washington society, which one journalist compared to "the last luxurious days of Louis XV," expressed quiet disapproval of the match.[61] Kate, along with Julia Grant, had continued to rule the capital's elites during the late 1860s and early 1870s. Although she was not the president's wife, Kate had many qualities the First Lady did not, including beauty, wit, and a complete understanding of Washington politics and protocol. After 1869 Kate voluntarily relinquished her post as Washington's preeminent hostess, choosing to spend more time in Rhode Island or abroad. Washington hostesses like Elizabeth Blair and Violet Blair Janin stopped receiving Kate after 1876, particularly as she was seen more frequently in public with Roscoe. "They were so much seen together," Violet Janin explained, "that it was generally supposed that she was his mistress."[62] Other Washingtonians, less hostile to the Chases than to the Blairs, continued to receive Kate. Jane Gray Swisshelm, a journalist, interpreted Kate's declining social power as politically motivated slander:

> It is declared that Mrs. Sprague went into Conkling's office alone. She went in on business but gossips say she went in to make love to Conkling. They say she nearly fainted the day of the Lamar-Conkling episode. The day Benton attacked Foote, one-fourth of the ladies showed alarm. They say Kate Chase rose, leaned over the gallery with blanched face— . . . that she is singled out among others . . . shows the deadly malice, jealousy and hatred of the "petticoated brigadiers" in Washington society. 'Tis said Kate Chase sends notes to Conkling . . . a common thing for ladies to send notes to members of the floor, common also are the smiles of approval exchanged.[63]

Not only did some Washingtonians disapprove of Kate as a political actor, but she also served as a convenient conduit for attacks on the men with whom she was connected. Salmon's overreaching ambition, William's unseemly behavior, and Roscoe's heavy-handed political maneuvering had all created enemies who attacked their opponents by sullying Kate's good name. Most Washington women associated with politicians would have been off limits to these kind of attacks, but Kate's position, both as an unofficial public politician and as the not-quite wife of two men, made her an exception.

Whatever Swisshelm's interpretation of Kate's and Roscoe's behavior, she clearly documents the actual events—that they exchanged notes, that they met privately in his office, that she showed alarm over the conflict with Lamar. In 1876, after Roscoe's friend Ulysses S. Grant left office and his enemy Hayes took up residence on Pennsylvania Avenue, both he and Kate had less socially at stake. Neither was likely to be invited into Hayes's social circle, even if they were circumspect, particularly while Hayes made repeated attacks on Roscoe's control of the New York Custom House. Also, Roscoe no longer had to maintain a basic level of decorum around the Grants, who were out of the country.[64] Essentially, Hayes's ascension accomplished for Roscoe what William's violent repudiation of his wife had accomplished for Kate—it freed him to act as he pleased. Conveniently, their emancipations came only months apart. As to hedging bets for the future, Roscoe had his eye on the presidency and believed so firmly in his eventually gaining that position that he did not feel he had to worry about the social approval of the next regime. He and Kate would be Washington's next great power. Thus after the spring of 1877 Kate and Roscoe began appearing together in public more often, though they received fewer invitations to official and private functions. Men continued to make morning calls at Edgewood, as Kate's house continued to be a veritable mecca for political counsel throughout the second half of the 1870s, but the wives stayed away. As much as any other evidence, this censure speaks volumes to the public nature of Kate and Roscoe's passion.

In early 1878, William's mother, Fanny, visited Kate at Edgewood and pleaded with her to go home to Canonchet, both to give up her public affair and to save William from his almost continuous drunkenness. Kate must have listened, because she briefly moved back to Canonchet that summer. A few weeks later, law enforcement officials of Nantasket Beach in Massachusetts arrested Mary Viall Anderson and William in a "drunken orgy." Although the press would not reveal the matter until the next year, all of Rhode Island knew of their former governor's shame. Kate packed up her daughters and returned to Edgewood—the one place where she felt secure.[65] Not coincidentally, the move brought her back in proximity with Roscoe Conkling. The results would be disastrous.

SIX

"Whiskey, Economy and Disregarded Wishes"
The Narragansett Affair, Domestic Abuse,
and State Politics,
1879

~

People marry through a variety of reasons, and with varying results;
but to marry for love is to invite tragedy.

James Branch Cabel

THE SCANDAL

Kate and Roscoe's relationship became public with the Narragansett affair, a scandal involving a sordid mélange of sex, violence, and politicians. These ingredients have always made for a potent tale of public dishonor, though perhaps never more than during the Gilded Age. In the decades that followed the Civil War, the breakdown of Kate and William's marriage gained as much notice as any of the now well known political scandals. Some newspapers printed a new version of the story every day for weeks. Jokes, songs, and poems made farcical reference to shotguns and senators. The Narragansett affair was neither the first nor certainly the last time the fertile combination of sex and politics engaged the country's puerile interest—Victorian Americans showing the same kind of rapt disgust and fascination at the affair that contemporary Americans have with the seamier side of public life.[1] Under the headline "Gunning for a Senator," a Cincinnati newspaper summed up the affair as "one of whiskey, economy and disregarded wishes."[2] When the dust had settled on Kate's escape from her marriage, none of the participants could claim the social authority they once had. The *Washington Post* noted, "It has taken six working days to reduce Mr. Roscoe Conkling to the rear end. In twenty or thirty years, if excessively prudent in his daily walk, he may be able to recover a small portion of his prestige . . . possible, but not probable."[3] Each actor would be besmirched by his or her role in the affair, and the ship of state and national politics would subtly but surely alter its course—proving that the affairs of men and women have much to do with political economy.

The events surrounding the Narragansett affair also illustrate how Kate and William Sprague, Roscoe Conkling, and the New York and Rhode Island political machines operated with little regard to restrictive notions of separate spheres. Kate, William, and Roscoe all challenged normative conventions with scandalous behavior. Kate both relied upon and rejected traditional modes of womanhood, depending upon the demands of the situation, while William's confrontation with Roscoe suggests competing visions of nineteenth-century manhood. The mixing of the political and domestic spheres that occurred in the working out of the scandal might have provided a challenge to existing social norms, but the titillating nature of the imbroglio obscured any lessons it might have taught.[4] Rather, the Narragansett affair offered Gilded Age majority culture a chance to reinforce accepted gender roles.

The scandal began innocently enough. Late in July 1879, Kate moved her household from steamy Washington to the Sprague mansion on breezy Narragansett Bay. As she often did, Kate invited a number of houseguests to enjoy the cool ocean air. For over a week the party enjoyed itself immensely. Mr. Throop Martin, a seventy-year-old invalid, spent the afternoons on Canonchet's wide piazza, while fitter members of the household enjoyed ocean bathing and lawn bowling. Kate had seen little of her husband that summer. William spent the majority of his time in Providence, probably at Young Orchard, his mother's estate.[5] William later claimed he was in Providence to attend to business matters, though Zechariah Chaffee, the trustee, said he paid William no salary "for the reason he has done no work." In contrast, Amasa, William's older brother, reported to the firm's offices every day and drew a salary.[6] Whatever William did in Providence, he went down to Narragansett that first weekend in August, and though the locals later reported that he acted a bit erratically, he harmed no one.[7]

At the same time, the local newspaper at Narragansett reported that Roscoe was across the bay in Newport—a guest of Levi P. Morton, a congressman and friend from New York. Morton was the founder of Morton, Rose and Co., the firm that had supplanted Jay Cooke's banking house in American finance after Cooke's disastrous 1873 failure. Morton probably held some of the paper on the indebted Sprague Company.[8] During his first

August visit William hung around in local taverns, talking about his intense personal hatred for Conkling and broadcasting his intention to confront the senator. William sometimes made these threats "when perfectly sober and in a normal condition, but more frequently under the influence of liquor."[9]

The first Sunday morning in August found William at the Studio, a local Narragansett watering hole, restaurant, and billiards hall. He declared to the men there: "I hope he [Conkling] will not come over here, for I will not have him." Undoubtedly under the influence of alcohol, William decided to go over to Newport, ostensibly on business. Before he went he declared that if he happened upon Senator Conkling in Newport their meeting would be "a tall row."[10] He returned to Canonchet, had breakfast, and collected his son. Willie's tutor, Professor Linck, objected: "Well Governor, you intend taking our boy to Newport and leaving me here all alone?" "He will have more fun there," Sprague retorted.[11] Once across the bay, William nearly encountered his foe at the Newport post office, where Roscoe had been a minute before to collect his mail. His quarry having, evidently, too great a lead, William eschewed pursuit. Fearing that someone might doubt his intentions, William assured the postmaster and a few bystanders that "it was time someone brought the duel back to the North, for there are matters which can only be adjusted by that means."[12] He also claimed that he would deal similarly with any reporters who interfered with his plans. Soon after his near miss with William, Roscoe took the ferry across the bay to Narragansett to visit R. G. Dunn, an old fishing partner. If William knew where his nemesis went he did not follow him.[13]

The whole thing might have ended there if William had not left Rhode Island and then returned three days before he was expected. He came home early, not to catch his wife and Conkling together, but because the legal system compelled him to do so. Since the panic of 1873 a host of lawsuits had entangled the Sprague estate. Prominent among these was a suit by William Sprague Hoyt (Nettie's husband) and Charles G. Francklyn (who had married William Hoyt's sister Susan) against William and his brother, Amasa. This suit charged that both Fanny M. Sprague (William Sprague's mother) and Mary W. Sprague (William Hoyt's grandmother) had failed to administer the estate when appointed to do so after the deaths of their respective husbands, both founders of the original A. & W. Sprague. The two widows failed to fulfill their tasks as administratrices, the suit charged, when they procured no settlement of the estate upon the death, in 1856, of William III (William Sprague's uncle, Hoyt's grandfather). As if this were not genealogically convoluted enough, Hoyt and Francklyn claimed that Byron Sprague, yet another cousin, had schemed with the Sprague brothers to defraud the Hoyts and Francklyns of assets from the original firm. The three Spragues had created a new corporation under the name of A. & W. Sprague Manufacturing Company in 1862, consequently dissolving the original firm of A. & W. Sprague. Thus the lawsuit claimed that the new founders had prevented the original founders' children and grandchildren from enjoying the assets and property which they believed rightfully theirs. These assets were not inconsiderable, for the company had been conservatively valued at $4 million after its incorporation and over $19 million before its 1873 failure. While A. & W. Sprague's value continued to exceed its liabilities, the same could not be said of the Hoyt family companies. Thus the Hoyt branch of the family hoped to recoup its losses with a windfall from the Sprague branch of the business.[14]

After a delay of over two years, a Newport circuit judge ruled against the Hoyt side of the family. Judge Lowell noted that even though the Sprague side of the family had lost much of the company's assets through bad investments, the 1862 incorporation was legal. The judge understood that had he ruled the incorporation illegal, the Spragues would have been relieved of responsibility for the firm's debts. The small state of Rhode Island could hardly stand such a loss and had, in fact, gone to great lengths to keep A. & W. Sprague afloat.[15] The court also found no evidence of fraud by either the administratrices or the Sprague partners. The new corporation had fulfilled the intentions of the original founders, the judge contended, by keeping the business in the hands of the three men with whom the elder William Sprague had formed a partnership just before his death. The circuit court dismissed the case and charged the costs to Hoyt and Francklyn.

On the face of it none of this would seem particularly significant to the Spragues' personal life, especially since their side of the family won the case and retained nominal control over the estate. On the positive side, the value of paper held on A. & W. Sprague could substantially increase once the suit was settled. The company's stock had been valued as low as sixteen cents per share while title to the corporate deed remained unclear. Having purchased great quantities of stock while it sold at its lowest point, the Spragues now stood to recoup some of their 1873 losses. This benefit to the Spragues, though, did not outweigh the debt that the company would now be forced to settle. Creditors, representing over $8 million in debt, had gone without payment for the duration of the lawsuit. These creditors included a bank that held the title on William's Narragansett house. The bank had no reason to support loans on Canonchet, for unlike the mills at Cranston and Providence, Canonchet contributed little to the Rhode Island economy. The huge mansion, sitting on 350 beachfront acres, represented a sizable sum of cash.

The court settled the lawsuit on Monday, 4 August. Eleven days later a notice appeared in the local newspaper stating that Canonchet "is advertised by the U.S. Marshal to be sold at auction on the 4th of September to satisfy a judgment in behalf of the National Bank of Commerce of New York." [16] Kate's distress at the news may explain why Roscoe left the safe confines of R. G. Dunn's house and went to stay at Canonchet. A second newspaper notice warned, "It will of course be understood that any sale by the United States Marshall of the A. W. Sprague property must be made subject of the creditors under the trust-deed and assignments to Mr. Chaffee." [17] William would see no profit from the sale of his estate. His legal victory in Newport's circuit court must have seemed a Pyrrhic one indeed.

William left Canonchet on Monday, 4 August, for business in Portland, Maine, and Kate, the children, and houseguests believed that he would return the following Saturday evening. [18] From Maine William heard about the settlement of the suit, most probably by telegram, sometime on Tuesday, 5 August. Meanwhile, Roscoe arrived at Canonchet on Wednesday afternoon. Unfortunately, William cut his trip short and returned home late Thursday night, after the household had retired for the evening. He sent no word of his early return, nor did he seek out his wife that evening or the next morning. Instead, he rose early Friday morning, before the rest of the household, and went into town. At the Studio he told his friends he had not slept all night, or the night before. He then spent the morning forgetting his troubles with beverages and billiards, having no idea that he had been under the same roof as Roscoe Conkling. [19]

Around midday someone at the Studio mentioned Roscoe's presence at Canonchet. Already upset about the imminent loss of his home and fueled by a heady mixture of drink and exhaustion, William became "angry beyond measure." The cuckolded husband told his drinking partners, "Senator Conkling was trying to do for [my] home in Rhode Island what he had already done for [my] home in Washington and [I am] determined to put an end to it once and forever."[20] No doubt William had reached a breaking point in his personal life, a point created or exacerbated by his business troubles, because he had tolerated Kate and Roscoe's relationship for almost three years. Indeed, his pursuit of Conkling in Newport the weekend before had a kind of ritual quality—a de rigueur public protest against a man he had no intention of really confronting. This hot Friday morning in August, though, only days after it became clear that he would have to settle his company's debts and lose his Rhode Island home, William snapped.

On his way back to Canonchet, William worked up quite a temper. He met Professor Linck outside the house and told the tutor to leave. William later admitted that "probably he did speak angrily [to Linck] . . . but his indignation was against Conkling."[21] The tutor's presence at Canonchet did irritate William, no doubt in part because he viewed Linck as an unnecessary expense. Perhaps more important than financial constraints, especially in light of the fact that the Spragues were anything but broke, was William's view of education. William had not had the same rigorous education as Kate. As the *New York Times* delicately put it, "In Providence and Newport he does not have the reputation of being a scholar." While in letters to his son William wrote of the importance of education, he seems to have found the reality of academic achievement irritating. William frightened the tutor so badly that Linck made haste for a nearby boardinghouse and never again returned to Canonchet.[22]

Having confronted one of the men who had been a burr under his saddle, William went in search of the other. When he found Roscoe on Canonchet's piazza with the Martin family and other houseguests, he commenced threatening Roscoe and "acting wildly." He asked the New Yorker if he was armed, to which Roscoe responded "No sir, I am not."[23] Kate later reported that Roscoe rose from his chair and walked across the room to stand in front of her. "Mrs. Sprague, your husband is very much excited and I think it better for all of us I should withdraw. If my departure puts you in any danger, say so, and I will stay whatever the consequences." Kate urged him to go. "If Mr. Sprague [is] in a passion it is useless to argue with him," she warned, "and might only lead to violence."[24] Roscoe later corroborated Kate's assessment of the situation, telling friends that her husband had seemed "unmanly" and "not the master of himself."[25] In the middle of this confrontation, the Sprague carriage pulled up in front of the house for Kate and Roscoe's afternoon ride. Kate called for her shawl, but William forbade his wife to leave the porch. He then told Roscoe he had five minutes to vacate the premises before bullets started flying. [26] Roscoe retrieved his hat and walking stick from the house and went down the stairs to the carriage platform. Ethel, the eldest Sprague daughter, followed him down the stairs. While her father looked on, Ethel threw her arms around Roscoe and begged him not to go. Kate told her daughter, "No, Ethel; Mr. Conkling will go, but no one shall hurt him or us." [27] Incensed by this tender scene, William shouted at his daughter's hero, "Now you have left this house you must leave this place. If you want to save your own life you must leave Narragansett Pier, for —— —— shan't stay here." William added that if he ever found the senator in his house again he would kill him, armed or not. [28] With this warning ringing in Roscoe's ears, the senator's carriage sped away.

This scene eloquently suggests that Ethel had every reason to fear her father, though if she feared for herself or her mother remains unclear. In March 1867, when Willie was only two, Kate wrote a diatribe against child cruelty, which she clipped to a newspaper article extolling the need to be kind and loving toward children. She wrote: "The personal grievings which cloaks its annoyance with the garb of punishment expressing its possession upon the helpless little one, cowardly oppression used by the stronger against the weaker are so obnoxious so detestable so cruel that the world should be made to ring with such abuses. The seeds of rebellion & crime are often sown by cruelty. I believe if I ever live to see the hand of the father of my own child raised to strike it would arouse in me something dangerous." [29] This fragment suggests that less than four years into the marriage Kate had reason to believe William capable of violence. Her cold reference to "the father of my own child" and the fact that she saved this scrap of paper suggest that William had already breached the boundaries of acceptable behavior toward family as early as 1867. The extent to which his domestic violence had escalated in the ensuing years remains open to conjecture.

As William, armed with his shotgun, pursued Roscoe into Narragansett, Kate did some quick thinking. [30] Declaring that she would "never sleep under the same roof with Mr. Sprague again," Kate ordered her guests and children to prepare to leave Canonchet that afternoon. She left her maid behind to pack the family's and Roscoe's trunks and took her children and guests to Tower Hill House, a hotel in Narragansett. Although some of the guests registered, Kate did not. The hotel maid overheard her say, "I hope I shall be able keep this out of the papers." Then, in an effort to turn her hopes into realities, she summoned Professor Linck. What passed between the two remains a mystery, but Linck was clearly willing to cooperate with Kate in her efforts to conceal the day's events.[31]

In the meantime, Roscoe, awaiting a train out of Narragansett, stopped at Billingtons' Cafe for a lunch of crackers and milk.[32] Soon afterward, William arrived in his carriage, shotgun at the ready, and called Conkling out into the street where all could see and hear the next installment of their altercation. W. C. Clarke, a local druggist whose shop stood less than a block from the café, watched the ensuing argument with great interest. All the onlookers had stories to tell the press in the coming days.[33] "Have you not gone yet, —— —— you? I want you," William demanded. The angry husband denounced Roscoe in "epithets unfit to publish and such as one seldom uses without blows resulting." Roscoe responded in tones too low for anyone but William to hear, after which the cuckolded husband yelled, "I will accept no apology for what you have done, —— —— you." "You are acting like an insane man," Roscoe admonished William, warning, "you will think better of all this to-morrow."[34] William again asked Roscoe if he were armed. Roscoe said he was not. "Then go and arm yourself," William yelled, "and hereafter go armed. I don't intend to shoot an unarmed man; but I tell you now that if you ever cross my path again I will shoot you at sight."[35] After what one newspaper called "this disgraceful exhibition by a drunken man," William sped away in his carriage. Soon afterward Roscoe's trunks arrived from Canonchet, and within three hours the train to Providence pulled out of Narragansett Pier with the senator onboard.[36] The *Newport Daily News* succinctly summed up its opinion of William's behavior that day: "Reports have said for a longtime [*sic*] that ex-Governor Sprague is not always in a condition to be held strictly responsible for his conduct. It is not even now understood that he belongs to the prohibition party. A reform club at Narragansett might possibly be a good thing."[37] Certainly the locals knew enough about William to understand that he could be erratic and self-destructive, particularly when drunk.

In fact, the whole scene reads like a dramatic set piece, a ritualistic display of manhood. William's rage drove him into the streets of Narragansett, armed with a gun. In order to regain mastery over his family, William had to engage in a vivid performance of masculinity. More important than the performance was the audience. American men defined themselves in adversarial relationships with other men, particularly after the "Age of Jackson." [38] Masculinity maintained itself as a "homosocial enactment," that is, a man knew he was "a man" when he acted a certain way in front of other men. William had to prove his manhood, not just for his wife and her guests, but in front of Narragansett townsmen. Kate, the children, and the servants did not have sufficient social worth to measure manhood. William needed male validation. The homosocial qualities of manhood not only explain William's public performance but suggest why he had not acted before. Roscoe's physical presence at Canonchet meant not only that William had caught him in the act but that Roscoe became the primary witness to William's "unmanning." [39]

Unfortunately for William, the way he reasserted his manhood disqualified him as a "true man." Many post–Civil War Americans discredited notions of an honor-based manhood, vilifying white southern men as feminized creatures who had failed the ultimate test of war. Additionally, nineteenth-century culture placed an increasingly high value on self-control, a trait that seemed essential in an industrializing world seen as increasingly out of control. [40] While William intended his performance to shore up his manhood, it proved to be a terrible miscalculation. His method and timing did not match.

The newspapers contrasted William's behavior to Roscoe's, emphasizing the New Yorker's reasonableness and sobriety. Roscoe's public use of gendered language—calling William "unmanly," for example—symbolically feminized his rival, a significant slur given the importance of gender roles to nineteenth-century Americans. In feminizing his rival, Conkling portrayed himself as the benevolent patriarch of Canonchet—a more sober and industrious father than William. [41] Kate used much the same pejoratives, suggesting that feminizing one's male enemies was not strictly the province of men. Kate and Roscoe would have understood that William was vulnerable to attacks on his masculinity given the failure of his business and his political career. When Kate said that her husband "was not the master of himself," she played on century-old notions that equated business reversals with failures in manhood. At the same time she claimed that William had become a slave to his passions; nineteenth-century Americans would have understood that if William were not his own master he had become a slave, and as a result he could no longer be considered a legitimate citizen. [42]

William had threatened a rival with a duel on at least two earlier occasions. The *code duello* had been considered an "instrument of honorable vindication" earlier in the century, particularly in the South. Duels like the ones fought by Andrew Jackson and Aaron Burr illustrate how often matters of honor and personal combat became embroiled in politics. [43] William's references to dueling and his willingness to confront his rival with armed violence suggest that he acted under a code of ritualized honor which sought to restore sullied reputations and prevent political chaos. Male virtue and honor demanded that men defend themselves against the sexual misconduct of "their" women. Even in a Republican state like Rhode Island the law (and William's political enemies) never charged William with assault. However bad the shotgun episode made William look to those who espoused a more Republican and control-oriented notion of manliness, he was never confronted by the law. His behavior was considered bizarre, but it remained within the boundaries of acceptable behavior.

William may have believed that his behavior would elevate him from his "not-quite-gentleman" status to a more socially elite position. Unfortunately, he did not understand the rules that governed masculinity, or else he was unable to properly enact the rules because of chronic drunkenness. Gentlemen, even southern Democrats, did not go about willy-nilly threatening duels. A man whose honor had been besmirched was supposed to behave with cool self-control, exchange letters with the other party, attempt a written rapprochement, and only when all else had failed arrange terms of the duel through his second. William did not follow these codes. [44] While his response to Roscoe (and earlier with Senator Abbot) may have created an avenue for him to think of himself as an authoritative and powerful man, he did it wrong. This, more than anything else, is why people viewed him as a fool.

Kate's adultery also threatened William by putting another man in his house, implicitly challenging his authority over Kate and the children. Remember, Ethel turned to Roscoe, not her father, in the moment of crisis. At the same time, Kate's willing infidelity breached the legal and political covenant of marriage. Nineteenth-century legal experts likened a woman's adultery to treason—a physical violation of a man's political authority. Underlying these ideas was the legal concept of coverture, that women were the property of their husbands. Naturally, men had a right to defend their property, particularly if some other man trespassed on that property.

Under the legal principle of "criminal conversation" or *trespass vi et armis*, husbands could bring civil action against seducers on the same principle as if the latter had stolen some real piece of property. Thus a husband's rights of possession not only allowed some men to treat their wives as objects but were foundational to determining how a "real man" should react to adultery.[45] William did not sue Roscoe for criminal conversation, but he did make it publicly and brutally clear that he would no longer allow the New Yorker sexual access to his wife. Kate's public adultery caused him loss of reputation and self. This staggering loss makes William's rage comprehensible, and in nineteenth-century minds it gave legal justification to his behavior.

Both local knowledge and a quick dissemination of the events through the press acted in Kate's favor. However clear it seemed that she and Roscoe had been caught *in flagrante delicto*, the cultural script for condemning adulterous wives demanded an innocent husband. "Good women" deserved protection from dissolute husbands, while fallen women were viewed as heartless betrayers of morally pure men.[46] Nineteenth-century Americans saw morality tales as pure dichotomies and had few tools to deal with a story where both parties had erred. William's public loss of control made it easy for people to cast him in the role of offender, while Kate's private transgressions created an imaginative space where people could think of her as the innocent party. Unsurprisingly, politics would play a large a part in determining culpability for the imbroglio.

THE COVER-UP: POLITICS AND SACRIFICE

Newspapers almost immediately speculated that there was "an agreement, either tacit or expressed, on the part of those who know personally anything about the encounter to say nothing about it."[47] Later, when silence failed, each actor told a different version of that summer's events, creating a twisted tale of wrangling for political supremacy that pitted the New York and Rhode Island political machines against the Sprague fortune. Each faction attempted to exculpate the players they championed, and in so doing they obscured the events at Canonchet for over a century. The cover-up began in Narragansett when Kate ensured Linck's cooperation, and in Providence when Conkling, after checking into the Narragansett Hotel, made his way to Senator Henry B. Anthony's house.[48]

One of the great powers in Rhode Island, Anthony had long contended with the Spragues for what one newspaper called the "chief honors in that lilliputian state."[49] The son of a cotton manufacturer, Anthony became the editor for the *Providence Journal* in 1838 and turned it into the most influential newspapers in the state. The social authority he and his newspaper gained made the paper a rallying point for conservative interests during the Dorr Rebellion (1842) and ultimately made Anthony governor at the tender age of thirty-four. Elected to the U.S. Senate in 1858, Anthony served his own interests and his country until his death in 1884, making him the most senior member of that body for over a decade. Called "a scrupulous trafficker in votes," Anthony ruled Rhode Island with the motto, "What are we here for if not to get offices?"[50]

In spite of Anthony's political ascendancy, the Spragues had possessed the economic advantage in Rhode Island, at least until the panic of 1873 leveled the playing field. One newspaper inadvertently (or so it was designed to appear) linked the Sprague-Anthony power struggle to the cover-up. On the same page as a story about the Narragansett affair ran this tidbit: "The great men of Rhode Island select various methods of gratifying their ambition. Mr. Anthony and his crowd keep on top by the disenfranchisement of thirty or forty percent of their fellow citizens. Mr. Sprague has decided that the dominating influence of the shot-gun shall keep him from oblivion."[51] Anthony's place in the cover-up has been obscured—a not unremarkable fact considering that even one of his admirers admitted that Anthony "was content to do his share in accomplishing public results, and leave to others whatever fame or glory might result from having accomplished them."[52]

The day after Conkling arrived at Anthony's house, Anthony's primary henchman, Nelson W. Aldrich, sent a telegraph to Professor Linck. Aldrich, a Rhode Island congressman, had worked his way up from clerk in a grocers firm to partner in that firm, then president of the First National Bank, and finally top man at the Providence Board of Trade. His political career had been assisted by his considerable personal wealth, his wife's inheritance, and Anthony's favor. The Anthony faction had installed Aldrich in the U.S. House the year before the imbroglio at Canonchet. The handsome Aldrich, with his classic nineteenth-century sideburns and mustache, acted as point man for the cover-up, a service for which Anthony would later reward him with a seat in the U.S. Senate.

The scandal at Canonchet quickly became as much about public politics as about the private peccadilloes of a few public people. Aldrich and Anthony had good reason to get involved, for not only did they want supreme control over Rhode Island, but they supported Conkling and his New York political machine. Roscoe hoped to place one of his men in the New York governor's mansion that fall, and, if he passed that test of power, attempt the Republican nomination for president. With both the New York and national Republican conventions fast approaching, Conkling's political future depended on keeping him out of the Canonchet scandal.

But the Anthony/Aldrich camp had another compelling reason for attempting to control any damage to Roscoe's reputation. After 1873 the Journal Ring increasingly dominated Rhode Island. Members of the ring included Henry B. Anthony, still a majority owner of the *Providence Journal;* Nelson Aldrich; Ambrose Burnside, Rhode Island's junior senator; and George W. Danielson, the *Journal*'s current editor. Few state machines more adroitly manipulated the Republican Party or bought more votes in Gilded Age America than the Journal Ring.[53] These men could ill afford to pass up such a heaven-sent opportunity to finish off their main rival for control of Rhode Island—the man who had been a thorn in their side since his fortune put him at the governor's desk almost twenty years before.[54]

The day after the first confrontation, Kate went to Providence, where she installed herself and her family at the very same hotel that had received Conkling the previous afternoon. Strangely enough, though different newspapers reported the whereabouts of Kate and Roscoe at different times, no one kept close enough score to notice that both of them resided, albeit briefly, at the same hotel. Conkling did take the boat to New York and check into the Fifth Avenue Hotel, but not until the following day.[55] The two had to have come in contact with each other, though privately. Saturday, then, found Linck, Kate, and Roscoe all in Providence cooperating with William's political enemies. Kate clearly staked herself out in opposition to her husband from this point forward.

Anthony and Aldrich acted quickly. They sent Professor Linck to see George Danielson, and together the men concocted a story that "gave the world the impression that Mr. Conkling was a much abused man and innocent of the charges gossipers had already begun to make against him."[56] The story also put William in an extremely bad light. Having cooperated with Danielson, Linck applied to the editor for advice "as to whether it was best to get out a writ for the Governor's arrest, charging him with assault."[57] Not wanting to see the thin tissue of Linck's story torn by close scrutiny or to draw more attention to the affair by encouraging the arrest of a former governor, Danielson sent Linck to a lawyer, E. H. Hazard, for advice. This move represented a masterful stroke of misdirection, for Hazard was one of William's most intimate friends.[58] Naturally, Hazard discouraged Linck from bringing charges against William, warning the tutor that "Sprague's great influence, together with the money he could command, and the great cost he [Linck] would be put to, would make it rather embarrassing for him."[59] Thus, ironically, the Anthony camp's efforts to shield Conkling inadvertently protected their enemy as well.

After sending a copy of Linck's statement to Kate for her revision, Danielson printed the statement in the Sunday edition of the *Journal*. Tortuous in its convolutions, Linck's and Danielson's multicolumn story contained a clever mix of real and fictional events designed to obscure the truth. Danielson's prefatory remarks claimed that "it appears that Gov. Sprague has a violent antipathy towards a German gentleman . . . ordered him from the house, and loading a gun, it is said, even attempted to shoot him." As to Conkling's role in the disturbance, this first version claimed that he "was at the Spragues' house during this situation, but saw nothing of it, as he was in the library." But since this was not a heroic enough portrayal of their man, the editor added, "There was an invalid gentleman in the party of guests and Senator Conkling took him in his arms and removed him to the carriage." Conkling also supposedly soothed all the frightened ladies, sent them away in a carriage, and then manfully walked the mile and a half to Narragansett. Linck's statement, which follows these remarks, makes no mention whatsoever of Conkling, though it does go into excruciating detail about the professor's dealings with the Spragues. The statement begins with a June 20 letter engaging Linck's services and proceeds through all of his movements in July. A *Journal* reader could learn how Willie did on his exams, that Linck sometimes felt "extremely lonesome," and that Canonchet seemed "gloomy" that summer. The governor comes and goes throughout the narrative, always combative and ungentlemanly, while "Mrs. S." appears as a cool voice of reason and Linck himself is revealed as an innocent victim of the governor's ire.

Newspapers from New York to Ohio picked up the *Journal* version of the events and printed them as gospel, but the story did not stand up to scrutiny. The *New York World* headlined "No German Teacher Concerned" the next day, and other major newspapers soon followed.[60] Narragansett residents like W. C. Clarke and Mr. Wood appeared eager to tell newspaper correspondents what they saw, and both assured the press that they could recognize Conkling on sight. Even at this early date the paper added its deduction about the source of the false story: "The whole affair would most likely have passed off without comment had not some foolish person invented and sent to the Associated Press a preposterous story about it. . . . Senator Conkling or his friends seem to have been able not only to procure the transmission of false information through the channels of the Associated Press, but also to control the columns of nearly every one of the New York journals."[61] The first effort to disguise the scandal had failed.

The Conkling conspirators next tried another tack. The *Providence Journal* claimed it had received a private letter from Kate to "a friend." Danielson lamented, "We deeply regret that any exigency should have arisen which seems to any person to demand or warrant the publication of a statement of such a painful nature." This disclaimer out of the way, Anthony's paper published a second version of the preceding Friday's events. Although long, Kate's letter deserves to be reprinted in full here, both for the truths she tells about her life and for the lies she tells in order to protect her lover's political prospects. Kate's missive also illustrates how she appealed to different cultural tropes of womanhood—victim of an immoral husband, selfless mother, obedient daughter, concerned nurse, and woman with "powerful friends." Careful to claim no power in her own right, Kate nonetheless struck some powerful blows against her husband by impugning his manhood. She wrote:

> As you must have surmised, Gov. Sprague's dissolute life and dissipated habits long ago interrupted our marital relations, though I have striven hard through untold humiliation and pain to hide from the world, for my children's sakes, the true condition of a blighted, miserable domestic life.
>
> About a year ago, even this poor semblance abruptly culminated, after a disgraceful orgy and arrest at Nantasket Beach, with the circumstances of which many people in Rhode Island are now unfamiliar.
>
> I then sought, with my little girls the neighborhood of old friends, and the shelter of my honored father's former home. There, dwelling almost within the shadow of his tomb, I felt more secure, less unprotected. Here

kindly sympathy sought me out, and though covert malice pointed some censorious comments, relief came, and our circumscribed means were adequate to our simple and quiet mode of life.

Gov. Sprague's irregularities having been visited upon him by the trustee administering this embarrassed estate, the contribution toward the maintenance of myself and children, without a word of explanation to me, was suddenly cut down to a palpably inadequate sum. Even this was remitted but for a few months; then, owing to a complete rupture between Gov. Sprague and the trustee, all remittances ceased, and for six months past no money has been contributed toward the maintenance of his family or household by Gov. Sprague. In addition to greater wrongs, trades people to whom he was indebted have been urgent in their demands for payment, but he gave no heed to the indebtedness, even answering when pressed by me to find a way to meet these just demands and relieve me of importunities that "I must look to my powerful Washington friends for aid," and, to my deep distress and mortification, permitted after a long delay, a bill for carriage hire for his mother's use during a visit to me in Washington, to be paid by the gentleman who had recommended to us the stable from which the carriage was hired.

This and other more unmanly exhibitions have been incidental to the past year, while the brutality of recent events—repetitions of similar scenes of violence and outrage enacted in the former years—has finally driven us from the door, and filled the public prints of the country with a scandal too cruel to be endured without redress.

Gov. Sprague's causeless and shameful persecution of the children's teacher is literally true as he tells the story, the real animus being, as confessed, Gov. Sprague's unwillingness to be subjected to the restraint at the table and in the household observances, of the constant presence of a gentleman.

The attempt to implicate Mr. Conkling with this matter is absurd. The two men never met, I believe, have never seen each other.

Gov. Sprague's indecent affront to the guests in the house was most gross and without excuse. Mr. Martin, whom I had met in a very precarious condition of health, en route for Narragansett Pier, I induced to go to Canonchet for quiet and good nursing. He was removed under Gov. Sprague's threats of "murder to be done," at the imminent risk of his life.

Mr. Conkling was, of course, as unconscious as I that Gov. Sprague sought occasion to enact the tragic role of the injured husband; for at their last meeting, not long since, Gov. Sprague had sought from Mr.

Conkling not only legal counsel, but accepted at his hand a favor, such as only the friendliest confidence could warrant.

In his determination to overthrow Mr. Chaffee as trustee, and hoping to join forces with the creditor interest to drive him from his post, Gov. Sprague had carried away from the counting room of A. & W. Sprague the books of the Quidnick Company, refusing to return them.

Mr. Chaffee in turn refused, until these books were returned, to permit Gov. Sprague to hold any business relations with the concern, and of course, refused to permit him to draw any money.

This was the situation of affairs which, by coming to Rhode Island, I had hoped, through some influence or other to bear on Gov. Sprague, to help to set right, and to secure, by some means, a maintenance for the four children for whose wants and needs I have been and am now bearing the undivided burden.

A conference with counsel employed by the firm achieved no results. Prof. Linck, under a contract with me for three months, was neither permitted to perform his duties nor paid and dismissed. We had no ostensible means for living at Canonchet without incurring additional indebtedness, to which I refused to be a party. In this awkward and painful dilemma I requested Mr. Conkling, who had already been consulted by Mr. Sprague, and upon whose judgment and advice I have safely relied in my own matters, to see Gov. Sprague and try to ascertain what point there was in this proposed programme of opposition, and what results were likely to follow that would benefit or provide for the children. Mr. Conkling stopped at Canonchet for this purpose, and was awaiting Gov. Sprague's return to seek an interview with him, when the now notorious outbreak occurred.

If any hostile words were exchanged between Mr. Conkling and Gov. Sprague at Canonchet, they alone know what they were, for no one else heard them. What transpired in the village I do not know beyond what is reported in the sensational accounts given in the newspapers.[62]

In painting a picture of her husband as a sexually immoral man who failed to provide for his family, Kate assailed William's masculinity, emphasizing at the same time the many ways in which she had continued to conform to the normative standards of womanhood. Ironically, she did so in a public forum, in the defense of a man who was not her husband, at a time when a real lady could expect to have her name in the newspaper only when she wed and when she died.

Meanwhile, Linck continued to send letters to the press. To the *New York Sun* he wrote, "I have made my statement to the *Providence Journal* to give a true account of all that happened . . . for my sake, but not to be made a cat's paw of." In a third letter he protested, "If Gov. Sprague, in his mad frenzy, had shot me dead, I would have been spared the mortification of finding myself grossly insulted."[63] Each version of Linck's story varied slightly, giving increasing attention to Conkling's whereabouts that weekend. Rather than convincing anyone, Linck's increasingly strident letters had the opposite effect, making his story appear more ridiculous with each passing August day.

Unlike most of the larger East Coast newspapers, the two main Republican newspapers, the *New York Herald* and *New York Tribune*, maintained silence regarding the affair.[64] In reference to Conkling, the *New York Sun* noted that "the inference is that if they spoke they would tell the truth, and that the truth would be destructive to him."[65] The *Providence Journal* further joined the fray by suggesting that William be removed as trustee of the estate and be replaced by Kate. At one point the *Journal* actually printed a notice "that Mrs. Sprague was appointed by the trustee custodian of Canonchet" and that "Gov. Sprague has no right to remain in the house," a statement that represented no more than wishful thinking on the part of the Anthony/Conkling faction.[66] In reality the bulk of Sprague creditors "warmly opposed" this plan, with one notable exception—Nelson Aldrich. Aldrich held a portion of the Sprague debt through his banking investments, and he hoped Kate would be placed in sole control of Canonchet.[67] Unfortunately for Aldrich and his cohorts, he did not hold enough Sprague paper to effect this particular power shift. Thus it became increasingly clear to the Anthony/Conkling camp that damage control would have to expand beyond mere rhetoric into action. They again called upon the only person who could counter Conkling's growing reputation as the despoiler of women and the American family—Mrs. William Sprague. Five days after she arrived in Providence, Kate went back to Narragansett's Tower Hill Hotel, despite the fact that she had told many people she feared for her life if she was left alone with her husband.[68]

Kate arranged an afternoon meeting with William. Her lawyer, Mr. Thompson, accompanied William to the house of Mr. Hale, a local Republican and conductor of the Little Narragansett Pier Railroad. Miss Emma Fosdick (probably the children's governess) accompanied Kate to the meeting, while Kate's cousin Ralston Skinner stayed with the children. Mr. Hale described the meeting as "stormy," though William, for once, was "not under the influence of liquor." William accused his wife of poisoning the children's minds against him and using Linck to alienate young Willie's affections. He demanded custody of his children, declaring himself "deeply wrapped up" in their welfare.[69] No law could keep him from his children, he insisted, and they would never leave him again "so long as he was willing to pay for their support."[70]

Kate countered that William had acted "with general brutality" toward the family on numerous occasions and had even "presented a loaded pistol at her head." They squabbled about Kate's infidelity, she denying everything. Nonetheless, Thompson advised her to return to Canonchet. The lawyer summoned Ralston, who surrendered the children to their father. William took them and left for Canonchet. By nightfall Kate succumbed to the pressure and, accompanied by Thompson, Skinner, and Miss Fosdick, followed her children to Canonchet. She either feared for the children's safety more than her own or she had some other reason for returning that was unrelated to her children.[71]

Kate's actions may support the press's claims that Conkling and Kate conspired to send her back to her husband to quell the scandal—in effect sacrificing her to Roscoe's political career.[72] As a Narragansett correspondent put it, "It is difficult to find any one here who knows anything about this matter who does not declare that when Mrs. Sprague returned to Canonchet, she did so against her own wishes and merely because she desired to comply with the request of some influential person whom she is anxious to please."[73] Coincidentally, Conkling held the fort at the Fifth Street Hotel in New York until Wednesday, 14 August. Then, the day before Kate went back to her husband, Roscoe left his central base of operations and returned to Utica and took up residence with his wife, Julia, something he rarely did. He had done all the damage control he could do.

Many people failed to understand why Kate had returned to Canonchet. The press, Washington gossip, and her biographers all excoriated her as a duplicitous, lying, cheating, and generally untrustworthy person. Recalling her recent letter to the press, critics wondered how she could return to a "blighted and miserable domestic life." One newspaper even reminded readers that Kate had "four times been made a happy mother," a fact that ruled out the possibility of domestic abuse in the minds of many Victorian

Americans. Kate's class status made it difficult for many people to think of the Sprague household as violent. Late-nineteenth-century Americans generally believed that only poor men abused their wives and children.[74] Kate's relationship with Roscoe further confused the issue because she could not be portrayed as a virtuous victim of a debased man. In this black-and-white world, the Sprague family story was shaded in gray. "Fortunately," the *New York World* piously reasoned, "women are not held so sternly as men to the logical outcome of their angry rhetoric."[75] Society did not protect women when they stepped outside the bounds of middle-class respectability, as Kate had done with Roscoe.

William's reason for forcing Kate back to Canonchet seems more obscure. Raised in a society that viewed women as civilly under the control of their husbands, William undoubtedly based his sense of himself on his ability to conform to a nineteenth-century notion of marital custodianship. A real man controlled not only his wife's behavior and sexuality but quite literally had legal custody of her body.[76] It was one thing for William to have his wife privately live a separate life, but the public exposure of their informal separation may have forced him to reassert his physical control over Kate and their children—particularly when she had convincingly and publicly charged him with failure to provide for his family.

The family violence that encircled the Sprague family illustrates the perils of embracing the companionate family model as empowering to nineteenth-century women. Men abuse women and children, in part, because they view them as property—as symbols of male power and status. The family conflicts from which William's violence arose were about power relations within the marriage.[77] William's violence against Kate served to coerce her subservience and to force her to acquiesce to his view of her as a means to political and social gain, and Kate's continued resistance only fueled William's anxiety about his inability to control his family. In this context, William's abuse served to reassert what he viewed as his failing masculinity. Companionate marriage norms did little to ameliorate male power, particularly in the light of the fact that Victorian society had difficulty acknowledging abuse outside the working class. Indeed, the rise in the last third of the century of activist organizations devoted to addressing domestic violence among the working class suggests not only the presence of considerable family dysfunction but many people's recognition of the failure of companionate family ideals in a deeply unequal society.[78] Kate had little recourse for her situation. Trained to think of herself as a political handmaiden, she had embraced that role and found power in it. Although she acted that role as much for herself as for Salmon, William, and Roscoe, she had nonetheless spent a lifetime serving the public and private needs of political men. She went back to Canonchet because she could not yet imagine for herself a course of action independent of public and private politics. Once Kate had put herself under William's control she would find she could not rely on anyone to rescue her. She would have to do it herself.

THE GREAT ESCAPE

Late on Thursday night, 14 August, William admitted his wife to Canonchet, though he turned away her companions Fosdick and Skinner. His reasons for doing so soon became clear. William held his wife prisoner at Canonchet. He locked Kate in her room, denied admittance to friends and servants, and opened every telegram and letter that came for her. He further instructed the servants of the house to take no orders from Mrs. Sprague, though this order seemed only to provoke those loyal to Kate to offer clandestine help. One maid, caught carrying a message from her mistress out of the house, lost her job. William held his wife not only with physical force but with threats as well. He declared that he would "under no circumstances at all allow Mrs. Sprague to take charge of the children," though she was free to leave at any time, providing she left alone.[79] William disingenuously claimed that Kate could see anyone she wished and professed that he kept her isolated only to "insure her peace and quiet." To this end he forbade her to correspond with her friends. Such husbandly solicitude left Kate in "a very excited condition."[80]

A number of newspapers carried the story of Kate's imprisonment. Paradoxically, William found he had to cooperate with the Conkling faction to justify his behavior. The weekend immediately after Kate's return, Sprague and three lawyers allowed a *New York Sun* correspondent to interview Kate. The reporter first spoke to William, who asserted that he did not keep his wife under "lock and key" but only kept her "quiet . . . to induce a frame of mind in which she would come to understand her future position to him." In her sitting room at the top of Canonchet's winding oak staircase, Kate received her first guest since returning home. Pale but composed, she told yet another version of her story:

I have sent for you because I wish to correct some false impressions which have gone abroad in regard to my conduct at Thursday's meeting. I did not charge my husband, as has been stated, with untruthfulness, nor did I make the verbal attacks upon him which I have been represented as doing. On the contrary, I bore with meekness the unmanly sneers and reproaches that he showered upon me, not responding save when my children's relations to me were touched upon. I have my story to tell, and when the truth of this terrible business is known I know that I shall be justified. God knows that I have no reason to fear the truth, though for 13 long years my life has been a constant burden and drag upon me. For years I have had this thing weighing upon me, and have striven with all my might to stand between my husband's wrong-doing and the public. I have done it for the sake of my children, not for any affection that existed between us, for there has been none for years. This whole miserable affair, into which Senator Conkling has been wantonly dragged without a particle of reason or excuse, originated in a business transaction between himself and my husband, of so trivial a nature that you would be astonished that any sane man could consider it a source of jealousy. For years I have known Senator Conkling just as, from the position of my father and of my husband, I have know scores of other public men in Washington.

She went on to describe some relatively obscure business dealings between Conkling and her husband, matters which had required that Roscoe pay some of William's debts. She also described how the senator offered economic assistance to her when her husband refused to support her or the children. She hastened to add that she had refused all offers as improper and that "there is not a word of truth in all of these atrocious reports. Mr. Conkling never paid me any attention that a wife could not honorably receive from her husband's friend, and it is false to say otherwise. Mr. Sprague was simply worked upon by his business troubles, which had been culminating for years, and by his indulgences in strong drink. He regarded everyone, no matter how honorable, who was a friend of mine, as an interloper and intriguer against him." Kate continued by describing the preceding Friday's events yet again, though this latest account varied considerably from the original story she had helped to concoct with Linck. She placed Conkling at the scene and described the confrontation between the two, continuing to absolve Conkling of any wrongdoing. She then attempted to obscure Conkling's role in the aftermath of the affair: "There is another falsehood that has been extensively circulated, and that is that Mr. Conkling indorsed [*sic*] that statement which attributed the whole affair to my husband's hatred of Mr. Linck. I know from gentlemen who were present when that dispatch was written that Mr. Conkling disapproved of it. He was neither sought to conceal nor to spread any knowledge he possesses of the wretched matter." Having essentially admitted that the first version of story had been nothing more than fiction, Kate also contradicted several other stories about her involvement with Conkling. She vehemently asserted that "these outrageous slanders" represented "monstrous falsehoods" and concluded the interview. Kate never spoke to members of the press again about the Narragansett affair, and in fact she published no other information on the "true character" of the imbroglio except that which she included in her divorce petition.

Kate's reticence suggests that her bouts of volubility were not of her own making or for her own benefit. Instead, Kate made a conscious choice to sacrifice her public reputation and put herself in physical danger in order to protect Conkling's political fortunes. The possibility also exists that William allowed his wife this interview on the condition that she excuse him from any wrongdoing, which Kate singularly failed to do. Certainly William was not the kind of man to allow his wife repeated opportunities to accuse him of unmanly and barbarous behavior, particularly while under his control. We can only guess at the private ramifications of this last interview.

For the next two weeks no word of Kate issued from Canonchet. At the beginning of her second week of imprisonment, with assistance from her driver Thomas Handy, she began surreptitiously moving valuables out of the house. Handy shipped at least two trunks containing jewelry and personal effects to New York, while another servant collected packages Kate left hidden about the house and took them into town.[81] Meanwhile, in the face of his wife's intransigence, William's self-control gradually melted away. One night at the end of the second week, after a night of hard drinking, he came home in a particularly violent temper. He found Kate in the children's room, helping the nurse dress the three girls. When he knocked for admittance, Kate called, "Don't come in."[82] Incensed at this command, William rushed into the room and shouted, "I'll show you who is master here." While the children screamed in fear, he grabbed Kate around the neck and shoulders, dragged her across the room, and attempted to throw her out a second-story window.[83] Kate, with the help of the nurse, successfully resisted his assault, and the gallant war hero retired to his room.

Believing that her husband had a sailing engagement the next afternoon, Kate ordered trunks packed in preparation for an immediate escape. Unfortunately, William canceled his sailing plans, either because he suspected Kate's plan or because he was simply too hung over to brave the waves of Narragansett Bay. The next morning Handy carried a bundle of letters and telegrams out of the house while Kate planned her escape for the afternoon, when William usually went down to the beach. Again, he foiled her plans by returning from his bathing venture sooner than usual. Later that afternoon, while William lay sleeping on the front piazza, Kate, the nurse, and the three girls, assisted by the aptly named Handy, made their escape out the back of the mansion. [84] Not more than twenty minutes later, William discovered Kate's precipitous escape and, in an action oddly reminiscent of the confrontation that had started the whole affair, gave chase. He raced his horse into Narragansett, where he accosted the train conductor, Mr. Hale, asking, "Have you lugged off my children?" The mud-spattered former governor searched the train, remounted his horse, and raced back along the Kingston Road, sending Willie toward Wakefield. Their quarry eluded capture, disappearing as surely and quietly as a fox down a hole.[85]

When Kate escaped from Canonchet, she also escaped her husband. This action, as much as the events of the previous weeks, placed her outside the bounds of respectability. Just as William had a right to keep his wife in his house under the legal tenets of marital custodianship, society expected that Kate would conform to her husband's control. Men's rights to restrain their wives have been compared, by both historians and nineteenth-century reformers, to the Fugitive Slave Act (part of the Compromise of 1850), which gave slave owners the right to compel fugitive slaves to return to bondage. Although the law did not actually compel women to return to their husbands, it did provide negative reinforcement for rebellious wives, often denying them alimony, child custody, or dower property. These realities explain why Kate had to clandestinely escape—she was stealing herself in a society that did not approve of married women's self-emancipating. Her actions must have had tremendous resonance for the daughter of Salmon P. Chase, the noted prosecutor of numerous fugitive slave cases.

Newspaper reports had Kate making off on a fast yacht from Newport, or to Boston by a relay of carriage horse, even going as far as Jamaica. Where she went remains a mystery. There is no mystery, though, in the accumulated evidence of domestic abuse revealed by the affair at Canonchet. William bore many of the hallmarks of a domestic abuser. He had the ability to be charming and manipulative in order to get what he wanted and hostile when faced with failure; he felt threatened by both major and minor changes in his life, particularly in the financial and political realm; he also exhibited a strong need to control situations and an intolerance of the disparity in status that existed between himself and Kate (or his own perception of that disparity); and, most significant, William was an alcoholic. Both alcohol and stress act as characteristic rationalizing agents for abusers, and this, combined with the fact that alcohol acts as a depressant, inhibiting adherence to social mores, makes a potent tonic for family violence.[86]

Domestic violence takes many forms—physical, sexual, and emotional—and few abusers limit themselves to only one category of violence. William proved no exception. Aspects of the violence that took place at Canonchet that August, as well as his attacks on Kate in 1877 and 1878, prove that William was no stranger to physical abuse, though what other episodes of physical abuse Kate endured can only be guessed. The same can be said for sexual abuse. William withheld affection from Kate throughout their marriage. In his 1869 speeches he publicly humiliated her in sexualized terms, and he made no secret of his extramarital infidelities. Marital rape, in an age that had no category as such, eludes the record. We simply cannot know if William raped Kate.

The affair at Canonchet also illuminates the emotional abuse William leveled at Kate. William engaged in a number of different kinds of emotional abuse. First, he isolated his wife by sequestering her in Canonchet. Second, he engaged in "monopolization of perception" when he isolated her, and he used the children as his personal possessions with which to torture their mother. Third, he used threats, both specific and vague, to gain Kate's cooperation and denied Kate power over her own life. Last, as the meeting with the *Sun* reporter attests, William occasionally indulged his wife, then reverted to isolation and violence, thus encouraging Kate to hope the abuse would cease. Psychological abusers may also keep their victims in financial isolation.[87] Kate cited time and again her financial strain, and though her biographers charge her with frivolous and exorbitant spending, it seems clear that the Spragues were anything but destitute. Even after

1873 William could afford to travel, drink in town, frolic with women who were not his wife, and consider railroad investments. He could have drawn a salary from A. & W. Sprague Manufacturing but chose not to. He also chose not to economically support his wife and children. There can be little doubt that even one hundred years before psychologists started defining domestic abuse, William understood its power and nuances and used it to batter his wife again and again.

As a couple, Kate and William fit other hallmarks of domestic violence. Abused women most often lack strong female support and kin networks. Kate, who had no cohesive extended family, no living parent, and was estranged from her sister, certainly found herself in a vulnerable position. Conversely, male abusers most commonly have well-developed male alliances and control of family resources. William, who moved in the manly worlds of business and politics and who had a considerable family with whom he spent large amounts of time, had at his disposal far more economic and familial resources than did his wife. William's sense of his own manliness also exacerbated his abusive tendencies. As he increasingly came to believe that Kate's behavior threatened his patriarchal birthright, he engaged in a "compulsive masculinity" whereby he used violence to establish his superiority over Kate. More than simply uncontrollable, drunken rage, William's abuse may be framed as intentionally dominating behavior.[88]

What turned out to be tragedy for those personally involved seemed less so to their Gilded Age contemporaries. Reading day after day about the scandal allowed Victorian Americans to contemplate the forbidden. The story's sexual and violent components only fueled the public's fascination with the scandal. Penny papers like the *Sun* and *World* in New York sensationalized the affair, but even serious newspapers covered these events of August 1879. The press often gave the drama a comedic cast. Far away in St. Paul, Minnesota, one paper described the matter as a melodramatic farce: "The Conkling-Sprague affair belongs to the largest class of scandalous domestic intrigues, to which the three parties are a somewhat worthless husband, a disappointed and neglected wife and a masher. . . . The masher is essentially the same creature, whether he is senator or a barber's clerk, and the generic similarity is particularly apparent if, being a senator, he affects the external appearance and manner of a barber's clerk. He is a curious combination of peacock and goat, with the ingredients variously proportioned according to temperament and social rank."[89] The contrast between the simultaneous seriousness and levity with which the press treated the story of the affair at Canonchet speaks to the manner in which Victorian society treated sexual matters. The Spragues had forced an intensely private part of Victorian life into the public forum, had transgressed the normative boundaries of the companionate family. The reaction of the press suggests that few cultural tools existed for understanding such a clear case of domestic violence and political maneuvering rolled into one. The decades following the imbroglio did little to clarify the matter. Rather, commentators often cite the story as a fantastic example of the social chaos that could surround a "woman gone bad." The multitudes of meanings ascribed to this story have depended upon the social and temporal locations of the teller, the interpretive conventions, and the differing needs of communities of readers. Making fun of the imbroglio served much the same cultural need as did its more serious treatment—humor countered a perceived resistance to patriarchal norms and class categories, making the whole imbroglio seem silly and beneath critical attention. The actors in this domestic drama/farce, though, found little humor in their situations. They all approached the autumn of 1879 with the utmost seriousness, attempting to survive the scandal with their reputations and futures intact. Each tried to act as if his or her political status remained intact. That Kate, William, the children, and Roscoe would never escape the stigma of the shotgun was not immediately apparent.

SEVEN

"Extreme Cruelty and Gross Misbehavior"
Divorce and Politics,
1800

~

Discontent is the want of self-reliance: it is infirmity of the will.
Ralph Waldo Emerson

WINNING AND LOSING DIVORCE

It did not take long for the ramifications of 1879 to come to light. In December 1880 Kate sued William for divorce. In her petition to the Rhode Island courts, she accused her husband of having "committed adultery with divers women at divers places and times," of having repeatedly assaulted her, of having tried to kill her by throwing her from a window, and of suffering from "habitual drunkenness." She added that William had falsely accused her of "gross improprieties with other men." He had claimed to not be the father of her children, had imprisoned her within their Narragansett mansion, and had sought "frequently to have criminal intercourse with the female domestics and guests in the family, causing them to leave the house."[1] Kate requested reasonable alimony, custody of their four children, and the right to return to her maiden name (see appendix A for her complete divorce petition). A month later William countersued his wife. His divorce petition alleged that Kate had "been on terms of close and improper intimacy with other men" and "that she had willfully and without cause deserted the bed and board of your petitioner," while "absenting herself from his home and household for long periods of time." William also claimed that she had failed to attend to the domestic duties "incumbent on her as a wife and mother" (see appendix B).[2]

In the ensuing battle, Kate won her divorce. She received no alimony, no settlement from the still considerable Sprague estate, and no child support for their three daughters, of whom she gained custody. Willie chose to remain with his father, preferring loose-living Dad to the discipline his mother required. During the last decades of the nineteenth century Kate lived off the proceeds from the sale of her china, paintings, statuary, jewelry, and even dresses—a financial remedy once sought by Mary Todd Lincoln. Even before her divorce many Washingtonians knew of the precariousness of Kate's position. In 1879, before the fall scandal, Roscoe sponsored a bill exempting Edgewood from future taxes "together with all interest and penalties now due and unpaid." [3] But even without property taxes Kate gradually became impoverished. By the 1890s she had exchanged the brilliant social life of Washington for the company of her dogs and occasionally her children and grandchildren on a decaying suburban farm.

William, on the other hand, continued to live at Canonchet. Ten months after the divorce he married Dora Inez Weed Calvert, a singer of dubious talents twenty-eight years his junior. [4] His new bride reportedly spent over $30,000 to redecorate Canonchet, and in 1890 the state of Rhode Island assessed the estate's value at $120,000. [5] Inez had the resources to redecorate. A local newspaper reported, "The ceiling of the sleeping room was adorned with a panel named 'Love Awake,' while the chief wall panels featured 'Music of the Sea.' The bathroom showed an ocean scene at sunset in blue and pink, with mermaids sporting in the water while Love rode a dolphin." [6] William ran for office one more time, though with a spectacular lack of success. [7] However frustrated his attempts at resuscitating his political career might have been, William lived a comfortable and economically secure life with his new family.

How did Kate, who had once shone so brightly, fall so far, and why did William, an alcoholic failure with predilections to domestic violence, continue to live fairly well? The prominence of the actors in this public drama makes the Sprague divorce unique, while the outcome of the divorce largely mirrors the fate of divorced men and women in Victorian America. In some ways, though, all nineteenth-century divorces may be viewed as exceptional, for each marital breakdown represented a failure of domestic ideals as well as an individual failure of gender roles. Because divorce undermined the contractual aspect of marriage, it also represented a breakdown of legal order. Divorce suits gave Americans a public forum for discussions about acceptable and unacceptable adult behavior, clarifying community norms of manhood and womanhood. [8] Both Kate and William used their divorce to define themselves as the injured and respectable party and to indict the other for failing respectability.

One female journalist blamed Roscoe's enemies for the bad press Kate suffered in the years surrounding her divorce: "Year after year, this accomplished woman sat in the gallery, apparently deeply interested in the debates, without the slightest departure from the most rigid decorum. In the late years, she was rarely seen without one of more of her children. History is full of martyred women who have been used to crush obnoxious men. Conkling had enemies who wished to crush him. They used slander to bring him into disrepute with his constituents and destroy his hope of the presidency." [9] In reality Kate hardly needed special enemies to attain martyrdom; as a publicly political woman she had always inhabited a tenuous space, one she maintained by virtue of her political pedigree and refined appearance. Kate's "rigid decorum" had justified her womanly interest in political debates. Once the events of August 1879 came to light, she became sexualized to a degree that no amount of social civility could disguise. The scandal highlighted Kate as a female physical body, susceptible to animal passions, and thus it ruled out the possibility that she might maintain her position in the rational realm of public life. [10]

If the view the Canonchet imbroglio afforded of Kate as a physical body disqualified her from much of public life, William's role in the scandal accomplished much the same, but for different reasons. Just as the facade of civility allowed Kate entrée into elite politics, so too did it underwrite William's public manliness. What his repeated misbehaviors failed to do, his reckless disregard for rules of conduct accomplished. By chasing Roscoe through the streets with a shotgun, particularly while drunk, William evidenced a fatal lack of self-mastery. His behavior made him appear a slave to his baser appetites, and nineteenth-century Americans did not recognize slaves, real or metaphorical, as "real men." In effect, the Canonchet affair disqualified William and Kate as legitimate political actors, for both had exposed traits that damaged their claims to citizenship. Kate's downfall, though, stemmed from the exposure of her physical femaleness, while William's came from the disappearance of his manhood. [11] In essence, one had to be a "categorical man" to act as a political person, and both Kate and William had fallen out of that realm.

In the spring of 1880, months before she filed for divorce, Kate hosted a luncheon at Edgewood for Washington's female journalists. Emily Edson

Briggs, a noted society columnist, wrote of Kate, "No woman in Washington excels her as a lady 'to the manner born,' or can surpass her in the graces which make her the reigning queen of her own home." Evidently Kate pulled out all the stops in an effort to prove that although she might be down, she was not altogether out. As Briggs described the event:

> High Noon. The heavy doors are opened displaying an elegant table in the center of a perfect dining room, recalling thoughts of the royal days of sunny France; ancient Gobelin tapestry once in the palace of Marie Antoinette. Persian rugs conceal the inlaid floor. . . . An elaborate service of silver and gold upon the sideboard; upon the table, Irish damask soft and sheeny as satin, around which are placed eight heavy mahogany chairs. All are seated, the hostess leading the way and taking her stand at the head of the table, while her ebony assistant stands at her right, a white-gloved, machine-like Ethiopian who understands at a glance from the Princesses eye. The courses follow in silent procession.
>
> French bouillon in bowls, gems brought from the heart of Persia, made from the dust of garnets from the Palace of the Shah—that had found their way into the Chase home; oyster patties served on plates, each a handsome hand-painted portrait by a French artist—one a head of Lafayette, another of Napoleon I—which Mrs. Sprague had secured from a sale of royal pottery belonging to a reigning family of the old world; sweetbreads on plates designed by Kate Chase as a present to the Chief Justice, made at a celebrated pottery near Paris, no two alike, and each embellished by a gorgeous bouquet.[12]

The luncheon, while a great success, proved an immense show of false bravado, a last hurrah for the once reigning queen of Washington. No amount of terrapin, Virginia ham, or charlotte russe could mask the "visible gulf, like a hideous skull at a feast, between the days of the young millionaire's wife . . . and the cold bereavements and change of fickle fortune of today."[13] The glowing reports of the luncheon even may have generated a backlash, for the picture of wealth that Kate created seemed to substantiate William's claims of his wife's profligacy.

Not long after the luncheon, Kate attempted to regain many of the personal items she had left at Canonchet after her hasty departure. She wanted not only clothing and jewels but also her personal papers. William refused her trustee, Robert Thompson, admission to the estate, claiming that Kate had already packed all of her belongings and transferred them to Edgewood. In the face of William's intransigence, Zechariah Chaffee, trustee for A. & W. Sprague, promised to "take charge of Canonchet, and, if possible, eject the ex-Senator." [14] On 6 November 1880 Thompson attempted to gain entry to the house from the beach side, but fifteen-year-old Willie saw him, drew his pistol, and fired. Five days later the local sheriff arrested Willie for "murderous assault" on his mother's trustee. William posted a two-hundred-dollar bond for the boy and took him back to Canonchet. At the trial, three witnesses supported Thompson's version of the events. In his defense Willie insisted that he had only been "firing the pistol for fun" and had, in any event, missed his mother's agent by shooting over his head. Willie's friend (or accomplice) corroborated his story. The Narragansett judge dismissed Thompson's case for insufficient evidence. [15] Kate never did recover all of her belongings. The *New York Times* suggested that she and her lawyers knew there were no belongings to reclaim and had merely been attempting to make William look bad, but the evidence suggests that this interpretation is incorrect. Soon after Thompson's unsuccessful foray to Canonchet, William repurchased some of the household items that had recently been auctioned to meet his debts, among them Salmon P. Chase's signed commission from Abraham Lincoln appointing him chief justice of the Supreme Court. [16] It does appear that Kate left some of her things at Canonchet and that she sincerely believed they were still there.

TIMING DIVORCE: PARTISAN POLITICS AND THE LAW

Kate did not file her divorce petition with the Washington County Supreme Court in Rhode Island until December 1880. [17] The multifaceted explanation for the time lag between her flight from Canonchet and her filing for divorce involves a complicated web of national politics, post–Civil War divorce reform, and child custody laws. Most important, Kate's timing for the divorce suit depended upon the vagaries of Roscoe Conkling's political career. By the 1870s and 1880s Roscoe's considerable efforts bent toward the development and continuation of his political machine, upon which rested his future control of the U.S. Senate and New York politics. He was, as well, in pursuit of the Republican presidential nomination, while feuding with the current president. Rutherford B. Hayes had been attempting to reform the civil service (and in so doing appoint his own men to civil service posts) since taking office in 1877. Hayes and others believed that the New York Custom House stood as a model of an institution that needed to be reformed. The president dismissed three New York customs officials, among them Roscoe's close friend and henchman Chester Arthur, and in February 1879 Roscoe failed to block the installation of Hayes's replacements.[18] This struggle between the president, whom Roscoe called "His Fraudulency," and the New York Republican machine represented an attack on Roscoe's political power that he could ill afford to ignore. In fact, Hayes was probably less averse to machine politics than he was to Conkling personally, who had refused to campaign for him in 1876. In taking the New York Custom House out of Conkling's hands, Hayes and other like-minded Republicans took the first steps toward crippling the New York senator's political power base.

With the attacks on Roscoe's patronage power and his well-publicized role in the affair at Canonchet in the summer of 1879, the New York senator had much at stake in the presidential election of 1880. Conkling's silence on the Sprague affair, though an attempt to deny accusations by declining to dignify them with a response, had left his reputation in tatters. Ditty after ditty appeared in newspapers, each lampooning the Senate's Adonis as a coward and a fool. The following appeared in the midst of the Canonchet episode, portraying the New York senator in a light that could not possibly have helped his political aspirations.

> *The good ship Conkling bore*
> *All down on a friendly coast,*
> *And as it neared the shore,*
> *With its sails and banners spread*
> *And a clear sky overhead*
> *And sailors chaff'd,*
> *And many a toast and many a boast*
> *Went up from the nobby craft.*
>
> *A man stood out on a pier*
> *With a Shot-gun in his hand*
> *And cried "git out of here!*
> *I say just what I mean,*
> *This shot-gun quarantine—*
> *You shall not wait*
> *To fumigate—*
> *Your try to land or to anchor and*

I'd scuttle you sure as fate!"

To the shot-gun on the pier
That good ship Conkling wailed,
"There is no infection here,
I am as pure as the noonday sky
And I pri'thee let me by!"
But the shot-gun swore
It was "git" or "gore;"
And the Conkling quailed and back it sailed
To its distant and native shore.[19]

Silly but dangerous, this rhyme suggests how tenuous Roscoe's political power had become. Any move on Kate's part to file for divorce immediately after her escape would have kept the matter in the papers and foremost in people's minds, finishing the work begun by William's shotgun. By retiring quietly to Edgewood after her escape, Kate gave her lover a chance to recoup his political losses.

For Roscoe, the first order of business was New York's 1879 elections. He wanted to ensure that New Yorkers elected loyal Conkling men to key state offices, most particularly Alonzo Cornell to the governorship. One of Roscoe's most trusted underlings, Cornell desired the position as much as Roscoe needed one of his own men in the governor's mansion. The New York elections tested Roscoe's power, and he must have been pleased when Republicans won every state office but state engineer. But the senator could not help but notice that Tammany Hall boss (and thus Democrat) John Kelly, who had run a third-party campaign, had siphoned off just enough Democratic votes to account for Cornell's victory.[20] This fact, combined with the continuing power vacuum at the custom house and the past summer's scandal, made Roscoe's victory less than decisive.

Next Roscoe attempted to make Ulysses S. Grant, in lieu of himself, the 1880 Republican presidential nominee. In this effort Conkling led the "Stalwarts," men who opposed Hayes's southern policy and civil service reform. The "Half-Breeds," or reform element of the Republican Party, supported civil service reform. The divide in the party, though, relied as much on the enmity between Conkling and Hayes/Blaine men as it did upon ideology. Conkling counted Grant among his closest friends and probably genuinely wanted to see his friend in ascendancy as much as he hoped to restore his own political power by placing an ally in the White House.

It did not take long, however, for Roscoe's camp to realize that both the party and the public would not accept Grant for a third term. At the Chicago convention the nominating seesawed between Grant, James G. Blaine, John Sherman, and others.[21] Conkling and his men worked feverishly for Grant, but they lost several crucial battles over rules to the anti-Grant faction of the party. On the third day of the convention, Kate wrote a remarkable letter to Chester Arthur:

> Dear Genl. Arthur,
>
> I venture to recall myself to you & to tell you in confidence upon which I fully repose, that I am here strictly incognito, our friends being ignorant of my presence in the city—an ignorance I am specially anxious to preserve.
>
> I am with the sister of the Honorable Richard Crowley—but Mr. C—— is not a Delegate & has not succeeded this far in obtaining preferred seating. You will appreciate the interest I feel in the outcome of this convention, & the importance of my preserving my incognito.
>
> My I ask you to see that Miss Corbett and myself have seats, not of course upon the platform, or too forward, but in over the section say O. or P. to the right of the Platform, or D. on the left.
>
> We are now seated where we can neither see nor hear.
>
> Trusting you will not be embarrassed by my request or the confidences it imposes, pray accept my assurances of respect.
>
> Most Cordially yours
> Katherine Chase Sprague[22]

The contents of this letter are stunning for several reasons, among them the fact that Kate continued to involve herself in matters of Republican politics, however clandestinely, after the scandal of the previous summer. Although ostensibly in disguise, she was in Chicago and at the convention. It is difficult to believe that the men at the convention did not know the identity of the veiled woman, but no one exposed her.

Of even greater interest, though, is her reference to Richard Crowley, who was one of Roscoe's most loyal Stalwart lieutenants and a man Roscoe could have visited without undue notice.[23] Although this letter does not clearly state that Kate and Roscoe continued their affair into 1880, it strongly suggests the two had some kind of connection. Roscoe had made several motions the day Kate wrote Arthur, and her letter says she could not hear the speakers. She probably could not hear Roscoe. The chances are also good that Kate knew that Roscoe would make Grant's nominating speech the next day and wanted to be better positioned to hear his oration. In fact, the speech turned out to be one of Conkling's finest. He leapt atop a table and several times evoked wild applause—at one point he had to wait twenty minutes for the clapping and yelling to die down. Unfortunately, the nominating went on into the next day, and by the time the convention began balloting the fervor Roscoe had created for Grant was gone. Impassioned conventioneers had plenty of time to remember the string of scandals that had attended Grant's administration, as well as the informal rule set by George Washington that a man should serve only two terms as president. [24]

Kate and Roscoe and their co-conspirators must have been extremely discreet, for no hint of their continued relationship ever became public. Indeed, most people assumed that the senator had abandoned Kate after 1879, leaving her brokenhearted and alone to face the scandal that had become her life. [25] Nothing could be further from the truth. Instead, Kate traveled to Chicago and was there to watch the ballots seesaw back and forth until finally, on the thirty-sixth ballot, Republicans nominated James A. Garfield as a compromise candidate. Garfield, an old family friend and fellow Ohioan, had once been the beneficiary of Salmon's patronage, but he bore Kate's paramour no particular affection. [26] Roscoe's faction of the Republican Party had been defeated. In an effort to placate the Conkling machine, Garfield offered the vice-presidency to Chester A. Arthur, one of the Conkling men whom Hayes had removed from the New York Custom House. Billy Hudson reported that Arthur's acceptance enraged Roscoe, who regarded Arthur's ascendancy as an inappropriate alignment with the enemy rather than a nod to Conkling's party power. [27]

In November, Garfield won the popular election by ten thousand votes. Upset at his inability to force Grant on the Republican Party, Roscoe refused to campaign for Garfield until he pledged to "reward the men who do the work" in New York. Roscoe waited until September to begin campaigning against the Democratic candidate, Winfield Scott Hancock, but his tardy efforts helped carry New York for the Republicans. Garfield consulted with Conkling about cabinet appointments, promising that Stalwarts would occupy key positions in the new government. His promises would prove empty. [28] Thus, while Conkling hoped his political star might remain in the ascendancy, his politics and association with Kate had begun his eclipse. The shotgun had been engraved on too many minds, a fact that the New Yorker only slowly came to understand. After Garfield's election he wrote to a friend, "A thief breaks into your house, steals your watch and is sent to Sing Sing. The newspaper man breaks into the casket which contains your most precious treasure, our reputation, and goes unscathed before the law." [29] Kate, however, saw the writing on the wall with the results of the presidential election in November 1880 and filed for divorce a month later.

Other events and circumstances probably conspired to make late 1880 a propitious time for Kate to file for divorce. Considering the fact that Roscoe continued to lobby for key political appointments, Kate's timing must have been prompted by issues other than partisan politics. Rhode Island, where Kate would file, had always been a liberal divorce state. As early as the 1640s, the Rhode Island General Assembly involved itself in divorce requests. In 1655 the legislature permitted "a general or town magistrate to grant a bill of divorce." [30] This shift from legislative to judicial divorces marks Rhode Island as well ahead of other states in the adjudication of marital disputes. Maryland, for example, continued to rely on the cumbersome legislative process, with its individual divorce bills, until 1841. [31] By 1747 each county's superior court considered Rhode Island divorce decrees on the grounds of either adultery or desertion. In 1798 the state added impotence, extreme cruelty, and "gross misbehavior and wickedness in either parties repugnant to and in violation of the marriage covenant." [32] These last grounds illustrate the relatively liberal nature of Rhode Island divorce laws, since most states did not begin to allow for omnibus clauses like extreme cruelty or gross misbehavior until the 1870s. [33] By the time Kate filed her request for "reasonable alimony out of the estate of said Sprague," Rhode Island had also been awarding alimony for over eighty years. [34] Thus by midcentury Rhode Island had seven grounds for the dissolution of marriage, five of which Kate would cite in her petition.

In many states, though, the progressive trend in divorce law since the Revolutionary War was partially reversed after the Civil War. Social and economic upheaval caused by the war, combined with a perception of rising divorce rates, caused a movement toward divorce "reform." With its confidence in the social order shaken by cataclysmic violence and a forced refashioning of political and racial institutions, the nation faced the 1870s and 1880s with some anxiety. The Gilded Age was politically conservative, disillusioned by the failures of Reconstruction, and anxious about repeated economic depressions.[35] As localism, laissez-faire, and racism reasserted themselves, Republicans retreated from both social egalitarianism and their broad definition of federal power. Thus, as the 1870s progressed, and into the 1880s, Americans turned away from egalitarian reform, seeking a hiatus from the rigors of the Reconstruction years. Conservative reformers believed that the nation needed to turn its attention away from problems that stemmed from the dissolution of the Union and toward the issues that came from dissolution of marriage.

However much postwar divorce reformers sought to limit divorce as a marital remedy, their efforts were largely unsuccessful. After the Civil War, increasing numbers of Americans ended their marriages in divorce. During the 1870s the U.S. population rose 30.1 percent, while the divorce rate rose a precipitous 79.4 percent. The following decade saw another severe jump; as the population rose 25.5 percent, divorces rose 70.2 percent.[36] Rhode Island, with its relatively liberal divorce laws, was one of six states with a divorce rate of over .75/1,000 population.[37]

Both the notoriety of the Tilton-Beecher affair and the popularity of "divorce novels" like William Dean Howells's *A Modern Instance* (1882) illustrate the tangled nexus between reform rhetoric, public sentiment, and people's lives. Considering the prevailing social climate, Kate may have worried that her chances to obtain an easy divorce in Rhode Island would slip away if she waited any longer. The Rhode Island General Assembly did change state divorce law in 1882. The law stipulated that "divorce from bed, board and cohabitation, until the parties be reconciled, may be granted for any of the causes for which by law a divorce from the bond of marriage may be decreed, and for such other causes as may seem to require the same."[38] This law provided for "bed and board" (*mensa et thoro*) divorces. Unlike complete (*a vinculo*) divorces, bed-and-board divorces functioned as legal separations and did not allow for remarriage. Bed-and-board divorces freed men and women from living together, while continuing men's economic responsibilities for their families and granting *femme sole* authority to wives in business transactions. For many women a partial divorce left them in a better economic position than women who obtained a complete divorce with no accompanying financial support.[39] Although it was interpreted as "reactionary legislation" and as a reversal of 250 years of liberal legislation, the *mensa et thoro* law extended people's divorce options.[40] The 1882 law should not have adversely affected the Sprague divorce, but it is unclear how much Kate knew about the general assembly's plans to change Rhode Island divorce law. Because other states had attempted divorce reform, she had every reason to believe that Rhode Island's meddling with its divorce laws would lead to tighter legal strictures.

The timing of Kate's divorce petition may have also been linked to Rhode Island's child custody laws. An 1879 legal decision stated, "The well-being of a child is a primary consideration in awarding custody, and a female child of tender years could be awarded to the mother despite any superior right of the father and despite fault on the part of the mother."[41] Ethel, Portia, and Kitty were under age twelve and fell under the domain of this law. Despite William's repeated threats to take the children from Kate, he never stood much of a chance in the light of the law, his waning political ability to bend that law, and his occasional claim that he was not the girls' father. Kate's greatest custody weakness lay with her oldest child. Willie's age and gender made the nature of his legal guardianship ambiguous, and his mother had good reason to worry about the boy's custody and future. When he was ten, for example, Willie had hung his sister Ethel out a window and threatened to drop her two stories, in direct imitation of his father's abusive behavior toward his mother.[42] It appears that at some time in his youth Willie had also begun to emulate his father's drinking habits and would become an alcoholic. In December 1880, when Kate first filed for divorce, Willie was fifteen years old. Under Rhode Island law, children age sixteen or older could not be considered wards of their parents or the court, and thus neither parent could be awarded legal custody of that child.[43] In waiting until after the Republican convention to file for divorce, Kate gambled Willie's future against her lover's.

William filed a divorce countersuit in January 1881—partly as a bid to gain custody of Willie, partly to accuse Kate as she had accused him. Through her lawyer George Hoadly, a former law student of her father's, Kate vehemently denied William's charges of sexual and domestic misconduct. Hoadly collected the testimony of witnesses who would attest to the veracity of Kate's version of the marriage. According to Hoadly, "she was ready for trial at an early date, but upon one pretext and another and against her opposition, the trial was postponed throughout the year, without apparent preparation by him."[44] William and his lawyers were stalling the courts on purpose, knowing that delay brought Willie's sixteenth birthday ever closer. When the court insisted on setting a trial date, William's lawyer offered to withdraw his client's divorce action if Kate would withdraw the charges of adultery against her husband, allowing her a divorce on the grounds of cruelty and nonsupport. William had no desire to go to court.

The fact that William was willing to withdraw his petition as plaintiff and become the divorce defendant speaks volumes. In the nineteenth century, great significance was attached to who initiated the divorce and who was legally to blame. Victorian divorces contained a standard set of narrative elements: a victim (or plaintiff), a villain (or defendant), a claim of fault, and a final decree. In instigating the divorce suit Kate cast herself as the victim and, more important, William as the villain. The court assigned the grounds for divorce to him, making William legally responsible for the failure of the marriage. [45] The importance of this divorce narrative was underscored in 1883, when William petitioned in the state of Virginia to be remarried. In his petition he stated that the divorce had been charged against Kate, for adultery. Kate and Hoadly found this inaccuracy important enough send a letter to the paper that had printed William's intent to remarry:

> A copy of your paper of the 16th of March, 1883, has been placed in our hands, from which it appears that William Sprague, of Rhode Island, in order to procure a license to marry again and to induce a clergyman to perform the ceremony, made certain statements in regard to his divorce condition to the clerk of the court . . . which statements have been published by you, and being not only false, but also libelous of the most honorable and worthy lady we, her counsel, in her suit for divorce from Gov. Sprague, feel it our duty, in justice to her, to ask you to publish this statement of the facts in the case. [46]

Hoadly stressed that the court had granted an "absolute divorce in the favor of Mrs. Sprague, with permission, at her discretion, to resume her maiden name of Katherine Chase, a privilege seldom granted in Rhode Island, and never when a cloud rests upon the fair repute of a lady." [47] Although he portrayed his client as an innocent and wronged woman, Hoadly also knew that courts made it difficult for men to prosecute their wives for adultery. The judiciary took a protective role over women that stemmed from the court's awareness of the deep asymmetry in family power relations. Judges assumed a women's innocence of adultery charges in the absence of direct, irrefutable evidence—men quite literally had to catch their wives in bed with another man to prove adultery. When William withdrew his divorce countersuit, he signified that he understood the importance the courts placed on a woman's sexual reputation and the cultural significance of not being the divorce defendant—an understanding he underlined when he later lied and claimed he had divorced Kate for adultery.

When the Washington County Supreme Court finalized the Sprague divorce on 27 May 1882, Willie was weeks from his sixteenth birthday. He did not figure in the custody agreement and elected to remain with his father. Kate lost her delicate game of timing when she waited until December 1880 to file for divorce. She decided to risk her son in an attempt to rejuvenate Roscoe's political life. This fact, more than Washington gossip, the accusations of her husband, or the guesses made by her biographers, suggests that Kate sought solace from her unhappy marriage in the love and companionship of the handsome New York senator.

WHY DIVORCE? MARITAL POWER AND REPUBLICAN IDEOLOGY

Although we may understand why Kate divorced her husband when she did, this does not tell us why she chose to divorce him at all. Salmon P. Chase had not raised a "bad woman," a daughter who failed to live up to nineteenth-century standards of femininity. Nor had he trained Kate to defy social convention. During all of Kate's marital trouble, Chase had never counseled her to leave her husband, but rather he had stressed reconciliation or had ignored the problem all together. Yet Kate decided to divorce William. Certainly she experienced her union with William as a failure of romantic love and companionate marriage. She was not alone in her disappointment. Increasingly high expectations for marriage in the nineteenth century exacerbated the divorce crisis because increasing numbers of married couples fell short of the affectionate ideal. Thus rising national divorce rates suggest a close correlation between "prescription and description," between companionate standards and real marital expectations. For Kate and many other Victorian Americans, cultural values may not have translated into particular behavior, but they did influence expectations of that behavior.

Nevertheless, many Americans felt that their spouse had fallen short of expectations yet remained married.[48] Violet Blair Janin, for example, a woman about Kate's age and social location, also contracted a less-than-felicitous marriage. She lived apart from her husband, Albert, for most of their marriage, maintaining her individual identity in a manner that balanced affection and marital power. George ("Autie") and Libbie Custer also had their problems. Although they often described their marriage in romantic terms, Autie's problems with gambling and infidelity, as well as their inability to have children, had, by 1870, terribly strained their union. Libbie always forgave him his transgressions though, in part because she had a great fear of being alone. Ellen and William Tecumseh Sherman suffered through almost four decades of deeply unhappy marital life, but they never divorced. Certainly Ellen's Catholicism played a part in the poorly matched couple's continued association, but the two only briefly and temporarily separated from each other. They would live apart for a few months at a time, then move back in together and even take trips with each other. "Cump" found solace and affection with other women, while Ellen remained reclusive in her habits, ignoring her husband's extramarital activities until her death freed them both.[49]

Kate and William proved unwilling to live as miserably as the Shermans, nor could they create a workable truce as did the Custers and Janins. Notably, Kate did not set the terms of her marriage to reject romance, as Violet did, or to reject reality, as Libbie did. At the root of Kate's decision to divorce lay her personal politics. She was committed to the Republican ideal of autonomy and self-ownership that she had learned at her father's knee. How she reconciled her divorce with social prescriptions reveals much about both Republican and pro-divorce rhetoric.

To fully understand Kate's decision to divorce, we must examine her alternatives more fully. Many women, like Violet Blair Janin, instead of divorcing their husband, created an extralegal divorce. They removed themselves from their husband's households, pretended to be single or widowed, or simply ignored the existence of their legal mates. Certainly the Shermans, Janins, and Conklings utilized this strategy to varying extents. Roscoe and Julia Conkling established almost completely separate lives; in essence, they created a de facto divorce. From her house in Utica, Julia seems to have borne her husband's infidelities stoically, although in 1881 Roscoe chastised her for "discussing family affairs of a private nature" with acquaintances. Outraged, Julia wrote back, "I have heard no end of disagreeable, intensely annoying things. My course has been to love gently,

& to endeavor to sustain my dignity and yours. These 'family difficulties'—a phrase I copy from the newspapers, have not been of my making, & my best efforts have been made to refrain comment." [50] Julia was not a doormat. Many American couples did what the Conklings did—created informal bed-and-board divorces that left them socially separate but legally married.

For a while Kate had attempted to do the same with William. She left the country for long periods of time, seeking to remove herself from William, to obtain an affordable yet good education for her children, and to rekindle their romance through separation. But after 1876 Kate did not have the economic support Julia Conkling or Ellen Sherman had. [51] Nor did she have recourse to a family fortune, as did Violet Blair Janin. Kate did have a husband who drank excessively and refused to provide for his family. And although divorce proceedings are often acrimonious and couples falsely accuse each other of heinous activities, it does appear that Kate and her children were intimately acquainted with domestic violence. She had, as well, been subjected to William's numerous marital infidelities, which she took great care to enumerate in her divorce petition.

Interestingly, Kate never accused William of marital rape, though his propensities toward drunken rages certainly create the possibility that she endured some forced sexual contact. Although American common law made marital rape an impossibility (on the basis that marriage automatically created voluntary consent between partners), social standards held that women ought not be forced into unwanted sex—standards further upheld by the tenets of masculine self-restraint. At the same time, legal and moral theorists believed that a husband's free use of his wife's body functioned as a deterrent against adultery. If William had ever raped Kate she understood that claiming those episodes could backfire on her by raising the specter of the frigid wife whose sexual unwillingness forced her husband to seek release with other women. [52] Calling attention to forced marital relations also would have highlighted her as a sexual body, something to which the mistress of an ambitious politician would not want to call attention. The possibility also exists that William's binges caused impotence, which may have fueled his anger at his wife enough to cause him to attack her and the household furniture. In her divorce petition, though, Kate hinted at egregious violations of morality. After enumerating William's marital infidelities, she accused him of "other gross misbehavior & wickedness repugnant to and violation to the marriage covenant," and again later, after accusing him of sexually attacking servants, she claimed he had made "other violations of decency." Both times she accused him of some unspecified transgression, she did so after describing his sexual acts with other women. These hints, along with his and Mary Viall Anderson's arrest for a "drunken orgy," suggest that alcohol-induced impotence did not always, if ever, affect William.

The violence and abuse that became public during the 1879 Canonchet imbroglio proved to be Kate's watershed. After that date she no longer contented herself with Ellen's, Julia's, or Violet's solution to marital problems. Nor did a growing number of women. By 1867 women instigated 64 percent of all the divorces awarded in the United States. From 1867 to 1886 the courts granted 65.8 percent of all divorces to women. Men created extralegal divorces by abandoning their families, while women sought legal remedies in a culture increasingly sympathetic to women's accusations of cruelty, intemperance, and adultery. Clearly, by the Gilded Age, divorce had become "a woman's remedy."[53] Certainly Kate's and William's radically different accusations in their divorce suits support this trend. Kate and many other women sued husbands for nonsupport, cruelty, and gross misbehavior. Kate's claim of nonsupport was a particularly strong accusation. As middle-class and upper-middle-class white Americans increasingly valorized women's domestic and moral roles in the family, men faced increasing pressure to support their families. Failure to do so indicated a failure of manliness.[54] Divorce could result when gender roles broke down in a marriage, much as they did between the Spragues. Kate accused William of failure to support his family, both economically and emotionally, of chronic drunkenness, and of serial adultery. Each of these accusations directly responded to divorce courts' definitions of what constituted grounds for dissolution of marriage. William, on the other hand, claimed that Kate had failed to provide adequate domestic services and that she had "violated her marriage covenants" by an act of adultery. This last charge had particular resonance because Victorian culture remained committed to the sexual double standard and would have found Kate's sexual infidelity far more shocking than William's.[55] In effect, the Spragues accused each other of failing to act out their respective womanly and manly roles.

Although Kate's recourse to divorce fits into rising divorce rates, the total number of divorced women in the Gilded Age remains minuscule when compared to modern statistics. Rhode Island had only three divorces per four thousand people (.075 percent) during the 1870s, with women instigating two-thirds of these divorces.[56] This tiny percentage reflects the stigma that late-nineteenth-century Americans attached to divorce. Divorce represented a fundamental failure of the individuals to live up to "normal" behavior. Many Americans viewed divorced people social degenerates. The spirit of Victorian democracy theoretically provided that any one individual could, with adherence to the dominant ethos, join respectable society. This very fluidity created powerful fears about anyone not absolutely committed to the Victorian code of respectability. States that allowed divorce were far less interested in personal freedom from a bad marriage than they were in perfecting the marriage script. Those who failed to enact the correct script for marriage were punished. After her divorce, Kate became a social and political outcast, living proof that downward mobility could be more than economic.[57]

Kate was not alone in her insider-turned-outsider status; Gilded Age society stigmatized divorced women in particular, treating them as a category of "fallen women," disgraced and outside the bounds of respectability. While the northern, Republican model of manhood urged men to stay chaste before marriage, most of Victorian America maintained a sexual double standard. Discreet sexual indiscretions, like William's with Mary Viall Anderson, enhanced young men's masculinity, while the same activity in a young woman placed her indisputably outside the bounds of respectability.[58] The results of the 1872 Tilton-Beecher affair provided a moral lesson to all women: Henry Ward Beecher recovered his respectability after his extramarital affair with Elizabeth Tilton, while she lived out her life in quiet disgrace.[59] The Sprague divorce ran a parallel course. That William remarried and resumed his public life (albeit in a truncated version) while Kate slipped through the cracks of elite society into a social limbo illustrates both society's conservative reaction to divorce and the gender specificity of that reaction. What stigma William lived with might just as well be attributed to the dubious social status of his second wife, his multiple attacks on the political status quo, his aberrant post-divorce behavior, and the decline of his fortune. Kate's loss of status, on the other hand, may be unerringly pinned on the public exposure of her extramarital affair and subsequent divorce. As one historian has suggested, "relief from misery cannot be equated with autonomy and independence. An abiding asymmetry in divorce outcomes marked divorce in Victorian America. Men ended their marital woes and enjoyed the power that had always been their birthright, while divorced women faced a society that systematically denied them autonomy and independence." [60] The liberalized divorce laws that allowed Kate her divorce did little to counteract these patriarchal realities.

Kate lost economic as well as social status when she divorced, forfeiting any chance of ever regaining access to the Sprague fortune—a fortune that remained considerable despite Sprague's 1873 financial setbacks. She did retain Edgewood. Divorcing wives almost always recovered any property they brought into the marriage and received no share of the husband's assets. No alimony or child support accompanied the dissolution of the Sprague marriage. Men who did not (or could not) support their families while married were unlikely to do so after divorce, particularly when not compelled to by the legal system. But William was not destitute, and he most certainly could have paid Kate alimony. The courts considered a wife's behavior and need when assigning alimony. However much the legal divorce narrative cast Kate as victim, the exceedingly public nature of her affair with Roscoe and the fact that she had run away from her husband placed her outside the category of women likely to receive alimony. Most women's only chance at support lay in remarriage. Although Kate's economic standing was threatened before the divorce by her husband's intransigence, and her social standing was threatened by the public exposure of her affair with Roscoe, divorce cost her whatever chances she had of ever recouping any of these economic and social losses. [61]

Perhaps the best explanation for why Kate chose almost certain ostracism lies in the kind of woman her father and her temperament had made her. Calvinistic language about duty shifted in the nineteenth century as ideas about the rights of individuals to own their bodies became a central tenet of antebellum political theory and reform ideology. Liberal feminists in particular adopted slavery imagery, and "bondage became the metaphor of choice for pro-divorce feminists." Many nineteenth-century Americans saw the experiences of wives and slaves as structurally parallel. Husbands/masters had absolute power to command their dependents, wife and slave alike. Pro-divorce activists used the slavery/freedom dichotomy as a gendered metaphor with which to criticize nineteenth-century patriarchy, while southern apologists justified slavery because of its likeness to marriage. Reformers genuinely felt that forced marital servitude degraded the human spirit as much as slavery degraded African Americans. It was the power disparity between men and women to which women's rights advocates objected.[62]

In this ideology, the absence of violence did not abrogate the need for divorce, for the right to one's body transcended the conditions of servitude. As Elizabeth Cady Stanton, one of the leading proponents of the slavery/marriage analogy, expressed it, "our evolution thus far is but a struggle to stretch ourselves while bound hand and foot, to fly with clipped wings . . . the oneness of man and woman is a oneness than makes woman a slave."[63] As post–Civil War marriage underwent a reconstruction of its own, so did women's impetus for divorce. Women began to claim self-ownership in greater numbers, especially under the rubric of "voluntary motherhood" and the birth control movement. Some women came to view marriage as enslavement (and thereby antithetical to self-ownership), and as citizenship became tied to free labor, activists recast marriage as a "contract dissoluble at will." This view of marriage as a contract became an ideal of personal freedom in an age that had survived a war for individual rights. Thus while more conservative Americans used divorce as "a trope for moral decay," more radical citizens approached the topic as "an emblem of personal liberation."[64]

As a result, while reformers called for the restriction of divorce, the language of pro-divorce activists made divorce a partisan issue. The Republican Party responded to the rhetoric as Democrats did not. Indeed, in the early years of the Republican Party, before Kate's father and others crystallized the party's stance against slavery, many Democrats viewed Republicans' willingness to intercede in matters of family with considerable alarm. Democrats believed that marriage and slavery were both institutions that should brook no governmental interference. In their defense of slavery, Democrats elevated the patriarchal family, insisting upon the submission of wives, children, and slaves to white husbands and fathers. Many Democrats, particularly those in the South, resisted divorce as a matter of manly honor as well. Southern states made it almost impossible for a woman to successfully pursue a divorce action, while a husband's chances of ending a marriage proved better. Thus it was not necessarily the ending of a marriage that some Democrats found so repugnant, but rather the erosion of patriarchal prerogative, manly self-image, and individual male reputations. Simply put, female-instigated divorces challenged white male authority. As Kate knew from personal experience in her father's household, many Republicans rejected this conservative stance as an inappropriate use of male power that could lead to sexual corruption and marital tyranny.[65]

Few women in America would have been as susceptible to the post–Civil War divorce discourse as Kate Chase Sprague. She had been weaned on abolition, had learned the importance of free labor at her father's knee, and was educated as the intellectual equal of any man. Antislavery men like James G. Birney, Cassius M. Clay, Gerrit Smith, and Joshua Giddings often visited her father's house in the years before Kate left Ohio for school in New York.[66] The larger social environment in which Kate developed was no less political. The years from 1840 to 1860 witnessed the full maturation of the Jacksonian two-party system, with its intersection of mass culture and politics. Kate's home state, Ohio, boasted the highest voter turnout in the country between 1840 and 1860, while New York, where she went to school for eight years, ranked fourth. Nor was political enthusiasm in the mid–nineteenth century limited to enfranchised men. Women went to tremendously popular (and long) political speeches, participated in parades, and joined in party celebrations. [67] Kate, no less than any other political citizen, subscribed to the tenets of her partisan community, and her community included her father, William, and Roscoe—Republicans all. Republican tenets included free soil, free labor, and a crusade for individual freedom. The party's rhetoric based free-labor ideology on the claim that all Americans, black or white, "could achieve social advancement if given equal protection under the law." [68] White freedom and social advancement, for *some* Republicans, included suffrage for women. Ironically, even William concurred with this rhetoric. "The Governor is well too," Salmon wrote Nettie in 1866, "and has been making a little speech on women's suffrage, which seems to me very good." For women's rights advocates and some Republicans, marriage, like labor, had to be based on freely given consent.[69]

Although Salmon supported much in the women's rights program, he had never counseled his daughter to consider divorce. In 1867 he advised a friend's wife about divorce, suggesting he found the remedy a mixed blessing: "Everything, almost, should be borne before seeking separate lives & a suit for divorce. If you have resolved on that course, however you should note the counsel of someone with whom you can confer personally and who [word illegible] to the qualities of a good lawyer, than of a judicious friend. He could tell you what would be the probable course of application & what action will be necessary to serve you against impoverishment during the hesitancy of litigation by the loss of your income."[70] This letter, while not an enthusiastic endorsement of divorce, stands in sharp contrast to conservative rhetoric about the evils of divorce. Indeed, Salmon seems to have been far more concerned with the economic realities of divorce than with any moral stance. The intersection between pro-divorce and Republican rhetoric created a discourse in which Kate had been raised to participate. Indeed, though leading Republicans often insisted that they were not women's rights advocates (just as they insisted that they were not abolitionists), many Republican-controlled states liberalized divorce and remarriage restriction, weakened a husband's rights to his wife's earnings, and strengthened women's access to alimony.[71] For Kate and women like her, Republican rhetoric about individual freedom and consent-based relationships increasingly outweighed prescriptions of womanly submissiveness and self-denial. In this light Kate's divorce becomes a partisan act. This is not to say that women who did not identify with the Republican Party never divorced, but rather that the Democratic Party provided little ideological impetus for divorce. Democrats were more likely to figure divorce as a failure of true womanhood and an attack on patriarchal prerogative, while Republicans, whether they intended to or not, created an environment favorable to marital emancipation.[72]

The connection that Stanton and other divorce advocates made between marriage and slavery probably had particular resonance for Kate after William's attempt to keep her prisoner. Having grown up with a father who argued fugitive slave cases, Kate may have felt some connection with the plight of escaping slaves during the hours and days surrounding her flight from Canonchet. Just as the fugitive slave laws privileged the rights of slave owners in the recovery of human property, so did a husband's right to "protect" his wife by constraining her freedom outweigh a woman's civil rights. The law condoned a husband's coercive actions, as one historian suggests, "as a measure of his attachment and affection, the normal desire and possessive devotion of a husband for his wife." As long as William did not attempt to kill Kate, the nineteenth-century society viewed his enslavement of her as a moral offense but not a legal one.[73] This would explain why, though everyone knew that Kate was being kept at Canonchet against her will, no one intervened on her behalf. It must have come as a great shock to find herself in such a position, she who had acted so freely and independently throughout her life. William's insobriety compounded the insult of Kate's imprisonment. Feminists and moralists alike likened a drunkard to an animal. Elizabeth Cady Stanton, for example, described the intemperate husband as a "coarse, beastly and disgusting drunkard."[74] Thus the master of Kate's imprisonment was no master at all, making her position all the more degrading and untenable.

Certainly Kate's decision to divorce William cannot be ascribed solely to her political affiliation any more than the gender gap in divorce can be accounted for by partisan politics. That women had fewer recourses from bad marriages than did men, that the law did not protect them from marital rape, and that women suffered more often from the effects of male violence than vice versa also explain the divorce imbalance. Marriage was simply a better deal for men than for women. Kate's request to revert to her maiden name also gives us some clue. Women rarely reverted to their maiden names, particularly when they had children. Kate, and women like her, expected their husbands to provide for them. Kate divorced William on the grounds of nonsupport, not alienation of affection. Most other divorcing Victorian women cited the same grounds. Republican ideology provided Kate with the intellectual grounds to consider divorce as an alternative, but it was an alternative she did not make use of until William abandoned his role as family breadwinner. When William failed to support her and the children, she saw no need to remain a Sprague—either literally or figuratively. Kate's divorce and her return to her maiden name, more than any other actions in her life, suggest the centrality of Republican politics in her life. She was a party woman to the core, and a Chase to the end.

PARTY WOMAN IN ACTION AGAIN

Only weeks after Kate filed for divorce, and eighteen days before William filed his countersuit, she sat down at her writing desk at Edgewood and wrote Chester Arthur, the newly elected vice-president, a letter. Heading the letter "STRICTLY CONFIDENTIAL," she proceeded to illustrate not only her command of the current political situation but her continued relationship with Roscoe Conkling. Although this letter is highly political in nature, it reveals not only that Kate and Roscoe were still in the same political camp but that they were literally still in the same bed. However bold the letter, Kate's careful use of language also suggests one of the ways in which political women operated. For example, her effusive protestations of friendship illustrate how many women used correspondence to transform strangers into confidants—playing on a notion of mutual sympathy that allowed women entrée into the political venue.[75] She began her letter by assuring Arthur that she would rather see him in person and then reminded him of his old boss's continued friendship:

> Our mutual friend brought the other day from New York, two excep-tionally good lithographs of our Vice President elect. One was brightly festooned at Edgewood & the Senator, YOUR FRIEND, never passes the table where the likeness stands, that he does not apostrophize it with some hearty expression of real affection, such as is rare in man to man & a tribute from this self-contained, but noble & true nature that any man may feel bound to possess. I have never been more struck with any manifestation I have seen of devotion to friends—a distinguishing individuality in Mr. Conkling—than with his special feeling for you.

Arthur had good reason to disbelieve Kate's story. Roscoe had not approved of Arthur as Garfield's running mate, and he liked the deal even less when the president-elect named Roscoe's nemesis James G. Blaine the future secretary of state. But however irritated the New York boss might be with Arthur, he understood that the future vice-president remained in his camp. Blaine's faction of the Republican Party, the Half-Breeds, wanted to keep Conkling men out of the cabinet, though the Stalwarts had good reason to believe that Garfield had promised Levi Morton, another Conkling man, the post of treasury secretary (Kate's father's old job).[76] At the same time, New York's second Senate seat had opened, with five candidates vying for the job, three of them Stalwarts. Kate addressed these issues in her letter.

> I think of you a great deal in the heated contest in which you are now engaged.
> Partly because personally my preference and sympathy are identical with yours, & further because I see so plainly that the paramount embarrassment resides in the reformers unwillingness to ask a sacrifice of you, or to have you disappointed.
> But my dear friend consider are you using good, generous, but inde-pendent Mr. Crowley for his own best advantage in the long run? Were it this or nothing in his case it would call for different logic—but I leave it here—
> Mr. Morton is too small a man for the position. New & untried in

politics, an apprentice at legislation business. Not a man to decorate the Senate, or prove all that could be desired in a colleague.

Roscoe had most probably been grooming Arthur for the Senate seat, creating another reason for him to be irritated with Arthur. With Arthur out of the running, Thomas Platt, Levi Morton, and Richard Crowley led the field, with different factions of the Stalwart camp favoring a different man.[77]

Chester Arthur, for example, favored Crowley—a loyal party man with good political experience but no personal fortune. Politicos privately wondered how he could make a good senator when he had not prospered in his private law practice. Crowley was also a Catholic, which Kate may have been referring too when she called the loyal party man "independent." Some Victorian Americans believed that Catholics' loyalty to the pope compromised their loyalty to the nation. Kate appealed to both Arthur's and her friendship with Crowley to suggest that Crowley might be better used elsewhere. Conkling wanted Levi Morton for the cabinet and thus did not want the New York State Assembly to nominate him to the Senate. Morton, on the other hand, desperately wanted the Senate seat, perhaps not believing that Conkling could override Blaine's power over Garfield to put a Stalwart in the second-most-influential cabinet position. Having disqualified two of the top contenders, Kate left the matter of Thomas Platt silent. Thus she subtly but surely apprised Arthur of Roscoe's choice for the Senate. Three days after this letter the New York State Assembly elected Platt on the first ballot. Platt would prove himself a loyal subject of Lord Roscoe. In her letter to Arthur, Kate also addressed the battle over cabinet appointments:

> The mutterings of distant thunder & approaching storms already becloud the disc of the political horoscope. Garfield and Sherman & Blaine (as it looks to private forecast) are to combine forces to overthrow & crush the power that saved them, but which they recognize only to fear & hate.
>
> Surely the Senators friends, his tried friends, & true will not cripple or soon embarrass the man to whom they owe so much?
>
> If you think me venturesome—perhaps I should say meddlesome— forgive it—it is well meant.
>
> Do not reply to this, unless you can do so without the least constraint. It is entre-nous STRICTLY & shall remain so.

You and I are destined to be good friends & will no doubt as time rolls on discuss many serious questions in confidence.

You will always find me straight forward or silent & you shall elect which it is to be. I write hastily but in the utmost sincerity

Yours truly

Katherine Chase Sprague.[78]

Thus Kate made Arthur responsible for protecting Conkling's interests against the growing power of the rival Republican camp. She also solidified her "friendship" with Arthur by figuring herself as a kind of political soul mate to him, placing herself firmly in the vice-president's cadre of advisers. Garfield eventually offered Morton a cabinet post, but Roscoe encouraged him to him refuse. Morton would become minister to France, and the position at the Treasury Department went to Senator William Windom of Minnesota.[79] New York Stalwarts, Conkling chief among them, regarded the whole business as a grim disappointment and a harbinger of rough times.[80]

Kate and Roscoe did not have to wait long before Garfield launched another attack on the Conkling machine. On 22 March he sent a list of several Conkling men to the Senate for appointment to minor patronage posts, prompting a vociferous protest from anti-Conkling forces. The next day the wavering president sent another list that nominated William Robertson to the collectorship of the New York Custom House. No friend of Conkling's, Robertson had been in politics all his adult life and was no more untainted with patronage than any benefactor of Conkling's, but he did support Garfield and Blaine, and he stood positioned to wreak havoc over the New York senator's patronage power.[81] Robertson's appointment also indicated the power Blaine had over the president, for it was at the secretary of state's urging that Garfield made the nomination.[82]

Although Roscoe and his friend Chester Arthur attempted a series of maneuvers to cancel Robertson's nomination, including threatening the president, little came of their efforts. If anything, Stalwart indignation over the matter only strengthened Garfield's resolve, even causing him to withdraw his previous nominations of Conkling men. The battle lines were drawn. By early May, Robertson's confirmation looked all but certain and Conkling's power nearly at an end. Then on 16 May 1880 Arthur read two letters to the Senate. The first contained Conkling's resignation, while the second announced the resignation of New York's newest senator, Thomas Platt.[83] The senators believed that their resignations would call attention to the president's duplicity and appall fellow politicians. Then, having made the grand gesture, the two believed the New York State Assembly would return them to the Senate as their own replacements. Thus Roscoe and Thomas Platt hoped the whole episode would function to rebuke President Garfield and restore Conkling's supremacy in the political patronage game.

Unfortunately, while the plan had a certain amusing elegance, the senators did not cooperate as the New Yorkers had expected. Rather than being aghast at the resignations, almost to a man other senators thought the whole maneuver foolish. The *New York Times* summed up political and public sentiment when it editorialized, "In this city the most common sentiment was impatience and disgust that the State should have been made the laughing-stock of the country by the childish display of temper on the part of its Senators." Kate's old suitor John Hay wrote to a friend that "Roscoe is finished. That Olympian brow will never again garner up the thousands of yore."[84] What Kate thought may only be guessed. Certainly the situation must have seemed eerily similar to the circumstances surrounding her father's cabinet resignation. Both Salmon and Roscoe had challenged a president over a New York Custom House appointment, both men gambled their careers in the quest for power, and both men lost their games of chance. By late May it became clear that the New York State Assembly would decline to return Conkling and Platt to the U.S. Senate. Not even the New York Stalwarts could consider the two men serious political figures. This must have come as quite a shock, not only to the former Adonis of the Senate but to Kate as well. For the first time in her adult life she was connected to no man in a position of political power.

EIGHT

"Baleful Grief and Bitter Bread"
Surviving Divorce in the Gilded Age,
1881–1915

~

What is writ is writ—
Would it were worthier.

Childe Harolde

A DEPLORABLE LEGACY

Roscoe Conkling did not easily quit the field. In late June 1881 Richard Croweley became a candidate for one of the Senate seats, but Roscoe made a special trip to Albany to kill the movement. Next, Platt announced his retirement from the campaign. Coincidentally, several Blaine supporters had happened to observe (through a transom window) Platt in a highly compromising position with a lady of dubious moral standing. Apparently Conkling's circle had kept Kate and Roscoe's ongoing association secret, for that news would certainly have forced him out of the race as well. It would take an entirely different kind of tragedy to accomplish that feat. On 2 July, the same day Platt's withdrawal letter was read to a joint session of Congress, Charles Guiteau fired two shots at President Garfield. One bullet merely grazed his arm, but the second lodged in his spine. Rumors of the president's death circulated throughout Washington but proved premature. Garfield lingered on through the summer, sometimes rallying, sometimes drifting toward death.

The president's would-be assassin had a long history of erratic behavior, compounded by recurrent delusions of grandeur. Psychosis seems to have run in the family—his aunt died in an asylum, and his father believed he would never die. By his mid-thirties the assassin had been divorced on the grounds of abuse and nonsupport, had been convicted of fraud, had chased his own sister with an ax, and had engaged in various other activities of dubious moral and mental uprightness. Having written a pamphlet supporting Stalwart candidates in the 1880 election, Guiteau came to believe not only that he was single-handedly responsible for Garfield's election but that he would soon marry an heiress, receive a plum political appointment from the president, and eventually become the ruler of the world. When his plans failed to come to fruition, the increasingly delusional Guiteau persuaded himself that "if the President was removed it would unite the two factions of the Republican Party, and thereby save the Government from going into the hands of ex-rebels and their Northern allies." [1] After purchasing a gun, Guiteau stalked President Garfield for weeks before shooting him. Taken into custody almost instantly by an alert policeman, the crazed shooter shouted, "I did it, and will go to jail for it. Arthur is President and I am a Stalwart." [2]

During the two and a half months that Garfield resisted death, Chester Arthur balanced between president-in-waiting and public enemy number one. Many believed Arthur unworthy of the highest office in the land. Indeed, many Americans viewed him as having risen to presidential heights on the back of a corrupt spoils system that rewarded venal partisans rather than qualified men genuinely interested in public service. Most Americans understood that his vice-presidency had been a sop to Conkling and viewed Arthur as his boss's puppet. Rutherford B. Hayes summed up many people's sentiments when he wrote, "Arthur for President! Conkling the power behind the throne, superior to the throne!" [3] Guiteau's public pronouncements had only exacerbated the public's negative assessment of Arthur and Conkling.

From jail Guiteau wrote Arthur letters making suggestions for cabinet appointments. He thought the ministry of Paris or Vienna would serve as a suitable reward for his political loyalty and believed Conkling would champion his appointment once the country understood the assassination as a political necessity. [4] Although some people actually believed that Conkling and Arthur had hired Guiteau to kill the president, most Americans recognized that the spoils system, and the tremendous political schism that had grown out of the fight for the right to award patronage, had only encouraged a madman to shoot Garfield. This view did little to exculpate either the New York boss or his trusted lieutenant. Even Conklingites in the New York State Assembly distanced themselves from their boss that July, and by the end of the month Elbridge Lapham had been elected to fill Roscoe's Senate seat.

President Garfield died just before midnight on 19 September 1881, leaving Arthur in charge of a grieving nation that little believed the White House was in good hands. To make matters worse, Garfield's cabinet was openly hostile to Arthur and Conkling. Treasury Secretary William Windom resigned first, followed by Attorney General Wayne MacVeagh and Secretary of State James G. Blaine.[5] Rumors abounded about Arthur's possible replacement appointments, but the new president approached his task fully aware of the political minefields that lay ahead. At this point Kate stepped into the fray to lobby for Roscoe. On 15 October 1881 she wrote her father's old friend Samuel Pomeroy:[6]

> My dear Sir
>   Hastily as I must write I cannot fittingly reply to your letter just received & to which my feeling so strongly responds. I agree with you, of course, & am almost surprised to hear especially with those long familiar with the public service & interests, such ardor & solicitude expressed for Mr. Conkling's active cooperation in the new Government.
>   Indeed I am pretty well persuaded after watching critically & closely the progress of this fierce struggle for political preferment, that among those who do their own thinking, to find a score of men wise enough to discover the truth, that ONE intrepid enough in the face of opposition to stand up for the same.

Evidently Pomeroy had given Kate reason to believe that he supported Conkling's bid for a cabinet appointment. He also seemed aware that Kate and Roscoe were still close and that Kate earnestly desired to see her lover's political advancement. Although Pomeroy was an old Chase family friend, he was in neither Conkling's nor Arthur's circle of confidants, suggesting that Kate and Roscoe's relationship had become a fairly open secret among their friends. In the light of these realities, her letter became more politically explicit:

> Mr. Conkling's bitterest foes are among the most dangerous enemies to our political brothers. He is dreaded by the plunderers, hated by the licentious, ridiculed by the sycophants, & ephemera. With the honest, the high-minded his virtues, like his services, plead trumpet tongued for recognition and reaction against the unparalleled injustice which cries "crucify him," in my judgment is not remote. "Like some tall cliff etc., the

sunshine of Militus still glows upon the higher summits, & the proportion both of thanks & payment will be his."

You refer to my Father's incumbency of this great office. "There were giants in those days." Since then high places have been too frequently OCCUPIED and not FILLED. There seems to be so little proved, staunch, strong timber available, with which to oppose, a bulwark against, the carnival of crudity, the masquerade of hypocrisy, the corrupt intrigue which surges about the foundations of our political system & threatens its destruction, that were Mr. Conkling much less my friend, had I not seen him tried on a crucible which proves manhood's highest virtues & emerge at each new test firmer in loyalty, more gallant in courage, stronger & brighter in the faith that was in him, I should still feel sure that at this crisis, the value & importance of his services to the country, the cause & the Executive is incalculable.

Closer contact & association during a period of twenty-five of the most momentous years of our national existence, with men who darkened nations when they died, & who, when they lived magnified their great offices into positions of highest trust, has inherently moved me with and interest in public affairs & this must plead for my earnestness now.

In comparing her lover to her father, Kate paid him her highest tribute and revealed the depth of her devotion. Salmon had also shamelessly jockeyed for political power and advancement, but his ambition had always been underwritten by very real principles. He truly believed in antislavery, sound fiscal policies, and fair judicial proceedings. Roscoe's singular cause had always been Roscoe Conkling, yet Kate believed him a "true man." However much she believed in Roscoe, she did not think she should take her case to Arthur. As she explained it:

But it would not excuse, it might not satisfactorily explain my obtruding my views upon the President.

His position is beset with difficulties & his task extremely delicate and perplexing. "He stands in honorable trust"—& it behooves those who have kept the faith with those in the past to show him their unreserved, whole-hearted support now. To through the self-seeking hollow truce, that masks continuous factional strife, too bitter in its rivalries to be allayed, too fraught with the danger of disgrace, not to be treacherous.

What an exceptional opportunity for the "Leadership"—but the margin between politics & statesmanship is so broad—It is my belief that the

Republican Party as NOW KNOWN, will never elect another President, nor does it deserve to, but the elements are fast reforming for recrystallization.

But to return to the suggestion of your letter. As I estimate Genl. Arthur any plea with him for Mr. Conkling's recognition would be a grave affront. I cannot doubt that Genl. Arthur, President, is the pure, true, upright, intrepid man as Genl. Arthur, Collector and Candidate. I assume that none better than he appreciates that but for the [word illegible] catastrophe which elevated him in the first place of power, his tried friend & champion could not have been, even for an internal [show] of his great strength. "Power wins golden opinions, From all kinds of men," Shakespeare tells us & so potent a spell is not likely to operate less promptly or kindly in Mr. Conkling's behalf than in Genl. Arthur's.

Believing implicitly in Gen. Arthur's rectitude & courage as I do my only fear is for the misconstruction consequent upon delay. The enemy score their first triumph when they discover that their hostility causes the President to hesitate or deters him from finalizing his power to do at once, this act of poetic justice—"If it were done, when 'tis done, then it were done quickly."

But perhaps the President has marked out for himself a different mode of procedure however anxious his friends may be to see him promptly freed from the shadows & toils—a deplorable legacy. They will rejoice to see him jealously guard his independence.

Kate went on to describe President Arthur as friendly, chivalric, earnest, and gentlemanly, perhaps aware that Pomeroy would pass this letter to Arthur for his perusal. Six days later, and in spite of saying she could not write him without "a grave risk of being misunderstood," she addressed a letter to the president.[7]

New York, Oct. 21, 1881
Dear General Arthur,

So much gratuitous & doubtless unwelcome advice is thrust upon you that one shrinks from joining the ranks of busy bodies & intruders.

I have been urged, importuned, entreated by more than a score of earnest men, many of whose experience & zeal has instructed the needs & interests of executive government, to bring before you, in my poor way, the vital importance of placing a robust, courageous, clean-handed man at the head of the treasury, the Portfolio of which is responsibility & power bestows priority among your ministers. To dwell upon Mr. Conkling's eminent qualifications for this high office would be idle &

audacious; you know them better than I, but pray bear with me when I say that notwithstanding the whirlwind of passion, the malignant fury of blind abuse, that has swept in a craze over the length and breadth of the land; for a host of reasons, unless honor, honesty & patriotism have become empty traditions, Mr. Conkling's association *upon the threshold* of your new administration would become a tower of strength at once a glory & a defense.

That which she had hinted at in her letter to Pomeroy she made more explicit in the letter to Arthur—that Roscoe wanted the Treasury post. In true political style she pretended she was a disinterested party and not another of Roscoe's political lieutenants. She also referenced her practical political experience as Salmon P. Chase's daughter to give weight to her recommendation.

Were Mr. Conkling less my friend, I could speak with less constraint. His assent I never could have obtained to my addressing you in his behalf & should the act ever come to his knowledge, I should have little hope of his forgiveness. But, subject to the still small voice of the human conscience, acquitted of any spirit of impulsiveness, or inclination to self-assertion, a sense of long familiarity stronger than the perception of change, intensity desired from a detailed practical knowledge of the growth of this great trust, rehabilitated & dignified by my Father's undaunted courage & sagacity & never since adequately filled—I venture to ask, is not the interest of the nation, some higher requirement to be met, than political preferment, or the liquidation of the personal indebtedness, more specifically under the abnormal conditions now prevailing under the administrations of public trusts.

I will not tire you with dwelling here upon the political aspects upon which this bears. With the burial of the famous dead, issues will change. Bloodless battles will be fought by the [enemies] of the Republic, a narrow scene of corporate action, suddenly becomes an area wide enough to embrace a nation & the future is bright with portentous issues. The greatest opportunities of a Century are yours! The most brilliant & masterful stroke of diplomacy & statecraft presented itself when it became possible for you to right two great houses of York & Lancaster in your cabinet. At once & for all you would have [word illegible] the charges & silence the organized opposition in the Press & while commended for your courage & loyalty to your own tried friend & champion. You would promptly have allowed the claims of "Garfield's residuary legatees." But I am told, By your own judgment did not sanction this course.

These may seem to you bold words. Believe me they are not meant as bold & trust they will not offend. It would be easier to join the multitudes who say pleasant things, but to speak & speak effectively I can no speak half-truths. It is in a spirit of true loyalty & prayerful interest for your highest success that I write. . . .

In my belief the Republican Party is hopelessly rent asunder & will never again, intact, elect another President. Its last effort was strained & indefensible. The Cohesion of momentum, or the craze of sentimental hypocrisy, will not carry it much further & after the Deluge, what then?

Here Kate touched upon an exceptionally real concern. The Republicans could not hope to increase or even maintain their power while locked in a vicious battle between Stalwarts and Half-Breeds, between conservatives and reformers. Without some kind of reconciliation the breech would divide the party, much like the slavery issue split the Democrats in 1860, leaving the field open to the opposition. Kate then made an interesting claim.

I have long believed that Mr. C—— was *the victim of Grantism*, & the condemned "machine," and *not its beneficiary*.

Had he after the Chicago Convention, asserted his independence, thrown off the old yoke of party allegiance, declared unequivocally for the vital issues upon which new parties will be formed, he would have had the better part of the old party in its defeat, solid & strong at his back instead of hounding him as the ruling faction has done ever since for its concessions that he made & the sacrifices & suffering it has cost.

It is difficult to know how much of this Kate really believed and how much was political expediency. The picture of "Lord Roscoe" as a victim of machine politics could only provoke amused skepticism among those who knew better. While it is certainly true that Conkling's support of Grant in 1880 did the New Yorker no favors, no one had foisted the cause upon him—Roscoe had always steered his own course. Kate next addressed the question of Conkling and Arthur's quarrel over Garfield.

Mr. C's loyalty *to you*, you bring into question, over the old argument. Fate, he said, had taken a bond of him when you accepted the candidacy & like the true knight he is he entered the lists, only to be cruelly wounded & to be rewarded with base ingratitude.

Fortuitous circumstances put it in your power to make full restitution to vindicate the man, who when you were assailed never stopped to weigh the chances of the popularity in your defense. There will never again come a time when your hearty appreciation of such services will possess the same value AS NOW. There is no other preferment in you gift which in my belief Mr. Conkling would or should accept but the one already NAMED. . . .

Probably no one but you & I know how illjudged & unfortunate Mr. C's last visit to Washington was. Once there, it was by my advice that he went to you, his trusted friend & with utter frankness laid bare his heart. Then I saw him AFTERWARDS, & saw HOW HE WAS SUFFERING. I urged his quitting Washington without delay. Friends who have seen him with in a day or two, report him as very ill. It is this, more than all else, that prompts this letter. I do not address it to you as President, but to undertake it at the dictate of the source of obligation to loyalty & friendship.[8]

Kate referred to Conkling's visit to Arthur at the White House the previous week. Clearly, Roscoe and the president had had a frank talk about the former senator's political future. Arthur could not nominate his old boss for any federal position. Not only would the confirmation hearing have precipitated a tremendously divisive debate in the Senate, but any such appointment attempt would have given Arthur's detractors an opportunity to further mark him as Conkling's puppet.

For those same reasons, Arthur could not gratify Roscoe's other pet wish, that Robertson be removed from his position as collector at the New York Custom House. Thus Kate's strategy contained within it severe limitations. In appealing to the power of sympathy and by marking herself as a subjectively interested party, Kate stepped outside the traditional political realm. Personal feelings had no official place in public policy. As Roscoe's champion, Kate invoked the private realm of friendship and love, which opened the door for Arthur or others to view her letters as the apolitical pleadings of an emotional enthusiast.[9] The weaknesses of her approach, though, should be weighed against its strengths. In appealing to the power of sympathy she created a venue in which she could demonstrate considerable political acumen and partisanship that might have otherwise gone unexpressed. Rather than assuming a male role in the political process, Kate utilized a feminine language in an attempt to accomplish her goal.

Unfortunately for her, no approach, no matter how skillful, would have gotten Roscoe a cabinet post.

Charles Guiteau had also believed that Conkling would make an excellent cabinet addition. Starting in mid-November 1881 and lasting until late January 1882, Guiteau's trial was probably the most sensational insanity case of the nineteenth century. The assassin defended himself, and in the process he implied on several occasions that he spoke either to or for God and that Arthur had been his personal confidant. The new president, not surprisingly, ardently desired Guiteau's conviction and execution, if for no other reason than to silence him. After a swift deliberation the jury delivered a guilty verdict, and Arthur soon afterward refused a plea for stay of execution. Guiteau, who was beyond a doubt mentally ill, went to the scaffold shouting, "I saved my party and my land, Glory Hallelujah!"[10] That claim alone should have been enough to prove his insanity. The assassination had not only sullied all Republicans by highlighting the dangerous effects of intraparty squabbling, but it had also exacerbated the divisions between the party's warring factions.

Although Roscoe received no cabinet appointment, Arthur did not utterly abandon his political mentor. On 27 October Arthur nominated longtime Conkling supporter and chief justice of the New York Supreme Court Charles Folger for the treasury position. The Senate confirmed Folger the same day, so that finally a Stalwart held the coveted secretary of the treasury post. More Stalwarts soon filled other cabinet positions, causing Mrs. James G. Blaine to write, "All the Stalwarts are going in, and though the mills of Arthur may seem to grind slow, they grind exceedingly fine."[11] By the end of 1881, Roscoe had retired to New York and taken up his private law practice in earnest.

It is surprising that Kate did not recognize the wreck of her lover's political career as quickly as did the newspapers and the Republican Party. In her defense, though, Roscoe appears to have been just as blind to the reality of his situation. All the actors in the 1879 drama seem to have failed to understand how their behavior had ultimately doomed them to political ignominy. The affair had much the same effect on Kate's reputation as it did on William's or Roscoe's, though Kate held no official public office from which she might be repudiated. After she filed for divorce she became a social, rather than political, pariah.

DOMESTIC WARFARE AND FATHERING

While Kate practiced politics, William and Willie continued a lively existence at Canonchet. Although news that Canonchet would be sold to meet A. & W. Sprague's debts had precipitated the events of the summer of 1879, the estate was not scheduled for auction until 15 August 1882, only months after the divorce became finalized. As proof of Kate's extravagance and domestic failure, William had once told a reporter that Canonchet was "no home . . . it requires an army of servants to keep in order." [12] Nonetheless, he zealously defended his non-home against auction. The auctioneer, trustee Zechariah Chaffee, and those prepared to bid on the estate arrived the morning of the fifteenth to find the gates locked, the bridge over a stream that crossed the front drive destroyed, and armed squads of mill employees patrolling the grounds. A sign on the gate read "No Admittance. Canonchet and grounds are closed to all carriages and persons." [13] William had trained the troops himself, invented a system of codes and signals, and even designed his own flag. The former governor took his stand from a tower on the grounds while Willie patrolled the front lawn on his gray pony, fortified with a club and a pistol. At one point in the morning the auctioneer attempted to climb the fence, but Willie called out, "I have orders not to let any person enter these grounds," then fired a shot over the heads of the gathered crowd. Wisely, Chaffee decided to move the auction into town.

Interestingly, William's solution to this problem harkens back to his childhood fondness for the martial world. Pushed seemingly beyond his limits, William reverted to the place where he had been most happy—a "boy culture" that did not admit adult rules of property and authority. In designing flags and secret codes and enlisting his adolescent son as his prime henchman, William once again became a child, or at least a person who predated the collapse of his business and marriage. In the process he neglected his son. Denizens of Narragansett Bay reported young Willie running amok, drinking to excess (particularly for a seventeen-year-old), and going about fully armed at all times.

It seems that William's fathering style, like so much of his personal ideology, had much to do with ideas more often associated with parenting in the plantation South. White southern fathers generally held to a more patriarchally based fatherhood than did their northern counterparts, using shame to inculcate in their sons a sense of family hierarchy and individual honor. "Duty to fathers came first." Traditional southern fathers distrusted maternal indulgences and religious training as "feminizing" to male children and thus debilitating to male prowess and honor.[14] William clearly adhered to some version of southern honor-based notions of fatherhood. He disliked Kate's emphasis on higher learning for William, particularly the language arts, and rejected religiosity in any form. He wanted Willie to learn to ride, shoot, and drink with the same skill displayed by himself. William also demanded a particularly dangerous kind of loyalty from his son, one that entailed direct defiance of New England law. People in nearby Narragansett Pier found Willie "an object of great annoyance" that summer, a young man chiefly remarkable for his "ungovernable temper and vicious propensities."[15] Willie, it would seem, tried exceedingly hard to please his father. Alienated from his mother by the divorce and denied a stable male role model, Willie was poorly prepared for manhood.

In spite of the Spragues' considerable and frankly violent resistance, the businessman Frank E. Moulton purchased Canonchet for $62,250. Although the purchase price was a tremendous bargain, about $30,000 less than the estate's appraised value, Moulton never managed to take possession of his new property. William would not let him approach the grounds. Coincidentally, Moulton had been intimately involved in the Beecher-Tilton affair, having acted as go-between for Henry Ward Beecher and "Lib" Tilton after her husband forbade them communications. Moulton had also worked with Henry Ward Beecher to quiet the scandal.[16] As Canonchet's new owner he applied to the courts to validate his title, but he died before a decision could be reached. His wife, Emma, seeing little good in a prolonged legal battle, eventually quitclaimed the property back to William.[17]

Not surprisingly, the *Providence Journal* vehemently decried the Sprague approach to real-estate deals. "If this man may, with force, resist the just rights of his creditors and the mandate of the Court, any other man may follow his example." William had not only threatened Rhode Island's system of debt collection, the paper claimed, but he defied due process. Local law enforcement had refused to serve the papers "for the recovery of a woman's clothes and her children's illegally withheld from her. The connivance at that outrage naturally led to this," the *Journal* warned, "and the connivance at this will lead to others, if not greater ones." The newspaper concluded by describing the terrible condition of the estate and young Willie, suggesting that both suffered from the lack of a woman's care.[18]

While William and Willie carried on their private war, Kate and her daughters continued to live quietly at Edgewood. That fall, in the light of her ex-husband's recent scandalous behavior, Kate gave an interview to a local newspaper. Her interview offered quite a contrast in parenting styles. The reporter gushed about Edgewood's fabulous view and the "refined and elegant tastes" of Kate's interior decorating. The reporter found the little girls' playroom particularly noteworthy. He described "the degree of maternal tenderness which shows that love for her offspring is the ruling passion of her heart and that her real enjoyment is not found in the material splendor which surrounds her, and the luster of which is dimmed by the beauty of her own person and the grace of her manner and conversation." Portia and Kitty would "revel for several hours each day in this room which contains dolls of every conceivable size and style, many of which were purchased in France and Germany, and the room abounds with curious toys, cribs, cradles, and carriages. The floor is strewn with them, and the shelves of little cabinets are filled with these tokens of a mother's love." The little girls also gave the reporter a tour of the yard, including a swing in a grove of trees and a pair of pet goats whom they harnessed to a small carriage. Kate carefully conveyed the impression that although her son was gone, he was not forgotten—she kept a portrait of him on the parlor wall and proudly pointed it out to the visiting journalist. Completely captivated by Kate, the writer extolled her youthful beauty, charm, grace, elegance, and "silvery voice."[19] No doubt she created just the picture she had intended, skillfully continuing her battle with William for their son even after the divorce became final.

The news of the William and Willie's next scandal could not have reassured Kate about her son. In 1882 William took a Christmas Day temperance vow, and in March 1883 he remarried.[20] His second wife, Inez Weed Calvert, was as beautiful as she was disreputable. The *New York Times* reported that "the new Mrs. Sprague attracted a good deal of attention in her promenades up and down the streets . . . and [her] bathing costume furnished seaside correspondents with material for many letters."[21] She was twenty-five and he fifty-eight years old. Although she was variously reported as being from both Virginia and Connecticut, Inez had spent several years in Washington and had visited Narragansett Pier during the fateful summer of 1879. She had "been presented to the ex-governor" in Washington, despite the fact (or perhaps because of it) that she was "not in society."[22] After the wedding Inez brought her younger sister, Avice, to live at Canonchet. The fifteen-year-old Avice counted among her admirers the oil magnate Colonel Gerritt Wheaton, who often stayed at Canonchet; her brother-in-law, William Sprague; and William's son, Willie. Soon after Avice arrived at Canonchet, nineteen-year-old Willie began reading her poetry and taking her for walks along the shore. Newspapers reported that the boy "forsook his mustang and rifle, and was no longer seen making his wild dashes over hedge and ditch." The two quietly married on 25 July 1885.[23]

Willie stayed on at Canonchet for a short time, but soon he noticed that his young bride was pregnant. An indignant Willie hastily decamped, suggesting that he did not believe himself the father. Avice gave birth to Inez Sprague within months of the wedding.[24] Willie then sued her for divorce, alleging that he had not been a free agent at the time of the wedding.[25] Many believed Willie had been made a scapegoat for his father's sins, and certainly William's track record with women, especially those under his own roof, does little to exculpate him. Colonel Wheaton, whom Avice married soon after her divorce from Willie, should also be considered a candidate for the baby's paternity. Although the child was legally a Sprague, no one—not Willie, his father, his stepmother, or his ex-wife—ever asserted that Willie had become a father or should be held to the responsibilities of fatherhood. Certainly Kate never considered Avice's baby her grandchild. Nonetheless, William never forgave his son his lack of cooperation, nor did Willie forgive his father's continued alliance with the Weed sisters. Several years later Willie wrote his mother that he had been thinking of arranging a meeting with his father, "without coming into contact with those detestable parasites," but Willie and his father never reconciled.[26] William turned his back on his son, having no use for a boy who would not comply with his every wish, however sordid.

PERSONAL AND PUBLIC POLITICS IN DISGRACE

Not long after William remarried, Kate took her daughters and once more sailed for Europe. Perhaps she left to escape the social isolation that had become hers since the summer of 1879, despite her attempts to regain her social position. Perhaps Kate wanted to secure for her daughters the same high-quality education that Willie had received. She probably left for a combination of these reasons, and because Europe offered her a venue where she had never fought with William, a place that had always provided her a haven from domestic discord. Roscoe most probably fit into Kate's decision to leave the country as well. Although they had discreetly maintained their relationship at least into late 1881, Roscoe's fall from power eventually took its toll. During the summer of 1883, soon after Kate put the Atlantic between her and her old life, Roscoe and Julia Conkling took a trip to Yellowstone country together.[27] Although the joint vacation did not reflect a rebirth of the Conkling marriage, for they would continue to live apart, it may have signaled an end to Roscoe's extramarital attachment.

Kate would stay abroad for several years. She rented a small villa on the edge of the Fountainebleau Forest, thirty-seven miles from Paris. Foreign correspondents wrote that Kate lived quietly, seldom went into Paris, and devoted herself to raising her children, painting, and mastering local history. She reportedly "looks well, and wears all the old gaiety and brightness which once gave such charm to Washington society." Another correspondent described her in detail. "Her face is a face that, once seen, is seldom forgotten." Her eyes still changed from dark brown to amber, her nose remained small and feminine, and her smile was "bewitching," though her hair had dimmed from golden red to brown. He added: "She is, in the loftiest sense, a politician, and if she had been of the other sex, she would have been certain of an extraordinary following. He would be, indeed, obdurate and insensible whose vote she could not command. What a magnificent lobbyist she would make! Any measure she should advocate would be sure to pass. Her magnetism, when she chooses to exercise it, is well-nigh irresistible. She has so many charms and gifts that she may be considered one woman in a hundred thousand."[28] This article meant so much to Kate that, unlike the other interviews with journalists she had granted over the years, it was found in her private papers after her death.

Kate's house lay close to Mlle Dussant's school for young ladies. After attending Dussant's, Ethel spent a year in Leipzig and Berlin, perfecting her German and French. A governess came daily to attend to Portia's letters and numbers and to give music and voice lessons. Time made it clear that Kitty's mental development precluded any attempts at advanced education. She would remain childlike, her mother's perpetual companion.[29] Kitty had her mother's looks and her grandmother's "tubercular tendency," requiring Kate's constant care. After his parents' separation, Willie thought Kitty should come live with him and his father at Canonchet because "It is said that those with weak lungs can only be healed on the salt water." Ten years later Kitty was still under a doctor's care for "chest development."[30] Thus she became the family pet, the daughter who did not (and could not) worry about her future.

In August 1886 Kate returned to Washington to arrange for the transfer of her father's remains from Washington to Columbus, Ohio, where Kate's mother also lay. Eighteen-year-old Ethel accompanied her mother on this trip, while Portia and Kitty stayed in France. During that visit, twenty-one-year-old Willie agreed to visit his mother and sister Ethel, though he felt "very reluctant" to appear in public with them. "I look so shabby and generally dilapidated," he wrote his mother. He also worried that "the birth of the child" had strained their relationship. Willie believed it had been his duty to leave Canonchet and Avice, but he felt "utterly alone."[31] Kate also had a private audience with President Grover Cleveland, though the First Lady pled illness and declined to meet with her. Soon afterward, Kate told a reporter that she was impressed by Cleveland's "manliness," though she met him "not as a bridegroom, but as a statesman." Always the political women, Kate spoke to the journalist about affairs in France. "Speaking of exile," she quipped, "I am well acquainted with the exiled princes of France. . . . I do not regard these princes as the degenerate scions of a dying dynasty, but as men who have suffered the martyrdom of a popular prejudice. . . . I expect to live to see the day when France shall be ruled by an Orleans King. There will be no revolution of blood, but a growth from natural causes. The French republic is a misnomer. There is no Freedom and manhood, only restraint and espionage."[32]

Not only did Kate write and talk about political issues, but she continued to offer advice to powerful men, even occasionally stepping into the fray herself. According to one story, Roscoe's friend Levi Morton, then the U.S. minister to France, needed to obtain certain delicate information. Morton invited Kate to dinner and posed to her his request, which Kate politely but firmly refused to honor. Nonetheless, she asked a good number of questions about the matter, leaving Morton in hopes that she might change her mind. Several days later he received an anonymous letter containing just the information he had wanted, and his sources told him it came from

Kate. [33] After Kate returned to the States, a reporter asked her what she thought of the women involved with the suffrage movement. They had her entire sympathy, she replied, though she believed women "will do whatever they want to do; whenever they want to vote they will vote, and no power on earth will stop them."[34] Kate's belief in women's political power explains why she never became involved in women's suffrage. Her statement comes close to suggesting that she believed women, not men, had kept women out of the official exercise of political power. Certainly she had personal reasons to hold such a belief, for she had always been a political woman, despite her inability to actually cast a vote. Given Gilded Age politics, she may also have viewed the importance of voting with a somewhat jaundiced eye. Machine politics did seem to make voting an overrated political exercise. Kate's social position, though, had created for her opportunities for political power to which very few other women had access.

William did not entirely give up politics either, though his efforts would bear only the bitterest of fruit. His temperance vow of December 1882, carefully planted in the newspapers, was probably as motivated by political aspirations as by his impending matrimony. A week after his second marriage, William allowed himself to be nominated for governor by a coalition of Democrats and Independent Republicans, and newspapers around the nation erupted with indignation. "His record is beyond shameful," the *Cleveland Leader* proclaimed. "It is not even certain that he is a person of sound mind, and if not legally insane, then he is at least dangerously 'cranky.' There is nothing in his history as a public character to inspire admiration among any but the thoughtless and vicious, and yet it is as a husband and a pretended gentleman that he has been the farthest from all that right-minded people approve." The *Leader* added, "Cruelty and drunkenness and neglect of all the properties of life characterized his unhappy career." A Cincinnati paper quipped, "The Great Persecuted will endeavor to wreak vengeance upon his enemies. The shot gun is to be taken from Canonchet to the State House." The *Providence Journal* suggested that William had cloven hooves, while another local paper that a vote for Sprague "is to encourage robbery, cheating and repudiation." Even those who thought William might make a good governor had acknowledged his eccentricities. "It has been the fashion of late years to speak of the ex-Governor as half crazy or half witted," the *New York Tribune* wrote, "but he has flashes of uncommon sagacity, and whoever picks him up for a fool is apt to get burned fingers for his pains." [35] The *Providence Journal* reprinted negative editorials from across the nation as the Journal Ring continued its unremitting assault on the vestiges of Sprague power. The onetime "boy governor" overwhelmingly lost the election. Like Roscoe, William underestimated the debilitating effects of the shotgun on a career in politics—even in the Gilded Age.

Kate's quietly dignified life abroad created a tremendous contrast to William's path to infamy. Newspapers praised her for her continued beauty, charm, and intelligence. William, not one to tolerate life in the shadow of his ex-wife's fame, and perhaps seeing the coattails by which he might drag himself back into polite society's good graces, gave an interview in which he expounded on Kate's virtues:

> Mrs. Katherine Chase is a woman of rare attainments. She has a brilliant mind and many accomplishments, she is a woman of ardent affections and nature has been munificent in bestowing upon her rare charms of person and manner. She will bring up her daughters well, and they will make fine women. . . . The world has been very inconsiderate in its treatment of her. She is devoting herself to her children, to bring them up to be noble women, in honor to their blood and parentage, and she should be permitted to follow these instincts of maternity without intrusion of public comment or scandal. . . . Mrs. Chase was always a high-spirited woman accustomed to exercising her own will, and she will always do that.

William excused his failure to support this exemplary woman and her charming daughters by claiming that Kate's mother and father had left her a fortune of over $50,000. He also noted that her "usual conservatism" with regard to money matters made him sure she had a comfortable living. [36] Not only was the $50,000 a figment of William's imagination, but it seems William's tune had changed considerably from the days when he had charged Kate with moral and economic profligacy. Despite the fact that his praise also couched several rather backhanded compliments (imputing that Kate was unwomanly in her willfulness, and essentially disclaiming the girls' paternity), Inez was not pleased with the interview. Her rebuttal suggests William's interview had landed him in quite a bit of trouble at home:

> Since Katherine Chace [*sic*] has been agitating the removal of her father's body, she has beguiled the interim by entertaining reporters with

reminiscences, and shadowing forth her charms, assuring the public she married Governor Sprague to further her father's political interests, thus martyring herself on the altar of Mammon. By her own confession, purity, refinement, and all the other instances of womanhood were warped and blighted when she sold herself to Governor Sprague. Treachery and deceit were the parents of disloyalty and disunion, from which naturally issues treason and continued spite. I have ever felt kindly towards her—for her actions have given me the love of the noblest and grandest of men, and would only ask her to hesitate ere she bring into connection with her a name that belongs wholly and entirely to another.

I do not object to her regaling her friends by expatiating on her personal attractions (if she permits fondness for the antique to carry her to such length) neither do I object to her reveling in past conquests, if she can find listeners, but I demand that she does not refer to my husband in any form whatever. We extend to her our united pity, which she ever and always commands.[37]

Inez also claimed that William's recent interview had been a fraud perpetrated by Kate in her indecent quest for fame. In reality, Kate had not referred to her ex-husband in any of her interviews, nor did she ever refer to herself as "Mrs. Sprague." She unerringly refused to comment on her personal life, except to extol her father's accomplishments. In fact, Kate's 1886 unwillingness to give personal details probably explains why newspaper articles concentrated on her father's career and the state of French politics. Rather, the bitter tone of Inez Sprague's answer to her husband's friendly comments about Kate suggests a deep jealousy—one perhaps provoked by William's continued admiration for a woman whose public stature Inez would never attain.

Whatever the second Mrs. Sprague's shortcomings might have been, Inez had accomplished what Kate never could—she made a lasting and apparently happy marriage with William. Undoubtedly William's new sobriety greatly assisted the Spragues' marital felicity, cutting down on his problems with abuse and infidelity. But more than that, Inez and William were simply a much better match. Inez never made William feel as deeply inadequate or undeserving as Kate did, however much Kate did not intend to inspire such feelings. Inez, with her gaudy murals and morals, never made William feel like a social climber. Her acceptance of the goings-on among Avice, Willie, and either Colonel Wheaton or her husband indicates in Inez a certain moral flexibility that no daughter of Salmon P. Chase could ever master, a pliancy William must have viewed with considerable relief. Inez also simply handled William better. Kate's inability to make William conform to her vision of manhood not only exacerbated his vast insecurity but signified a certain clumsiness on her part when handling such a potentially explosive substance as William Sprague. This is not to suggest in any way that it was Kate's fault that she fell victim to a myriad of domestic abuses, but rather that she seemed almost incapable of connecting with her husband in ways that did not enrage him. Of course, the possibility also exists that William did not appreciably change his ways after his 1883 marriage but that Inez simply tolerated the situation more than Kate had. Certainly more domestic abuse has taken place than has been documented, and we only know of William's penchant for domestic violence because Kate broke the code of silence.

Not long after Inez's outburst, she had William divest himself of the art Kate had collected in Europe. The *New York Times* announced the sale of 160 of William's paintings to be auctioned "for Mrs. Sprague's benefit." Although the collection included works by many American artists, most were of French origin, including some by Corot and Courbet. The two-day sale netted Inez $23,660, which she promptly spent on improvements at Canonchet.[38] The next year notices appeared that the Spragues intended to sell Canonchet, hoping to realize a tidy profit of $800,000. A consortium of New York capitalists proposed to purchase the property and turn it into a resort, with the mansion serving as a summer clubhouse, but nothing ever came of the plan.[39]

In the spring of 1888 it once again became clear that years of alcoholism had done little to improve William's reasoning abilities or temper his paranoia. This time his fight centered on Rhode Island's desire to make a memorial of a Bull Run cannon on the statehouse lawn. The aged war hero became incensed at the proposal, saying the gun had been his and that he had given it to his old artillery company—but not for them to donate to the state. In a letter to the state government, William vented his ire:

> It cannot, of course, be the State's intention to erect a memorial to myself, since it has during the past 20 years driven me nearly into the ocean, where I think I am impregnable against all its assaults. If, however, the contrary should prove to be the case, I have already designated my last retreat, that

between Beaver Tail Light and the lightship, and the gun must be near me for that eventuality. We will then lay thee as a personal memorial, face downward; we will lie down together, forcing the State to enact the early rebel role when burning our dead face downward, to indicate the malignity of the ounce of its power. Bullets are crude but effective antidotes in the one case, as they were in the other.[40]

However incoherent his letter was, the former governor's meaning was well taken. Sadly, he had actually given permission for the project earlier in the year. Several of his admirers had proposed that the cannon be used as a memorial to William's brave and voluntary service during the war. Brooding within the halls of "Castle Canonchet," William had forgotten the project's original purpose. This episode also suggests that William may have been in violation of his 1882 temperance pledge.

In the spring of 1887, about the time Inez was auctioning the Sprague art collection, Kate and the girls moved back to Edgewood. In his will Salmon had left his estate jointly to Kate and her sister, but Nettie, who was happily married and economically well off, wanted nothing to do with the property. In 1873, right after Salmon's death, she offered to sell her half of Edgewood to Kate, but the failure of A. & W. Sprague complicated matters. Not only did Kate have a difficult time acquiring the funds, but the feud between the Hoyt and Sprague branches of the family embroiled the Chase sisters. Nettie and Will Hoyt showed little inclination to smooth the way for a Sprague, and they slowed the sale of Edgewood into 1876. The Hoyts even made arrangements to sell Edgewood to another buyer, but the estate's lawyer "persuaded them to wait." Kate wrote letters to her sister assuring her that she wished no misunderstandings to foul their relationship. Nettie thought her sister was stalling the deal for some mysterious and nefarious purposes, though Kate tried to explain that "I did my utmost with the material I had to work with & the impediments I found in my way." Finally, in early 1876 Kate took a quick trip to Washington in an effort to secure her rights to Edgewood, leaving her girls in France under a nanny's care.[41] Although Kate eventually purchased Nettie's half of the estate for $16,875 (at 6 percent interest), the enmity between the two branches of the family poisoned the sisters' relationship for the rest of their lives.[42] Kate would die unreconciled with her only sibling.

By 1887 the Sprague girls had become young women. Portia, fifteen, and

Kitty, almost fourteen, had spent many of their formative years abroad, and Kate believed they needed to become familiar with their own country. Ethel would be eighteen in the fall and wanted to begin acting. When she announced her intention to take to the stage, a journalist asked her if her mother approved. "Oh yes! She makes no objections," Ethel proclaimed. "She sees that I am determined and she has not at any time absolutely tried to dissuade me from my purpose."[43] Many found evidence of Kate's moral degradation in the fact that she would allow her daughter to become an actress. Rather, Kate may have, for obvious reasons, encouraged Ethel's efforts to become financially independent. Also, Kate had relished acting in parlor productions herself, once enjoying the part of Mary, Queen of Scots so much that she had her picture taken in costume.

Willie needed his mother's assistance as well. Once again unemployed, the young man had finally broken off all contact with his father. Apparently William had once promised Willie a portion of A. & W. Sprague, going so far as to sign over to his son a trust deed to the Quidnick mill. But Inez would not have it (or rather, would have it all) and ensured that the Sprague men remained estranged. Not long after Kate arrived home in 1887 the prodigal son visited his mother. She arranged a job for him as a photoengraver for the Long Island Railroad Company, but Willie soon quit. His wild habits were not conducive to steady employment.[44] Kate sent money to him when he needed it, let him stay at Edgewood when unemployed, and continually reminded him how much she loved him. She suffered through his alcoholic binges, and each time he sobered up he would tell his mother he felt "heartily ashamed" about his behavior.[45]

In 1889 Ethel encouraged her mother to take a final trip abroad. Kate had been unwell, and her daughter hoped the trip would restore her health to its old vibrancy. Ethel and a governess took charge of the younger girls so that Kate could travel alone. Ethel wrote to Willie: "The trip will no doubt do Mother lots of good & she needed it badly, we are awfully broken up about the parting. I feel so awfully about Mother, she seemed so ill that I really felt it unsafe for her to travel alone."[46] Kate arrived back in New York by Christmas, but no amount of travel could cure her of what ailed her. By 1890 ill health had begun to take its toll, and in her fifties Kate began to look like an old woman. Mrs. Henry Villard, who had not seen Kate since the halcyon days of the mid-1860s, described the contrast:

Kate Chase was the most bewitching of the queens in the garden of roses. . . . I a simple young home body from New England never before had seen so beautiful and brilliant a creature as Kate Chase; and it seemed to me then that nothing could blight her perfection. That was the only time I ever saw her until towards the end of her life when she was overtaken by misfortune and poverty, and my husband was exerting himself in her behalf. One day, he said to me, "Would you mind inviting Kate Chase to our home for a few days?" I replied that I would be happy to receive a woman I had so much admired years before. She came with my husband; I never would nave recognized her otherwise. The glorious eyes were dull and inflamed as though scalded by salt tears; she apologized for her looks, saying that she had been on the coast and the air did not agree with her— a subterfuge, I felt sure. Poor broken woman! She elicited my pity, but not my admiration. [47]

Not long after Kate's visit to the chilly Mrs. Villard, Willie headed west. First he went to Chicago, where he took a job with an electrical supply house as a "mechanic." He optimistically wrote his mother about the alarm clock he had invented and assured her that "I have met a great many nice fellows (who dont drink)." He believed he had a promising future. [48] That job did not last either, and within three months he moved to Seattle to take a job with the local paper. In October 1890, at the age of twenty-five, Willie killed himself.

"A Wild and Reckless Career Brought to a Close," read the *New York Times*. Willie had failed to show up for his new job as the manager of the engraving department for the *Seattle Journal*. A co-worker went to Willie's boardinghouse and found him in bed, sheets in disarray, his naked body exhibiting the "torture of self-destruction." He had cut his wrists, lost his nerve, and tried to stanch the flow of blood with a shirt; when that failed, he soaked a sheet in chloroform and wrapped it around his head, falling unconscious while his life ran out with the gushing blood at his wrist. The *Times* concluded that Willie "was a pretty wild boy, but was thought to have settled down." [49] Reporters for the Seattle paper quickly telegraphed the news around the country.

Journalists and readers found the news particularly shocking because popular theory in the last two decades of the century held that suicide resulted from the evils of modern social conditions. Poverty, dirt, and disease encouraged self-destruction in a world that had lost its moral center, or so social theory held. "Suicide is often regulated by the price of bread," one psychologist quipped. That William Sprague's heir, a child of privilege and not the streets, would find himself subject to such mental stresses surprised and shocked many people. Ten years earlier, the son of successful journalist Ambrose Bierce had committed murder-suicide. Observers found the act so incomprehensible that one journalist thought the deed might be a "moral lesson" to his father, a man famed for his acerbic wit. Struck down with grief for months, Bierce seemed to agree, though he never moderated his journalistic style.[50]

A reporter found Kate at lunch and broke the horrible news, but she refused to believe the report. "I received a cheerful letter from him from Chicago only a few days before he left that city," she told the reporter. "There was nothing in it to indicate that he was not feeling well or happy."[51] Mid-nineteenth-century theorists had also linked suicide to ill health. A person who was well adjusted mentally had to be physically well. Doctors often treated those who attempted suicide with bleeding, laxatives, and purgatives to address the patient's somatic imbalance. Thus Kate's mention of Willie's being "well" references an earlier belief that only a physically ill person would contemplate self-destruction. The journalist assured Kate that the news was indeed quite correct and reported that he found her grief "quite affecting." Kate immediately wrote to Willie's father.

> Governor Sprague,
> This terrible blow ends our poor boys life of struggle & disappointment. If God forgives you, He will be merciful indeed, for at your door lies this unnatural crime.
> A home I have sacrificed, everything in life to maintain the heritage of the man who loved us all & died so full of confidence & hope. A mothers heart full of devotion, patience & hope, all were powerless to save this poor boy from what he called his "heritage of woe." A letter from him the day he left Chicago for Seattle dated Sept 19 was cheerful & hopeful.
> What a bitter disappointment & desolation of spirit must he have endured to have induced self-murder. I have telegraphed to friends in Seattle to do all that can be done to properly bestow the poor body.
> Will you meet me in New York within a few days to determine upon arrangements for its final internment.
> A broken hearted
> Mother

In this sad [role] I cannot but believe that you will wish to act with me.[52]

William, however, did not wish to act with his ex-wife in this or any other matter. Kate sent Ethel to Providence to make the funeral arrangements without her father.

The day after Kate wrote her letter, William told a reporter that he had not heard from his son in over a month and that he did not know his son's plans or what had caused such despair. "Will was always more with his mother than with me," the former governor coolly lied, adding, "He was always a restless, roving lad and impatient of disappointment. He very likely made an end to himself in a fit of despondency at having gone out there so far to no purpose."[53] If William's self-absolution convinced anyone but himself, his state of grace lasted only a short time. The friend who had found Willie also recovered three unfinished letters. There was one to Ethel and one to his mother, each "couched in the most affectionate terms."[54] The third letter Willie addressed to his father—a letter so damning that William's enemies at the *Providence Journal* printed it eight days after Willie killed himself.

I sent you a postal upon the eve of my departure as an item of news, as I imagine that news is pretty scarce down there—not that you don't have your little diversions and slight sensations in the matrimonial line, for instance, but then one always likes to hear from former friends and acquaintances. Not that you have given me any encouragement to spring my bright scintillation's of wit and humor upon you. Oh, no—quite the contrary. . . .

Your letter was one of those cold and chilling communications that pass between men when one gets a bill of goods charged more than is shown in the invoice. Talk to me about the howling blizzard of the North Pole, the awful absence of heat when a friend won't lend you a V! Lord Massey! take these seats away back in the rear, and hide their faces in very shame in the face of that letter! With my sensitive and highly considerate nature, I cannot conceive how a man can so ruthlessly knock a man down, or, in fact, no cause. But it really matters little, except to my feelings, and they are practically of no use, except to me. . . .

Out here I am thrown among strangers again, cast upon a desert isle, as far as soul communication is concerned. I cannot tell how I long for love and affection, that I have never experienced, and cannot describe, yet long for. Ah me, I fear my dream will never be realized. But this sentimental "biz" will never do. I had a lot of it stowed up and had to work it off. I have a boozy recollection of having written you a letter containing an outline of a proposition made me by these people, and there . . . [55]

Here the letter ended, as if young Sprague had run out of paper, hope, or both.

Willie's funeral illustrated the family's deep divisions. Kate, Ethel, Portia, and Kitty, Ethel's fiancée, Frank Donaldson, and the widows of William's cousin Byron and his brother, Amasa (who were also mother and daughter), sat on one side of the church, backed by past employees from the family estate at Narragansett Pier. Perry Greenman, who had known Willie as a boy and worked for the family for years, wrote to Kate that her ex-husband "has no friends at Narragansett."[56] William and Inez sat on the other side of the church, attended by Avice, young Inez (Willie's legal child), and Avice's second husband, Colonel Wheaton.[57] After the service a train took Willie's body to Providence, where the Swan Point Cemetery received the body.

Kate and the girls stayed with Willie's body until the end, and the crowds waiting in Providence saw a bereft mother "weeping and trembling under her sorrow."[58] William skipped the trip to Swan Point, causing Perry Greenman to write that "most everyone thinks that he did not care any thing for his only son and there is lots of people . . . that would like to have mobbed him after it was over[;] to think that he would not even go to the train to see his boys remains put on the train much more not to go to Swan Point."[59] Perhaps William needed to do his grieving in private, or perhaps he understood the indelicacy of foisting Inez and Avice upon Kate at such a time, or maybe he really had become a heartless and unloving father. He had once loved his son enough to write to Kate, "How is the little angel. Does your heart cling to him. Is he not a great comfort to you and is not your heart more free, more open from his freshness and his presence—My dear this should be a chain, the links of which should be eternal to bind our hearts together."[60] Willie's death, though, highlighted how these chains had eroded beyond repair.

William survived his son's death with little apparent personal trauma. He and Inez continued to live at Canonchet and occasionally traveled abroad. Avice and her husband visited so often that baby Inez became like a daughter to the Spragues. The former governor continued to believe himself a man of importance. In 1898, as thousands of men mustered for the Spanish-American War, he reminisced with reporters about his glorious Civil War experience and claimed he would soon go to Washington to tender the president his services.[61] If he did so, William McKinley declined the old war governor's help.

BITTER VICTORY

Roscoe died as he had lived, with a flamboyant flourish. On 12 March 1888, New York experienced one of the most spectacular blizzards of the decade. Although he was suffering from what was most probably a brain tumor, Roscoe spent three hours walking twenty-five blocks through waist-high snow from his office on Wall Street to the New York Club. He had refused a cab because he thought the driver asked too high a fee for the dangerous traverse. Arriving at his club covered in snow and ice, he staggered through the front door and collapsed in the hall. Club employees temporarily revived him and eventually moved him back to his rooms. For the next two weeks Roscoe attempted to act as if he suffered no ill effects of his trudge through the storm, but the lingering respiratory infection, combined with an abscess on his head, forced him to seek medical attention. Doctors opened and drained the abscess but found that it had "begun to press dangerously upon the membranes of the brain." Delirium and coma followed swiftly on the heels of the operation. Although doctors had hope that Roscoe's legendary strength might pull him through, his wife and daughter were summoned. Visitors streamed through his apartment, and crowds waited outside for the latest news from the bedside. The senator succumbed within a week of his operation, a victim of pulmonary edema.[62]

Roscoe maintained his silence about the scandal of 1879 until his death. One of his eulogists represented his silence as strength: "He was maligned, misrepresented and misunderstood—but he would not answer. He knew that character speaks louder and far more than words. . . . His silence, better than any form of speech, refuted every charge."[63] Others judged him more harshly, one critic claiming that "there is not the slightest evidence that his soul has ever risen above pap and patronage," adding that he thought the senator a "patriot of flesh-pots."[64] Indicative of both the admiration and the loathing Roscoe inspired, another man summed up his life as follows: "He was a man of much ability and too proud to sham or steal, but over-bearing and vain—not constructive on anything, but destructive—a political gladiator—nothing more. Quarreling with everybody—even to his wife and daughter, his only child. . . . Hardly worthy to be called a statesman, and as an orator very pompous and inflated, yet strong and wonderful at times in his rhetoric."[65] Clarence Darrow thought him "cold and selfish," but in 1875 when white senators snubbed a black senator from Mississippi, Roscoe made a public point to befriend the man. He had also used his physical might to protect the failing Thaddeus Stevens in 1860 in the House of Representatives from southern members intent on assaulting the old Radical, and whatever people said of him, he had not abandoned Kate in 1879. Although he was often excoriated as a man of little principle, nothing could be further from the truth. Roscoe had ideals and honor. He believed in black suffrage and women's rights. But he believed in power more than anything else, and that made him a quintessentially modern politician. What Kate thought of her lover's death remains a mystery.

Around the time of Roscoe's death, Kate, a longtime believer of temperance (given her parental training and her husband's habitual intoxication), supported legislation against saloons in the suburbs of Washington. The reform was successful in March 1891, and newspapers called it "Kate Chase's Victory." [66] Kate's involvement in local prohibition represents the logical outcome of her years as a Republican woman. Not only had the corruption of the Grant years morally tainted the Republican Party, but Kate's breach of respectability after 1879 made her an outsider among party elites. Her 1881 letters to Pomeroy and Arthur suggest that she repudiated the Republican Party for its treatment of Roscoe during the ruinous Stalwart/Half-Breed schism. The Prohibition (or "Home Protection") Party platform both repudiated drink and endorsed women's suffrage. Prohibitionists offered women unprecedented levels of direct partisan power. "No party," Rebecca Edwards claims, "had ever offered women so many possibilities for direct power."[67] Women made up over 30 percent of the delegates at most of the party's national conventions. Not only would this clear line to political power have appealed to Kate, but its stratagem of claiming that temperance protected women and children from male violence would have had significant personal resonance. The Woman's Christian Temperance Union (wctu) called sobriety measures "home protection," arguing that drunkenness ruined families by diverting resources to saloons and encouraging family violence. The wctu officially endorsed the Prohibition Party in 1885. Kate had yet another reason to find it a congenial political home. In the 1884 election, prohibitionists claimed to have siphoned off just enough of the Republican vote to ensure the defeat of Conkling's most powerful nemesis, James G. Blaine, at the hands of Democrat Grover Cleveland.[68]

By the mid-1890s Kate had sold almost everything she had of value, had asked every man of wealth she knew to invest in Edgewood, and had failed to find a buyer for the dilapidated estate. Her borrowing power exhausted, she attempted to turn Edgewood into a paying concern. She raised chickens and vegetables and drove her own carriage to deliver eggs in the city. Despite her considerable efforts, Kate could not make farming pay. Biographers have charged that Kate inherited her father's inability to manage money—a weakness exacerbated by years of profligate spending as the wife of William Sprague. It is difficult to judge the accuracy of this assessment, though Kate's letters to her husband and Will Hoyt after 1873 indicate that she understood a great deal about how a business worked and how to manage money.[69] More likely no one could have wrung enough money from asparagus, milk, and eggs to keep afloat an estate like Edgewood, which required constant upkeep.[70] In the years after Willie's death Kate borrowed $44,000 against Edgewood, but the failing farm gobbled up the capital. At one point she almost sold the property, but bad luck struck again. An old friend of her father's offered Kate $115,000 for the estate, but as he made a final inspection of the grounds a thief mugged the old gentleman. He died a few days later.[71]

In January 1895, Washington Loan and Trust, which held the mortgage on Edgewood, attempted to auction the estate's contents to cover delinquent payments on the loan. Kate protested the company's actions, saying that they "charged her with having borrowed larger sums than she ever received." The trust company managed to partially empty the house before Kate presented it with an injunction to stop the removal of her "family pictures and relics brought from all parts of the world and a bust of her father."[72] Six months later the bank foreclosed on the mortgage, giving Kate until 1 February 1896 to buy back the property.

However beneficent this offer might sound, the company required Kate and Kitty to immediately vacate the premises. Essentially homeless, Kate went first to Ohio, then to New York, hoping she could influence wealthy investors to part with their cash so that she might turn the property into a monument to her father. Henry Villard, J. P. Morgan, C. P. Huntington, Levi Morton, and others agreed to contribute to a fund that would pay the mortgage and allow Kate an income of four thousand dollars a year for two years. Politicians from Ohio each gave five thousand dollars, as did Kate's old friend Levi Morton. The consortium announced that they intended Edgewood as an investment, though observers believed the whole scheme was more a matter of charity. In reality the land Edgewood stood on, at the developing edge of the capital, had considerable value as part of a future suburb. Streets had been surveyed and laid up to the edge of the property, and eventually the estate was sold and developed.[73]

In the meantime, trustees believed that Kate could live off the proceeds of fifteen lots carved from Edgewood's grounds. Unfortunately, the trustees proved no more successful than Kate at wringing money out of the decaying estate, and they failed to pay her the second year's income as stipulated, leaving her in "straitened circumstances" once again.[74] Thus, though her home had been purchased by a trust that allowed her to live there as long as she desired, Kate had no income upon which to live except what she made from farming. Her efforts were real, as this note to a neighbor attests:

> I was sorry not to be able to send you the asparagus and rhubarb for your dinner today. Kindly give your order at night for the next day and we will be glad to fill it if we have what you wish. What we have is good and I am pleased to send it to one so appreciative as you always are. We have now milk—2 fresh cows and a good deal of milk and cream. Are there any of your neighbors who would care to have our milk and cream?
>
> My work this year is largely field work. My men go to work early and are constantly busy until six P.M. and we run no wagon so can only serve after working hours.[75]

This from a woman who had once been married to a millionaire, who had dined with princes and presidents, and who had been the queen of Washington society. No one ever heard Kate complain about the work, and she clearly did not believe herself above it.

Several days after hearing of the endowment that allowed the infamous Kate Chase to live in relative security, a reporter went out to Edgewood to survey the scene. He found the house partially empty, much of its furniture auctioned off, dust everywhere and the windows dirty. An empty frame hung above the fireplace, though the marble bust of Salmon P. Chase still held pride of place on the mantel. "Not a sound is heard about the house," the man reported, "and over the whole place hangs an air of solitude, of desolation that makes the dingy mansion seem a black cloud in a bright landscape."[76] Important men had once visited there, men like Garfield, Grant, Sumner, Sherman, and Conkling. The grounds where the First Rhode Island Regiment had camped so long ago also lay nearby, as did the hills and woods where Kate and her "boy governor" had once ridden— he on his white stallion and she on shining black Atalanta. At Edgewood Kate could keep Kitty safe and play with her grandson. Ethel had left acting after only a couple of years to marry a doctor named Frank Donaldson, with whom she had a son named Chase. Young Chase Donaldson was a great favorite with his grandmother, so much so that Ethel left him at Edgewood for days at a time. Ethel would complain to her mother that she spoiled the boy, who never wanted to leave his grandmother's house.[77]

Hard work and poverty exacerbated Kate's deteriorating physical condition. In 1899, after feeling ill for several years, she finally called in a doctor. Unfortunately, her condition had progressed too far to benefit from medical attention. She had developed what doctors then called Bright's disease, a generic term once used for all kidney ailments. Her symptoms suggested that she had end-stage renal disease and that kidney failure caused her death. The last three months of her life she weakened, suffering from congestive heart failure, severe high blood pressure, and decreasing nervous system function. This last problem caused her to have convulsions during her last days. Kate died just before dawn on 31 July 1899. The doctors predicted her demise sufficiently for her daughters to gather at her bedside during her last hours—Portia from Narragansett Pier, Ethel from Brooklyn. Obituaries extolled the charm and grace of her manner, her brilliant social career, and her great success with the political men of her time. The *New York Times* noted that "she had a rare personal magnetism, a faculty of drawing out the best traits in others, and while shining herself pre-eminently she was able to keep about her the most prominent leaders in politics." The *Times* went on to note the recent failure in Kate's fortunes: "Washingtonians of this generation recognize in the name of Kate Chase only the memory of a career of which many years of sadness followed a few years of youthful excitement and pleasure." The *Washington Post* also reviewed Kate's fall from grace but found virtue in her penury: "Mrs. Chase bore her comparative poverty without complaint. She might have relieved her condition if she had given to the world some of her father's secrets."[78] Loyal to the end, Kate took what secrets she knew to the grave. Her memoirs would have been fascinating, and she could have settled a myriad of scores, not the least with William. But Kate, who had said so much to help Roscoe, would say nothing to help herself.

Ethel arranged to have her mother's body temporarily interred at Glenwood Cemetery, the least prestigious of Washington's three cemeteries. The girls eventually moved their mother's body to Mount Auburn Cemetery in Columbus and laid her to rest beside her beloved father and the mother she never really knew.[79] Portia and Ethel closed up Edgewood, sold the animals, and gave their mother's dogs to a farmer several miles away. The house lay dark and empty, inhabited only by the ghosts of past glory. Few remembered the young war hero with the yellow plume in his hat, or the beautiful young woman who had dazzled him. William had nothing public to say about the death of the woman who had once had all his pulsations. Only the dogs remembered. After the funeral they found their way back across the city to Edgewood's porch, where they were found waiting for Kate.

The tragedy of Kate's life is not that it ended in poverty and obscurity but that Kate suffered from too little love in her life. Even Nettie, who had so adored her sister as a child, repudiated Kate in the family quarrel between the Spragues and the Hoyts. Not long after Kate's death a relative wrote Nettie a condolence letter. Nettie answered with bitterness:

> I feel as if an unhappy chapter of my life has been closed. What grieved me beyond everything, more than any injustice to me, was the way Kate (though she did not realize the harm she was doing) injured her father's memory.
>
> The unjust & grossly exaggerated criticisms of his great desire for "the presidency" came all through her intrigues with second rate politicians during the latter part of his life. And since his death it was very very hard for me to have her beg money in his name. However that is all over now. Poor soul, her life was certainly a tragic one.[80]

Nettie would be neither the first nor the last to blame Kate for her father's ambition, but that makes her no less wrong. There can be little doubt that Salmon chose his own course, and nothing indicates this better than his own voluminous correspondence. Nettie's letter also illustrates her inability to understand the difficulty Kate experienced after the divorce—the loss of income and respectability coupled with a family background and social situation which ill prepared Kate for making her own living. Certainly Nettie never had to face a similar challenge. Not too many sentences after she criticized her sister for "begging money," Nettie mentions moving out of their "country club house" and into town for the winter. From her comfortable social position she could find neither sympathy nor empathy for her sister, though Kate had devoted years to acting as a stand-in parent for Nettie. She must have known what kind of husband William had been, even if she did not know the extent of the abuse. In the end she failed her only sister and made herself as culpable as William and Salmon for Kate's end.

Like Nettie, the New Hampshire politician and Washington insider Benjamin Brown French knew Kate at the height of her powers. Having seen her at a New Year's Day reception only weeks after her marriage, he wrote in his journal, "I think her one of the most lovable women I ever saw, and I wished her many, many, happy years from my heart."[81] However lovable she might have been, in 1868, in the midst of the Spragues' first great marital crisis, Kate recorded her feelings on a scrap of paper—sentiments she kept among her personal papers until her death:

> I dwell so constantly upon the absence from my life of a [word illegible] kinder, devoted love. Perhaps I have no right to the only thing that gives real value to all my other blessings. They are many fold & very rich, it is true, but how gladly would I exchange them all & consider that I gained everything by that exchange could I awaken & possess the Governor's great treasure my soul craves. Whatever the fault my heart seems withering, dying. I feel now & then one warm glad impulse & then relapses into apathy & chill. One by one hopes fade away & happiness turns to solemn & melancholy which I can not resist is fastening itself upon me. Vigor & youth remain as yet & when they too, as time speeds on, fade away, God help me![82]

She had loved William, Roscoe, and her father more than they had loved her—and she connected the absence of romance in her life with her poverty.

On the flyleaf of a volume of verse, found after her death, Kate wrote these words.

> *Canst thou bear cold and hunger?*
> *Can these arms*
> *Framed for the tender offices of love*
> *Endure the bitter gripes of smarting poverty?*

It would be nice to believe that Kate found peace in her last few years, solace in a quiet life with her girls, dogs, and chickens. Some days she may have. But Kate had not been trained by the ambitious Salmon P. Chase to enjoy the pastoral advantages of genteel poverty, nor did her preeminence in the glittering political whirl of wartime and Reconstruction Washington prepare her for a life of quiet obscurity. Having made her choice, having been removed from the world of political power, Kate underlined the following lines of poetry in one of her books:

> *Ah, little think the gay licentious crowd*
> *Whom pleasure, power and affluence surround;*
> *They who their thoughtless hours in giddy mirth*
> *And wanton, often cruel riot waste—*
>
> *Ah, little think they while they dance along,*
> *How many fell this very moment death*
> *And all the sad variety of pain;*
>
> *How many drink the cup*
> *Of Baleful grief, or eat the bitter bread*
> *Of misery, sore pierced by wintry winds;*
>
> *How many shrink into the sordid hut*
> *Of cheerless poverty.* [83]

Kate's search for love and acceptance consumed her life. Politics functioned as a way to gain approval from her father, and when she found she had great talent for governmental intrigue, politics set her apart from other women, made her special and notable. She mastered public politics but failed at the private politics of marital life. Her union with William went down as an unmitigated disaster; however, the marriage did not fail because she did not love him, but rather because she loved him too well—too well to take his infidelities as a matter of course, too well not to rage against his repeated failure to live up to his written promises. "Funny Kate," her father had written when she was only three years old, "she desires love." [84] If her father could have foreseen where that desire would take his "accomplished" daughter, he might not have thought the matter so amusing.

THIS HOUSE OF TRAGEDY

After Kate's death, William and Inez continued to live in relative prosperity at Canonchet. In 1900 Narragansett elected the aging "boy governor" town council president. In 1904 a bearded and seventy-four-year-old William marched in a Grand Army of the Republic parade in Boston. [85] Despite his years of debauchery, he appeared strong and fit. Eight years after Kate died, William and Inez again attempted to sell Canonchet. With the improvements Inez had made at the house—the added greenhouses, stables, and 350 acres of grounds, all financed by Avice's husband—Canonchet was said to be worth $1 million. They had been planning to leave the estate to young Inez Sprague, Willie's legal daughter, but in 1907 she broke her engagement to J. Harold Winpenny of Philadelphia and eloped with Harry William Stiness, son of John H. Stiness, a retired Rhode Island Associate Supreme Court judge. The senior Stiness was an unofficial member of the Journal Ring, friend of manufacturing rival Brown & Ives, and, William believed, one of the men responsible for A. & W. Sprague's bankruptcy. "He did his utmost to accomplish my financial ruin," William declared of the elder Stiness. "I can never forgive her." [86] William and Inez then instructed their lawyer to forfeit young Inez's inheritance by selling Canonchet. The senior Spragues planned to use the proceeds to live abroad. "Yes, historic Canonchet is for sale," Inez told a reporter. "We are disappointed and broken in spirit. The Governor and I are going to put the Atlantic between us and the place's recurring tragedies." She melodramatically added, "All that years of family pride and our fighting spirit has preserved is now wrecked by Inez's surrender to the son of our old enemy. For us, it is finished." [87] The Spragues, it would seem, had learned nothing from Willie's suicide. Hubris and selfishness continued to rule the day.

Known as "the house of tragedy," Canonchet went unsold. William and Inez must have forgiven the new Mrs. Stiness, for she gave birth to her first child at Canonchet, a baby girl she named Avice. In the summer of 1909 the elder Avice solidified her daughter's position at Canonchet when she induced her third husband to purchase the property. [88] That October, William ordered fires kindled in Avice's suite of rooms, prefatory to her return to Rhode Island. A defective flue threw sparks onto the house's dry shingles, starting a blaze that eventually consumed the house. Michael Allen, the family coachman, discovered the fire at 2 A.M. and hustled the occupants to safety. Rash and impetuous to the last, seventy-two-year-old William rushed back into the burning house, determined to save his personal papers. Inez prevailed upon the coachman to follow her husband.

Almost overcome by smoke, Allen stopped on the second floor and wrapped wet cloths about his head, then went in search of the old governor. He found him in the bathtub of a third-story bathroom and carried him out of the house. Onlookers said the house was "almost a furnace" by the time the two emerged into the night air. The local fire department proved no match for four-story, sixty-eight-room wooden structure, particularly since the fire hoses did not reach from the nearest hydrant to the house. Firemen from nearby Wakefield and Peacedale (towns just west of Narragansett) brought more fire hose, but the delay doomed the mansion before any water could touch the inferno. The local newspaper reported that the building burned in under two hours, creating "a magnificent spectacle as the flames leaped from floor to floor and the column of flame soured high into the air." Inez estimated the loss at $650,000, though the Spragues carried only $200,000 worth of insurance.[89]

With the destruction of Canonchet went the last piece of property in the once-mighty Sprague empire. William and Inez, unwilling to face the wreak of their fortune, remade their lives abroad. Also, granddaughter Inez was in Paris and had filed for divorce. Not immune to Mrs. Stiness's beauty and fortune, a count and marquis were said to be ambitiously courting her attentions. The Spragues stood watch over young Inez until the divorce was final in 1910, then hustled her back to America, but not before the French suitors and William had angry words and threatened duels while at the train station. Inez (the younger) declared, "Husbands are nearly all failures. Husbands are bores. I prefer an aeroplane to a husband." Given the marriages she'd seen up close, was it any wonder?[90]

William claimed that Paris was "the only civilized place to live"— this from the man who in 1869 had publicly excoriated his wife for the "immoralities" she brought home from Europe. In early 1910 William suffered a stroke that left him partially paralyzed. The biographer Henry Shoemaker interviewed the governor that summer and found his mind "undimmed by the inroads of age." When the Germans threatened Paris in 1914, the aged war governor and his wife fled the city in "a dilapidated fiacre, drawn by a rheumatic horse." About twenty miles from the city, William saw German airplanes in the sky. He climbed out of his car and lashed an American flag to its roof—a flag they had brought with them at William's request so that Inez might wrap his body in it if he did not survive his last brush with war.[91] Thus equipped, the Spragues escaped their last brush with adventure, unscathed as always. The couple then sailed for Narragansett, where they spent the summer at Avice's cottage on the Canonchet property—a dwelling that had escaped the 1909 fire.

Asked about her father's midwar return, Portia, by then Mrs. Charles Whitney, told reporters that it was probably true that Inez Sprague-Stiness planned to marry French Baron D'Orsay. The elder Spragues "declined to comment on the engagement."[92] Evidently the younger Inez was allowing herself to be wooed by impoverished European nobility once again.

The Spragues returned to Paris after only a short stay in Rhode Island. As the war escalated, the couple converted their apartment on the Rue de la Pompe into a "convalescent hospital for the wounded of all nationalities." Inez assisted by giving up her dressing room for use as a pharmacy. A year later, one day short of his eighty-fifth birthday, William died, a victim of spinal meningitis complicated by old age. After a funeral service in Paris, Inez shipped her husband's body back to New York. Governor Beeckham sent an escort of prominent Rhode Islanders to meet Mrs. Sprague and escort her to Narragansett Pier. The Spragues had the funeral at St. Peters-by-the-Sea, just as they had for young Willie, and laid William to rest in the family mausoleum at Swan Point Cemetery. William and Willie lay under the same roof once more. A seventeen-gun salute and taps marked the end of William's tumultuous life. He had outlived his son by twenty-five years, Kate by sixteen. He was the last of the Civil War governors, and as one biographer observed, the country was less surprised by his death than by the fact that he had lived so long.[93]

Inez did not return to Paris, choosing instead to live out her life in the States. Six months after her husband's funeral, Anderson Galleries auctioned 236 pieces from the Sprague collection, netting the widow over $18,000. A set of Heppelwhite dining room chairs alone brought a staggering $1,800. Other items auctioned included Heppelwhite parlor chairs and matching settee, a tapestry-upholstered living room suite, a Louis XVI inlaid, mahogany commode, and a Queen Anne cut crystal chandelier with matching wall sconces. It is difficult to know if Inez needed the money this auction provided or simply wanted to get rid of items that had once belonged to either her husband or his first wife. The quality of the auctioned items, though, speaks volumes about the economic level at which William and his second wife lived during their last years. Inez did not remarry, and she died at Narragansett Pier in January 1938.[94]

Ethel took briefly to the stage, acting character parts in Richard Mansfield's troupe. [95] She gave up her dramatic career after three years and married Dr. Frank Donaldson, a man of middling means and a good sense of adventure. He served as surgeon for Roosevelt's Rough Riders during the Spanish-American War, returning home so battered that Ethel failed to recognize him at the train station. Donaldson refused to leave his sick "boys," so Ethel became a Red Cross nurse and joined her husband at Camp Wickoff in Long Island. The couple later received a commendation from President Roosevelt for their war services. Dr. Donaldson, who had never regained his health after the war, eventually made Ethel a widow. During World War I, Ethel, utilizing her expertise in French and German, acted as a translator at the Washington's Red Cross headquarters. After the war she became a journalist for a San Francisco newspaper, raised her son, Chase, survived the great 1906 earthquake, and, like her mother, relied on herself rather than a second husband. [96]

Portia, the small, dark-haired daughter who looked more like her father than her mother, eventually found a clerking job at the U.S. Treasury Department. She married twice, once to Charles Whitney of Washington and later to Mr. Browning of Narragansett Pier. Portia had no children by either husband, but she did take care of her sister Kitty for the few years she lived past Kate's death. Once, during her tenure in Washington, Portia arranged a meeting with her father. She had not seen him in the fourteen years that had elapsed since Kate took her and her sisters to France. When she arrived at her father's hotel Portia nearly missed the reunion—it took a desk clerk to point out that the shrunken man leaving the lobby was her father. William, too, had failed to recognize his flesh and blood. They had a friendly talk, but their familial relationship was never rekindled. [97]

Avice Weed Sprague Wheaton probably prospered the most in this cast of characters. Colonel Wheaton acted as father for baby Inez and provided the Spragues with continued infusions of cash. When the colonel died he left his widow a fortune of $7 million, some of which she used to finance renovations at Canonchet. In 1907 Avice married again—this time to millionaire Puerto Rican cattle baron and diplomat Wenseslac Borda Jr. Mr. Borda was said to be quite a bit younger than his bride and worth several million dollars. The wedding came as a complete surprise to members of both the Borda and Sprague families. Husband number three then purchased Canonchet from the Spragues for an undisclosed sum. This legal turn of events made Avice's daughter Inez the Spragues' heir. It was, as well, probably Avice's economic hold over the Spragues that encouraged her sister and brother-in-law to take young Inez back into the fold after her marital misadventures. Thus through a series of intelligent marriage choices Avice elevated herself from an attractive young female of dubious social background into a woman powerful enough to control William Sprague. Furthermore, unlike Kate, Avice parlayed a bad marriage and a scandalous divorce into not one but two marriages to wealthy men.

Indeed, Kate's failure to remarry speaks most eloquently of her desire for independence. She could have remarried—throughout the 1880s observers commented on Kate's continued beauty. Her looks alone could have guaranteed her a rich husband willing to overlook a scandalous past (particularly during the Gilded Age). Add to that her continued ability play politics, in both the public and private forum, and she might surely have attracted the kind of man who would have saved her from the indignities of genteel poverty. But she did not. She chose chickens, dogs, and grandchildren over the glittering life she had once lived. On 20 December 1880, when she filed her divorce petition, Katherine Chase Sprague declared her emancipation, an act she emphasized by requesting a legal name change. The Rhode Island senator's wife took back herself when she took back her name. This power of naming speaks to the political nature of Kate's life. When Kate manipulated political and social systems to her own ends, she engaged in a self-empowering act. Many believe that Kate's story is full of pathos, a sad tribute to a woman gone bad, but we have just as much reason to believe her life was a kind of simple triumph. From 1880 onward she alone directed her life. For Salmon P. Chase's daughter, a woman raised on Republican politics, self-determination came before the easy happiness of economic respectability. Thus, while many might point to her days as the treasury secretary's hostess or her postwar years as a leading Washington socialite as the greatest indicators that Kate was first and foremost a political woman, her divorce from William and her last years make an eloquent testament to the power of politics in her life.

Afterword

~

However important politics was to Katherine Chase Sprague, there are those who remain unconvinced that she was a political or partisan woman. Unfortunately, for historians and general readers alike, Kate never joined any women's rights organization, nor did she leave any nice, neat memos summarizing her political ideology. Despite occasionally visiting wounded soldiers, she did not work for any of the prominent ladies aid organizations that existed during the Civil War. Because she never voted or held office, we cannot track her ideology through her voting record. Nor did she have a cadre of female friends with whom she might have shared her political ideals. Even her sister left no helpful record of Kate's ideology. Indeed, Nettie's privileged position, both as Salmon Chase's second daughter (and thus exempt from the full glare of his dubious attentions) and the beloved wife of a financially solvent man, created a woman incapable of understanding her sister. Nonetheless, Kate was a committed and passionate partisan woman. The political play in the Chase household when the girls were young, the Kansas newspaper tacked to Kate's bedroom wall, her association with her father, William, and Roscoe, her temperance work, and her divorce and refusal to remarry—all these point to a woman with deep political ideals. It's all there, if one is able to look beyond traditional women's political culture for evidence.

To think that Kate spent her whole life in partisan politics and was nothing more than a hostess for political men is to assume that all political hostesses were (and are) empty-headed women incapable of serious thought. If we change the parameters of "political," it is not difficult to see ladies who use their social skills to influence political men as political persons in their own right. These ladies, and there are hundreds in addition to

Kate, did not need to make public statements of ideology, and indeed such declamations may have been counter to their purposes. Just because historians do not know a person's political ideology, be that person male or female, it does not mean that person had no ideology. For example, historians working in the confluence of women's history and political history have found that people have difficulty conceptualizing women as political creatures at all. I suggest that people have trouble thinking of Kate as a political person precisely because she was a woman. If she had been a man no one would have ever questioned her political status, regardless of the obscurity of her personal political ideology or her absence from traditional venues of women's political culture. No one has ever questioned William Sprague's or Roscoe Conkling's status as a political person. William is seen as an incompetent politician, but a politician nonetheless, while Roscoe's lack of guiding principles might qualify him as an archetypal Gilded Age politician. If Kate had been a man, the need to defend her political status would quite simply never have arisen. It is Kate's gender, not her lack of political ideology, that has hidden her from view as a serious political actor.

The paucity of meaningful analysis of Kate and women like her has ensured that women's very real contributions to the national political landscape has, until very recently, been obscured. This has reinforced people's difficulty in conceiving of women as political actors (creating a kind of chicken-and-egg argument) and, perhaps more seriously, contributed to women's continued underrepresentation in public and partisan politics. As Melanie Gustafson so cogently put it, "An absence of history, of social memory, has meant that women have had to repeatedly establish and prove, to themselves and to others, that they have the ability to make political contributions and the right to pursue their individual political paths." [1] This argument echoes Gerda Lerner's larger arguments about feminist consciousness—that the systematic suppression of women's knowledge of women that came before them has caused women to waste valuable energy justifying their activities. Worse, women's ignorance of female "cultural knowledge" has caused them to begin from scratch every generation, rather than building on the analysis and skills of those who came before them. Thus, Lerner argues, the absence of women's history has created a barrier to women's intellectual growth in both the past and the present. [2] Likewise, a political history that not only excludes women but fails to recognize particularly female modes of political activity creates a barrier to women's political participation.

Kate's ambition for the men in her life was fundamentally partisan and political, particularly when compared to her life decisions. Wives, and to a lesser extent daughters and mothers, have often acted as political adjutants for the men in their lives. Certainly we can look at the birth of the American Republic and find women acting just as Kate did. Politicians' wives, far from being vapid society women interested only in their own social power, were political persons of the highest order.[3] Political wives are politicians too. One might even make the argument that political women's disenfranchisement makes their political commitment all the more central and essential to understanding both womanhood and politics in American history. Before the Nineteenth Amendment, influence was American women's only avenue to political power. To disqualify women like Kate for their "backdoor approach" seems shortsighted in the light of their alternatives, or lack thereof. Thus, like Roscoe, Kate was an archetypal political woman, or at least one type of political woman.

Kate's status as a political woman can be determined, though, by so much more than her association with political men. We understand resistance to slavery as a political act. To resist bondage, to escape from an institution fundamentally at cross-purposes to American liberty, is to make a political claim—a claim to independent personhood and American citizenship. Nineteenth-century women's rights activists saw the parallels between American slavery and womanhood. Additionally, divorce, like love, marriage, and the Republican Party, has changed meaning in the last century. Kate would have seen her marriage as a kind of bondage, despite her access to all the privileges of her race and class. Her divorce was the penultimate partisan act of her life, particularly when understood in the context of the nineteenth century.

Indeed, viewing Kate's divorce as a political act opens the door to numerous other women who did not have access to politically powerful men, who never joined any reform organization, yet who were, nonetheless, political women. Although lost to the historical record, literally hundreds of thousands of faceless and voteless women were probably as political as their fathers, husbands, and sons. Indeed, one might wonder why a historian must muster evidence to *prove* political womanhood rather than to support an *absence* of political womanhood. Historians recognize that the nineteenth century was a hotbed of political activity and that women made up at least half of that population. Thus, in the absence of patriarchal assumptions about women's political inabilities we would assume that women were political unless proven otherwise. If the story of Kate's life had been written assuming her political involvement, my work here would have been done before it began.

Appendix A
Katherine Chase Sprague Divorce Petition

~

February Term, 1881, Washington ss.:
To the Honorable Justices of the Supreme Court to be beholden in South Kingston, within and for the county of Washington, in the State of Rhode Island, on the third Monday in February, A.D. 1881.

Katherine Chase Sprague, of South Kingston in said County of Washington, respectfully represents: That she is a domiciled inhabitant of the State of Rhode Island, and has resided therein for one year next before the filing of this petition. That she was married to William Sprague on the 12th day of November, A.D. 1863, at Washington, in the District of Columbia, and has ever since kept and performed on her part all the obligations of the marriage covenant, but that said William Sprague has violated the same, in this: That he has committed adultery with divers women at divers places and times since the said marriage, to wit: With one Mary Eliza Viall, alias Mary Eliza Anderson, at divers times in each and every year from the year 1864 to the year 1879, in the city of Providence, in said State, and elsewhere, and especially at Nantasket Beach, in the State of Massachusetts, in the year 1878; with one Elizabeth R. McCue, formerly Elizabeth Rhing, at South Kingston aforesaid, in each year from the year 1877 to the year 1880; with one Harriet Brown, in the year 1869, at Washington, in the District of Columbia; with Maggie English, in South Kingston and elsewhere, in the years 1866 and 1867; with one Fannie Adams, in March, 1876, at Providence aforementioned, at the house of one Ann M. Ballou, commonly called Maria Ballou, said house being a house of prostitution; with one Minnie Wilson, in January, in 1878, at a house of prostitution in Providence aforesaid; and with divers other lewd women, whose names are not known to your petitioner, at Washington and Providence aforesaid, and at Alexandria, in the state of Virginia, and at Philadelphia, in the state of Pennsylvania, and at New-York City, in the State of New-York, between the years 1863 and 1878.

That said Sprague has been guilty of extreme cruelty toward your petitioner in this: That he has personally assaulted her with great violence, and especially at the house known as "Canonchet" in South Kingston, in the year 1877, in that he entered her room at night in a state of intoxication, seized and dragged her to the window, which was in an upper story, and attempted to throw her therefrom; that in the year 1879 he forcibly laid hands on her and threatened to kill her; that he has been guilty of continued drunkenness.

That since the early part of the year 1879 he has neglected and refused, being of sufficient ability to do so, to provide necessaries for the subsistence of your petitioner and her children, to wit: In the year 1873, owing to depression in business, the manufacturing companies and firms with which said Sprague was connected, and in which he was largely interested, suspended payment, and conveyed all their property to a trustee for the benefit of creditors, claiming however, to have a surplus of some $6,000,000; that after said conveyance said Sprague at once entered the employ of said Trustee, and received from him a considerable compensation for the services so rendered up to the year 1879, a part of which was applied and paid by said Trustee for the support and maintenance of your petitioner and her children; that since the early part of the year 1879 said Sprague, though of sufficient ability, has refused to earn any money whatever, though said Trustee was ready and willing to employ him and continue said occupation; and said Sprague has since lived in idleness, and though of sufficient ability to do so, has neglected and refused to contribute in any way for the support of your petitioner and her three daughters, whereby your petitioner since the early part of 1879 has been deprived of the moderate provision she had theretofore received through said Trustee for the subsistence of herself and her children.

That said Sprague has been guilty of other gross misbehavior and wickedness, repugnant to and in violation of the marriage covenant, in this; That he has repeatedly applied the vilest and the most opprobrious epithets to your petitioner, both alone and the in presence of others; that he has threatened to kill her; that he has broken up and destroyed the furniture in their house, at one time collecting bedding and furniture in the night time and making a bonfire of the same; that he has often said to his children that he was not their father, and that they were not his children; that he has repeatedly falsely accused your petitioner of gross improprieties with other men—sometimes one man, sometimes another; that he has intercepted and returned letters addressed to your petitioner by her counsel; that in August, 1879, While your petitioner and said Sprague were at Canonchet, he refused to allow her friends, including her legal adviser, to see her; that he at said time refused to permit your petitioner to leave said you to go anywhere with her said children, and sought to imprison her and them therein; that from the year 1865 to the year 1877 said Sprague frequently attempted to have criminal intercourse with the female domestics and guests in the family, causing them to leave the house; that prior to February, 1877, said Sprague by indecent advances to female servants, and other violations of decency, which had increased in frequency and enormity, had made said residence at South Kingston an unsuitable abode for your petitioner and her children, and your said petitioner did, in February, 1877, with the assent of said Sprague, leave said house with her three daughters, her son Willie being then absent in Europe.

In the year 1879, urged by said Sprague to do so, your petitioner obtained permission from Zachariah Chaffee, Trustee of the property of the corporations and business firms aforesaid, and who was possessed of Canonchet as a portion of the property included in said trust, to occupy said house with her children during the Summer months; that the said Sprague urged that by so doing it would be of material pecuniary benefit to him in adjusting his affairs with his creditors; that on her way to Canonchet your petitioner remained with her said children on Sunday at Watch Hill, in the State of Rhode Island; that said Sprague then came to Watch Hill grossly intoxicated; that he was violent and offensive, and with a stick menaced and assaulted the attendant of said children. On the arrival of your petitioner at Canonchet, by virtue of the permission of said Trustee as aforesaid, said Sprague presented himself at that place from time to time, often intoxicated, menacing, wild, and otherwise offensive, and at length assumed authority over and control of said premises. Finally, it became impossible for your petitioner to remain longer, as said Sprague caused her to fear for her personal safety and that of her children and even her life. He threatened to carry away her children to Europe. Influenced by her fears and his threat aforesaid, and as the only escape from indignity and danger, your petitioner, by the aid of friends, was enabled to fly with her daughters, Ethel, Katherine, and Portia, to a place of safety. That for more than two years past said Sprague has in every possible way sought to annoy and disturb your petitioner and to make her life wretched. That said Sprague, since he so drove her from Canonchet, has persistently refused to deliver to her wearing apparel and that of her children and that of her servant, and that he has refused to permit said property, and other personal property of your petitioner, including gifts from her father, and the portraits of her parents, to be delivered to a Trustee of the property of your petitioner, duly appointed, or to the Sheriff of the said County of Washington, holding a writ of replevin for the same, and has resisted said officer, and has prevented him from entering the house where said property, or any property of your petitioner there situated by closing and barring the doors of said house, and has threatened personal violence to any person attempting to take possession of said property, or of any property of your petitioner there situated. That having made it impossible for your petitioner to remain at Canonchet as aforesaid, said Sprague has occupied said house as a place of resort for persons of vicious reputation and bad character, consorting with them in revelry and drunkenness, and has allowed the only son of your petitioner and said William Sprague, named William Sprague, Jr., to consort and associate with persons of bad character, and to become addicted to bad habits and idleness, withholding form him all educational advantages, thereby tending to corrupt his morals and vitiate his future life.

Wherefore your petitioner prays for the causes aforesaid that she may be divorced from the said William Sprague, and that the bond of matrimony now subsisting between your petitioner and said William Sprague may be Dissolved and that the custody of their four children, issue of said marriage—to wit, William Sprague, Jr., aged 15 years; Ethel Sprague, aged 11 years; Katherine Chase Sprague, aged 7 years, and Portia Sprague, aged 7 years—may be awarded to your petitioner, and that she may be allowed reasonable alimony out of the estate of said Sprague, and that she may be permitted to resume her maiden name, Katherine Chase, and for such other or further order or decree herein as to your Honors shall seem meet and just.

KATHARINE CHASE SPRAGUE

E. H. HAZARD
C. H. PARKHURST,
Attorneys for the Petitioner

Appendix B
William Sprague Divorce Petition

~

Providence, Rhode Island, January 27. February Term, 1881, Washington ss.;
To the Honorable Justices of the Supreme Court to beholden in South Kingston, within the County of Washington, in the State of Rhode Island, on the Third day of February, A.D. 1881.

William Sprague, of South Kingston, in Washington County represents that: he is a domiciled inhabitant of Rhode Island, and has resided therein for one year next before filing this petition. That he married Katherine Chase on the 12th day of November, A.D. 1863 at Washington, in the District of Columbia, and has ever since, on his part, kept or performed all his marriage covenants, but that Katherine Chase Sprague, unmindful of her marriage vows and disregarding her marriage covenants, hath violated the same.

That she has willfully and without cause deserted the bed and board of your petitioner, which desertion, although not for a continued term of five years, yet was under such circumstances as to entitle him to a decree for divorce; that she has been guilty of other gross misbehavior, and wickedness, repugnant to and in violation of her marriage covenants in this, that she has persistently and against the express wishes and commands of your petitioner, and after great public scandal had been occasioned thereby, kept company of, and been on terms of close and improper intimacy with other men, and of the same men whose names had been associated with hers in the public scandals aforementioned; that she has repeatedly declared, without cause, that she would never live with your petitioner again; that she had denied to him and his household the cares and duties incumbent on her as a wife and mother to fulfill; that she has, without cause, turned and driven her oldest child and son out of doors; that she has persistently and against the will for your petitioner squandered his property and means by engaging in the most lavish, extravagant, and foolish expenditure of money; that since financial embarrassment of your petitioner in 1873, and after repeated entreaty, request, demand, and command to the contrary by your petitioner, and after full explanation to her by him of his financial situation, and the inevitable effect of such proceedings on her part, yet the same respondent, notwithstanding all the same, has still persisted so far as possible, has persisted in the same reckless, extravagant, lavish and foolish expenditure of money and style of living, thus further (as explained and pointed out to her in the manner aforesaid) embarrassing and defeating your petitioner in his effort to extricate himself and any remnant of his estate (commingled with the estates of others) from said financial difficulties and embarrassments; that she has many times since her marriage with your petitioner and against his wishes absented herself from his home and household for long periods of time, living abroad and at hotels, thereby subjecting your petitioner to further greater expense and depriving him of her society and assistance, to which, as her husband, he was entitled; that she has willfully persisted in a course of slanderous and abusive language and publications of and concerning your petitioner with the view and purpose of harassing, vexing, and annoying him, and with such effect, thus rendering his life miserable, and thus destroying his domestic peace and all the happiness incident to the marriage relation. Wherefore, your petitioner prays your honors to pass a decree dissolving the bond of marriage between him and Katherine Chase Sprague, and for such other and further relief as to your honors may seem meet.

Notes

❦

BDC *Biographical Directory of the United States Congress, 1774–1989*. Bicentennial edition. Washington DC: Government Printing Office, 1989.

BUL William and Katherine Chase Sprague Papers, 1850–1900. Brown University Library, Providence, Rhode Island.

Chase Papers John Niven, James P. McClure, and Leigh Johnson, eds. *The Salmon P. Chase Papers*. 5 vols. Kent OH: Kent State University Press, 1993–98.

DAB American Council of Learned Societies. *Dictionary of American Biography*. 20 vols. New York: Scribner, 1928–36.

JCH Janet "Nettie" Chase Hoyt

KCS Katherine Chase Sprague

LC Arthur Chester Arthur Papers, Library of Congress, Washington DC.

LC Chase Salmon P. Chase Papers, Library of Congress, Washington DC.

LC Conkling Roscoe Conkling Papers, Library of Congress, Washington DC.

OR *The War of the Rebellion: A Compilation of the Official Records of the Union and Confederate Armies*. 128 vols. Washington DC, 1880–1901.

Phi-Chase Salmon P. Chase Papers, Historical Society of Pennsylvania, Philadelphia.

SPC Salmon Portland Chase

WS William Sprague

INTRODUCTION

1. Henry Villard, *Memoirs of Henry Villard, Journalist and Financier, 1835–1900* (Boston: Houghton Mifflin, 1904), 175.

2. Thomas Belden and Marva Robbins Belden, *So Fell The Angels* (Boston: Little, Brown, 1956); Mary Merwin Phelps, *Kate Chase: Dominant Daughter* (New York: Thomas Crowell, 1935); Ishbel Ross, *Proud Kate: Portrait of an Ambitious Woman* (New York: Harper Bros., 1955); Alice Hunt Sokoloff, *Kate Chase for the Defense: A Biography* (New York: Dodd and Mead, 1971); Thomas Belden, "William Sprague: The Story of an American Tragedy" (M.A. thesis, George Washington University, 1949); Donald D'Amato, "William Sprague: Rhode Island's Enigmatic Governor and Senator" (M.A. thesis, University of Rhode Island, 1956).

3. Phyllis Rose, *Parallel Lives: Five Victorian Marriages* (New York: Random House, 1983), 5–6.

4. Jack Plano and Milton Greenberg, eds., *The American Political Dictionary*, 6th ed. (New York: Holt, Rinehart, and Winston, 1982), 16–17; Michael S. Kimmel, "Masculinity as Homophobia: Fear, Shame, and Silence in the Construction of Gender Identity," in *Theorizing Masculinities*, ed. Harry Brod and Michael Kaufman (Thousand Oaks CA: Glenwood Press, 1994), vii–viii, 131–35; Michael Kimmel, *Manhood in America: A Cultural History* (New York: Free Press, 1996), chaps. 1 and 2.

5. Notable exceptions are Jo Freeman, *A Room at a Time: How Women Entered Party Politics* (Lanham MD: Rowman and Littlefield, 2000), 6; Catherine Allgor, *Parlor Politics: In Which the Ladies of Washington Help Build a City and a Government* (Charlottesville: University of Virginia Press, 2000).

6. Elizabeth Varon, "Tippecanoe and the Ladies Too: White Women and Party Politics in Antebellum Virginia," in *A Shared Experience: Men, Women and the History of Gender*, ed. Lara McCall and Donald Yacavone (New York: New York University Press, 1998), 141.

7. Paula Baker, "The Domestication of Politics: Women and American Political Society," in *Unequal Sisters: A Multi-Cultural Reader in U.S. Women's History*, ed. Vicki Ruiz and Ellen Carol DuBois, 2nd ed. (New York: Routledge, 1994), 94. See also Allgor, *Parlor Politics;* Rebecca Edwards, *Angels in the Machinery: Gender and American Party Politics from the Civil War to the Progressive Era* (New York: Oxford University Press, 1997); and Varon, "Tippecanoe and the Ladies Too," 143–69.

8. P. Baker, "Domestication of Politics," 86.

9. Pamela Herr and Mary Lee Spence, eds., *The Letters of Jesse Benton Frémont* (Urbana: University of Illinois Press, 1993), xx–xxiii; Rebecca Ed-

wards, "Gender and American Political Parties, 1880–1900" (Ph.D. diss., University of Virginia, 1995), 18–70; R. Edwards, *Angels in the Machinery;* Elizabeth Varon, *We Mean to Be Counted: White Women and Politics in Antebellum Virginia* (Chapel Hill: University of North Carolina Press, 1998).

10. Harry Brod, "Some Thoughts on Some Histories of Some Masculinities," in Brod and Kaufman, *Theorizing Masculinities*, 82–88.

11. P. Baker, "Domestication of Politics," 86.

12. Theda Skocpol, *Protecting Soldiers and Mothers: The Origins of Social Policy in the United States* (Cambridge: Harvard University Press, 1992); Linda Gordon, *Pitied But Not Entitled: Single Mothers and the History of Welfare, 1890–1935* (New York: Free Press, 1994); Ellen Carol DuBois, *Harriot Stanton Blatch and the Winning of Woman Suffrage* (New Haven: Yale University Press, 1997).

13. R. Edwards, *Angels in the Machinery;* Varon, "Tippecanoe and the Ladies Too"; Norma Basch, "Marriage, Morals, and Politics in the Election of 1828," *Journal of American History* 80 (1993): 890–918; Robert J. Dinkin, *Before Equal Suffrage: Women in Partisan Politics from Colonial Times to 1920* (London: Greenwood Press, 1995); Mark E. Kann, *On the Man Question: Gender and Civic Virtue in America* (Philadelphia: Temple University Press, 1991); Michael McGerr, "Political Style and Women's Power, 1830–1930," *Journal of American History* 71 (1990): 864–85.

14. Eric Foner, *Free Soil, Free Labor, Free Men: The Ideology of the Republican Party before the Civil War* (London: Oxford University Press, 1972), 300.

15. Christine Stansell, *City of Women: Sex and Class in New York, 1789–1860* (New York: Knopf, 1986), 20–24; Linda Kerber, *Women of the Republic: Intellect and Ideology in Revolutionary America* (New York: Norton, 1980), 10–11; Glenna Mathews, *Just a Housewife: The Rise and Fall of Domesticity* (New York: Oxford University Press, 1987).

16. Ellen Carol DuBois, *Feminism and Suffrage: The Emergence of an Independent Women's Movement in America, 1848–1869* (Ithaca: Cornell University Press, 1978), 57–63; DuBois, *Harriet Stanton Blatch*, 122–25.

17. Elizabeth B. Clark, "Matrimonial Bonds: Slavery and Divorce in Nineteenth-Century America," *Law and History Review* 1 (spring 1990): 31–32.

18. Elizabeth Cady Stanton, editorial, *Revolution*, 8 April 1869, in DuBois, *Feminism and Suffrage*, 184.

19. Katherine Chase Sprague Divorce Petition, *New York Times*, 20 December 1880.

I. BEFORE THEY MET

1. *Chase Papers*, 1:142.

2. In his family memorandum Salmon spelled Kate's full name with a "C," but she would always write her name as Kate, Katie, or Katherine. Family Memorandum, LC Chase.

3. John Quincy Adams (1767–1848), sixth U.S. president, *DAB*, 1:84–93.

4. SPC to Charles D. Cleveland, 1 October 1845, *Chase Papers*, 2:121–22. Eliza's brother Edmund and her sisters Caroline and Maria all died of tuberculosis. Eliza's parents were also deceased by the time she gave birth to Kate. *Chase Papers*, 1:135, 136, 151, 189.

5. Josephine Ludlow (1838–66), *Chase Papers*, 1:578; John Niven, *Salmon P. Chase: A Biography* (Oxford: Oxford University Press, 1995); Frederick Blue, *Salmon P. Chase: A Life in Politics* (Kent OH: Kent State University Press, 1987); Jacob W. Schuckers, *The Life and Public Services of Salmon Portland Chase* (New York: Appleton, 1874); Albert Bushnell Hart, *Salmon Portland Chase* (Boston: Houghton Mifflin, 1899); Robert Bruce Warden, *An Account of the Private Life and Public Services of Salmon Portland Chase* (Cincinnati: Wilstack, Baldwin, 1874); David H. Donald, ed., *Inside Lincoln's Cabinet: The Civil War Diaries of Salmon P. Chase* (New York: Longmans, Green, 1954).

6. Catherine Garniss Chase (1811–35), *Chase Papers*, 1:81–103; Bernard Engel, "Why So Doleful?: The Funereal Poetry of the Early Midwest," *Old Northwest* 7 (summer 1981): 152; Karen Haltunen, *Confidence Men and Painted Women: A Study of Middle-Class Culture in America, 1830–1870* (New Haven: Yale University Press, 1982); Ann Janine Morey, "In Memory of Cassie: Child Death and Religious Vision in American Novels," *Religion and American Culture* 6 (winter 1996): 104; Ann Douglas, *The Feminization of American Culture* (New York: Knopf, 1979), 202–14; Blanche Linden Ward, *Silent City on a Hill: Landscapes of Memory on Boston's Mount Auburn Cemetery* (Columbus: Ohio State University Press, 1989).

7. *Chase Papers*, 1:81–102.

8. Catherine Jane Chase (1835–40), *Chase Papers*, 1:148.

9. Eliza Ann Smith Chase (1821–45), her second and third daughters Lizzie Chase no. 1 (1842), Lizzie Chase no. 2 (1843–44), Josephine "Zoe" Ludlum Chase (1849–50), and lastly Sara Bella Ludlow Chase (1820–52). In his journal Salmon wrote that he had recorded the details of Eliza's death "in separate sheets," but that account has never been found. See the *Chase Papers*, 1:120, 164, 171, 179.

10. SPC to KCS, 13 August 1850, LC Chase.

11. SPC to KCS, 5 December 1851, LC Chase.

12. SPC to KCS, 6 February 1853, Phi-Chase.

13. Linda Rosenweig, *The Anchor of My Life: Middle-Class Mothers and Daughters, 1880–1920* (New York: New York University Press, 1993), 22–25, 82–90; Nancy M. Theriot, *The Biosocial Construction of Femininity: Mothers and Daughters in Nineteenth-Century America* (Lexington: Greenwood Press, 1988), 64.

14. *Chase Papers*, 1:161.

15. Noah Webster to SPC, 5 September 1842, LC Chase; Family Memorandum, LC Chase; *Chase Papers*, 1:170, 188, 189–90.

16. Harry B. Weiss, *The Great American Water-Cure: A History of Hydropathy in the United States* (Trenton NJ: Past Times Press, 1967); Susan E. Cayleff, *Wash and Be Healed: The Water-Cure Movement and Women's Health* (Philadelphia: Temple University Press, 1987).

17. *Chase Papers*, 1:311.

18. Carol Smith-Rosenberg, "The Female World of Love and Ritual: Relations between Women in Nineteenth-Century America," in *A Heritage of Her Own: Towards a New Social History of American Women*, ed. Nancy F. Cott and Elizabeth Pleck (New York: Simon and Schuster, 1979), 311–42.

19. Theriot, *Biosocial Construction of Femininity*, 2, 12–18, 25–36; Robert Griswold, *Fatherhood in America: A History* (New York: Harper Collins, 1993), 16–17; Kathleen Brown, *Good Wives, Nasty Wenches, and Anxious Patriarchs: Gender, Race, and Power in Colonial Virginia* (Chapel Hill: University of North Carolina Press, 1996), 347–48.

20. SPC to Charles D. Cleveland, 29 August 1840, *Chase Papers*, 2:69–71.

21. R. Edwards, *Angels in the Machinery*, 3–38; Varon, "Tippecanoe and the Ladies Too."

22. *Chase Papers*, vol. 1; John Todd, *The Student's Manual: Designed by Specific Directions to Aid in Forming and Strengthening the Intellectual and Moral Character and Habits of the Student* (Northampton and Boston, 1835).

23. Belle Chase to KCS, 29 August, 12 November 1850, Phi-Chase.

24. Harry B. Weiss and Howard R. Kemble, *The Great American Water-Cure Craze: A History of Hydropathy in the United States* (Trenton NJ: Past Times Press, 1967), 128–29, 146–50; Cayleff, *Wash and Be Healed*, 78–79, 98–99; *Chase Papers*, 2:271, 278.

25. SPC to KCS, 12 February 1852, Phi-Chase.

26. School bills, Maria Eastman to SPC, 17 February, 29 June 1855, LC Chase; Henrietta B. Haines to SPC, 5 July 1851, 1 July, 2 September 1853, LC Chase.

27. Mary Kelley, "Reading Women/Women Reading: The Making of Learned Women in Antebellum America," *Journal of American History* 83

(September 1996): 401–24; William J. Gilmore, *Elementary Literacy on the Eve of the Industrial Revolution: Trends in Rural New England, 1760–1830* (Worcester MA: American Antiquarian Society, 1992); William J. Gilmore, *Reading Becomes a Necessity of Life: Material Culture and Cultural Life in Rural New England, 1780–1835* (Knoxville: University of Tennessee Press, 1989).

28. SPC to KCS, 13 August 1850, Phi-Chase.

29. SPC to KCS, 13 April 1855, *Chase Papers*, 2:403.

30. Bernard Wishy, *The Child and the Republic: The Dawn of Modern American Child Nurture* (Philadelphia: University of Pennsylvania Press, 1968); Jane Turner Censer, *North Carolina Planters and Their Children* (Baton Rouge: Louisiana State University Press, 1984); Brett E. Carroll, " 'I Must Have My House in Order': The Victorian Fatherhood of John Shoebridge Williams," *Journal of Family History* 24 (July 1999): 275–303.

31. Jannette Ralston Chase (1773–1832), Abigail Corbet Chase Colby (1799–1838), *Chase Papers*, 1:19. Elizabeth Washington Gamble Wirt (1784–1857), James Grant Wilson and John Fiske, eds. *Appletons' Encyclopedia of American Biography*, 6 vols. (New York, 1887–89), 6:579. Salmon probably transcribed early versions of *Flora's Dictionary*, and he contributed over a dozen poems to the 1835 edition of the book. Anya Jabour, "Masculinity and Adolescence in Antebellum American: Robert Wirt at West Point, 1820–21," *Journal of Family History* 23 (October 1998): 393–415; Niven, *Salmon P. Chase*, 202–3; *Chase Papers*, 1:5.

32. Philander Chase (1775–1852), *DAB*, 4:26–27; Niven, *Salmon P. Chase*, 11–12.

33. William Wirt (1772–1834), U.S. attorney general (1817–29), *DAB*, 20:419–20. Wirt authored the tremendously popular*Letters of the British Spy* and *Sketches of the Life and Character of Patrick Henry.*

34. Foner, *Free Soil, Free Labor, Free Men*, 73; Julius Yanuck, "The Garner Fugitive Slave Case," *Mississippi Valley Historical Review* 40 (1953): 47–66.

35. SPC to JCH, 15 September 1854, Phi-Chase.

36. SPC to JCH 10 August 1860, LC Chase.

37. KCS to JCH, 25 July 1860, LC Chase. In Kate and Salmon's defense, Nettie maintained a particular disdain for spelling and punctuation well into adulthood.

38. JCH to SPC, 26 January 1862, LC Chase.

39. SPC to KCS, 5 July 1854, Phi-Chase.

40. Although these course listings were taken from a 1872–73 catalog for Eastman's Brooke Hall Female Seminary, established in 1856, there is little reason to believe that Eastman drastically altered her teaching philosophy and course requirements in the years after Kate left school. Catalogue Text,

Brooke Hall Female Seminary, Media, Delaware County, Pennsylvania, 1872, Philadelphia Historical Society, Special Collections.

41. SPC to KCS, 15 September 1854, Phi-Chase.

42. SPC to KCS, 8 January 1855, Phi-Chase.

43. SPC to Edward Pierce, 29 April 1858, bMS Am 1, Houghton Library, Harvard University.

44. Virginia Tatnall Peacock, *Famous American Belles of the Nineteenth Century* (Philadelphia: Lippincott, 1901), 212; *Chase Papers*, 1:252, 253, 257, 260, 277–78, 292, 309.

45. Herr and Spence, *Letters of Jessie Benton Frémont*, xxii–xxiii; Varon, "Tippecanoe and the Ladies Too," 166; R. Edwards, *Angels in the Machinery*, 26.

46. R. Edwards, *Angels in the Machinery*, 29.

47. Salmon described Kate's wall decoration in a letter to Sumner, who was convalescing in Europe after the Brooks caning. *Chase Papers*, 2:444, 451–52.

48. Julia Foraker, *I Would Live It Again: Memories of a Vivid Life* (New York: Arno, 1932), 76.

49. Isabella Strange Trotter, *First Impressions of the New World on Two Travelers from the Old in the Autumn of 1858* (London: Longman, Brown, 1859), 191–93.

50. Carl Schurz, *The Reminiscences of Carl Schurz* (New York: McClure, 1907–8), 169–70.

51. SPC to Abraham Lincoln, 17 May 1860, *Chase Papers*, 3:28–29.

52. SPC to Charles Sumner, 10 September 1859, *Chase Papers*, 3:18–19.

53. Niven, *Salmon P. Chase*, 26–28, 234.

54. In 1891 Nettie wrote a series of five autobiographical reminiscences for the *New York Tribune*. JCH, *New York Tribune*, 22 February 1891.

55. Elizabeth Keckley, *Behind the Scenes, or Thirty Years as a Slave* (New York: G. W. Carleton, 1868), 124–25; Ruth Painter Randall, *Mary Lincoln: Biography of a Marriage* (Boston: Little, Brown, 1953), 217–18.

56. *Frank Leslie's Illustrated Newspaper*, 22 February 1862, 214; Schurz, *Reminiscences*, 169–70.

57. Christie Anne Farnam, *The Education of the Southern Belle: Higher Education and Student Socialization in the Ante-bellum South* (New York: New York University Press, 1994), 180; Anne Firor Scott, *The Southern Lady: From Pedestal to Politics, 1830–1930* (Chicago: University of Chicago Press, 1970), 23. Theodosia Burr (b. 1783), for example, has been touted as one of America's famous belles, and though she gained her fame in the late eighteenth and early nineteenth centuries, the rhetoric used to describe her closely follows the superlatives used in relation to Kate. Peacock, *Famous American Belles*, 18–38.

58. Jean Baker, Mary Todd Lincoln's most recent biographer, suggests that Mary's problem with negative press lay in her political intelligence. This assessment fails to account for a definition of politics that includes an ability to skillfully negotiate the other facets of politics. In short, the fact that the president's wife had the ability to discuss patronage details does not mean that she understood the nuances of mid-nineteenth-century political culture. Also, Baker suggests that Mary was a better conversationalist than Kate, for she could speak French and Kate could not. Kate did, however, have years of French lessons, and she sometimes corresponded with her father in that language. See Jean H. Baker, *Mary Todd Lincoln: A Biography* (New York: Norton, 1987), 160, 198.

59. JCH, *New York Tribune*, 8 March 1891.

60. JCH, *New York Tribune*, 8 March 1891.

61. JCH, *New York Tribune*, 5 April 1891; Charles Pettit McIlvaine (1799–1873), Episcopal bishop of Ohio, 1832–73, *DAB*, 12:64–65. McIlvaine replaced Salmon's uncle Philander Chase at the bishop's post.

62. JCH, *New York Tribune*, 5 April 1891.

63. JCH, "Salmon P. Chase's Home Life," 22 February 1891, *New York Tribune;* James A. Garfield (1831–81), U.S. president, 1881, *DAB*, 13:170–71.

64. JCH, "Salmon P. Chase's Home Life," *New York Tribune*, 22 February 1891.

65. William Sprague III (1799–1856), speaker of the Rhode Island House of Representatives, member of the U.S. House, governor of Rhode Island, and U.S. senator, 1842–44. Benjamin Knight Sr., *History of the Sprague Families of Rhode Island* (Santa Cruz CA: H. Coffin, 1881), chap. 9.

66. Belden and Belden, *So Fell the Angels*, 52–53.

67. WS to KCS, 31 December 1863, BUL.

68. Peter J. Coleman, *The Transformation of Rhode Island, 1790–1860* (Providence: Brown University Press, 1963), 124–29.

69. The Sprague family used the names Amasa and William in every generation, but without the clarifying numerical additions to successive names. This creates a deeply confusing family history.

70. William G. McLoughlin, *Rhode Island* (New York: Norton, 1978), 128–35; P. J. Coleman, *Transformation of Rhode Island*, 254–94.

71. Arthur May Mowry, *The Dorr War: The Constitutional Struggle in Rhode Island* (New York: Preston and Rounds, 1901), 123, 211–12; Marvin E. Gettleman, *The Dorr Rebellion: A Study in American Radicalism, 1833–1849* (New York: Random House, 1973), 53, 100, 129.

72. Anthony E. Rotundo, "Boy Culture: Middle-Class Boyhood in Nineteenth-Century America," in *Meanings for Manhood: Constructions of Masculin-*

ity in Victorian America, ed. Mark C. Carnes and Clyde Griffen (Chicago: University of Chicago Press, 1990), 15–36; Anthony E. Rotundo, *American Manhood: Transformations in Masculinity from the Revolution to the Modern Era* (New York: Basic Books, 1990); Joseph R. Kett, *Rites of Passage: Adolescence in America, 1790 to the Present* (New York: Basic Books, 1977).

73. See Marcus Cunliffe, *Soldiers and Civilians: The Martial Spirit in America, 1775–1865* (Boston: Little, Brown, 1968), 208–12.

74. John Russell Bartlett, *Memoirs of Rhode Island Officers* (Providence: Little, Brown, 1867), 108.

75. Rotundo, "Boy Culture," 15–19; Kett, *Rites of Passage*, 91–92.

76. Bertram Wyatt-Brown, *Honor and Violence in the Old South* (New York: Oxford University Press, 1986), vii–x; Bertram Wyatt-Brown, *Southern Honor: Ethics and Behavior in the Old South* (New York: Oxford University Press, 1982), 166–78; Nicole Etcheson, "Manliness and the Political Culture of the Old Northwest, 1790–1860," *Journal of the Early Republic* 15 (spring 1995): 59–77.

77. *Congressional Globe*, 41st Cong., 1st sess., 24 March 1869, 242–46.

78. Knight, *History of the Sprague Families*, chaps. 7 and 8.

79. WS to KCS, 8 August 1866, BUL.

80. Knight, *History of the Sprague Families*, 30–33, 38.

81. Oliver Payson Fuller, *The History of Warwick, Rhode Island* (Providence: William, Archie, Wheeler, 1875), 204–5; Jonathon Prude, *The Coming of the Industrial Order: Town and Factory Life in Rural Massachusetts, 1810–1860* (Cambridge: Cambridge University Press, 1983), xv, 51.

82. Fuller, *History of Warwick*, 254–55; Richard M. Bayles, *History of Providence County, Rhode Island*, vol. 1 (Boston: Little, Brown, 1891), 754.

83. Vincent Sprague, *Sprague Families in America* (Rutland CT: Tuttle Co., 1913), 389.

84. Kimmel, *Manhood in America*, 16–42; Toby L. Ditz, "Shipwrecked; or, Masculinity Imperiled: Mercantile Representations of Failure and the Gendered Self in Eighteenth-Century Philadelphia," *Journal of American History* 81 (June 1994): 51–80; Kathleen Brown, "Brave New Worlds: Women and Gender History," *William and Mary Quarterly* 50 (April 1993): 325; Anthony E. Rotundo, "Learning about Manhood: Gender Ideals and the Middle-Class Family in Nineteenth-Century America," in *Manliness and Morality in Britain and America, 1800–1940*, ed. J. A. Mangan and James Walvin (New York: St. Martin's Press, 1994), 36–37.

85. *Providence Daily Post*, 2 February 1860.

86. Henry W. Shoemaker, *The Last of the War Governors* (Altoona PA: Altoona Tribune Press, 1916), 6–7; Belden and Belden, *So Fell the Angels*, 42.

87. Mary Viall Anderson, *The Merchant's Wife, or He Blundered: A Political Romance of Our Own Day* (Boston: privately printed, 1876), 21. Hardly more than a pamphlet at only fifty pages, this was printed privately for the author, who identified herself as Miss Viall. In the work she called her autobiographical heroine Miriam and never named the Sprague character, but contemporaries saw through this thin disguise almost from the moment the book came off the presses. See Belden and Belden, *So Fell the Angels*, 291–92; Sokoloff, *Kate Chase for the Defense*, 70–71.

88. Anderson, *The Merchant's Wife*, 13, 18, 20, 23.

89. Mary Merwin Phelps, whose biography of Kate is based on a number of interviews with people who knew Kate and William, claims that Mary Viall Anderson had a son whom she named Hamlet. Phelps adds that because Mary's addiction to alcohol, as well as her life of vice, did not allow her to take care of her boy, she tried to get her sister to adopt him. The sister refused, but a pension was arranged for Hamlet that encouraged his Anderson relatives to take care of him. Phelps does not say who arranged the pension, though she clearly creates the impression that the Spragues were behind it. No source provides more information. See Phelps, *Kate Chase*, 301.

90. Barbara Goldsmith, *Other Powers: The Age of Suffrage, Spiritualism, and the Scandalous Victorian Woodhull* (New York: Knopf, 1998), 208, 300–301.

91. Goldsmith, *Other Powers*, 22.

92. Spencer Klaw, *Without Sin: The Life and Death of the Oneida Community* (New York: Allen, Lane, 1993), 57–64; Mary Lockwood Carden, *Oneida: Utopian Community to Modern Corporation* (Baltimore: Johns Hopkins University Press, 1969); Dolores Hayden, *Seven American Utopias: The Architecture of Communitarian Socialism, 1790–1975* (Cambridge: MIT Press, 1976).

93. Ronald G. Walters, *American Reformers, 1815–1860* (New York: Hill and Wang, 1978), 39–60; Nathan O. Hatch, *The Democratization of American Christianity* (New Haven: Yale University Press, 1989), 65, 113–22, 187–88; DuBois, *Feminism and Suffrage*, 25–27; Elizabeth Griffith, *In Her Own Right: The Life of Elizabeth Cady Stanton* (New York: Oxford University Press, 1986), 102–11.

94. Etcheson, "Manliness and the Political Culture of the Old Northwest," 63; P. J. Coleman, *Transformation of Rhode Island*, 247–48; McLoughlin, *Rhode Island*, 150, 166–67.

95. *Congressional Globe*, 41st Cong., 1st sess., 8 April 1869, 617, 670; George B. Peck, "Life and Character of William Sprague" (MS at Rhode Island Historical Society, Providence, 1906).

96. McLoughlin, *Rhode Island*, 144–45; *Providence Evening Press*, 25 January 1860.

97. *Congressional Globe*, 41st Cong., 1st sess., 8 April 1869, 614; Richard P. McCormick, *The Presidential Game: The Origins of American Politics* (New York: Oxford University Press, 1982), 5–13; Jean H. Baker, *Affairs of Party: The Political Culture of Northern Democrats in the Mid–Nineteenth Century* (Ithaca: Cornell University Press, 1983); Jeffrey K. Tulis, *The Rhetorical Presidency* (Princeton: Princeton University Press, 1987).

98. *The Speech of William Sprague in the Senate of the United States, April 8, 1869* (New York, 1869), 22.

99. *Providence Daily Journal*, 29 February, 9 March 1860.

100. *Providence Daily Post*, 2 April 1860.

101. *Providence Daily Post*, 4 April 1860; John J. Turner Jr., "The Rhode Island State and National Elections of 1860" (M.A. thesis, University of Rhode Island, 1955), 55.

102. Peck, "Life and Character of William Sprague," 5.

103. Brooks D. Simpson, *America's Civil War* (Wheeling IL: Harlan Davidson, 1996), 7–8; James McPherson, *Ordeal by Fire: The Civil War and Reconstruction* (New York: Knopf, 1982), 125.

104. *Chase Papers*, 1:xxviii; Niven, *Salmon P. Chase*, 149–52; Foner, *Free Soil, Free Labor, Free Men*, 103–48. The terms "abolition" and "antislavery" are by no means universally defined as reflecting different ideologies. Ronald Walters, for example, appears to use them interchangeably. Walters, *The Antislavery Appeal: Abolitionism after 1830* (New York: Norton, 1978).

105. David M. Potter, *The Impending Crises, 1848–1861* (New York: Harper and Row, 1976), 430, 436–40, 442–47; McPherson, *Ordeal by Fire*, 125–29.

106. McLoughlin, *Rhode Island*, 146.

107. WS to Abraham Lincoln, 11 April 1861, Abraham Lincoln Papers, Library of Congress.

108. "Little Rhody," Sprague Collection, Cranston Historical Society, Cranston, Rhode Island; Thomas Aldrich, *The History of Battery A, First Regiment Rhode Island Light Artillery* (Providence: Little, Brown, 1904), n.p.

109. Schurz, *Reminiscences*, 227.

110. Tyler Dennett, ed., *Lincoln and the Civil War Diaries and Letters of John Hay* (New York: Dodd, Mead, 1939), 12.

111. Dennett, *Diaries and Letters of John Hay*, 14.

112. *Washington Evening Star*, 25 April 1861.

113. WS to Simon Cameron, 13 May 1861, *OR*, series III, vol. 1, p. 193; Simon Cameron to WS, 15 May 1861, *OR*, series III, vol. 1, p. 207; WS to Simon Cameron, 17 May 1861, *OR*, series III, vol. 1, p. 212. Lincoln had already appointed Benjamin Butler as major-general, a far wiser political choice given

the fact that Butler came from Massachusetts, a larger and more politically important state than Rhode Island.

114. D'Amato, "William Sprague," 24.

115. John Barnard to Irvin McDowell, 29 July 1861, *OR*, series I, vol. 51, pt. 1, p. 328–31.

116. Robert E. Denney, *The Civil War Years: A Day-by-Day Chronicle of the Life of a Nation* (New York: Sterling, 1992), 59–60.

117. *Congressional Globe*, 41st Cong., 1st sess., 8 April 1869, 618.

118. *Congressional Globe*, 41st Cong., 1st sess., 8 April 1869, 618; *Washington Evening Star*, 22 July 1861.

119. Richard Chappel Parsons (1826–99) became, under Chase, the internal revenue collector of Cleveland, 1862–66, and marshal of the U.S. Supreme Court, 1867–72, as well as a U.S. congressman, 1873–75. *BDC*, 1614.

120. *Narragansett Times*, 28 May 1883; Peacock, *Famous American Belles*, 16–17; Ross, *Proud Kate*, 51; Phelps, *Kate Chase*, 124–25.

121. WS to KCS, 27 May 1866, BUL.

2. "MY FORMER SELF HAS LOST ITS IDENTITY"

1. Francis T. Miller, ed., *The Photographic History of the Civil War*, vol. 1 (New York: Review of Reviews Co., 1912), 28; Margaret Leach, *Reveille in Washington*, 2nd Graf ed. (New York: Carroll and Graf, 1991), 68–69.

2. WS to KCS, 27 May 1866, BUL.

3. Leach, *Reveille in Washington*, 69.

4. WS to KCS, 8 June 1863, BUL. William probably misdated this letter, as he identified its writing on Sunday evening, 7 June.

5. Ellen K. Rothman, *Hands and Hearts: A History of Courtship in America* (New York: Basic Books, 1984), 9; Karen Lystra, *Searching the Heart: Women, Men, and Romantic Love in Nineteenth-Century America* (New York: Oxford University Press, 1989), 13; Lucia McMahon, "While Our Souls Together Blend: Narrating a Romantic Readership in the Early Republic," in *An Emotional History of the United States*, ed. Peter N. Stearns and Jan Lewis (New York: New York University Press, 1998), 68; Steven Stowe, "The Rhetoric of Authority," *Journal of Family History* 73 (March 1987): 916–33; Patricia Cline Cohen, *The Murder of Helen Jewett: The Life and Death of a Prostitute in Nineteenth-Century New York* (New York: Knopf, 1998), 278–79.

6. Shoemaker, *Last of the War Governors*, 15–16.

7. Shoemaker, *Last of the War Governors*; WS to KCS, 27 May 1866, BUL.

8. Sokoloff, *Kate Chase for the Defense*, 69–70. Sokoloff cites for this theory a letter that does not exist, though she may have been incorrect in her dates

in this matter. If this is so, the letter to which she may mean to refer contains only the most veiled of references to some "old story" of six years prior. See WS to KCS, 22 May 1866, BUL.

9. *Cincinnati Enquirer*, 13 August 1879.

10. Edward Bates, *The Diary of Edward Bates, 1859–66*, ed. Howard Beale (Washington DC: Government Printing Office, 1933), 238.

11. John Hay, 17 September 1862, Senate Executive Document no. 10, 41st Cong., 3rd sess. [hereafter cited as SED], 4:2.

12. SED, 3:6.

13. James M. Goode, *Capital Losses: A Cultural History of Washington's Destroyed Buildings* (Washington DC: Smithsonian Institution Press, 1979), 171.

14. SED, 3:6.

15. Mansfield French to SPC, [March 1862], *Salmon P. Chase Papers*, 3:147–48; Belden and Belden, *So Fell the Angels*, 58; Willie Lee Rose, *Rehearsal for Reconstruction: The Port Royal Experiment* (Indianapolis: Vintage Books, 1964), 152.

16. WS to SPC, 14 October 1862, *Chase Papers*, 3:297–98; William H. Reynolds to SPC, 17 October 1862, LC Chase.

17. SED, 3:20–22, 80, 82–86.

18. Shoemaker, *Last of the War Governors*, 15, 19.

19. In neither his letters nor his diary does Salmon mention which relatives were visiting. WS to SPC, 14 October 1862, *Chase Papers*, 1:420, 422, 3:297; Theodore Clarke Smith, *The Life and Letters of James Abram Garfield*, vol. 1 (New Haven: Yale University Press, 1925), 238–40, 265–66.

20. Rothman, *Hands and Hearts*, 117–19, 122–24; Lystra, *Searching the Heart*, 157–83.

21. *Narragansett Times*, 6 March 1863.

22. McPherson, *Ordeal by Fire*, 345–48; Simpson, *America's Civil War*, 148–49.

23. The *Springfield (Ill.) Republican*, quoted in Kathryn Allamong Jacob, *Capital Elites: High Society in Washington D.C. after the Civil War* (Washington DC: Smithsonian Institution Press, 1995), 50.

24. Jacob, *Capital Elites*, 46–47.

25. *Washington Evening Star*, 22 July 1861.

26. Edward Winslow Martin, *Behind the Scenes in Washington* (Washington DC: National Publishing, 1873), 64–65.

27. *Chase Papers*, 1:426; John D'Emilio and Estelle B. Freedman, *Intimate Matters: A History of Sexuality in America* (New York: Harper and Row, 1988), 75.

28. He used "My Bridy" on 19 and 23 October 1863 as an opening salutation.

29. WS to KCS, 18 May, 10 June, 5 November 1863, BUL; Lystra, *Searching the Heart*, 19–20; Ellen Plante, *Women at Home in Victorian America: A Social History* (New York: Facts on File, 1997), 18–20.

30. Lystra, *Searching the Heart*, 30; D'Emilio and Freedman, *Intimate Matters*, 75–76.

31. Rothman, *Hands and Hearts*, 103; Peter Ward, *Courtship, Love, and Marriage in Nineteenth-Century English Canada* (Montreal: McGill-Queen's University Press, 1990), 148.

32. Serena Ames to George Wright, 2 March 1860, quoted in Rothman, *Hands and Hearts*, 111.

33. WS to KCS, 14 July 1863, BUL.

34. WS to KCS, 17 June 1863, BUL.

35. Rothman, *Hands and Hearts*, 159–60.

36. Rothman, *Hands and Hearts*, 161–62. Two years before I researched this chapter I was set to the task of finding out exactly when Kate and William had become engaged by my then boss at the Salmon P. Chase Papers. I spent hours in primary and secondary sources looking for an engagement announcement, searching the Washington papers for the months of May and June, all to no avail. We make a critical methodological mistake in assuming that an engagement announcement, particularly of a socially prominent couple, would receive the same kind of public notice then as it does now.

37. P. Ward, *Courtship, Love, and Marriage*, 104.

38. WS to KCS, 16 June 1863, BUL.

39. Other young women engaged in similar struggles. See Anya Jabour, " 'It Will Never Do for Me to Be Married': The Life of Laura Wirt Randall, 1803–1833," *Journal of the Early Republic* 17 (summer 1997): 193–236.

40. KCS Diary, 11 November 1868, BUL.

41. SPC to James Garfield, 31 May 1863, *Chase Papers*, 4:47.

42. WS to SPC, 31 May 1863, *Chase Papers*, 4:50.

43. D'Emilio and Freedman, *Intimate Matters*, 76–77.

44. WS to SPC, 31 May 1863, *Chase Papers*, 4:49–50; SPC to KCS, 7 July 1863, Phi-Chase.

45. WS to KCS, 8 June 1863, BUL.

46. WS to KCS, 10 July 1863, BUL.

47. WS to KCS, 22 and 25 July 1863, BUL; SPC to Jay Cooke, 29 July 1863, *Chase Papers*, 4:97–98; SPC to KCS, 12 August 1864, Phi-Chase.

48. Salmon was quite put out with the girls for getting Nettie back to school several days late, and he expressed his disfavor in at least two letters.

spc to Charlotte Eastman, 22 August 1863, and spc to nch, 19 September 1863, *Chase Papers*, 4:112–13, 141; *Rhode Island: A Guide to the Smallest State*, written by the Workers of the Federal Writers' Project of the W.P.A. for the State of Rhode Island (Boston: Little, Brown, 1937), 349–50.

49. ws to kcs, 22 and 23 October 1863, bul.

50. Cissie Fairchilds, "Female Sexual Attitudes and the Rise of Illegitimacy: A Case Study," *Journal of Interdisciplinary History* 3 (1977–78): 627–67; Mary Beth Norton, *Liberty's Daughters: The Revolutionary Experience of American Women, 1750–1800* (Boston: Little, Brown, 1980); P. C. Cohen, *The Murder of Helen Jewett*, 226–29.

51. Elisabeth Hardwick, *Seduction and Betrayal: Women and Literature* (New York: Oxford University Press, 1974); Jan Lewis, "The Republican Wife: Virtue and Seduction in the Early Republic," *William and Mary Quarterly* 44 (1987): 689–721.

52. ws to kcs, 17 and 30 October, 1 November 1863, bul.

53. Smith-Rosenberg, "The Female World of Love and Ritual."

54. McMahon, "While Our Souls Blend Together," 68–74.

55. *Chase Papers*, 1:458–60.

56. ws to kcs, 20 September 1863, bul.

57. Kimmel, "Masculinity as Homophobia," vii–viii, 121–22.

58. ws to kcs, 22 September 1863, bul.

59. Nancy F. Cott, *Public Vows: A History of Marriage and the Nation* (Cambridge: Harvard University Press, 2000); Mark E. Kann, *The Gendering of American Politics: Founding Mothers, Founding Fathers, and Political Patriarchs* (Westport ct: Praeger, 1999), 79–85; Dana D. Nelson, *National Manhood: Capitalist Citizenship and the Imagined Fraternity of White Men* (Durham nc: Duke University Press, 1998), 21–22; Laura F. Edwards, *Gendered Strife and Confusion: The Political Culture of Reconstruction* (Urbana: University of Illinois Press, 1997), 142–43.

60. ws to kcs, 28 October 1863, bul.

61. ws to spc, 30 October 1863, lc Chase.

62. ws to kcs, 22 October 1863, bul.

63. ws to kcs, 2 November 1863, bul.

64. *New York Times*, 12 November 1863; Denney, *Civil War Years*, 339; McPherson, *Ordeal by Fire*, 338–39.

65. Virginia Jeans Laas, ed., *Wartime Washington: The Civil War Letters of Elizabeth Blair Lee* (Urbana: University of Illinois Press, 1991), 319.

66. Richard Bickerton Pemell Lyons (1817–87), minister to United States, 1858–65. Leslie Stephen and Sidney Lee, eds., *The Dictionary of National Biography*, reprint ed., 21 vols. (London: G. K. Hall, 1973), 12:358–59.

67. Michael Burlingame and John R. Turner Ettlinger, eds., *Inside Lincoln's White House: The Complete Civil War Diary of John Hay* (Carbondale: Southern Illinois University Press, 1997), 111; *Daily National Intelligencer*, 13 November 1863.

68. Denney, *Civil War Years*, 340–41.

69. *Washington Evening Star*, 13 November 1863.

70. *Washington Evening Star*, 13 November 1863.

71. Probably Virginia Rolette Cameron (d. 1920), who later married Wayne MacVeagh. *Who Was Who in America* (Chicago: Marquis–Who's Who, 1943–), 1:766.

72. KCS Diary, 11 November 1868, BUL.

73. *Chase Papers*, 1:72, 81–94, 120, 179.

74. Rothman, *Hands and Hearts*, 164–66; WS to KCS, 26 October 1863, BUL.

75. SPC to KCS, 24 and 30 September 1863, Phi-Chase.

76. C. W. Cambell et al. to SPC, 10 and 11 November 1863, LC Chase.

77. Plante, *Women at Home in Victorian America*, 23–26.

78. Plante, *Women at Home in Victorian America*, 23–26; *Washington Evening Star*, 12 November 1863; WS to KCS, 20 and 28 October 1863, BUL.

79. Irvin McDowell to WS, 18 September 1863, BUL; *Harper's Weekly*, 28 November 1863; *New York Times*, 13 November 1863. Chase's biographer John Niven reported that the tiara alone cost $50,000. Niven, *Salmon P. Chase*, 343; WS to KCS, 19 September 1863, BUL.

80. Rothman, *Hands and Hearts*, 170; WS to KCS, 19 October, [3 or 4] November 1863, BUL.

81. WS to KCS, 2 November 1863, BUL.

82. Etcheson, "Manliness and Political Culture of the Old Northwest," 69–70; Caroline Gebhard, "Reconstructing Southern Manhood: Race, Sentimentality, and Camp in the Plantation Myth," in *Haunted Bodies: Gender and Southern Texts*, ed. Anne Goodwyn Jones and Susan V. Donaldson (Charlottesville: University of South Carolina Press, 1997), 132–55.

83. Thomas Poynton Ives to WS, 30 October 1863, BUL; *Washington Evening Star*, 13 November 1863.

84. WS to KCS, 23 October 1863, BUL.

85. William Tegg, *The Knot Tied* (1877; reprint, Detroit: Singing Tree Press, 1970), 298.

86. Rothman, *Hands and Hearts*, 168–70; P. Ward, *Courtship, Love, and Marriage*, 110–11; *Washington Evening Star*, 13 November 1863.

87. Laas, *Wartime Washington*, 319.

88. Niven, *Salmon P. Chase*, 340.

89. Janet A. Bigglestone and Carolyn Schultz, *Victorian Costuming, 1840–*

1865 (New York: Other Times Productions, 1980), 53–70; James Laver, *Costume and Fashion: A Concise History* (London: H. N. Abrams, 1969), 177–88.

90. Harvey Green, *Light of the Home: An Intimate View of the Lives of Women in Victorian America* (New York: Pantheon, 1983), 25.

91. KCS Diary, 11 November 1868, BUL.

92. L. F. Edwards, *Gendered Strife and Confusion*, 128–29, 138–40; Catherine E. Beecher, *A Treatise on Domestic Economy, for the Use of Young Ladies at Home, and at School* (Boston, 1841), 308–19.

93. *Washington Evening Star*, 12 November 1863; *New York Times*, 12 November 1863.

94. Thorstein Veblen, *Theory of the Leisure Class* (New York: Penguin, 1994), 35.

95. *Washington Daily National Intelligencer*, 13 November 1863; *New York Times*, 13 November 1863.

96. C. W. Cambell to SPC, 10 and 11 November 1863, LC Chase.

97. Burlingame and Ettlinger, *Inside Lincoln's White House*, 111; Laas, *Wartime Washington*, 319.

3. NO FUTURE BRIGHTER

1. *Washington Evening Star*, 14 November 1863; Mary Sprague died four months later, leaving a daughter, Fanny. See WS to KCS, 9 and 22 March 1864, BUL.

2. *Chase Papers*, 1:454–55; Smith to SPC, 26 September 1863, Phi-Chase.

3. Iver Bernstein, *New York City Draft Riots: The Significance for American Society and Politics in the Age of Civil War* (New York: Oxford University Press, 1990), 4, 25; Adrian Cook, *The Armies of the Streets: The New York City Draft Riots of 1863* (Lexington: University Press of Kentucky, 1974).

4. *New York Times*, 18 and 19 November 1863.

5. *Chase Papers*, 1:450–54.

6. Simpson, *America's Civil War*, 116–18; McPherson, *Ordeal by Fire*, 338–39.

7. Alice Skinner to SPC, 22 November 1863, and WS to SPC, 21 November 1863, LC Chase. Alice was the daughter of Salmon's sister Jeanette. *Chase Papers*, 1:302.

8. Phelps, *Kate Chase*, 142–43.

9. P. Ward, *Courtship, Love, and Marriage*, 115.

10. P. Ward, *Courtship, Love, and Marriage*, 116–17.

11. WS to KCS, 22 October 1863 (one of three), BUL; SPC to KCS, 9 September 1863, Phi-Chase.

12. SPC to WS, 18 November 1863, Phi-Chase; the report was the "Report

of the Secretary of the Treasury on the State of Finances, for the Year Ending June 30, 1863," which Salmon delivered to the first session of the 38th Congress as House Executive Document no. 3.

13. SPC to Nettie, 18 and 23 November 1863, Phi-Chase.

14. P. Ward, *Courtship, Love, and Marriage*, 116–17.

15. Ross, *Proud Kate*, 145. Ross identifies Columbus as the site of the Parsons visit and party, but this seems unlikely, for Chase's old friend lived and worked in Cleveland. See *Chase Papers*, 1:268.

16. Jane Auld to SPC, 7 December 1863, Phi-Chase.

17. WS to SPC, 2 December 1863, Phi-Chase.

18. Ishbel Ross, one of Kate's biographers, asserts that the two spent additional time in New York after returning from Ohio and before returning to Washington, and that while there they visited with Henry Ward Beecher. However, a letter from Beecher to Chase written after Christmas makes it clear that he had not yet met the Spragues. Also, if they had just left Loveland on 6 December, as Jane Auld's letter indicates, they would not have had time to tarry in New York, for they arrived in Washington on the tenth at the very latest. See Henry Ward Beecher to SPC, 28 December 1863, *Chase Papers*, 4:231.

19. KCS to WS, 11 December 1863, BUL.

20. KCS to WS, 12 December 1863, BUL.

21. WS to KCS, 17 December 1863, and Mary Ann Sprague to KCS, 20 December 1863, BUL.

22. KCS to WS, 29 December 1863, BUL.

23. WS to KCS, 31 December 1863, BUL.

24. WS to KCS, 1 January 1863, and Fanny Sprague to KCS, 2 January 1864, BUL.

25. Mary P. Ryan, *Cradle of the Middle-Class: The Family in Oneida County, New York, 1790–1856* (New Haven: Cambridge University Press, 1977); Carl N. Degler, *At Odds: Women and the Family in America from the Revolution to the Present* (New York: Oxford University Press, 1980), 14–16, 42; Alexis de Tocqueville, *Democracy in America*, ed. Phillips Bradley, 2 vols. (New York: Knopf, 1945), 1:315, 2:202–4; Steven Mintz and Susan Kellog, *Domestic Revolution: A Social History of American Family Life* (New York: Free Press, 1988), chap. 3; Robert E. McGlone, "Suffer the Children: The Emergence of Modern Middle-Class Family Life in America, 1820–1870" (Ph.D. diss., UCLA, 1971), chap. 2; Robert Griswold, *Family and Divorce in California, 1850–1890: Victorian Illusions and Everyday Realities* (Albany: State University of New York Press, 1982), chap. 7; Lawrence Stone, *The Family, Sex, and Marriage in England, 1500–1800* (New York: Harper and Row, 1977), chaps. 6–8.

26. D'Emilio and Freedman, *Intimate Matters*, 73–78; Anya Jabour, *Marriage in the Early Republic: Elizabeth and William Wirt and the Companionate Ideal* (Baltimore: Johns Hopkins University Press, 1998).

27. D'Emilio and Freedman, *Intimate Matters*, 78–80.

28. Janet Farrell Brodie, *Contraception and Abortion in Nineteenth-Century America* (Ithaca: Cornell University Press, 1994), 3–5; Griswold, *Family and Divorce in California*, 186; Degler, *At Odds*, 178–226.

29. The house at Sixth and E Streets was constructed in 1851 and used as a boardinghouse during the last quarter of the nineteenth century. The Catholic Church used it as a clubhouse and offices until it was razed in 1936 to provide space for a parking garage. Goode, *Capital Losses*, 51–52; Martin, *Behind the Scenes*, 53–54, 57.

30. ws to Kate Chase, 15 June 1863, BUL.

31. SPC to Nettie, 19 August 1863, SPC to KCS, 9 September 1863, and SPC to ws, 6 June, 14, 21 July 1863, Phi-Chase; ws to KCS, 22 July, 26 September 1863, ws to KCS, 27 October 1863, and ws to KCS, 7 and 8 November 1863, BUL; Varnum to John Graham, 20 November 1863, LC Chase.

32. ws to KCS, 22 March 1864, BUL.

33. ws to KCS, 9 June 1864, BUL.

34. SPC to Lincoln, 22 February 1864, and Lincoln to SPC, 29 February 1864, *Chase Papers*, 4:303–5; Niven, *Salmon P. Chase*, 349–62.

35. Albert G. Riddle, *Recollections of Wartime: Reminiscences of Men and Events in Washington* (New York: Putnam, 1895), 266; Niven, *Salmon P. Chase*, 350–51; Laas, *Wartime Washington*, 385.

36. SPC to Lincoln, 29 June 1864, and Lincoln to SPC, 30 June 1864, *Chase Papers*, 4:409–11.

37. *Congressional Globe*, 38th Cong., 1st sess., 3543; SPC to NCH, 5 July 1864, SPC to KCS, 11 July 1864, and KCS to SPC, 26 July 1864, Phi-Chase.

38. ws to KCS, 24 November 1864, BUL.

39. ws to KCS, 25 December 1864, BUL.

40. KCS Diary, 27 December 1868, BUL.

41. The story first surfaces in Warden's biography of Chase. Warden was one of two biographers who vied to produce the first Chase book. Kate supported Jacob Schuckers's biographical efforts and actively interfered with Warden's work. Warden is the source for many of the unflattering stories about Kate. See Frederick Blue, "Kate's Paper Chase: The Race to Publish the First Biography of Salmon P. Chase," *Old Northwest* 8 (1982–83): 353–63; Belden and Belden, *So Fell the Angels*, 139–40; Niven, *Salmon P. Chase*, 374–75; Warden, *Salmon Portland Chase*, 630.

42. John Adams Dix (1798–1879), secretary of the treasury, 1861, com-

mander of Department of Maryland and Department of the East, 1861–65, minister to France, 1866–69. *dab*, 3:325–27; SED, 3:46–47.

43. *Congressional Globe*, 38th Cong., 2nd sess., 77, 642, 690.

44. WS to Major General Dix, 10 February 1865, SED, 3:47–48, 4:2; Belden and Belden, *So Fell the Angels*, 141–46.

45. United States Archives, War Department Records Division, Adjutant General's Office, 134, in Belden and Belden, *So Fell the Angels*, 148.

46. WS to KCS, 31 December 1864, BUL.

47. James McPherson, *Battle Cry of Freedom: The Civil War Era* (New York: Oxford University Press, 1988), 848; Denney, *Civil War Years*, 553–54, 557.

48. *Chase Papers*, 1:529; Denney, *Civil War Years*, 559. Salmon had gone to bed at about 10 P.M. but was awoken soon after. Unable to sleep, he recorded the news in his journal that night. His reference to the tramping "all night" and "a night of horrors" suggests he actually wrote part of this journal entry early on the morning of the fifteenth.

49. *New York Herald*, 20 April 1865; *Chase Papers*, 1:531.

50. Champ Clark, *The Assassination: Death of the President* (Alexandria VA: Time-Life Books, 1987); *New York Herald*, 20 April 1865.

51. *Chase Papers*, 1:587; South County Museum brochure (Rhode Island Arts and Tourism Commission); *Providence Daily Journal*, 12 October 1901; *Narragansett Times*, 15 October 1909.

52. SPC to KCS, 24 June 1865, LC Chase.

53. *Chase Papers*, 1:587; NCH to SPC, 26 August 1865, LC Chase.

54. *Chase Papers*, 1:601–4.

55. Ida Nichols, the daughter of William's sister Mary Ann and her first husband, was married to a Mr. Tillinghast in a hasty and small May wedding, then promptly sent off to Europe with her mother. They returned to Rhode Island in the fall with a "premature" baby. See WS to KCS, 22 May, 12 July, 22 September 1866, BUL.

56. WS to KCS, 18 May 1866, BUL.

57. WS to KCS, 8 and 11 June 1866, BUL.

58. WS to KCS, 12 July 1866, BUL.

59. WS to KCS, 8 May, 11 June 1866, BUL. English politician John Bright (1811–89) was a leading figure in nineteenth-century British radical reform agitation and a prominent supporter of the Union during the Civil War. *Encyclopedia of World Biography* (New York: Random House, 1973), 167–68; Donald Read, *Cobden and Bright: A Victorian Political Partnership* (Oxford: St. Martin's Press, 1967).

60. ws to kcs, 22 May 1866, BUL.

61. D'Emilio and Freedman, *Intimate Matters*, 69–70.

62. ws to kcs, 22 May 1866, BUL.

63. Lafayette Square is a small park on the east side of Pennsylvania Avenue, opposite the White House. A bronze statue of a horse-bound Andrew Jackson stands in the middle of the park, which was a popular place for elite Washingtonians to take their exercise. Martin, *Behind the Scenes*, 60–61; ws to kcs, 29 June 1866, BUL.

64. *New York World*, 20 February 1870. The *World* was a Democratic paper and released the story years after it reportedly happened. The newspaper suggests the story had been a legend of Washington gossip for years. The story could nonetheless be apocryphal, but the large amount of supporting data with regard to William's alcoholism makes it just as probable.

65. ws to kcs, 14 April 1866, BUL.

66. ws to kcs, 18 and 22 May 1866, BUL.

67. ws to kcs, 14 April, 9, 10, 11, 12 May 1866, BUL.

68. ws to kcs, 27 and 28 May 1866, BUL.

69. spc to kcs, 12 October 1866, Phi-Chase.

70. Degler, *At Odds*, 18–28; Lawrence Stone, "Family History in the 1980s," *Journal of Inter-disciplinary History* 12 (summer 1981): 51–88; Mintz and Kellog, *Domestic Revolution*, 46.

71. Jeanne Boydston, *Home and Work: Housework, Wages, and the Ideology of Labor in the Early Republic* (New York: Oxford University Press, 1990); Nancy F. Cott, *The Bonds of Womanhood: "Woman's Sphere" in New England, 1780–1835* (New Haven: Yale University Press, 1977).

72. David H. Donald, *Charles Sumner* (New York: Da Capo Press, 1996), 269–71, 289–91, 374–76, 314–20.

73. Charles Sumner to Mrs. John E. Lodge, 14 and 19 July 1868, Charles Sumner Papers, Massachusetts Historical Society, Boston.

74. Donald, *Charles Sumner*, 317–18.

75. L. F. Edwards, *Gendered Strife and Confusion*, 27–32.

76. spc to jch, 15 October 1866, LC Chase.

77. Many dances, or "Germans," did not get under way until 9 P.M. and went on until early morning. Elizabeth Fries Ellet, *The Court Circles of the Republic, or the Beauties and Celebrities of the Nation* (1873; reprint, New York: Arno, 1975), 550–54. See also Mary Clemmer Ames, *Ten Years in Washington* (Chicago: A. D. Worthington, 1875), 243–59; and Mark Twain, *The Gilded Age*, chaps. 13–30.

78. Mary Logan, *Reminiscences of a Soldier's Wife: An Autobiography* (New York: Scribner, 1913), 229, 236–39; Ames, *Ten Years in Washington*, 244–46.

79. Adele Cutts married Stephen Douglas in 1856. She was, at the time, the belle of Washington. *DAB*, 3:401; SPC to NCH, 31 January 1867, LC Chase; Ellet, *Court Circles of the Republic*, 253; Niven, *Salmon P. Chase*, 204.

80. SPC to NCH, 24 January 1867, LC Chase.

81. SPC to NCH, 1 January 1867, Phi-Chase.

82. SPC to NCH, 23 March 1867, LC Chase.

83. SPC to NCH, 12 September 1867, LC Chase.

84. Eric Foner, *A Short History of Reconstruction, 1863–1877* (New York: Harper and Row, 1990), 86–87, 104–5.

85. McPherson, *Ordeal by Fire*, 497–501.

86. McPherson, *Ordeal by Fire*, 518–20; David M. Jordan, *Roscoe Conkling of New York: Voice in the Senate* (Ithaca: Cornell University Press, 1971), 61–65.

87. SPC to NCH, 15 February 1867, LC Chase. Congress passed the first two Reconstruction acts in March 1867, the third in July 1867, and the fourth in March 1868. See Brooks D. Simpson, *The Reconstruction Presidents* (Lawrence: University Press of Kansas, 1998), 112–19.

88. Gideon Welles, *Diary of Gideon Welles*, vol. 3 (Boston: Houghton Mifflin, 1911), 16.

89. Charles Daniel Drake (1811–92), U.S. Senate, 1867–70, and Oliver Hazard Perry Morton (1823–77), U.S. Senate, 1867–77, *BDC*, 1101, 1596; *Congressional Globe*, 40th Cong., 1st sess., 42, 100, 148–49, 155.

90. Foner, *A Short History of Reconstruction*, 142–43; McPherson, *Ordeal by Fire*, 528–30.

91. *Congressional Globe*, 40th Cong., 2nd sess., 1405–6, 1523; Niven, *Salmon P. Chase*, 415.

92. SPC to Gerrit Smith, 2 April 1868, *Chase Papers*, 5:199.

93. SPC to Gerrit Smith, 19 April 1868, *Chase Papers*, 5:207–9.

94. SPC to August Belmont, 30 May 1868, *Chase Papers*, 5:221–24.

95. McPherson, *Ordeal by Fire*, 529–30; Niven, *Salmon P. Chase*, 420; Simpson, *The Reconstruction Presidents*, 119–20.

96. Senators were allowed four tickets per day for gallery seats. Emily Edson Briggs, *The Olivia Letters* (New York: Neale, 1906), 51, 70.

97. Briggs, *The Olivia Letters*, 400.

98. Nancy Isenberg, *Sex and Citizenship in Antebellum America* (Chapel Hill: University of North Carolina Press, 1998), 45–55; Helene E. Roberts, "The Exquisite Slave: The Role of Clothes in Making of the Victorian Woman," *Signs* 2 (spring 1997): 557–62; Sylvia D. Hoffert, *When Hens Crow: The Woman's Rights Movement in Antebellum America* (Bloomington: University

of Indiana Press, 1995), 23; Robert E. Reigel, "Women's Clothes, Women's Rights," *American Quarterly* 15 (fall 1963): 391–93.

99. *Philadelphia Evening Star*, 15 May 1868; Sokoloff, *Kate Chase for the Defense*, 136–38; Belden and Belden, *So Fell the Angels*, 181.

100. Belden and Belden, *So Fell the Angels*, 190–91; Welles, *Diary*, 349, 356; William Archibald Dunning, *Reconstruction: Political and Economic, 1865–1877* (New York: P. Smith, 1907), 107.

101. spc to kcs, 10 May 1868, lc Chase.

102. *New York World*, 4 May 1868; *Frank Leslie's Illustrated Newspaper*, 30 May 1868; spc to Horace Greeley, 19 May 1988, *Chase Papers*, 5:216–17.

103. Theodore Tilton, "A Folded Banner," *Independent*, 16 April 1868. Chase wrote back that he would not have accepted the nomination even if Grant were "out of the way." He added that he had not told Tilton he would accept the Democratic nomination, only that he had refused to say he would not accept it. "It would have been ridiculous in me to say that I would not accept what had not been offered, and was not likely to be. It would have savored strongly of vanity." *Chase Papers*, 5:210–11.

104. Brooks D. Simpson, *Let Us Have Peace: Ulysses S. Grant and the Politics of War and Reconstruction, 1861–1868* (Chapel Hill: University of North Carolina Press, 1991), 225; John Bigelow, *Retrospections of and Active Life*, vol. 2 (New York: Baker and Taylor, 1909), 110.

105. *New York Times*, 16 May 1868; *New York Herald*, 16, 17, 18, 30 May 1868; Niven, *Salmon P. Chase*, 436.

106. *New York Herald*, 22 March 1868.

107. *London Daily News*, 27 March 1868, in Charles Coleman, *The Election of 1868: The Democratic Effort to Regain Control* (1933; reprint, New York: Octagon Books, 1971), 80.

108. R. Edwards, *Angels in the Machinery*, 12–33, 35–36; Dinkin, *Before Equal Suffrage*, 32–37, 44–45; Stephanie McCurry, *Masters of Small Worlds: Yeoman Households, Gender Relations, and the Political Culture of the Antebellum South Carolina Low Country* (New York: Oxford University Press, 1995), 208–304.

109. *Chase Papers*, 1:xliv, 536–74; spc to Edwin M. Stanton, 20 May 1865, and spc to Charles Sumner, 20 May, 25 June 1865, *Chase Papers*, 5:52–57.

110. spc to Johnson, 17 May 1865, *Chase Papers*, 5:47–52; Brooks D. Simpson et al., eds., *Advice after Appomattox: Letters to Andrew Johnson, 1865–66: Special Volume No. 1 of the Papers of Andrew Johnson* (Knoxville: University of Tennessee Press, 1987), 3–16.

111. *Chicago Tribune*, 21 and 22 May 1868.

112. spc to Alexander Long, 8 and 19 April 1868, *Chase Papers*, 5:202, 206.

113. SPC to August Belmont, 30 May 1868, *Chase Papers*, 5:221.

114. SPC to August Belmont, 30 May 1868, *Chase Papers*, 5:221.

115. Niven, *Salmon P. Chase*, 426–28; C. Coleman, *Election of 1868*, 28–33, 39.

116. *New York Times*, 1 and 3 July 1868.

117. William C. Hudson, *Random Recollections of an Old Political Reporter* (New York: Cupples and Leon, 1911), 18–19.

118. Susan and Edwin lived at 94 Fifth Avenue, and the hotel was at 190 Fifth Avenue. Several of Kate's letters to her father are written from 94 Fifth Avenue, which all of Kate's and Salmon's biographers have incorrectly assumed to be the hotel's address. H. Wilson, comp., *Trow's New York City Directory. Vol. LXXVI for the Year Ending May 1, 1863* (New York, 1862), 420; H. Wilson, comp., *Trow's New York City Directory. Vol. LXXXIV for the Year Ending May 1, 1871* (New York, 1870), 577; KCS to SPC, 2, 10 July 1868, LC Chase; *Chase Papers*, 1:612.

119. KCS to SPC, 2 July 1868, Phi-Chase.

120. John Bigler (1805–71), governor of California, 1851–55, three-time delegate to National Democratic Convention; August Belmont (1816–90), prominent Democrat until 1872, when Democrats nominated Horace Greeley. *DAB*, 1:263–64, 169–70; KCS to SPC, 2 July 1868, Phi-Chase.

121. KCS to SPC, 5 July 1868, Phi-Chase.

122. Hamilton Smith to SPC, 5 July 1868, *Chase Papers*, 5:254–55; *New York Herald*, 5 July 1868.

123. C. Coleman, *Election of 1868*, 224–26.

124. C. Coleman, *Election of 1868*, 224–26.

125. William Hudson overheard this conversation and reported that both his editor, who used it in the next day's paper, and Kate, who read it there, were delighted with his work. Hudson, *Random Recollections*, 19–20.

126. SPC to KCS, 7 July 1868, *Chase Papers*, 5:257–59.

127. See Simpson, *Let Us Have Peace*, 245–48.

128. KCS to SPC, 10 July 1868, Phi-Chase.

129. Niven, *Salmon P. Chase*, 430–32, 525; C. Coleman, *Election of 1868*, 128–29.

130. *New York Times*, 3 July 1868.

131. Alexander C. Flick, *Samuel Jones Tilden: A Study in Political Sagacity* (New York: Greenwood Press, 1939), 167, 171; John Bigelow, ed., *The Writings and Speeches of Samuel J. Tilden*, 2 vols. (New York: Harper and Brothers, 1885), 1:212.

132. SPC to John Dash Van Buren, 10 July 1868, LC Chase.

133. Flick, *Samuel Jones Tilden*, 177.

134. Carl Schurz, *Intimate Letters of Carl Schurz*, ed. Joseph Shafer (1929; reprint, New York: Da Capo Press, 1970), 433.

135. *Cincinnati Daily Enquirer*, 20 March 1868, cited in Frank L. Klement, *The Limits of Dissent: Clement L. Vallandigham and the Civil War* (New York: Fordham University Press, 1998), 224; C. Coleman, *Election of 1868*, 131.

136. Schuckers, *Salmon Portland Chase*, 568–700.

137. Warden, *Salmon Portland Chase*, 705.

4. "ARGUMENT AND PERTINACITY"

1. KCS to SPC, 5 October 1868, Phi-Chase.

2. Ellet, *Court Circles of the Republic*, 881–83.

3. Helen Nicolay, *Our Capital on the Potomac* (New York: Arno, 1924), 406; Ames, *Ten Years in Washington*, 253–54; James Dabney McCabe, *Behind the Scenes in Washington* (1873; reprint, New York: Arno, 1974); Mary Logan, *Reminiscences of the Civil War and Reconstruction* (Carbondale: Southern Illinois University Press, 1970); Mark Twain, *The Gilded Age, or The Adventures of Colonel Sellers* (1873), and Henry Adams, *Democracy* (1879).

4. Briggs, *The Olivia Letters*, 391.

5. Ellet, *Court Circles of the Republic*, 568, 581; Peacock, *Famous American Belles*, 214.

6. Logan, *Reminiscences of the Civil War*, 167.

7. Katherine Chase Sprague Divorce Petition, *New York Times*, 20 December 1880.

8. SPC to KCS, 9 August 1868, Phi-Chase. What William had done remains unclear from the content of existing letters.

9. Some of Kate's biographers have suggested that William fathered only Willie and that the three girls were products of Kate's infidelity. The Beldens offer as proof that the second child, Ethel, was a Sprague only in name the fact that William was absent from the Senate 18–30 January and 4–10 February. Ethel's exact birthday remains unknown, but she was certainly born in late October. But William was often missing from the Senate, and Kate was in Narragansett during this period. There is little reason to believe that William did not spend some of that time at Canonchet with Kate. The Beldens also cite William's later claim that he was not the father of Kate's children, but he did so only after he lost custody of them during the divorce. Before that he tried on several notable occasions to take possession of "his" children. Lastly, the Beldens suggest that William, in his 1869 Senate speeches, was obsessed about the fidelity of American women because Kate was cuckolding him. This argument, if one considers the full content and context of the speeches, must

be viewed as the weakest proof of Ethel's illegitimacy. See Belden and Belden, *So Fell the Angels*, 26–27, 381.

10. KCS Diary, 4 November 1868, BUL.

11. KCS Diary, 11 November 1868, BUL.

12. KCS Diary, 4 November 1868, BUL.

13. KCS Diary, 27 December 1868, BUL.

14. SPC to KCS, 15 and 17 April 1869, Phi-Chase.

15. Joseph W. Nye (1815–76), Republican U.S. senator from Nevada, 1864–73, BDC, 1625; *Congressional Globe*, 41st Cong., 1st sess., 19 March 1969, 156–59.

16. *Congressional Globe*, 41st Cong., 1st sess., 24 March 1869, 243–45.

17. *Frank Leslie's Illustrated Newspaper*, 24 April 1869.

18. J. H. Baker, *Affairs of Party*, 253–58; McCurry, *Masters of Small Worlds;* Martha Hodges, "Wartime Dialogues on Illicit Sex: White Women and Black Men," in *Divided Houses: Gender and the Civil War*, ed. Catherine Clinton and Nina Silber (New York: Oxford University Press, 1992), 230–32; R. Edwards, *Angels in the Machinery*, 20–24.

19. *Congressional Globe*, 41st Cong., 1st sess., 30 March 1869, 400–402.

20. *Congressional Globe*, 41st Cong., 1st sess., 8 April 1869, 613–20.

21. P. F. Henderson, *A Short History of Aiken and Aiken County* (Columbia SC: R. L. Bryan Co., 1951), 1–6.

22. SPC to KCS, 17 April 1869, Phi-Chase.

23. SPC to KCS, 29 April 1869, Phi-Chase.

24. Joseph Carter Abbot (1825–81), Republican U.S. senator for North Carolina (1868–71), BDC, 759; *Congressional Globe*, 41st Cong., 1st sess., 22 April 1869, Special Session, 744, 776.

25. SPC to KCS, 26 April 1869, Phi-Chase; *New York Herald*, 27 April 1867.

26. SPC to NCH, 4 May 1869, LC Chase.

27. Alexander Gilmore Cattell (1816–94), Republican U.S. senator from New Jersey, 1873–77; Willard Warner (1826–1906), Republican U.S. senator from Alabama, 1868–71, BDC, 960, 1977; R. Edwards, *Angels in the Machinery*, 25; Etcheson, "Manliness and the Political Culture of the Old Northwest," 66–67; Kenneth Cmiel, *Democratic Eloquence: The Fight of Popular Speech in Nineteenth-Century America* (New York: W. Morrow, 1990), 60–63; Elliott J. Gorn, " 'Gouge and Bite, Pull Hair and Scratch': The Social Significance of Fighting in the Southern Backcountry," *American Historical Review* 90 (February 1985): 18–43; Dickson D. Bruce Jr., *Violence and Culture in the Antebellum South* (Austin: University of Texas Press, 1979); Basch, "Marriage, Morals, and Politics."

28. James L. Crouthamel, *Bennett's "New York Herald" and the Rise of the Popular Press* (Syracuse: Syracuse University Press, 1989), 138–54; Douglas

Fermer, *James Gordon Bennett and the "New York Herald": A Study of Editorial Opinion in the Civil War Era, 1854–1867* (New York: Boydel Press, 1986), 5–10.

29. *New York Herald*, 16 April 1869.

30. Crouthamel, *Bennett's "New York Herald,"* 145–49.

31. Briggs, *The Olivia Letters*, 112–14.

32. John S. Crosby left the army in 1870 and in 1876 took up an appointment as American consul in Florence, which he held until 1882. Philip Sheridan (1831–88), Civil War general, also famed for campaigns against Plains Indians. *DAB*, 2:568–69, 9:79–81.

33. SPC to KCS, 4 May 1869, Phi-Chase.

34. SPC to WS, 2 May 1869, LC Chase.

35. SPC to KCS, 1 October 1869, Phi-Chase.

36. Martin, *Behind the Scenes*, 58.

37. Goode, *Capital Losses*, 52.

38. SPC to KCS, 15 September 1869, Phi-Chase.

39. SPC to KCS, 7 November 1869, LC Chase.

40. Niven, *Salmon P. Chase*, 447, 449. Most of Kate's and William's biographers place Portia in third birth order, with Kitty as the last baby. Sokoloff cites birth record evidence that reverses this order, making Portia the fourth. See Belden and Belden, *So Fell the Angels*, 262; Phelps, *Kate Chase*, 237; Sokoloff, *Kate Chase for the Defense*, 200, 304. No letter or journal evidence exists to contradict either birth order, except that when Kate does refer to the girls together it is almost always as "Portia and Kitty" rather than vice versa.

41. By mid-December Chase began describing the weather as "too cold" and "cold in house." *Chase Papers*, 1:662.

42. SPC to NCH, 15 October [1870], LC Chase.

43. William R. Thayer, *The Life and Letters of John Hay*, vol. 1 (Boston: Houghton Mifflin, 1915), 258–59.

44. *New York World*, 10 February 1870.

45. Thomas Allen Jenckes (1818–75), Republican to U.S. House, 1863–71, *BDC*, 1369; *Providence Journal*, 31 October 1870; *New York Times*, 5 January 1871.

46. *Providence Press*, 3 November 1870.

47. *Providence Journal*, 8 November 1870.

48. William Worth Belknap (1829–90), secretary of war, 1869–76; Senate Report 377, 41st Cong., 3rd sess., 1871, 6–16; *DAB*, 2:147–48; *Narragansett Times*, 16 January 1874; D'Amato, "William Sprague," 441–42; Belden, "William Sprague," 70–71.

49. Mark Wahlgreen Summers, *The Press Gang: Newspapers and Politics, 1865–1878* (Chapel Hill: University of North Carolina Press, 1994), 55–56.

50. *United States Statues at Large*, 10:655, 16:493; *Congressional Globe*, 41st Cong., 3rd sess., 1870–71, 2:1256, 1262.

51. SPC to Richard Parsons, 16 February 1871, *Chase Papers*, 5:342.

52. Walter Nugent, "Money, Politics, and Society: The Currency Question," in *The Gilded Age*, ed. H. Wayne Morgan (New York: Scholarly Resources, 1970), 109–28; William S. McFeely, *Grant: A Biography* (New York: Norton, 1981), 288–89; Alexander McClure, *Our Presidents and How We Make Them* (New York: Harper Bros., 1900), 208.

53. Niven, *Salmon P. Chase*, 438–41; *Chase Papers*, 1:650–51, 668–69; SPC to James S. Pike, 24 December 1869, *Chase Papers*, 5:322–23.

54. *Congressional Globe*, 41st Cong., 1st sess., 15 March 1869, 360–62.

55. David R. Roediger, *The Wages of Whiteness: Race and the Making of the American Working Class* (London: Verso, 1991), 173–81; Simpson, *The Reconstruction Presidents*, 133–34; McFeely, *Grant*, 280–81, 36–87.

56. William Sprague Hoyt (1847–1905), in *Representative Men and Old Families of Rhode Island*, 3 vols. (Chicago: J. H. Beers and Co., 1908), 1:416; *New York World*, 24 March 1871; *Washington Evening Star*, 24 March 1871; Peacock, *Famous American Belles*, 222; Briggs, *The Olivia Letters*, 282–85.

57. Mary Logan did not remember that Kate and Nettie had different mothers. *Reminiscences of the Civil War*, 222–23.

58. Quoted in Belden and Belden, *So Fell the Angels*, 259.

59. *New York Times*, 24 March 1871; *Washington Evening Star*, 23, 24 March 1871.

60. *Washington Evening Star*, 23, 24 March 1871; Briggs, *The Olivia Letters*, 282–85.

61. *New York World*, 20 February 1870.

62. At sixteen, Beatrix was the youngest woman to ever become the national women's golf champion, a title she held for three years (1896–98), as well as the only woman to win five successive qualifying rounds. Like her mother, she became a landscape painter. Her brother Franklyn Chase Hoyt was a judge at the Children's Court and chairman of the Federal Alcohol Control Board. *New York Times*, 14 November 1937, 15 August 1963.

63. KCS to SPC, 29 August 1871, LC Chase.

64. KCS to SPC, 29 August 1871, LC Chase.

65. Mrs. Ulysses S. Grant, *The Personal Memoirs of Julia Dent Grant*, ed. John Y. Simon (New York: Putnam, 1975), 189–92. See also Ames, *Ten Years in Washington*, 253–55; Briggs, *The Olivia Letters;* and Harriet Bailey Blaine, ed., *Letters of Mrs. James G. Blaine*, 2 vols. (New York: Duffield and Co., 1908), 1:81.

66. SPC to M. C. C. Church, 20 March 1872, *Chase Papers*, 5:352–53;

Belden and Belden, *So Fell the Angels*, 264–65; *New York World*, 28 April 1872; Schurz, *Reminiscences*, 187.

67. McClure, *Our Presidents and How We Make Them*, 221–43; Jordan, *Roscoe Conkling*, 178–81; Niven, *Salmon P. Chase*, 445–48.

68. SPC to JCH, 12 April 1873, and SPC to Richard Parsons, 5 May 1873, *Chase Papers*, 5:368–69, 370.

69. Niven, *Salmon P. Chase*, 449.

70. KCS to John Nicolay, 3 November 1876, BUL.

71. Charles Carroll, *Rhode Island: Three Centuries of Democracy*, 4 vols. (New York: Lewis Historical Publishing, 1932), 2:764; *New York Tribune*, 30 January 1867.

72. Ellis Paxson Oberholtzer, *Jay Cooke: Financier of the Civil War*, 2 vols. (Philadelphia: G. W. Jacobs, 1907), 2:415.

73. Martin L. Primach et al., *An Economic History of the United States* (Menlo Park CA: Benjamin Cummings, 1980), 277; Robert M. Robertson, *History of the American Economy* (New York: Harcourt, Brace and World, 1973), 426; Oberholtzer, *Jay Cooke*, 2:378–439.

74. Thomas A. Bailey, *The American Pageant* (Boston: Houghton Mifflin, 1956), 492.

75. C. Carroll, *Rhode Island*, 1:521; Zechariah Chaffee Jr., "Weathering the Panic of '73: An Episode in Rhode Island Business History," *Rhode Island History Journal* 28 (1930): 18–35.

76. Chaffee affidavit in *Latham v. Chaffee* (7 Fed. Rep. 520), 5–7; Land Evidence Transcript Record No. 1, District of Narragansett, 1868–1879, 329–36, Sprague Company Collection, Rhode Island Historical Society, Providence.

77. *Narragansett Times*, 10 April 1874, 9 June 1876, 23 January 1880.

78. D'Amato, "William Sprague," 75.

5. THE BEGINNING OF THE END

1. Venila Lovina Shores, "The Hayes-Conkling Controversy, 1877–1879" (Ph.D. diss., Smith College, 1919), 266.

2. Jordan, *Roscoe Conkling*, 91.

3. Briggs, *The Olivia Letters*, 107; Logan, *Reminiscences of the Civil War*, 255–56.

4. Belden and Belden, *So Fell the Angels*, 288.

5. Charles E. Russell, *Blaine of Maine* (New York: Cosmopolitan Books, 1931), 116–17, in Jordan, *Roscoe Conkling*, 145. Jordan says that Russell had the story direct from the editor's assistant but cites no source for the story.

6. *Philadelphia Press*, 12 March 1870.

7. Henry Adams, *The Education of Henry Adams: An Autobiography* (Cambridge: Cambridge University Press, 1961), 252.

8. Jordan, *Roscoe Conkling*, 3–7.

9. Robert G. Ingersoll, "Memorial Address," in *The Works of Robert G. Ingersoll*, 12 vols. (New York: Ingersoll League, 1900), 12:427–37; Jordan, *Roscoe Conkling*, 51.

10. Julia Seymour Conkling (b. 1830), Jordan, *Roscoe Conkling*, 13–20; Horatio Seymour (1810–86), Democratic governor of New York, *DAB* 17:6–9.

11. Jordan, *Roscoe Conkling*, 95–138. 139–43.

12. Elihu Root, "Addresses," in Jordan, *Roscoe Conkling*, 142.

13. Alexander B. Callow Jr., *The Tweed Ring* (New York: Oxford University Press, 1966), 5–6; Moisei Ostrogorski, *Democracy and the Organization of Political Parties* (New York: Macmillan, 1964), 179–180.

14. Welles, *Diary*, 16.

15. Grant to Conkling, 8 November 1873, LC Conkling.

16. Conkling to Grant, 20 November 1873, LC Conkling.

17. Jordan, *Roscoe Conkling*, 201.

18. Belden and Belden suggest that Kate and Roscoe began their physical relationship before William's 1869 speeches and that the speeches are a result of William's discovery of his wife's infidelity, but they offer little more than a deep antipathy toward their subject as proof. Phelps and Ross suggest that the relationship began around 1870, but both are exceedingly vague about details and proof. Conkling's early biographer discounts the relationship entirely, but Jordan also suggests that the relationship was in full sway by 1873, offering Phelps, Ross, and Bowers as evidence. Bowers, like other historians who repeat this story as a side tale, also cites Phelps and Ross. Phelps, *Kate Chase*, 240–44; Ross, *Proud Kate*, 231; Belden and Belden, *So Fell the Angels*, 290–91; Claude G. Bowers, *The Tragic Era: The Revolution after Lincoln* (New York: Houghton Mifflin, 1929), 252–55.

19. At one point Conkling's biographer Jordan says that by the fall of 1870 Kate and Roscoe's relationship had not yet begun. He later contradicts this statement, claiming that by the spring of 1870 "it became obvious that Conkling and young Mrs. Sprague were seeing each other." He also says that at this time Kate sent flowers to Conkling's Senate desk, offering Ross's biography of Kate as support. However, Ross does not substantiate this claim, saying that the relationship began after 1873 and peaked between 1875 and 1879. Jordan, *Roscoe Conkling*, 145, 204–5; Ross, *Proud Kate*, 231–37.

20. Johnson Brigham, *Blaine, Conkling, and Garfield* (New York: G. E. Steckert, 1919), 12; Ishbel Ross, *The General's Wife: The Life of Mrs. Ulysses S. Grant* (New York: Dodd, Mead, 1959), 222–23, 233.

21. Quoted in John D. Bergamini, *The Hundredth Year: The United States in 1876* (New York: Putnam, 1976), 110.

22. R. Edwards, *Angels in the Machinery*, 13–34; Kathryn Kish Sclar, *Florence Kelley and the Nation's Work: The Rise of Women's Political Culture, 1830–1900* (New Haven: Yale University Press, 1995); McGerr, "Political Style and Women's Power," 864–85; Kann, *On the Man Question*.

23. R. Edwards, *Angels in the Machinery*, 15–16; J. H. Baker, *Affairs of Party*, 297–98.

24. KCS to Amasa Sprague, 26 May 1875, BUL.

25. KCS to William T. Sherman, Letterbook, BUL. Kate did not date this letter, but it was written to Sherman while he was commanding general of the U.S. Army and after he moved his staff to St. Louis. This places the letter in the nineteen months after May 1874. Michael Fellman, *Citizen Sherman: A Life of William Tecumseh Sherman* (New York: Random House, 1995), 277–87.

26. KCS to WS, 2 December 1875, BUL.

27. KCS to Will Hoyt, 2 December 1875, BUL.

28. Nelson, *National Manhood*, 189–90; Rotundo, *American Manhood*, 194–205.

29. KCS to Willie Sprague, 1 January 1877, BUL.

30. KCS to Willie Sprague, 18 January 1877, BUL.

31. KCS to Willie Sprague, 18 January 1877, BUL.

32. WS to Willie Sprague, 15 November 1877, BUL.

33. John Demos, *Past, Present, and Personal: The Family and Life Course in American History* (New York: Oxford University Press, 1986), 50, 431–32; Cott, *The Bonds of Womanhood*, 63–100; Anthony Rotundo, "American Fatherhood," *American Behavioral Scientist* 29 (1985): 7–25.

34. Griswold, *Fatherhood in America*, 10–19; Steven Mintz, *A Prison of Expectations: The Family in Victorian Culture* (New York: New York University Press, 1983), 33–35; Demos, *Past, Present, and Personal*, 41–65; B. E. Carroll, " 'I Must Have My House in Order.' "

35. *Congressional Record*, 44th Cong., 1st sess., 219–28, 236–45, 2155–82; Allan Nevins, *Hamilton Fish: The Inner History of the Grant Administration* (New York: Dodd, Mead, 1936), 804–10; Julia Dent Grant, *Personal Memoirs*, 189–92; *DAB*, 2:147–48. The House impeached Belknap on 1 April 1876 of high crimes and misdemeanors. The Senate failed to convict him by a two-thirds majority on 1 August 1876.

36. Katherine Chase Sprague Divorce Petition, *New York Times*, 20 December 1880.

37. Linda Gordon, *Heroes of Their Own Lives: The Politics and History of Family Violence* (London: Virago, 1988), 3–7, 7–28, 252–57; Elizabeth Pleck,

"Feminist Responses to 'Crimes against Women,' 1868–69," *Signs* 3 (spring 1983): 465–69; Nancy Tomes, "A Torrent of Abuse: Crimes of Violence between Working-Class Men and Women in London, 1840–1875," *Journal of Social History* 3 (spring 1978): 328–45; Angus McLaren, *The Trials of Masculinity: Policing Sexual Boundaries, 1870–1930* (Chicago: University of Chicago Press, 1997), 4–5.

38. *Chase Papers*, 1:459, 554; Hendrik Hartog, *Man and Wife in America: A History* (Cambridge: Harvard University Press, 2000), 218–40.

39. Glenda Riley, *Divorce: An American Tradition* (New York: Oxford University Press, 1991), 64–65, 72–74; Nelson Manfred Blake, *The Road to Reno: A History of Divorce in the United States* (New York: Macmillan, 1962), 100–103; Hartog, *Man and Wife in America*, 218–40.

40. Goldsmith, *Other Powers*, 90–94, 224–82; Richard Wrightman Fox, *Trials of Intimacy: Love and Loss in the Beecher-Tilton Scandal* (Chicago: University of Chicago Press, 1999); Blake, *Road to Reno*, 110–15.

41. William Sprague Divorce Petition, *New York Times*, 28 January 1881.

42. Anderson, *The Merchant's Wife*, 26, 29, 44, 48.

43. Theodore Tilton, "Marriage without Love," *Independent*, 1 December 1870, in Goldsmith, *Other Powers*, 228.

44. Of New York's 70 votes, 61 switched to Hayes and 9 to Conkling's nemesis James G. Blaine. Jordan, *Roscoe Conkling*, 241.

45. McClure, *Our Presidents and How We Make Them*, 246–49; Jordan, *Roscoe Conkling*, 243–45; Arthur Schlesinger, *The Coming to Power: Critical Elections in American History* (New York: Chelsea House, 1972); Bergamini, *The Hundredth Year*, 160.

46. Michael P. Riccards, *The Ferocious Engine of Democracy: A History of the American Presidency* (New York: Madison Books, 1995), 308–9. Rutherford B. Hayes (1822–93), Republican president, 1876–80, *DAB*, 8:446–51.

47. McClure, *Our Presidents and How We Make Them*, 263–64; Jordan, *Roscoe Conkling*, 148–250; John Hope Franklin, *Reconstruction after the Civil War*, 2nd ed. (Chicago: University of Chicago Press, 1994), 202–7; Belden and Belden, *So Fell the Angels*, 295; Foner, *A Short History of Reconstruction*, 242–45.

48. Hudson, *Random Recollections*, 22–24.

49. The same reporter whom Kate had reassured about Conkling's speech wrote this story in his memoirs. So too did Alexander McClure, a Republican who recorded the story in his book about presidential elections. Hudson, *Random Recollections*, 22–23; McClure, *Our Presidents and How We Make Them*, 262–63. See also *Washington Post*, 12 August 1879; *New York World*, 10 August 1879; Belden and Belden, *So Fell the Angels*, 294–96.

50. KCS to Willie Sprague, 1 April 1877, BUL. The Beldens report that Kate left Washington immediately after Hayes's inauguration in order to celebrate her victory over Tilden. Her letters make it obvious that Kate was at Edgewood until at least mid-June. See BUL collection and Belden and Belden, *So Fell the Angels*, 296.

51. KCS to Willie Sprague, 8 and 14 June 1877, BUL.

52. Roscoe Conkling to Bessie Conkling, 1 July 1877, LC Conkling.

53. *Congressional Record*, 46th Cong., 1st sess., 802–5.

54. *New York Times*, 20 June 1879; *Congressional Record*, 46th Cong., 1st sess., 2142–44; James B. Murphy, *L. Q. C. Lamar: Pragmatic Patriot* (Baton Rouge: Louisiana State University Press, 1973), 206–9; Wirt Armistead Cate, *Lucius Q. Lamar: Secession and Reunion* (New York: Russell and Russell, 1935), 348–57.

55. Briggs, *The Olivia Letters*, 23 June 1879.

56. Steven M. Stowe, *Intimacy and Power in the Old South: Ritual in the Lives of the Planters* (Baltimore: Johns Hopkins University Press, 1987), 5–49.

57. Edward Mayes, *Lucius Q. C. Lamar: His Life, Times, and Speeches* (Nashville: Tennessee Publishing, 1896), 386–87.

58. Stowe, *Intimacy and Power*, 6, 47–49; Bruce, *Violence and Culture in the Antebellum South*, chap. 1; Wyatt-Brown, *Southern Honor*, 350–61.

59. Bessie Conkling married Walter Oakman in early 1879. The young man had once been a common laborer on the railroad, working his way up to an executive position. Though Walter came from a socially elite family, Roscoe expressed disdain for Walter's past and thought him below Bessie. After the marriage he referred to his daughter as "Mrs. Conkling's daughter," effectively repudiating his paternal status. See Jordan, *Roscoe Conkling*, 313–14.

60. Kate's biographer Mary Merwin Phelps is the main source for many of these stories. Phelps has only the scantiest of annotation, but she did speak to many of Kate's old friends and acquaintances in the course of writing the book. For example, she claims that a friend overheard Roscoe's comment about Kate's "bright mind," but she leaves the source of the quote unclear. Given the unofficial status of Kate and Roscoe's relationship, few standard sources record their behavior. Phelps's 1935 biography has the disadvantage and advantage of anonymous personal reminiscences. One society journalist wrote in her memoirs that Kate did send notes and have private conferences with Roscoe, but she dismisses the idea that anything inappropriate took place. See below and Phelps, *Kate Chase*, 244–48; Donald B. Chidsey, *The Gentleman from New York: A Life of Roscoe Conkling* (New Haven: Yale University Press, 1935), 119; *New York Evening Post*, 18 April 1888; Peacock, *Famous American Belles*, 114–15.

61. Briggs, *The Olivia Letters*, 48–49, 70.

62. Jacob, *Capital Elites*, 93–95, 111.

63. Jane Gray Swisshelm, in Phelps, *Kate Chase*, 251.

64. Jordan, *Roscoe Conkling*, 297–301. The Grants traveled the world from May 1877 to late 1879. Julia Dent Grant, *Personal Memoirs*, 201–319.

65. *New York Sun*, 17 August 1879; *New York World*, 14 August 1879.

6. "WHISKEY, ECONOMY AND DISREGARDED WISHES"

1. Patricia Cline Cohen's *The Murder of Helen Jewett* closely examines one such sensation, highlighting the case's mix of sex, violence, class, and the rise of the "penny press." The Tilton-Beecher affair and the McFarland and Sickles-Key murder trials also engaged the public's puerile interests.

2. *Cincinnati Daily Gazette*, 12 August 1879.

3. *Washington Post*, 19 August 1879.

4. Lyde Cullen Sizer, "Acting Her Part: Narratives of Union Women Spies," in Clinton and Silber, *Divided Houses*, 114–33.

5. *Providence City Directory*, 1880.

6. *New York Times*, 19 August 1879.

7. *New York Times*, 12 August 1879.

8. Chaffee, "Weathering the Panic." Levi Parsons Morton (1824–1920), governor of New York, 1895–97, *DAB*, 13:258–59.

9. *New York World*, 13 August 1879.

10. *New York World*, 13 August 1879.

11. *New York Times*, 12 August 1879.

12. *Cincinnati Gazette*, 13 August 1879.

13. *New York World*, 12 August 1879. R. G. Dunn was Chester Arthur's fishing partner and by extension a friend of Conkling's. Dunn had a summer home at Narragansett Pier during the 1870s. Conkling had stayed with Dunn many times before the events of the summer of 1879, and he continued to take him and Arthur fishing afterward. LC Arthur.

14. *New York Herald*, 7 August 1879; Chaffee, "Weathering the Panic," 274.

15. McLoughlin, *Rhode Island*, 167–68; *New York Herald*, 5 August 1879; Chaffee, "Weathering the Panic," 275–83.

16. *Providence Journal*, 15 August 1879.

17. *Providence Journal*, 16 August 1879.

18. *Washington Post*, 14 August 1879, *New York Sun*, 17 August 1879; affidavit in *Latham v. Chaffee* (7 Fed. Rep. 520), 5–7, mentions the Kennebec Land and Lumber Company in Maine as part of A. & W. Sprague's 1873 holdings.

19. *New York Sun*, 16 and 17 August 1879.

20. *New York Sun*, 17 August 1879.

21. *New York World*, 18 August 1879.

22. *New York Times*, 16 August 1879.

23. *New York World*, 14 August 1879.

24. *Providence Journal*, 18 August 1879.

25. *New York World*, 13 August 1879.

26. *New York World*, 14 August 1879

27. *Providence Journal*, 18 August 1879.

28. *New York World*, 13 August 1879.

29. KCS diary, 28 March 1867, BUL.

30. *New York Sun*, 17 August 1879. Whether he retrieved his shotgun at this point or had been carrying it with him remains unclear. Most newspapers reported that William wielded a gun during his first confrontation with Conkling. Kate's version of the event, published late the next week, does not mention any weapons. Given that she had no interest in protecting her husband's part in the affair, it is probable that the shotgun made its first appearance after Conkling's flight from Canonchet.

31. *New York World*, 14 and 15 August 1879.

32. It is from the waiter that we know what Conkling had for lunch. Newspapers had reported that the senator had clams, and the waiter was anxious to correct this error.

33. *New York Times*, 13 August 1879.

34. *New York Times*, 13 August 1879; *Cincinnati Daily Gazette*, 15 August 1879; *New York Sun*, 13 August 1879; *New York World*, 18 August 1879 (William's only account of the affair).

35. *New York World*, 18 August 1879. William himself admitted, in a short interview with a Narragansett correspondent, that he had threatened to shoot Conkling. See *New York Sun*, 15 August 1879.

36. *Cincinnati Gazette*, 15 August 1879.

37. *Newport Daily News*, 12 August 1879.

38. David G. Pugh, *Sons of Liberty: The Masculine Mind in Nineteenth-Century America* (Westport CT: Greenwood Press, 1983), chaps. 1 and 2.

39. Kimmel, "Masculinity as Homophobia," 129–31; Kimmel, *Manhood in America*, 7–8; Pugh, *Sons of Liberty*, 46–91.

40. Kimmel, *Manhood in America*, 75–78, 43–50; G. J. Barker-Benfield, *The Horrors of the Half-Known Life: Male Attitudes toward Women and Sexuality in the Nineteenth-Century* (New York: Harper and Row, 1976), chaps. 15 and 16; Rotundo, *American Manhood*, 404; Paul E. Johnson and Sean Wilentz, *The Kingdom of Matthias: A Story of Sex and Salvation in Nineteenth-Century*

America (New York: Oxford University Press, 1994); Stephen Nissenbaum *Sex, Diet, and Debility in Jacksonian America: Sylvester Graham and Health Reform* (Chicago: Dorsey Press, 1980).

41. Reid Mitchell, "Soldiering, Manhood, and Coming of Age: A Northern Volunteer," and David W. Blight, "No Desperate Hero: Manhood and Freedom in a Union Soldier's Experience," in Clinton and Silber, *Divided Houses*, 43–54, 55–75.

42. Ditz, "Shipwrecked; or, Masculinity Imperiled," 54–59; Isenberg, *Sex and Citizenship*, 41–45, 161–65; J. G. A. Pocock, *Virtue, Commerce, and History; Essays on Political Thought and History* (New York: Cambridge University Press, 1985), 68–70, 107–14; Ruth Bloch, "The Gendered Meanings of Virtue in Revolutionary America," *Signs* 13 (autumn 1987): 37–58.

43. According to Bertram Wyatt-Brown, northerners—especially after the Civil War—did not adhere to the honor ethic: "Increasingly, Northerners, driven by the so-called Market Revolution, made contracts, obtained loans and settled debts by institutional means," eschewing violence for calculation and restraint. Wyatt-Brown, "Andrew Jackson's Honor," *Journal of the Early Republic* 17 (spring 1997): 1–36.

44. Stowe, *Intimacy and Power*, 5–49; Bruce, *Violence and Culture in the Antebellum South*, chap. 1; Wyatt-Brown, *Southern Honor*, 350–61.

45. Hartog, *Man and Wife in America*, 136–43.

46. Isenberg, *Sex and Citizenship*, 128–29; P. C. Cohen, *The Murder of Helen Jewett*, 357–63.

47. *New York Sun*, 13 August 1879.

48. *New York World*, 15 August 1879; *Cincinnati Gazette*, 15 August 1879.

49. *Washington Post*, 20 August 1879.

50. The *Providence Journal* was a Whig organ until the mid-1850s, when it changed its allegiance first to the Know-Nothings and then to the Republican Party. Henry Bowen Anthony (1815–84), U.S. senator, 1858–84, *DAB*, 1:316–17; George F. Hoar, *Autobiography of Seventy Years* (New York: Scribner, 1903), 2:53; Nelson W. Stephenson, *Nelson Aldrich: A Leader in American Politics* (New York: Scribner, 1930), 4–5; P. J. Coleman, *Transformation of Rhode Island*, 247–49.

51. *Washington Post*, 14 August 1879. Anthony supported the conservatives in crushing a popular revolt over the limited and elitist nature of the franchise in Rhode Island. On the same page the *Post* also ran a notice that read, "WANTED—A few more Widow Olivers and Spragues to finish up a small 'job lot,' of Republican Senators. Nice second hand lot, and only offered because they do not 'match' with Lamar, Gordon and other 'plantation' Senators."

52. Hoar, *Autobiography*, 2:54.

53. John S. Gilkeson, *Middle-Class Providence, 1820–1940* (Princeton: Princeton University Press, 1986), 180–81; Stephenson, *Nelson Aldrich*, chaps. 1 and 2; McLoughlin, *Rhode Island*, 148–55.

54. *New York Times*, 16 August 1879; McLoughlin, *Rhode Island*, 166–67.

55. *Chicago Times*, 11 August 1879.

56. *New York Times*, 18 August 1879; Stephenson, *Nelson Aldrich*, 44.

57. *New York Times*, 11 August 1879.

58. Hazard also represented Kate in her divorce. Katherine Chase Sprague Divorce Petition, *New York Times*, 20 December 1880.

59. Katherine Chase Sprague Divorce Petition, *New York Times*, 20 December 1880.

60. *New York World*, 11 August 1879.

61. *Washington Post*, 13 August 1879.

62. *Providence Journal*, 14 August 1879. The letter was reprinted, in part or in full, in many of the major papers, excepting the *New York Herald*.

63. *New York Sun*, 14 and 15 August 1879.

64. On 14 August 1879 the *New York Times* answered for the *Herald* and the *Tribune*, saying, "we do not understand freedom of the press as to mean freedom from moral restraints," suggesting that good taste, not politics, muzzled the two Conkling papers. Given that both the papers printed a good amount of material about the sordid Newman-Hall divorce, this defense seems weak at best.

65. *New York Sun*, 13 August 1879.

66. *Providence Journal*, 15 August 1879.

67. *DAB*, 1:152; *Providence Journal*, 18 August 1879; *New York Times*, 19 August 1879.

68. *New York Times*, 16 August 1879.

69. James Ralston Skinner (d. 1893), known as Ralston, was the son of Salmon's sister Janette and Joshiah K. Skinner. *Chase Papers*, 1:155; *New York Times*, 16 August 1879.

70. *New York World*, 15 August 1879.

71. *New York Sun*, 15 August 1879.

72. *Washington Post*, 18 August 1879.

73. *Washington Post*, 20 August, 4 September 1879; *New York Times*, 18 August 1879.

74. Gordon, *Heroes of Their Own Lives*, 20–21, 27–58; Elizabeth Pleck, *Domestic Tyranny: The Making of Social Policy against Family Violence from Colonial Times to the Present* (New York: Oxford University Press, 1987).

75. *New York World*, 15 August 1879.

76. Isenberg, *Sex and Citizenship*, 106–11.

77. Gordon, *Heroes of Their Own Lives*, 2–4, 56–58; Linda Gordon, "Family Violence, Feminism, and Social Control," *Feminist Studies* 12 (fall 1986): 453–78; Bernadette Dunn Sewell, "Traditional Male/Female Roles Promote Domestic Violence," in *Violence against Women*, ed. Karin Swisher et al. (San Diego: Green Haven Press, 1994), 19–25; Suzanne K. Steinmetz and Murray A. Straus, eds., *Violence in the Family* (New York: Sage, 1974); David Finkelhor et al., eds., *The Dark Side of Families* (Beverly Hills: Sage, 1983); Murray Straus, Richard J. Gelles, and Suzanne Steinmetz, *Behind Closed Doors: Violence in American Families* (New York: Sage, 1980).

78. Gerald Hotaling et al., *Coping with Family Violence: Research and Policy Perspectives* (New York: Hotaling, 1988), 11–30.

79. *New York Sun*, 1 and 16 August 1879.

80. *New York Times*, 16 and 17 August 1879.

81. *New York Sun*, 5 September 1879.

82. *Washington Post*, 4 September 1879.

83. *New York Sun*, 1 September 1879; *Washington Post*, 2 September 1879; *Cincinnati Daily Gazette*, 2 September 1879.

84. *New York Sun*, 5 September 1879.

85. *New York Sun*, 5 September 1879; *Washington Post*, 2 September 1879.

86. Richard J. Gelles and Donilee R. Loseke, *Current Controversies in Family Violence* (Newberry Park CA: Sage, 1993), 171–87; Marti Laird McCue, *Domestic Violence: Contemporary World Issues* (Oxford: ABC-CLIO, 1995), 2–8; Lenore Walker, *The Battered Woman Syndrome*, 2nd ed. (New York: Spring, 2000), 10–11; M. Faulk, "Men Who Assault Their Wives," in *Battered Women: A Psychological Study of Domestic Violence*, ed. Maria Roy (New York: Van Nostrand, Reinhold, 1977), 121–22.

87. As many of 85 percent of modern abuse survivors report no access to any cash, bank accounts, or credit. Walker, *The Battered Woman Syndrome*, 27–30.

88. David Buss and Neil Malamuth, *Sex, Power, Conflict: Evolutionary and Feminist Perspectives* (New York: Oxford University Press, 1996), 241–49; Emilio C. Viano, *Intimate Violence: Interdisciplinary Perspectives* (Washington DC: Hemisphere, 1992), 5–19.

89. *St. Paul Pioneer Press*, 17 August 1879. The same paper, when mentioning Hayes's forthcoming tour of western fairs, said, "It seems as natural to meet Mr. Hayes at a fair as it does the premium bull or the two-headed calf."

7. "EXTREME CRUELTY AND GROSS MISBEHAVIOR"

1. Katherine Chase Sprague Divorce Petition, *New York Times*, 20 December 1880.

2. William Sprague Divorce Petition, *New York Times*, 28 January 1881. Two of Kate's biographers incorrectly cite 28 June 1881 as the date for the publication of William's countersuit. See Belden and Belden, *So Fell the Angels*, and Sokoloff, *Kate Chase for the Defense*.

3. *United States Statutes at Large*, 20:405–6.

4. *Narraganset Times*, 18 December, 15 October 1909. Though William Sprague was a governor for a only brief time before the Civil War, "Governor" remained his honorary title. In his letters to his daughter Salmon always referred to William as "the Governor."

5. *Tax Books*, Rhode Island, vol. 3, 1888–1917, 74.

6. *Providence Daily Journal*, 12 October 1909.

7. D'Amato, "William Sprague," 75–76.

8. Cott, *Public Vows*, 50–55, 107–33; Robert L. Griswold, "Divorce and the Legal Redefinition of Victorian Manhood," in Carnes and Griffen, *Meanings for Manhood*, 96–99; Norma Basch, *Framing American Divorce: From the Revolutionary Generation to the Victorians* (Berkeley: University of California Press, 1999), 2–3.

9. Uncited quotation from Phelps, *Kate Chase*, 251.

10. Isenberg, *Sex and Citizenship*, 41–55; Wendy Brown, *Manhood and Politics: A Feminist Reading in Political History* (Totowa NJ: Rowman and Littlefield, 1988), 24–35, 55–56.

11. Edmund Morgan, *American Slavery, American Freedom: The Ordeal of Colonial Virginia* (New York: Norton, 1975); Harry L. Watson, *Liberty and Power: The Politics of Jacksonian America* (New York: Hill and Wang, 1990); Lacy K. Ford Jr., *Origins of Southern Radicalism: The South Carolina Upcountry, 1800–1860* (New York: Oxford University Press, 1988); K. Brown, *Good Wives, Nasty Wenches, and Anxious Patriarchs*.

12. Briggs, *The Olivia Letters*, 15 April 1880.

13. Briggs, *The Olivia Letters*, 15 April 1880.

14. *New York Times*, 20 October 1880.

15. *Providence Journal*, 30 September, 15 November 1880; *New York Times*, 14 November 1880.

16. *New York Times*, 14 November 1880; *Narragansett Times*, 15 October 1909.

17. Many newspapers reprinted Kate's divorce petition in full, most notably the *New York Times*, 20 December 1880.

18. Shores, "The Hayes-Conkling Controversy." See also Johnson Brigham, "Blaine, Conkling, and Garfield: A Reminiscence and a Character Study," pamphlet of a paper read before the Prairie Club of Des Moines, 1914, Williams College Library Special Collections, Williamstown, Massachusetts; Jordan, *Roscoe Conkling*, 276–301.

19. *New York World*, 19 August 1879, originally in *St. Louis Times*, 16 August 1878.

20. *New York Times*, 13 December 1879.

21. James G. Blaine (1830–93) of Maine, Republican to U.S. House, 1863–76, U.S. Senate, 1876–81, secretary of state, 1881, unsuccessful candidate for president, 1884; John Sherman (1823–1900) of Ohio, younger brother of William Tecumseh Sherman, Republican to U.S. House, 1855–61, U.S. Senate, 1861–77, 1881–97. *DAB*, 1:322–29, 9:84–88.

22. KCS to Chester Arthur, June 1880, LC Arthur.

23. Richard Crowley (1836–1908), U.S. district attorney, 1871–79, U.S. House, 1879–83, *BDC*, 1038.

24. *New York Times*, 6, 7, 8, 9 June 1880; Thomas C. Reeves, *Gentleman Boss: The Life of Chester Alan Arthur* (New York: Knopf, 1975), 173–75.

25. All four of Kate's biographers, as well as William's and Roscoe's biographers, have made just this claim. David Jordan uses Roscoe's "complete termination" of the affair with Kate to illustrate the senator's narcissistic nature, his inability to care about anyone but himself, and his callous disregard for others' feelings. Oddly, Jordan apparently saw Kate's letters in the Arthur Papers, letters that make Roscoe and Kate's continued relationship explicit. See Jordan, *Roscoe Conkling*, 312–14.

26. James Abram Garfield (1831–81), major general at the end of the Civil War, Republican to U.S. House of Representatives for Ohio, 1863–80, U.S. president, 1881, *DAB*, 7:145–50.

27. Hudson, *Random Recollections*, 97–99.

28. Chester A. Arthur (1830–86), Republican president, 1881–84. Conkling and Garfield met on 16 February 1881 to discuss cabinet appointments. Roscoe wanted Oliver Morton for treasury secretary, but James G. Blaine prevailed upon Garfield to appoint Thomas James. *DAB*, 1:373–76; Jordan, *Roscoe Conkling*, 352–54, 372–76.

29. Alfred R. Conkling, *The Life and Letters of Roscoe Conkling* (New York: C. L. Webster and Co., 1889), 216.

30. Howard M. Chapin, *Documentary History of Rhode Island*, 2 vols. (Providence: Brown University Press, 1916–19), 2:152–53.

31. Richard H. Chused, *Private Acts in Public Places: A Social History of*

Divorce in the Formative Era of American Family Law (Philadelphia: University of Pennsylvania Press, 1994).

32. Sheldon S. Cohen, "The Broken Bond: Divorce in Providence County, 1749–1809," *Rhode Island History Journal* 67 (1985): 67–69. See also *The Public Laws of the State of Rhode Island and Providence Plantations* (Providence, 1798), 479.

33. George Elliott Howard, *A History of Matrimonial Institutions: Chiefly in England and the United States*, 3 vols. (Chicago: University of Chicago Press, 1904), 3:9.

34. *Public Laws of Rhode Island* (1798), 480; Katherine Chase Sprague Divorce Petition, *New York Times*, 20 December 1880.

35. Sean Dennis Cashman, *America in the Gilded Age: From the Death of Lincoln to the Rise of Roosevelt*, 3rd ed. (New York: New York University Press, 1993); Milton Rugoff, *America's Gilded Age: Intimate Portraits from an Era of Extravagance and Change, 1850–1890* (New York: Holt, 1989); Howard Wayne Morgan, *Unity and Culture: The United States, 1877–1900* (London: Penguin Press, 1971).

36. Carroll D. Wright, ed., *Report of Marriage and Divorce in the United States, 1867–1886* (Washington DC: Government Printing Office, 1891), 13–15, 157; Griswold, *Family and Divorce in California*, 1–16.

37. Alfred Cahen, *Statistical Analysis of American Divorce* (New York: Columbia University Press, 1932), 22–23. The six states with the highest divorce rates in 1870 were Rhode Island, Connecticut, Wyoming, Nevada, Oregon, and Washington. California, Montana, Utah, Colorado, and Kansas, with .5–.74/1,000, filled in the rest of the West.

38. *Public Statutes of Rhode Island* (1882), 427.

39. Chused, *Private Acts in Public Place*, 7–9, 60–67.

40. Howard, *A History of Matrimonial Institutions*, 3:15.

41. *McKim v. McKim*, 12 R.I. 462, 34 Am. Rep. 694 (1879), *General Laws of Rhode Island* (1956), 53.

42. *Providence Journal*, 9 October 1890.

43. *Public Laws of Rhode Island* (1851), 790.

44. George Hoadly Jr. (1826–1902), Superior Court judge of Cincinnati, 1851–55, 1859–65, Democratic governor of Ohio, 1884–86, *DAB*, 9:84–85; *New York Times*, 18 April 1883.

45. Basch, *Framing American Divorce*, 5–6, 99–120.

46. *Cincinnati Enquirer*, 17 April 1883, letter to the editor of the *Staunton (Va.) Vindicator*.

47. *Cincinnati Enquirer*, 17 April 1883, letter to the editor of the *Staunton (Va.) Vindicator*.

48. Griswold, *Family and Divorce in California*, 3–4; Griswold, "Divorce and the Legal Redefinition of Victorian Manhood," 97.

49. Violet Blair (1848–1933) married Albert Janin (d. 1928) in 1874. William Tecumseh Sherman (1820–91) and Ellen (d. 1888) married in 1850. Virginia Jeans Laas, *Love and Power in the Nineteenth Century: The Marriage of Violet Blair* (Fayetteville: University of Arkansas Press, 1998); Louise Barnett, *Touched by Fire: The Life, Death, and Mythic Afterlife of George Armstrong Custer* (New York: Henry Holt, 1996), 186–200; Fellman, *Citizen Sherman*, 29–50, 341–70; *DAB*, 9:93–97; Carol K. Bleser and Lesley J. Gordon, *Intimate Strategies of the Civil War: Military Commanders and Their Wives* (Oxford: Oxford University Press, 2001).

50. Roscoe Conkling to Julia Seymour Conkling, 29 June 1881, and Julia Seymour Conkling to Roscoe Conkling, 9 July 1881, LC Conkling.

51. D'Emilio and Freedman, *Intimate Matters*, 79–80; Jordan, *Roscoe Conkling*, 13.

52. Robert L. Griswold, "Sexual Cruelty and the Case for Divorce in Victorian America," *Signs* 11 (spring 1986): 529–33; Thomas Lacquer, "Orgasm, Generation, and the Politics of Reproductive Biology," *Representations* 14 (spring 1986): 15–19; Isenberg, *Sex and Citizenship*, 160–63.

53. Norma Basch, "Relief in the Premises: Divorce as a Woman's Remedy in New York and Indiana, 1815–1870," *Law and History Review* 8 (spring 1990): 12.

54. See also G. J. Barker-Benfield, "The Spermatic Economy: A Nineteenth Century View of Sexuality," in *The American Family in Social-Historical Perspective*, ed. Michael Gordon (New York: St. Martin's Press, 1978), 62–87; and Mitchell, "Soldiering, Manhood, and Coming of Age."

55. Michael Grossberg, *Governing the Hearth: Law and the Family in Nineteenth-Century America* (Chapel Hill: University of North Carolina Press, 1983), 289–307.

56. Grossberg, *Governing the Hearth*, 289–307.

57. Cott, *Public Vows*, 54; Walter Wilcox, *The Divorce Problem: A Study of Social Causation* (New York: AMSPress, 1891), 60–71.

58. Unrestrained promiscuity was, in general, frowned upon—discretion remained the watchword among respectable men. Wyatt-Brown, *Southern Honor*, 294–97.

59. Blake, *Road to Reno*, 114–15; See also Goldsmith, *Other Powers*, 5–6, 75–76, 88–89, 90–94, 224–82, 419–24.

60. Griswold, "Divorce and the Legal Redefinition of Victorian Manhood," 109–10.

61. Basch, *Framing American Divorce*, 107–9, 114–17.

62. As Cott points out, this is not to suggest that Victorians conflated the physical experience of marriage and slavery. Cott, *Public Vows*, 64–69; E. B. Clark, "Matrimonial Bonds," 31.

63. Elizabeth Cady Stanton to Isabella Beecher Hooker, 12 April 1871, in Patricia Holland and Ann D. Gordon, eds., *The Papers of Elizabeth Cady Stanton and Susan B. Anthony*, 45 microfilm reels (Wilmington DE: Scholarly Resources, 1991).

64. Linda Gordon, *Women's Body/Women's Right: A Social History of Birth Control* (New York: Grossman, 1976), chap. 5; E. B. Clark, "Matrimonial Bonds," 32; Basch, *Framing American Divorce*, 4; Cott, *Public Vows*, 64–78.

65. Wyatt-Brown, *Southern Honor*, 384–87; R. Edwards, *Angels in the Machinery*, 13–27; McCurry, *Masters of Small Worlds*, 208–300; Stansell, *City of Women*, 20–30, 75–82.

66. James G. Birney (1792–1857), publisher of the *Philanthropist*, Liberty Party presidential candidate in 1840 and 1844, and noted constitutional abolitionist. Cassius Marcellus Clay (1810–1903), publisher of the abolitionist newspaper the *True American* in the 1840s. Gerrit Smith (1797–1874), antislavery leader rumored to be one of John Brown's financial backers. Joshua Reed Giddings (1795–1864), Whig, Free-Soil, Republican congressman, 1838–59. *DAB*, 2:291–94, 4:169–70, 7:260, 17:270–71.

67. William Gienapp, "Politics Seem to Enter into Everything: Political Culture in the North, 1840–1860," in *Essays on American Ante-bellum Politics, 1840–1860*, ed. William Gienapp et al. (College Station: Texas A&M Press, 1982), 15–22.

68. Foner, *Free Soil, Free Labor, Free Men*, 300.

69. SPC JCH, 12 December 1866, LC Chase.

70. SPC to Rebecca Plumly, 3 April 1867, LC Chase. Rebecca was married to Benjamin Rush Plumly (1816–87), Ohio antislavery advocate and recruiter for Louisiana's Corps d'Afrique during the war.

71. Marlene Stein Worman, ed., *Women in American Law*, vol. 1 (New York: Holmes and Meier, 1985), 120–22; Grossberg, *Governing the Hearth*, 240–41, 348–49.

72. R. Edwards, *Angels in the Machinery*, 20; Basch, *Framing American Divorce*, 117–18.

73. Isenberg, *Sex and Citizenship*, 162–64.

74. Isenberg, *Sex and Citizenship*, 157–61; Stanton, "Divorce," *Lily*, April 1850, 1; W. Brown, *Manhood and Politics*, 24–26.

75. Isenberg, *Sex and Citizenship*, 67–68; for a discussion of the weakness of sympathy as a political strategy see the following chapter.

76. Levi Morton (1824–1920), minister to France, 1880–89, U.S. vice-president, 1889–92, governor of New York, 1895–97, *DAB*, 7:258–59.

77. Thomas C. Platt (1833–1910) began his long association with the Conkling machine by organizing New York's southern counties for Conkling in 1870. U.S. senator, 1881, 1904–10, and heir to the New York machine after Conkling's retirement. *DAB*, 8:4–6.

78. KCS to Chester Arthur, 10 January 1881, LC Arthur.

79. William Windom (1827–91), U.S. House, 1858–69, U.S. Senate, 1870–81, 1881–83, secretary of the treasury, 1881, 1889–91. *DAB*, 10:383–84.

80. T. C. Reeves, *Gentleman Boss*, 205–38; Jordan, *Roscoe Conkling*, 254–78.

81. William Robertson (1823–98), U.S. House, 1867–69, New York collector, 1881–85, New York Senate, 1881–89. In 1880, Robertson, who was a convention delegate for New York, announced that he would support Blaine rather than Grant. Stalwarts expressed shock at this bolt from machine (and Conkling) dictate. Other New York delegates soon followed his lead. T. C. Reeves, *Gentleman Boss*, 167; *BDC*, 1747.

82. Jordan, *Roscoe Conkling*, 381; T. C. Reeves, *Gentleman Boss*, 223–34; David S. Muzzey, *James G. Blaine: A Political Idol of Other Days* (New York: Dodd, Mead, 1934), 190–91.

83. T. C. Reeves, *Gentleman Boss*, 230–31; Jordan, *Roscoe Conkling*, 393–95. For the text of the resignation letters see *Congressional Record*, 47th Congress, Special Session, 459.

84. *New York Times*, 17 May 1881; Thayer, *Life and Letters of John Hay*, 451–52.

8. "BALEFUL GRIEF AND BITTER BREAD"

1. Charles Julius Guiteau (1841–82), *U.S. v. Guiteau*, 216, 727, 1108, in Allan Peskin, *Garfield: A Biography* (Kent OH: Kent State University Press, 1978), 582.

2. Peskin, *Garfield*, 584; Margaret Leech, *The Garfield Orbit: The Life of James A. Garfield*, ed. Harry Brown (New York: Harper and Row, 1978).

3. Peskin, *Garfield*, 599; Charles R. Williams, ed., *The Diary and Letters of Rutherford B. Hayes*, 5 vols. (Columbus: Ohio State Historical Society, 1922–26), 4:23.

4. *New York Times*, 3 July 1881; Peskin, *Garfield*, 581–94; Justus D. Doenecki, *The Presidencies of James A. Garfield and Chester A. Arthur* (Lawrence: Regents Press of Kansas, 1981), 53–55.

5. Elbridge Lapham (1814–90), U.S. House, 1875–81, U.S. Senate, 1881–85, *BDC*, 1437; Wayne MacVeagh (1833–1917), Republican minister to Turkey, 1870–71, U.S. attorney general, 1881, 1893–95, *DAB*, 7:170–71.

6. Samuel C. Pomeroy (1816–91), Republican senator for Kansas, 1862–73, headed committee to nominate Salmon P. Chase for president, 1863, unsuccessful candidate for president for American Prohibition Party, 1884. *DAB*, 8:54–55.

7. KCS to Samuel G. Pomeroy, 15 October 1881, LC Arthur.

8. KCS to Chester Arthur, 21 October 1881, LC Arthur.

9. Isenberg, *Sex and Citizenship*, 67–68.

10. Doenecki, *Presidencies of Garfield and Arthur*, 96.

11. Charles James Folger (1818–84), rival for Conkling's Senate seat in 1867, New York Senate, 1861–69, secretary of the treasury, 1881–84. Benjamin Harris Brewster of Pennsylvania became attorney general, Timothy O. Howe of Wisconsin became secretary of state, and Henry Teller became as secretary of the interior. All men were considered Stalwarts. T. C. Reeves, *Gentleman Boss*, 254–60; *DAB*, 3:486–87.

12. *New York Sun*, 3 September 1879.

13. *Providence Journal*, 16 August 1882. Another local newspaper reported that William and Chaffee got into a fight at a restaurant in Narragansett Pier, each man threatening the other until a Mr. Farmer intervened and threatened to dump William over a railing. See *Providence Press*, 16 August 1882.

14. Griswold, *Fatherhood in America*, 19. See also Wyatt-Brown, *Southern Honor*.

15. *Providence Journal*, 9 October 1890.

16. Goldsmith, *Other Powers*, 240–45, 261–62.

17. Phelps, *Kate Chase*, 268–69, 304–5.

18. *Providence Journal*, 28 August 1882.

19. *Washington Star*, 7 October 1882.

20. *New York Tribune*, 25 December 1882, 9 March 1883.

21. *New York Times*, 14 May 1887.

22. *New York Times*, 10 March 1883; *New York World*, clipping dated 1907 in Chase Papers files, A. K. Smiley Library, Redlands, CA. Phelps reports that Inez abandoned her sick husband at a hotel in Cincinnati, where he died soon afterward. The Beldens refer to Inez as a divorcée but offer no proof. See Phelps, *Kate Chase*, 269; Belden and Belden, *So Fell the Angels*, 331.

23. *New York Times*, 14 May 1887; *Providence Press*, 26 May 1887; *Boston Herald*, 26 July 1885, 24 October 1907.

24. *New York Tribune*, 12 October 1890; Belden and Belden, *So Fell the Angels*, 338–39; Phelps, *Kate Chase*, 269–70; Sokoloff, *Kate Chase for the Defense*, 274.

25. *New York Times*, 14 May 1887.

26. Willie Sprague to KCS, 20 January 1890, BUL.

27. Jordan, *Roscoe Conkling*, 412.

28. *Boston Herald*, 16 August 1886; undated clippings from BUL collection.

29. KCS to Willie Sprague, 11 July 1890, BUL.

30. See Willie Sprague to KCS, 7 September 1880, and KCS to Willie, 11 July 1890, BUL.

31. Willie Sprague to KCS, 2 and 4 November 1886, BUL.

32. Interview with KCS, unidentified newspaper clipping, BUL; Foraker, *I Would Live It Again*, 76.

33. *Cincinnati Enquirer*, 1 August 1899.

34. *Washington Evening Star*, 6 August 1886.

35. *Cleveland Leader* and *Cincinnati Times-Star* quoted from *Providence Journal*, 30 March 1883; *Providence Press*, 31 March 1883; *New York Tribune*, 15 March 1883.

36. *Philadelphia Times*, 11 October 1886; *Providence Evening Telegram*, 12 October 1886.

37. *Rhode Island Democrat*, 29 October 1886.

38. *New York Times*, 17, 18, 19 March 1887.

39. *New York Times*, 6 December 1888.

40. *New York Times*, 26 May 1888.

41. Clarkson Potter to KCS, 3 May 1875, KCS to Clarkson Potter, 22 November 1875, KCS to NCH, 2 November 1875, and KCS to Will Hoyt, 2 December 1875, BUL.

42. JCH to KCS, 13 October 1874, and KCS to JCH, 13 October 1874, BUL.

43. *New York Tribune*, 26 October 1887.

44. Willie Sprague to KCS, 20 January 1890, 16 February 1887, BUL.

45. Willie Sprague to KCS, 2 and 4 November 1886, BUL.

46. Ethel Sprague to Willie Sprague, 5 October 1889, BUL.

47. Villard, quoted in Ross, *Proud Kate*, 279–80.

48. Willie to KCS, 19 July 1890, BUL.

49. *New York Times*, 9 October 1890; William "Willie" Sprague (1865–90), *Chase Papers*, 1:579.

50. Robert N. Reeves, "Suicide and the Environment," *Popular Science Monthly*, June 1897, 186–91; Howard I. Kushner, *Self-Destruction in the Promised Land: A Psychocultural Biology of American Suicide* (London: Rutgers University Press, 1994), 58–63; Roy Morris Jr., *Ambrose Bierce: Alone in Bad Company* (New York: Oxford University Press, 1995), 209–10.

51. *Providence Telegram*, 9 October 1890.

52. Kushner, *Self-Destruction in the Promised Land*, 39–42; KCS to WS, 8 October 1890, BUL.

53. *Providence Telegram*, 9 October 1890.

54. *New York Times*, 9 October 1890.

55. *Providence Journal*, 15 October 1890.

56. Harriet Comstock married Byron Sprague and had six children, one of whom was named after her mother. This second Harriet married her uncle Amasa and bore him one son, also named Amasa. Perry Greenman to KCS, 1 December 1890, BUL.

57. N.d., 1907 newspaper article, BUL.

58. *Providence Journal*, 15 October 1890.

59. Perry Greenman to KCS, 1 December 1890, BUL.

60. WS to KCS, 26 June 1866, BUL.

61. *New York Times*, 9 May 1898.

62. *New York Times*, 18 May 1888; Brigham, *Blaine, Conkling, and Garfield*, 34–35.

63. Robert G. Ingersoll, "A Tribute to Roscoe Conkling," in *The Works of Robert G. Ingersoll*, 12:437.

64. *New York Tribune*, 14 May 1881.

65. Brigham, "Blaine, Conkling, and Garfield," 35–36.

66. Other than to say that Kate "instigated" the legislation, the newspapers give no hint as to what her involvement actually entailed. *Chicago Herald*, 10 March 1891.

67. R. Edwards, *Angels in the Machinery*, 39–45; Nell Irwin Painter, *Standing at Armageddon: The United States, 1877–1919* (New York: Norton, 1987), 12–13, 27–32; Ruth Bordin, *Woman and Temperance: The Quest for Power and Liberty* (Philadelphia: Temple University Press, 1981) and *Frances Willard: A Biography* (Chapel Hill: University of North Carolina Press, 1986); Jack S. Blocker Jr., *American Temperance Movements: Cycles of Reform* (Boston: Twayne, 1989); Barbara L. Epstein, *The Politics of Domesticity: Women, Evangelism, and Temperance in Nineteenth-Century America* (Middletown CT: Wesleyan University Press, 1981); Carol Mattingly, *Well-Tempered Women: Nineteenth-Century Temperance Rhetoric* (Carbondale: Southern Illinois University Press, 1998).

68. R. Edwards, *Angels in the Machinery*, 43; Painter, *Standing at Armageddon*, 133–34; Bordin, *Woman and Temperance*, 117–39; Jordan, *Roscoe Conkling*, 420–21; Dinkin, *Before Equal Suffrage*, chap. 5.

69. KCS to WS, 2 December 1875, and KCS to William Hoyt, 2 December 1875, BUL.

70. *Chase Papers*, 1:664–86, 680–87.

71. Sokoloff, *Kate Chase for the Defense*, 288–89.

72. *New York Times*, 7 January, 23 July 1895.

73. *New York Times*, 23 July, 2 August 1895, 1 August 1899; *Washington Evening Star*, 22 July 1895; *New York Sun*, 2 August 1895.

74. *New York Times*, 22 September 1897.

75. KCS to Mrs. Bancroft, 7 May 1897, Mary Merwin Phelps Papers, University of Michigan Library, Ann Arbor.

76. *Washington Post*, 28 July 1895.

77. Ethel Chase to KCS, n.d., Sprague Letter Collection, Cranston Historical Society.

78. *New York Times*, 1 August 1899; *Washington Post*, 1 August 1899.

79. Martin, *Behind the Scenes*, 71; *Washington Post*, 1 August 1899.

80. JCH to "Aunt Ammie," 17 August 1899, Ludlow-Dunlop-Chambers Collection, American Heritage Collection, University of Wyoming, Laramie. Aunt Ammie may have been Ruhamah Ludlow Hunt (1833–1913), the sister of Nettie's mother, Sara Bella Ludlow. Ruhamah married Randal Hunt (1825–92) of New Orleans, who became president of the University of Louisiana, 1867–83. See *Chase Papers*, 1:564.

81. Benjamin Brown French, *Witness to the Young Republic: A Yankee's Journal*, ed. Donald B. Cole and John J. McDonough (Hanover NH: University Press of New England, 1989), 443.

82. KCS fragment, 29 March 1868, BUL.

83. Both of the pieces of poetry are cited in Phelps, *Kate Chase*, 283–84. It appears that Phelps had access to Kate's personal papers and books after Kate's death, probably through Ethel Sprague Donaldson. These things may have been destroyed in the 1906 San Francisco earthquake and fire.

84. Phelps, *Kate Chase*, 237.

85. Photograph in Sprague Collection, Cranston Historical Society.

86. *Providence Daily Journal*, 12 October 1909; 1907 newspaper clipping, unidentified and undated, Chase Paper files, A. K. Smiley Library, Redlands, California.

87. *New York Times*, 3 November 1915.

88. *New York Times*, 14 July 1909.

89. *Narragansett Times*, 15 October 1909; *Providence Journal*, 12 October 1909; *New York Times*, 12 October 1909.

90. "What Next for the Tragic Spragues!" *Washington Post*, 22 October 1911.

91. *New York Times*, 12 September 1915; Shoemaker, *Last of the War Governors*, 62–63, 65; *Providence Daily Journal*, 3, 4, 5 November 1915.

92. *New York Times*, 13 April 1914. More than eighteen months later, an article about William's death referred to the second Inez as Mrs. Sprague-Stiness, suggesting that she had not married the baron after all. See *New York Times*, 3 November 1915.

93. Belden and Belden, *So Fell the Angels*, 355; *New York Times*, 12 September 1915.

94. *New York Times*, 12 March 1916, 23 January 1938. Little is known about where or how Inez lived in Rhode Island, or indeed if she did live out her years in that state. After William's death, except for the one auction notice, Inez Weed Calvert Sprague escaped public notice until her death.

95. *New York Tribune*, 26 October 1887; *Providence Daily Journal*, 12 October 1915.

96. *New York Times*, 20 December 1936; Phelps, *Kate Chase*, 273–74. Ethel died in 1936 of a "cerebral hemorrhage," most probably a stroke like the one that felled her grandfather Salmon.

97. Phelps, *Kate Chase*, 274; *New York Times*, 14 April 1914. One story has it that Portia spent a summer at Canonchet with her father and Inez, though the source contains no dates or sources. It may have been the summer 1899, when Kate died, because one of Kate's obituaries says that Portia came from Narragansett to attend her mother's deathbed. Portia lived in Washington at the time of Kate's death. See Paul Hacker, "The Story of Kate," Cranston Historical Society website at *www.geocities.com/heartland/4678/sprague.html*.

AFTERWORD

1. Melanie Susan Gustafson, *Women and the Republican Party, 1854–1924* (Urbana: University of Illinois Press, 2001), 4–5.

2. Gerda Lerner, *The Creation of Feminist Consciousness: From the Middle Ages to 1870* (New York: Oxford University Press, 1993), 3–12.

3. See Allgor, *Parlor Politics*.

Index